850 mc
N

THE ZAMBESIAN PAST

STUDIES IN CENTRAL AFRICAN HISTORY

THE
ZAMBESIAN PAST

Studies in
Central African History

Edited by

ERIC STOKES

and

RICHARD BROWN

MANCHESTER UNIVERSITY PRESS

© 1966, Institute for Social Research, University of Zambia
Published by the University of Manchester
THE UNIVERSITY PRESS
316-324 Oxford Road, Manchester 13

Distributed in the U.S.A. by
The Humanities Press Inc.
303, Park Avenue South
New York, N.Y. 10010

First published 1966
Reprinted 1969

GB SBN 7190 0261 3

Printed in Great Britain by
Butler and Tanner Ltd, Frome and London

FOREWORD

THE sixteen chapters of this book comprise revised and, in some cases, expanded versions of papers prepared originally for presentation at the Seventeenth Conference of the Rhodes-Livingstone Institute in May 1963. Unfortunately this significant occasion preceded my arrival in Zambia by a little over two months, but I have been gladly associated with the enterprise which results in this volume.

Recent events in central Africa make one realize afresh how far we have to go before the great majority of educated people throughout the world can be said to understand the origins of contemporary upheaval. It is my hope, shared with the Editors, that the studies gathered here will make a useful contribution to that understanding. The contents do make it clear that more is known than many realize: but equally that a great deal of work awaits the attention of archaeologists, historians and sociologists as their interest is aroused in this area.

The Institute is now—as the Institute for Social Research—the first element of a Centre for African Studies in the new University of Zambia: the 1963 history conference was therefore the last under the old name. In sponsoring the publication of this volume, the Institute has been privileged to bridge the gap between two eras of scholarship, and I should like to express our appreciation to the Editors and to the Manchester University Press for their collaboration in this venture.

ALASTAIR HERON
Director, Institute for Social Research,
University of Zambia

Lusaka, 25th November, 1965

CONTENTS

LIST OF FIGURES

CONTRIBUTORS

Editors:

ERIC STOKES
Fellow of St. Catharine's College, Cambridge, and University Lecturer in History. Formerly Professor of History, University College of Rhodesia and Nyasaland.

RICHARD BROWN
Lecturer in African History, University of Sussex; formerly University College of Rhodesia and Nyasaland.

PROFESSOR ALASTAIR HERON
Director of the Institute for Social Research, Zambia.

D. P. ABRAHAM
Senior Research Fellow in History, University College of Rhodesia and Nyasaland.

IAN CUNNISON
Professor of Social Anthropology, University of Hull; formerly University of Khartoum and Rhodes-Livingstone Institute.

G. KINGSLEY GARBETT
Lecturer in Social Anthropology, University of Manchester; formerly University College of Rhodesia and Nyasaland.

MUTUMBA MAINGA
Research Student, University of London and Cambridge; formerly student at University College of Rhodesia and Nyasaland.

L. S. MUUKA
Ministry of Foreign Affairs, Zambia; formerly student at University College of Rhodesia and Nyasaland.

TERENCE RANGER
Professor of History, University College, Dar es Salaam; formerly University College of Rhodesia and Nyasaland.

ix

J. K. RENNIE	Assistant Lecturer in History, University College of Rhodesia and Nyasaland.
K. R. ROBINSON	Historical Monuments Commission, Rhodesia.
REV. ANDREW C. ROSS	Post Graduate Fellow in History, University of Edinburgh; formerly Church of Central Africa Presbyterian, Malawi.
ANN TWEEDIE	St Anne's College, Oxford; sometime Research Officer, Rhodes-Livingstone Institute.
J. VAN VELSEN	Senior Lecturer in Sociology, University College of Rhodesia and Nyasaland.
P. R. WARHURST	Lecturer in History, University College of Rhodesia and Nyasaland.

ACKNOWLEDGEMENTS

ON behalf of the contributors the Editors would like to make acknowledgements to the separate National Archives in Lusaka, Salisbury, and Zomba, for the assistance and facilities they have provided.

On their own behalf the Editors would like to record their gratitude to Dr Audrey Richards, Mr K. J. MacCracken, and Mr A. Roberts for comment and advice on points connected with the Introduction. Responsibility for all statements of fact and opinion remains, of course, with the Editors.

They would also like to express their warm thanks to Dr A. C. Gifford for help in the preparation of the end-paper map of Zambesia, and to Mrs P. Thompson for executing the typing work with such admirable efficiency.

NOTE ON SPELLING OF
AFRICAN NAMES

IN view of the widely differing practice of the contributors and the absence of any fully accepted orthography, no attempt has been made to adopt a uniform system of transliteration except where serious risk of confusion to the reader might arise. The more modern academic usage of 'Ndebele' will, therefore, be found as well as the older and better known 'Matabele'; similarly 'Shona' as well as 'Mashona'. For the resolution of any difficulties arising from differences of usage the reader is referred to the Index.

EDITORS' INTRODUCTION

'ZAMBESIA' is a title of convenience though it was current during the period when the African societies of the region it describes were being unceremoniously bundled within frontiers drawn by European diplomats. Sometimes more austerely known as South Central Africa, it lies inland from the east coast, north and south of the great Zambesi river and roughly comprises the present Zambia, Malawi and Rhodesia, together with parts of Mozambique and other neighbouring territories. Its modern African peoples are almost wholly members of the Bantu-speaking section of the continent.

The main concerns of the historians of the pre-colonial period have been to reconstruct the peopling of the region throughout the two thousand or so years of the Zambesian Iron Age and to recover the histories of the various state systems to which this process gave rise. A major contribution so far has come from the archaeologists who, particularly in southern Zambesia, have made considerable progress in establishing the sequence of material cultures. Less success has been achieved in identifying the peoples associated with these cultures, and in both fields much remains to be discovered.

Before the beginning of the Christian era we have to picture Zambesia as thinly peopled by Late Stone Age hunter-gatherers of 'Bush-Boskopoid' stock who may have practised simple forms of vegeculture. The earliest Iron Age immigrants, identified by characteristic pottery, made their appearance by the 1st century A.D., and decisive economic changes began to make themselves felt. Iron tools and an agriculture benefiting from the introduction of Asian food crops led to increasing occupation densities. It used to be thought that the arrival of Iron Age cultivators spelt disaster for the Stone Age peoples, but recent authorities have stressed that the new immigrants were at first few in number and that for a long period coexistence and gradual absorption of the 'Bush' peoples is more likely. Indeed, J. Desmond Clark has argued for a fundamental continuity between the two eras and sees the spread of the Iron Age culture largely in terms of a change to the new economy by elements of the Late Stone Age population.[1]

The 4th century A.D. seems to mark the arrival in southern Zambesia of a further Iron Age culture (classified by the archaeologists as A2). It became particularly associated with the exploitation of the extensive gold deposits found between the Zambesi and Limpopo rivers. Given the limited technological resources available, exploitation was remarkably thorough and several thousand sites are believed to have been worked over a period of 1500 years. Export to Kilwa can be presumed for the earlier period, while a more regular trade developed after the establishment of Sofala by the Arabs in the 10th century. Little is known about the social and political organization of these peoples or to what degree they are ancestral to the modern inhabitants.

Difficulties in an outline history for southern Zambesia begin to appear more sharply with the fuller material available for the second millennium A.D. Surviving oral tradition, and (from the early 16th century) Portuguese documents, can now be set beside the archaeological record. A new Iron Age culture (B1) associated with building in stone made its appearance. There is general agreement that this is to be explained in terms of the arrival of new immigrant peoples who were definitely speakers of a Bantu language and who formed part of a succession of immigrations from the north. These seem to have been responsible for the development of a series of large-scale political organizations which in varying degrees dominated southern Zambesia until comparatively recent times. The first of them, the empire of Mutapa (known to the Portuguese as Monomotapa) is being exhaustively studied by D. P. Abraham through the media of oral traditions and Portuguese documents. 'It is difficult to identify another Bantu state or association of states', he writes elsewhere, 'which can vie with the Empire of Mutapa for length of historical development, variety of ethnic origins, and complexity of problems associated with the catalytic action of not one but two communities of exotic

---

[1] J. Desmond Clark, *The Prehistory of Southern Africa* (Pelican) 1959, Chap. xi; also *Journal of African History*, V, 1 (1964), p. 182.

origin . . . the Arabs and Portuguese'[1] (the latter having gained control of Sofala in 1505). Abraham reaches the conclusion that the nuclear Karanga—now part of the Shona-speaking peoples—arrived south of the Zambesi in the early 14th century and that the leader of one of the clans, under the title 'NeMbire', gained control in the north of what is now Rhodesia and gradually extended the Karanga sway southwards. The Mbire dynasty established an overriding authority over the Rozwi whom Abraham provisionally identifies as the bearers of Iron Age B1 and responsible therefore for the earliest stone walling phase at Great Zimbabwe. He presents the Mutapa state as the dual product of the Karanga and Rozwi peoples.

In the middle years of the 15th century, under the leadership of 'Mutapa' and his son and successor Matope, a vast empire was created by conquest stretching over most of what is now Rhodesia and over much of Mozambique. But the Mutapa empire was no sooner constructed than it began to disintegrate. A revolt by Changa, a provincial chief, led by the early 16th century to the emergence of a separate centre of power in the south based at Zimbabwe. The Mutapa empire steadily contracted into the north-eastern part of the country. Here it became increasingly involved with, and dependent on, Portuguese influence pushing up the Zambesi valley. By the end of the 17th century, after a series of attacks by the now powerful Changamire Rozwi empire, the Mutapa dynasty retained only a shadow of its former importance.

Of the Rozwi empire not deeply involved with the Portuguese little is known. A full investigation of the oral tradition is urgently required. K. R. Robinson's review of the archaeological evidence (Chapter 1) is therefore particularly valuable. However, it should be noted that Abraham's work has modified the archaeologists' views on the dating of the main building period at Great Zimbabwe. Despite the radiocarbon date of A.D. 1450 ± 150 for the beginning of the finer (Q-type) walling they continued to assign the splendours of Zimbabwe, the Great Enclosure Wall and Large Conical Tower to the relatively late period of the 17th

[1] *The Historian in Tropical Africa*, ed. J. Vansina, R. Mauny and L. V. Thomas, 1964, p. 106.

xvi   EDITORS' INTRODUCTION

or even 18th centuries.[1] Robinson now accepts the possibility of a date early in the 16th century, but still fails to meet Abraham's contention completely that 'the Great Enclosure and Large Conical Tower were already fundamentally complete by mid 15th century at the latest', that is, within the period of the undivided Mutapa empire at the height of its power, and not that of the separate Rozwi empire of Changamire, as Robinson suggests. If Abraham is proved correct the popular association of Zimbabwe with the 'Monomotapa' empire will remain valid.

Despite the difficulties of establishing an agreed picture of the earlier history of southern Zambesia, it is nonetheless very much clearer than the one available north of the Zambesi. Making its first appearance in the river valley in the 1st century A.D., the Iron Age was introduced simultaneously into both regions. A second Iron Age culture, designated that of the Kalomo people, supervened in the north around the 8th or 9th centuries, and lasted some five centuries. Its origins and its extent remain quite uncertain but the possibilities are that they lay further northwards. Superficially the Kalomo People culture appears to have had much in common with that of the earlier Leopard Kopje culture at Khami in the present Bulawayo region.[2]

Large scale political organization north of the Zambesi appears to have begun with the Maravi (Malawi) confederacy. The absence of a major historical investigation of this polity is perhaps the most notable gap in Zambesian historical studies. The name Maravi first appears on a Portuguese map of 1546, but its formation is believed to have taken place a century or more before. At its greatest extent it may have covered an area roughly bounded by Lake Malawi (Nyasa) and the Luangwa and Zambesi rivers. Ancestral Cewa, Manganja, Nyanja, Tumbuka, Cipeta, Nsenga and other peoples appear to have been loosely associated together in the confederacy under a paramount ruler known as the Karonga. Traditions of origin are conflicting, but it is not unlikely that these peoples were formed when groups of invaders from

[1] R. Summers, K. R. Robinson, A. Whitty, *Zimbabwe Excavations 1958*, National Museums of Southern Rhodesia Occasional Publications, Vol. 3, No. 23A, Dec. 1961, pp. 317 (Fig. 78), 322.

[2] Brian Fagan, 'The Iron Age in Northern Rhodesia', *Journal of African History*, IV, 2 (1963). Also *ibid.*, VI, 1 (1965), p. 111.

Luba country gained authority over previously established populations. Although there are scattered references from Portuguese travellers beginning in 1616 no very full documentary descriptions have yet come to light. The few writings there are create the impression of Maravi as a loosely structured entity—more loosely organized even than either of the major political systems of the south—in which there were constant shifts of power and allegiance. Its decline seems to have already been far advanced before the coming of major external challenges in the 19th century.[1]

Further west in northern Zambesia the central historical influence has been the Luba–Lunda diaspora of the 16th to 18th centuries which introduced new forms of political organization as well as many of the major peoples found in the region today. It seems that before the diaspora, much of Zambia was still thinly populated with groups mainly of 'Bush' stock, some practising an Iron Age economy and others still mainly hunters and gatherers. Towards the Zambesi the ancestors of the Tonga and perhaps other peoples were already established while the upper Zambesi valley (Barotseland) was occupied by many of the peoples later embraced within the Lozi polity.

Robinson mentions the similarities between the Rozwi and Barotse political systems, just as Clark has illustrated the extraordinary likeness of the plan of the Enclosure walling of Zimbabwe to that of the reed fences of the Litunga's villages.[2] Whether the Lozi state originated from the south or, as appears much more probable, from the Luba-Lunda complex in the southern Congo, is the question examined by Miss M. Mainga and L. S. Muuka in the light of oral tradition obtained and written up as an undergraduate exercise (Chapters 10 and 11). The problem remains unsolved, but the tradition has at least been stated more fully and precisely and valuable lines of enquiry suggested for future research.

Perhaps contemporary with the Luyi (Lozi) migration into

[1] For a summary of evidence on Malawi history, J. G. Pike. 'A Precolonial History of Malawi', *Nyasaland Journal*, XVIII, 1 (1965). Also cf. M. G. Marwick, 'History and tradition in E. Central Africa through the eyes of the N. Rhodesian Cewa', *Journal of African History*, IV, 3 (1963).
[2] J. D. Clark, *Prehistory of Southern Africa*, pp. 291-2.

Barotseland, were the similar movements of the Bemba and Kazembe's Lunda across the Lualaba and Luapula rivers from Mwata Yamvo's Luba–Lunda kingdom. The Bemba are today one of the two largest groups in Zambia and Miss A. Tweedie has endeavoured in Chapter 8 to fill out from oral tradition the 'middle period' of Bemba history from their arrival *c.* 1700 to 1850. In his study of Kazembe's Lunda kingdom (Chapter 9) I. Cunnison makes an important contribution to our knowledge of the effects of Arab penetration. Both these studies serve to underline the importance of long-distance trade in the politics of central Africa. If it was the importation of Portuguese firearms in the 16th century from the west coast which partially explains the rise of Mwata Yamvo's kingdom and satellite states like that of Kazembe, it was certainly the caravan trade with the east coast which brought about their undoing and the rise of new powers in the 19th century. The Nyamwezi-derived Yeke state of Msidi was established in the Katanga at the expense of both the Western Lunda (Mwato Yamvo's) and the Eastern Lunda (Kazembe's) who lay on either side; and the subsequent Arab intrusion brought internal dissension and further decline to both Lunda states. Meanwhile, the Bemba, like the Yeke, strong in Arab friendship and guns, extended their sway to its fullest extent.

Although the main migration period was completed beforehand, the pace of change quickened in the 19th century and reached its climax in the closing decade when the whole area fell under European rule. Some of the changes in the balance of power brought about north of the Zambesi by the development of east coast trade have already been touched upon. Equally significant were the consequences of the Nguni dispersion of the 1820's in the far south of the continent. The Zulu military revolution equipped the various groups who broke away from Shaka's empire with weapons and tactics which made them virtually invincible against all but opponents heavily armed with guns. A widely scattered group of 'snowball states' emerged, swelling their ranks and their extensive cattle herds by raids on weaker peoples. Zwangendaba and his followers put an end to Rozwi hegemony in the early thirties while thrusting their way north, and recovery was prevented when Mzilikazi and his Ndebele established themselves in part of Rozwi territory later in the decade. Away to the east the establishment of the Gaza kingdom brought uncertainty to the peoples lying between the Sabi river and the coast. The Kololo, a Sotho group also set in motion by Shaka's Zulu empire-building, conquered southern Barotseland and ruled for thirty years before being overthrown by the Luyi, or the Lozi as they called themselves after adopting the Kololo Sotho language. The cluster of Ngoni states which emerged in north-eastern Zambesia around the middle years of the century following Zwangendaba's death *c.* 1845 in Ufipa country near the southern end of Lake Tanganyika, contributed greatly to the pattern of ethnic and political fragmentation balanced by the rise of new powers which was characteristic of the times.

Indeed, the Lake Malawi region, already the most densely settled portion of Zambesia, bore the brunt of the 19th century disturbances. From the middle of the century the Yao, associates of the Arabs and traders in slaves and ivory, steadily penetrated Malawi from their homeland east of the lake. Lacking a central state structure, the Yao moved into the area in small, competing groups. A number of able leaders, skilled in trade and in the politics of attracting followers and obtaining captives, built up larger units to the point where individually, though not collectively, the Yao groups were able to offer stiff resistance to the establishment of colonial rule in the 1890's.

Meanwhile, the second half of the century saw the steady growth of European influences as a prelude to the era of the scramble for Africa. Matabeleland and Barotseland became linked to some extent with the economy of South Africa through the activities of a vanguard of Boer and English ivory-hunters and traders, while in Mashonaland furtive prospectors discovered gold deposits which could not immediately be worked. Portuguese of mixed ancestry and tribes under Portuguese influence like the Chikunda and Mambari were pushing north of the Zambesi from both east and west in search not only of ivory but also of slaves. Livingstone's journeys focused the attention of the outside world on to Zambesia and led to the despatch of the first Protestant missions three centuries after Catholics had launched their abortive attempt to win over the Mutapa empire. Of these initial

Protestant ventures the one in Matabeleland alone managed to survive though it failed to prosper; those in Barotseland (1859) and Malawi (1861-3) collapsed disastrously. Yet it was in these last two regions that missionaries were to play the more vital part. The French Protestant Coillard was at the centre of the negotiations which brought Barotseland under European overrule, while in Malawi the missionaries, mostly Scottish and low church, who arrived in increasing numbers from 1876 were indirectly influential, first, in keeping out the Portuguese and bringing in the British and, later, in preventing Malawi from coming under the British South Africa Company administration. Their effect on the nature of the colonial encounter was to be equally significant. In north-eastern Zambesia English and French missionaries performed a similar role, establishing what amounted to colonial enclaves on the Nyasa–Tanganyika plateau and decisively altering the relationships between the more powerful military states and the less organized peoples well before the commencement of European rule.

A high proportion of the contributions to this volume deal with the period of the partition of Africa and its immediate aftermath. Historians have for long studied the motives and objects of the European partitioners, but are increasingly concerned with trying to understand the motives and objects of the African polities in the face of the challenge of the partition to their independence. It is now seen that the varying ways in which the crisis was experienced helped to shape the colonial era and even to influence the African successor states which have or will emerge.

On the eve of the partition the African peoples of Zambesia to the outsider may have seemed to have much in common. At a very general level this is no doubt true: of more significance at the time were the wide variations not simply in custom, language and belief, but also the important differences in social and political structure. If one determinant of the outcome of the scramble for Africa was the vastly superior technological strength of the European powers, the other was Africa's political disunity, its fragmentation into a large number of separate, and often competing, polities. The Zambesian portion was no exception: it is almost impossible to give the number accurately since there is no clear method of classification, but there were something like two hundred 'tribal' groupings, and perhaps two dozen languages, each divided into many dialects. Though there were wide differences in size of populations, there was no overwhelmingly large Bantu nation. It is in terms of organization that the variations are most significant. At one extreme was the complex Lozi (Barotse) polity under whose hegemony a vast but ill-defined region on the Upper Zambesi was held together, comprising a wide range of ethnic groups with differing economic specializations. A developed and efficient agriculture exploited the peculiarities of the Barotse flood plain, while both the system of administration and the judicial procedures were highly sophisticated. Yet the near neighbours of the Lozi, the plateau Tonga, also large in number, were a 'stateless' society without a unifying system so that each village was an independent political unit.

Although the picture might thus appear to be one of a mass of heaving and jarring political atoms the degree of political fragmentation and instability should not be exaggerated. Zambesia was relatively rich in centralized state systems and these for the most part directed their energies towards maintaining and extending their control over 'marcher' lands and client peoples rather than attempting war *à outrance* against one another. Widely and fairly evenly distributed over the whole region there existed among them something akin to a balance of power which reduced the occasion for major conflicts. Ndebele and Lozi might clash on the middle reaches of the Zambesi, or Bemba and Northern Ngoni on the upper Luangwa, but in general the spheres of influence were well defined and respected. Even in the Lake Malawi (Nyasa) region where military-type states jostled each other almost cheek by jowl, the degree of disorder can all too easily be exaggerated. It is not accidental that the reports upon which the picture of a destructive anarchy on the eve of the colonial period has been constructed came from precisely those regions where Europeans were first welcomed as allies, that is to say, from among the interstices of the network of powerful states where peoples like the Lungu, the Mambwe, the Bisa, the Senga,the Lakeside Tonga, the Cewa, Nyanja and the

Amangoche Yao (of the Blantyre area), were all caught between powerful neighbours.

The major historical problem is to explain why Central African
peoples responded in such widely differing ways to European
colonial intrusion. Although many of the weakly-organized
peoples might welcome the European presence, they did not do
so uniformly. Where, like the more remote of the Ila and the
Plateau Tonga, they dwelt relatively unmolested by the raids of
neighbouring states, they could manifest protracted hostility to
white incursion, despite their inability to offer serious military
resistance. If it were then a case of the response being determined
by the strength or weakness of external threats from other
African peoples, one would suppose that the smaller or more
diffuse the political system and the more menaced it was from
without, then the friendlier would be its response to the white
man; conversely, the larger and more centralized the political
system and the more free from external menace, the more hostile
it might be expected to display itself. But often, in fact, resistance
on the part of what are usually regarded as large-scale centralized
political systems, such as the Lozi, the Bemba, and the Northern
Ngoni, did not materialize or was significantly weaker than from
small-scale systems, like the Yao. The question is, therefore, not
one of overall size as of internal structure and cohesion.

Sociologists have classified African political systems according
to the degree of centralization they exhibit. This tends to vary
inversely with the degree to which their internal political organization is regulated by lineage bonds. In proportion as 'diffuse
government gives way to minimum government and eventually
to yet more centralized forms', so 'kin-based, chiefless societies
develop into segmentary states and these to unitary states'.[1] The
historical process usually took the form of the successful assertion

[1] J. R. Goody, 'Feudalism in Africa', *Journal of African History*, IV, 1 (1963),
p. 9.
    A valuable general discussion of the classification of African political systems
according to rather different criteria is contained in P. C. Lloyd 'The Political
Structure of African Kingdoms', in *Political Systems and the Distribution of
Power*, Association of Social Anthropologists Monographs No. 2, 1965, and
I. M. Lewis, 'The Classification of African Political Systems', *Journal of Rhodes
Livingstone Institute*, No. 25, 1959.

of authority by a privileged descent group which established kingship, together with related chiefships.

The segmentary state thus brought into being was characterized by the absence of centralized sovereignty, power being shared between the central kingship and autochthonous local units or lineage heads. To proceed from this political form to that of the unitary state, the kingship had to assert itself as the overriding source of authority by monopolizing the power of appointment to office and by establishing the right to ignore the lineage framework. Abstractly considered, when this had been achieved, the lineage system had been entirely displaced as a political bond by the bureaucratic organization of the territorial state. The importance of this analysis lies in its implications for the type of political process which the whites encountered in different African societies. Segmentary states lean towards fission, the segment leaders seeking to resolve their competition with the centre by breaking away to form fresh states, or at least by asserting their autonomy. Conversely in unitary states politics tend to be centripetal, narrowed to a struggle for influence at court on the part of the king's officials.

Now these are all abstract models or ideal types with no direct correspondence to historical actuality. While the postulate of states emerging as the result of the successful assertion of authority by privileged descent groups fits the origins of the main Zambesian states of the Lunda, Bemba, Lozi, Ngoni and Ndebele, it is wrong to suppose that they each progressed cleanly though in varying stages along the continuum from segmentary to unitary state. Their segmentary character was never discarded but remained firmly embedded, so much so that Fallers has argued that even the most centralized of the southern Bantu states, the Zulu, remained essentially segmentary.[1] Given, therefore, that Zambesian kingdoms were necessarily mixed and not 'pure' in structure, it is still meaningful to examine their historical response to European intrusion in terms of their approximation to either the unitary or segmentary type.

Of the more powerful political systems usually classified as

[1] L. A. Fallers, *The King's Men*, 1964, p. 98 and p. 114 n. 41. Cf. Gluckman's most recent views, *Politics, Law and Ritual in Tribal Society*, 1965, pp. 135 ff.

centralized states, the segmentary character remained most marked perhaps among the Bemba and the Northern (Mbelwa's) Ngoni, and it is significant that these two military polities came under European control with barely a show of resistance. They deserve closer consideration. In both cases some decline in the effective authority of the central kingship seems to have occurred on the eve of the colonial period, bringing about a greater diffusion of power among the segment leaders. As a consequence interlocking strains and rivalries tended to cancel one another out, and in this state of comparative deadlock it appears to have been relatively easy for European missionary and then colonial authority to step in and assume direction of affairs almost bloodlessly.

It is an open question how far the internal strains were caused or heightened to a destructive pitch by European encroachment. In Chapter 13 Rennie argues strongly against the commonly held view that the Northern Ngoni were on the verge of political disintegration at the time of the first missionary settlement at the end of the 1870's. He takes up one strain of Ngoni tradition which stoutly maintains that the Europeans 'came too soon',[1] at a time when the Ngoni peoples were in a delicate transitional phase in their transformation from migratory to settled states. On this reading the absorption of solid blocks of subject peoples, like the Kamanga, Henga, Tumbuka and Tonga, and the resolution of difficulties between the paramount Mbelwa (Mwambera, Mombera) and his brothers, Mtwaro, Mperembe and Mauru, presented merely temporary difficulties. What this transitional phase did imply, Rennie acknowledges, was that the Northern Ngoni polity was peculiarly sensitive to external influences, but any decline in central power or tribal cohesiveness he sees as the result, and not the precondition, of European interference.

It would indeed appear that the difference in response between states of a predominantly segmentary character and those of a predominantly unitary character was most distinctly manifested not

---

[1] Margaret Read, *The Ngoni of Nyasaland*, 1956, pp. 17, 24. It is instructive that K. J. MacCracken of the University College, Dar es Salaam, in a forthcoming Cambridge Ph.D. thesis, inclines to the older view of incipient decline, confirming van Velsen's opinion, *African Studies*, XVIII, 3 (1959), p. 117.

in the first but in the second stage of contact with Europeans, that
is, when the influence of the latter had had time to exacerbate the
natural internal tensions of political competition and bring them
to breaking point. It was rare for African peoples to respond with
instinctual aggression on first encounter with the white man;
normally he was allowed to establish himself on the confines of
more powerful groups without interference, even if no closer
relationship in the form of missionary or trading station was
acceptable. The decisive reaction did not come until propinquity
had displayed its effects. The advance of the European missionary
or political frontier usually meant a steady contraction of an
African state's raiding grounds and consequential repercussions on
its military and economic organization. The material benefits
introduced by the European and obtainable by submission to
missionary authority or wage employment could also exercise a
powerful counter-attraction to traditional loyalties and ways of
life, so that the second phase of contact not only could throw up
critical problems for the traditional leadership but also strain the
very bases of its support. Where the leadership remained undivided as among Gomani's Southern Ngoni,[1] the ruler faced by
the threatened loss of his warrior class as migrant labour and mission subjects, might then suddenly change front, hurl a desperate
defiance at the colonial authority, and go down fighting. A more
powerful military polity, like that of the Ndebele, would show
less forbearance, the mere contraction of raiding grounds implicit
in the white occupation of Mashonaland in 1890 being sufficient
to bring them to the edge of war.

In a state where the segmentary tendencies were more marked,
the traditional leadership tended to be too divided among itself to
mobilize a concerted resistance against the gathering threat to its
independence. The Northern Ngoni, according to the reports we
possess, preserved central conciliar institutions and central control
of large-scale military operations under the paramount. They
differed apparently from Gomani's and Mpezeni's Ngoni in that
they managed to incorporate only the youth of subjugated peoples into the tribal structure and left the remainder under what

[1] The Maseko Ngoni were, of course, a unitary state only after the enforced
secession of Kacindamoto a few years earlier.

Chibambo calls a form of indirect rule. Central power was more widely shared with the royals who held the main chiefdoms, so tending to exclude from authority the other lineage heads (*alumuzana*), who in Gomani's state were the appointed chiefs or regional governors of the paramount.[1] Missionary contact coincided with the revolt of subject peoples, leading Rennie to argue with some plausibility that the Tumbuka and Henga insurrections of the later 1870's were prompted by the mere fact of the missionary 'protection' of the Tonga at Bandawe. Mbelwa's attitude to the missionaries seems to have been directed by a desire to monopolize their influence in order to contain it. At the same time he sought to utilize them for the purpose of strengthening his own internal position as well as giving him a better control over their relations with the revolted Tonga. Despite the severe limitations placed upon their activities, the missionary influence could not be so readily contained. Within Mbelwa's domain a tendency showed itself among the young men to split into modernizing and traditionalist factions, the one favouring the end of raiding and the other pressing Mbelwa to sanction its continuance, with those not of the pure Ngoni aristocracy tending to side with the modernists. The drought of 1886 also raised the issue of the effectiveness of the traditional spiritual authorities; Mbelwa's measured support of the missionaries and his partial recourse to their cult helped provoke a combined movement of protest from the traditionalist elements. These now found their leadership among the outer 'segments' of Mtwaro, Mperembe and Mauru, whose hostility to the missionaries had mounted with the visibly growing wealth of the Tonga on the lakeside, and their own inability to recover their ascendancy over them by war. They were equally jealous of Mbelwa whose position had been strengthened by his command of the cloth and trade goods dispensed by his missionary clients. The crisis was ended by a compromise solution that permitted raids against the northern Tonga outside missionary protection and that promised to distribute the material advantages more equally by throwing open the rest of Ngoniland to missionary settlement. The compromise in effect

---

[1] Read, *op. cit.*, pp. 13, 49–50. Barnes uses *alumuzana* to denote regional governors; J. A. Barnes, *Politics in a Changing Society*, 1954, p. 9.

spelt the final decision for collaboration. With their entry into the rest of the country the moral and material power of the missionaries proved irresistible to the people at large who abandoned their military system with little hesitation.[1] It would thus appear that in a state of this kind segmentary characteristics prevented not merely a concerted effort to preserve independence but permitted collaborationist tendencies to assert themselves among the body of the people and swing the traditional leaders into the peaceful acceptance of colonial overrule.

Just as the older view regarded the Northern Ngoni as a decomposing polity, so it tended to view the Bemba as a centralized military state at the height of its power on the eve of the colonial period.[2] There seem to be strong grounds for modifying this account. The Bemba bore all the characteristics of a segmentary state, divided as it was into some four or five major and over thirty minor chiefships under the paramount, succession to office being governed by lineage precedence in the royal clan. The power of the central ruler (Citimukulu) appears to have varied in proportion to the external danger, the period of Ngoni attacks throwing up a strong ruler in Citapankwa (ruled 1867–87) who not only warded off the Ngoni danger but expanded the Bemba frontiers at the expense of the surroundng Tabwa, Lungu, Mambwe, Bisa and Lala. In the period following his death the marcher lords, Mporokoso, Makasa, Nkula, Chikwanda, together with Mwamba, seem to have strengthened their own local position as against the central kingship which tended to lapse back as a mainly ritual and spiritual office.[3] Fissionary tendencies were, however, much less prominent than among the Ngoni, and to the end the control over the Citimukuluship remained a principal object of political contention. Close European contact coincided with a protracted feud between the Citimukulu, Sampa Mulenda

[1] Based almost entirely on W. A. Elmslie, *Among the Wild Ngoni*, 1899.

[2] Cf. *African Political Systems*, ed. M. Fortes and E. E. Evans-Pritchard, 1940, p. 5. Audrey Richards in *Seven Tribes of Central Africa*, ed. M. Gluckman and E. Colson, 1951, p. 168. Dr. Richards comments that she has since altered her view; letter to Editor.

[3] W. V. Brelsford, *The Succession of Bemba Chiefs*, Government Printer, Lusaka, 2nd ed., 1948, p. 5. Gluckman gives the date of Citapankwa's death as 1883; *Order and Rebellion in Tribal Africa*, 1963, p. 108. A. Roberts concurs.

Kapalakashya, and the strongest man to hold the Mwambaship, Mubanga Cipoya, both of whom succeeded to their offices upon the death of their predecessors in 1887. Mubanga appears to have gained the upper hand, winning territory from Kapalakashya, and on the latter's death in 1895 made a bid to oust his successor, the weakling Chimfwembe. Even before this European observers like Sharpe and Poulett Weatherley were reporting that Mwamba was 'the most powerful of the Awemba chiefs and has quite superseded Ketemukuru', and that Mwamba and Mporokoso were quite independent of him and paid him no tribute.[1] It was finally Mwamba Mubanga's death in 1898, by precipitating a succession dispute, that permitted the White Fathers and the Administration to step in and take over the country almost bloodlessly.

How far the peaceful collapse of Bemba power was a matter of internal weakness, whether temporary or more deep-seated, and how far the result of the action of corrosive external influences acting upon it, remains, as with the Ngoni, a matter for speculation. Unlike the Ngoni the final expansion of the Bemba after 1850 was effected through an active partnership of the chiefs with 'Arab' ivory and slave traders who supplied them with cloth and the munitions of war.[2] The strangling of the Arab caravan trade that began in the late 1880's was therefore bound to effect their position, coinciding as it did with the permanent establishment of missionary stations on the Nyasa–Tanganyika plateau, and the consequent constriction of the Bemba raiding grounds in Lungu and Mambwe country. It is conceivable that Mubanga Cipoya might have centralized the Bemba polity again as Citapankwa had done in the 1870's. He already controlled the appointment of Mporokoso and the other western chiefdoms, and in 1896 seems to have tried to push his son Dakura into the Nkulaship, the third great chiefdom in the kingdom.[3] But after 1895 the British South

[1] Sharpe's Report of 2 March 1891; F.O. Conf. Print 6178, incl. 3 in no. 58. Poulett Weatherley, *British Central Africa Gazette*, 15 September 1895, p. 6.
[2] Otto Genthe observed 500–600 men at chief Chikwanda's in 1898, all armed with guns, mainly Tower muskets, B.C.A.G., 5 February 1898, p. 5.
[3] 'Kitimkuru's Awemba', article signed by R. S. ('Bobo') Young; Chinsal District Notebook, p. 236. Brelsford states, however, that Mubanga's brother, Mutale Sichansa, was succeeded as Nkula by Chikwanda. Dakura's tenure of the Nkulaship may have been a brief interlude beforehand since Mackinnon was

Africa Company's administrative net was closing in. If 'Bobo' Young's somewhat confused account is to be relied upon, it was his intervention from the newly established boma at Mirongo in the upper Luangwa valley on behalf of Citimukulu and his allies that helped thwart Mwamba's design.[1] Political disintegration was therefore allowed to proceed unchecked, instability being heightened because of a feud between Mwamba Mubanga Cipoya and his putative heir, Ponde. The Bemba had tried to seal off their country from the white man, but in 1895 the White Fathers lavishly distributing presents gained over Makasa who agreed to the setting up of Kayambi mission station in his country in direct defiance of his overlord Citimukulu. The disarray of the chiefs went hand in hand with a slackening of the people's allegiance as the material advantages and security offered by the missionaries and the administration made themselves felt. By 1896 Bemba under Citimukulu's authority were coming forward in considerable numbers for employment as carriers with the administrative station at Fife on the Plateau road.[2] Both Young and Bishop Dupont were in no doubt that the peaceful collapse of Bemba power was also due to the harsh methods used by the chiefs to enforce their declining prestige and authority:

As the Administration's stations gradually surrounded the Awemba before the occupation of the country the chiefs took to raiding and selling their own people in outlying villages and punished them as formerly they had punished other people. The Awemba had for some time previously not been a united people. Internal quarrels and the cruel punishments inflicted on their people turned their own people against the chiefs, so the once . . . fearsome warlike Awemba became

---

presumably referring to Chikwanda's assumption of the Nkulaship in March 1898 when he wrote that Chikwanda had 'asked to settle in the Nsenga country, in fact to take over Dakura's old place'; Mackinnon to Daly, 14 March 1898; Lusaka Archives NER A6/2/2. Brelsford, pp. 29–30. But cf. Brelsford, *Aspects of Bemba Chieftainship*, Rhodes Livingstone Institute Communications, No. 2, p. 34. A. Roberts comments that Dakura could never have actually become Nkula, not being of the *Bena Ngandu*.

[1] 'Bobo' Young to Lt.Col. Gore-Brown, 20 July 1914; *Northern Rhodesia Journal*, II, 2 (1953), p. 66. Cf. Young's account in Chinsali District Notebook, *op. cit.* Brelsford records another tradition that Kafwimbe was maintained as Citimukulu because of his ritual and spiritual prestige; Brelsford, p. 8.

[2] J. M. Bell to Administrator, 31 August 1896; NER A/1/7/1.

with little trouble good subjects of the Empire and now pay taxes and carry transport as well as the tribes they formerly raided.[1]

As soon as the Bemba had come under administration there was a flight from the large stockaded villages and the control of the chiefs, so that the European officials found their first task to be a partial resuscitation of local tribal authority.[2] As with the Northern Ngoni the failure of the traditional political system to mount any serious resistance seems to be explained by a popular revulsion asserting itself against a hesitant and disunited leadership.

Both the Northern Ngoni and the Bemba possessed states with clear territorial segments. The same cannot be said of the Lozi. Yet if Barotseland must be regarded as much nearer to the unitary state of the model, the internal feuds and relative weakness of the kingship may well have reproduced in some measure the self-cancelling effects of a more segmentary polity. As Stokes shows (Chapter 12), the paper negotiations establishing the British protectorate reveal very little of the workings of the Lozi political system, and Lewanika's constantly shifting political stance is not properly explicable without further patient research on local sources, both written and oral.[3] It may well be, as Mutumba Mainga has hinted elsewhere,[4] that the unitary aspect of the Lozi state has been unduly exaggerated, and that fissionary tendencies were stronger than supposed. The Makololo conquest of 1838 left the tripartite split in the royal clan unresolved, and separate factions became established at three separate places, the Barotse valley, Nyengo, and Lukwakwa. A fourth faction centred on Sesheke made its appearance once the Makololo rule was overthrown in 1864. Nevertheless there seems good reason to suppose that these territorial tensions were ancillary and subordinate to the

---

[1] Chinsali District Notebook, p. 236. Cf. Dupont's Report, 4 September 1899; B.S.A. Co. Minutes, 13 December 1899, Salisbury Archives LO 1/1/13.

[2] Codrington to Under Secy. Salisbury, 27 June 1899; LO 1/1/13. Report on Systems of Native Administration in . . . N.E. Rhodesia, 1904; Lusaka Archives NWR IN/1/12.

[3] Mr G. Kaplan of the School of Oriental and African Studies, London University, is at present engaged in such a study.

[4] In a seminar paper, 'The Historical Structure of the Barotse State', given to the Commonwealth and Overseas History Seminar at Cambridge in March 1965.

main political battle for control of the kingship that was conducted in the capital Lealui and the central Barotse valley. The
intensity of political competition, although it left Lewanika's position constantly insecure, nevertheless probably gave him greater
freedom of manoeuvre and negotiation than was probably true of
a more tightly cohesive unitary state as that of the Ndebele.[1]

As Brown's paper makes clear (Chapter 4) the Ndebele approached most nearly to the model of the unitary state, where a
territorial administrative system had more or less entirely displaced genealogical affiliation as the political bond. The Ndebele
rulers had taken care to allow members of the royal clan only a
minor share in political office, and Lobengula's councillors and
provincial governors held their positions primarily by appointment and not birth. Nevertheless in this perfectly articulated despotism the freedom of manoeuvre enjoyed by the ruler was para-
doxically restricted. Like a miniature Prussia its organizing
principle and ethos was war, so that it proved impossible for
Lobengula with all his foreknowledge of disaster to prevent his
impis from giving the pretext which the Mashonaland pioneers
were seeking for the outright conquest of Matabeleland in 1893.

The major threat to almost all the offshoots of the Nguni
dispersion emanated from European encroachment, since within
themselves they were usually strong enough to dominate neighbouring African states. The threat became peculiarly acute when
complicated by the rivalries of competing European powers.
Neither Lobenguala, nor Gungunhana (*vide* Warhurst, Chapter 3), nor Mpezeni, met European advances with blank hostility;
rather their diplomacy sought to utilize the rivalries of Britons,
Boers and Portuguese in order to bolster their independence. Yet
by giving a lodgement to what they reckoned as the less dangerous
colonial power they merely ensured an intensification of European
competition, a heightening of internal strains, and the certainty of
a violent dénouement of the crisis. Involving as it did African
leaders of the highest stature the colonial reckoning in these circumstances worked itself out with the moving fatality of classical
tragedy.

[1] P. C. Lloyd's model of government by political association is apposite for
the Lozi in this connection, Lloyd, *op. cit.*, pp. 102–3.

Some of the fiercest and most protracted resistance to European control came, however, from societies seemingly innocent of centralized political organization. The Yao chiefdoms of eastern Malawi are remarkable in this respect. Upon a fissiparous matrilocal social structure that by normal processes produced no higher organization than a myriad of village republics, there had been superimposed by the action of war, migration and trade a fragile and shifting network of chiefdoms. It is probable that some of the larger of these 'caravan states' would have absorbed the smaller and settled down as enduring entities had European intervention not occurred. As it was, the Europeans encountered a welter of composite groups, lacking internal cohesion and riven by disunity among themselves. What is difficult to explain in these circumstances was the dauntless resistance of the more powerful chiefdoms, like Makanjira and Jalasi, and the loose measure of concert they achieved. No doubt they enjoyed exceptional strategic advantages in their mountainous habitat on the Anglo-Portuguese border, providing as it did ideal conditions for guerrilla warfare and the advantage of supply lines to the coast through territory which the Portuguese were for long unable to occupy or administer. The total loss of wealth and prestige which threatened them as warrior chiefs when once caught within the confines of colonial rule also perhaps acted as a constant spur to their resolution. All over eastern and central Africa it was the warrior trading class represented by Arabs and Swahilis who had most to lose and who proved the least assimilable. Perhaps another factor may have been at work deserving more attention than it has hitherto received. In a general African context it has been noted that the most determined resistance to the assertion of European control came from Islamicized societies. Certainly it was true among the Yaos that the strongest resistance came from those groups which bore the deepest traces of Islamic influence, although such influence found expression more in cultural than in purely religious terms.[1]

It may well be that in this way the Amacinga and Amasaninga

[1] Ronald Robinson and John Gallagher, 'The Partition of Africa', *New Cambridge Modern History*, vol. XI, pp. 618 ff. For specific reference to the Yao, cf. J. S. Trimingham, *Islam in East Africa*, 1964, p. 61.

Yao were supplied with a common sense of identity and purpose that encouraged a loosely concerted but unwearying opposition on the part of their more substantial chiefs, and that at the same time was free from the fatal check and counterbalance inhibiting resistance in centralized state systems of the segmentary cast.

The postulate that religion might act as an organizing agency capable of generating common action over areas much wider than the limits of normal African political systems has been explored by Ranger in his study of the Ndebele and Shona rebellions of 1896–7 (Chapter 5). Here the Zambesian historian encounters a concerted movement of popular resistance unique in scope and intensity. We have already observed that the second phase of colonial contact tended to show up strains in the allegiance of the people to their traditional leaders. With the Northern Ngoni and Bemba the tide of popular feeling seems to have carried the leaders towards peaceful collaboration with the whites. The reverse seems to have been true in southern Zambesia. While even the proud Ndebele *indunas* were skilful enough to recognize when further resistance became self-defeating, they were unable to maintain control. The second phase of contact produced what can be described as genuinely national revolutions in which for a time the traditional political leaders were set aside. The role of traditional religious authorities in supplying both the ideology and organization of popular revolt becomes a matter of key importance. In Mashonaland it is true there was no such clash of allegiance as in Matabeleland, the Shona paramounts giving their full support to the rebellion to the end; but Ranger's analysis leaves the strong impression that the initiative and direction lay throughout with the religious leadership, the Shona paramounts following in their wake. While the complexities of the relationship between secular and spiritual authorities among the Shona is further examined in historical depth by D. P. Abraham (Chapter 2), the value of modern sociological study for throwing light on the manner in which a particular society may have functioned in the past is illustrated by G. Kingsley Garbett's analysis (Chapter 6) of the contemporary role of the spirit mediums among the Korekore, a branch of the Shona-speaking peoples who once formed part of the Mutapa empire

Although the structure of Zambesian societies is of first importance in attempting to assess their historical development in the
modern period, the nature and intensity of the pressures generated
by European contact is clearly a dimension that needs to be held
steadily in view. A comparison north and south of the Zambesi
is instructive in displaying the significance of the varying intensity of colonial pressures. It is notable that north of the river,
in the area of modern Zambia and northern Malawi, initial resistance was exceptional and subsequent rebellion almost unknown. There seems little doubt that the rate of administrative
build-up, and, above all, the establishment of white settlement, in
southern Zambesia and southern Malawi supply the explanation.
It is relevant here to note that the British South Africa Company
did not at first extend its activities into north-eastern Mashonaland
and that the area was not involved in the 1896–7 rebellions, but
when it did so in the years after 1896 the result was the 'Mapondera Rising' of 1900–5. There is also the question of premeditated
design. The chapters by Ross and Stokes (Chapters 14 and 15)
serve to show how much of the policy of brusque military
pacification in southern Malawi was prompted by the particular
outlook and philosophy of the early commissioners, Johnston and
Sharpe. In a similar way, the attitude of Company officials bred
into South African traditions made certain that Barotseland
would not be developed into a partially self-governing state on
the lines of Buganda. Thus conscious European imperialism,
though differing according to origin, must still be regarded as an
independent reality exercising a far from negligible influence on
the fate of indigenous political systems.

The beginning of modern nationalist-type movements followed
hard on the collapse or overthrow of traditionalist resistance. In
Malawi Van Velsen argues that barely twenty years separated the
founding of the British protectorate in 1891 from the first modern
political associations led by an educated elite. Attention has
tended to fasten, he points out, on African 'separatist' church
movements as the most significant early expression of African
aspirations, but modern secular organization ran parallel. With
the surviving elements of the traditionalist leadership forced
increasingly into docile collaboration as the price of recognition

and pay, it is to be expected that the new elite of ministers, teachers and clerks would seek to assert their own claims to direct and represent the feelings of their people. The divergence of interest had become clear by the period which opened after the First World War, but in special circumstances the small handful of educated Africans might subordinate themselves to a movement which aimed at the partial resuscitation of the traditional order. Such circumstances were brought into existence where African state systems had been, or remained, so powerful that resentment against white pressures gravitated to the support of traditionalist leaders prepared to stand out against them. In this sense the obvious example of Buganda had its Zambesian counterpart in Barotseland where it would seem in the first two or three decades of the present century the educated Lozi rallied to the defence of their kingship. In the same period, as Ranger recounts (Chapter 7), an analogous movement sought vainly to revive the Ndebele kingship in Matabeleland. Van Velsen deals in the main with the period after 1920, and is at pains to make clear how the modern elite not merely detached itself from traditional leadership, but actively sought to break out of the tribal framework and construct a 'nation-wide' organization. In Southern Rhodesia, on the other hand, Ranger sees no such sharp cleavage. To him one stream of contemporary Zimbabwian nationalism emerges harmoniously from an older Ndebele patriotism, with some of the key members of the traditional elite successfully accomplishing the passage into the ranks of modern political leadership.

PART ONE

SOUTHERN ZAMBESIA

1

THE ARCHAEOLOGY OF THE ROZWI

by

K. R. ROBINSON

THE purpose of this chapter[1] is to examine the archaeological evidence relevant to the period of Rozwi dominance in Southern Rhodesia, and to discuss the possible implications of it, particularly with regard to the alleged association of the Rozwi with Zimbabwe and other ruin sites. I should like to stress the fact that anything like a clear picture is impossible until far more field work and excavation has been undertaken over a wider area.

The occupation sites of the Rozwi: starting point

The material culture contained in the vast majority of our Iron Age sites usually does not of itself inform us with regard to the identity of the people who were responsible for it. A link must first be established between the material culture and some known tribal group. Such a link may be difficult if not impossible to find, but fortunately with regard to the Rozwi we have one or two useful clues which enable us to connect up with reasonable certainty a number of ruin sites with the final period of Rozwi supremacy, and from that point it is possible to consider the significance of provedly earlier cultures which may or may not be ancestral to the more recent Rozwi period.

The starting point in this investigation is at Khami Ruins.[2] It is

[1] My thanks are due to Mr C. K. Cooke, Director of the Historical Monuments Commission, and to Mr R. Summers, Curator of the National Museum, Bulawayo, for kindly reading the text and making valuable suggestions. I am indebted to the Historical Monuments Commission for permission to make use of the distribution maps published by the Commission in *An Archaeological Survey of Southern Rhodesia*, supplement to the *Annual Report of the Commission for the Preservation of Natural and Historical Monuments and Relics*, compiled by Roger Summers, F.S.A., and C. K. Cooke, F.S.A.

[2] Robinson, 1959.

at Khami that the familiar band and panel pottery occurs in such profusion throughout the deposits. This class of pottery is still claimed by the living Rozwi as their own as it was by Chief Jirri during Hall's lifetime.[1] This same Jirri had actually lived at Khami, the home of his grandfathers and great-grandfathers, but according to Hall he had no idea who built the walls. However, excavation has demonstrated that there is only one class of pottery associated with the occupation of the building, i.e., Khami Ruins Ware. The only change which occurred in the pottery during the Khami Ruins occupation period was the greater development of polychrome decoration in the upper levels. The class of pottery remained the same throughout the deposits.

Thus Khami was occupied from beginning to end by people practising one pottery tradition. This fact certainly suggests that people of only one tribal group are involved. If there were any interruptions in the occupation they were of very short duration, and the place was re-occupied by descendants of the original stock. Pottery which belongs to the same general class as the Khami Ruins Ware occurs at a number of other ruins in Matabeleland. In most of these instances there are traditions claiming connection with the Rozwi. Important sites of this kind are Dhlo Dhlo, and Nalatali near Fort Rixon, Taba Zikamambo, Inyati, the Longwe Ruins on the Longwe river, and many others in the same districts. Similar ruins also connected with the Khami type culture may be found scattered over most of Matabeleland (Fig. 1/1) down to the Limpopo and across it, in the Tati Concession and as far east as the Belingwe district. The ruins on the Bumbusi River near Wankie are also of the same tradition but they are late. These are the ruins described by Schofield[2] as his western complex characterized by the building of hut platforms flanked by cattle enclosures, and also by the free use of wall decoration including the check pattern. Before going further, it is important to be quite clear as to the value of the Khami Ruins Ware as a reliable indication of Rozwi occupation. The pottery itself is distinctive and easily recognized, the real question is who actually made it? Was it made by the women of the ruling clan? First of all exactly what elements composed the Rozwi royal family during the

_____
[1] Hall, 1910, p. 37.　　　　[2] 1942, p. 82.

early 19th century when we know that the Rozwi power was
broken by invasions of Nguni from the south? All that is known
for certain is that Mambo was of the *Moyo* or heart totem. The
last of the important Mambos was probably killed by the impis of
Zwangendaba at Taba Zikamambo hill. The name of this man
was either Dhlembewu or Chirisamuru.[1] Jirri is the dynastic name
adopted by the descendants of this line after the Rozwi had been
driven from their ancestral homes. Originally all the paramount
chiefs were known as Mambo.

A glance at *Totems of Mashona Tribes*[2] shows that today all the
important Rozwi groups belong to the *Moyo* totem or *Mutupo*. It
can be stated with certainty that those ruins or other occupation
sites so far examined, which tradition associated with the *Moyo*
Mambos, invariably contain pottery of the same general class as
that represented at Khami. Therefore, whether or not made by
the women of the ruling clan, this class of pottery appears to have
been the kind of ware favoured by them. A fact worth bearing
in mind is that *mutupos* were sometimes changed. There is no
reason to suppose that such changes necessarily affected the type
of pottery made.

I have previously mentioned[3] the close affinity which appears to
exist between the Rozwi and Venda of the Northern Transvaal.
This has been recognized by many authorities, and is borne out
by the pottery,[4] and also by Venda building methods. Lestrade[5]
has stated his belief that the Venda are descended from the Rozwi,
and he further states that, 'The Balozwi are not a Karanga people'.
On the other hand, they were undoubtedly associated with the
Karanga, no doubt at first as rulers, but as time went on intermarriage may have brought about a more intimate relationship.
This is not the place, nor have I the qualifications to discuss in
detail the traditions of the Rozwi and Venda. My task is to attempt
an interpretation of the archaeological evidence. Now and then
it will be necessary to compare some aspect of the archaeological
evidence with recorded tradition or documentary evidence, but
this will be kept to a minimum.

[1] Robinson, 1957, p. 79.   [2] Bullock, 1927, pp. 96–115.
[3] Robinson, 1959, p. 114.   [4] Schofield, 1948, pp. 113–18.
[5] pp. 486–95.

To summarize:

1. Khami Ruins Ware was being used by the ruling people during the last days of the Rozwi Mambos of the *Moyo* totem, i.e., up to the early 19th century.
2. Stratigraphical evidence at Khami Ruins shows that this pottery was made during the whole period of occupation.
3. Many other ruin sites of the terraced type, with coursed and decorated stone walling are to be found in the Matabeleland area. Many of these contain pottery of the same class as Khami, and may reasonably be attributed to the *Moyo* Rozwi period.
4. The old pottery of the Venda and their building methods are very reminiscent of Khami and related ruins.

The Rozwi and Zimbabwe

It has been found necessary to begin this investigation from the wrong end, chronologically speaking, in order to examine the essential pottery link between the material culture revealed by the spade, and tribal identity. It is now proposed to view the stratigraphical evidence at Zimbabwe, and consider its possible bearing on the Rozwi.

Excavations during 1958 in the Western Enclosure of the Acropolis produced some vital stratigraphical evidence together with three radiocarbon dates.[1] These dates naturally require further checking, but there appears to be no reason to doubt that they are likely to be near the mark. The earliest date, A.D. 330 ± 150 years for the first Iron Age occupation of the hill by the makers of the stamp decorated pottery (Zimbabwe Class I) has already its counterpart from the Tunnel Site at Gokomere where similar pottery is dated A.D. 530 ± 120 years. The next Zimbabwe date is A.D. 1085 ± 150 years. Somewhere between 330 and 1085 the first settlers were superseded, probably after an appreciable time gap, by the makers of the Zimbabwe Class 2 pottery. The latter is very different from Class 1, and typologically belongs to the industries which succeed it rather than to that which precedes it. During this period of some 700 years there appears to have been

[1] Summers, Robinson, Whitty, 1961, pp. 159–235.

no stone walling. Walling began round about 1085, and was accompanied by a much improved potting technique (Zimbabwe Class 3), and substantial daga floors and huts. There is evidence of increased trade with the coast.

The third date is A.D. 1450 ± 150 years, and marks the end of Period III and the Class 3 pottery. This was followed by Period IV and Class 4 pottery which may be ancestral to the Khami Ruins Ware. In addition the stone building technique changes from style P to Q.[1] There are also changes in the pole and daga building methods. Period V is modern and represents the Mugabe occupation during the 19th century.

Gundiro or Murinye Mugabe (Duma) left the lower Sabi on hearing that the Rozwi had been driven out of Zimbabwe by the VaManwa under Chief Charumbira (*mutupo* Tshibgha). The latter was eventually attacked by Chipfuno Mugabe and his younger brother Haruziweshe about 1820, and driven from the Acropolis. This information was given to me by Vengai, the grandson of Haruziweshe Mugabe. The exact relationship between the Mugabe, Charumbira and the Rozwi is not clear.

The big question is the relationship between Classes 2, 3 and 4 pottery. Class 1 can be disregarded here as something not directly connected with what followed at Zimbabwe.

I have already remarked[2] that, although distinct from one another, there is nevertheless a link between Classes 2 and 3. I have stated that Class 2 may be ancestral Karanga pottery. I see no reason to change my view (of course there may have been no tribe called Karanga at that time). Class 3 may be Class 2 plus, but plus what? I have used the term 'Shona' to distinguish this

---

[1] For a full description of Zimbabwe walling see Whitty, *Zimbabwe Excavations*, 1958, pp. 289–305. A brief description of P and Q wall styles is given below:

(a) P walling: The stone blocks are irregular in size and shape, and there is little or no signs of dressing of the blocks. The courses are uneven and tend to fade out. In spite of these features the wall face is usually more or less vertical.

(b) Q walling: The blocks are well sized, and usually show obvious signs of having been dressed or knapped. The courses are level and continuous for many yards. High walls frequently show a characteristic batter.

P style walling has been proved to be the earlier of the two styles at Zimbabwe.

[2] *Ibid.*, pp. 214–18.

new element because the Class 3 pottery has some affinities with
certain pottery made by the Mazezuru. It also has affinities with
material from Mapungubwe hill (M1)[1] and perhaps with some
of the material from old kraal sites in Matabeleland provisionally
termed later Leopard's Kopje (Fig. 1). These latter sites appear
to be either contemporary with the Khami Ruins period or
earlier, and have been termed 'later' Leopard's Kopje sites because,
while retaining some of the features typical of the Leopard's
Kopje culture,[2] there is evidence of development. The cause of
this change may have been due to contact with a superior culture.
The following changes may be noted:

The appearance of new pot forms alongside the old ones.

The replacement of the stamp form of decoration by carefully
applied incised designs, often geometric in style, mainly in
narrow bands.

Increase in the use of black (not graphite) burnish.

A bead series which differs from that associated with the earlier
Leopard's Kopje sites, and has typological affinities with the
beads from the lower levels in Zimbabwe Period III.

Increased use of stone in the kraal construction.

Change in the type of clay figurines.

In addition, the stratigraphical evidence obtained from four
sites supports the conclusions drawn from the typological evidence (not yet published).

It may be significant that at Zimbabwe the Class 3 wares belong
to the P style walling period, while the later Leopard's Kopje sites
frequently contain rough walling which could conceivably be
related to the Zimbabwe P style walls. The same may be said of
the stone walling on Mapungubwe hill.[3] In saying this it is not
intended to imply that the walling which occurs at the later
Leopard's Kopje sites exactly resembles the Zimbabwe P walling;
it is much inferior, and as a rule shows no signs of coursing. There
are instances, however, where an attempt at coursing the slabs is

[1] Schofield, 1937.   [2] Robinson, 1957, pp. 25-39.
[3] Fouche, 1937, Plate VIII.

evident as at Mapungubwe hill, and perhaps certain ruins in the Plumtree district. Rough walling has been recorded from the earlier Leopard's Kopje sites as well. The supposition is that the Zimbabwe P walling may have had its prototype which may have continued in use outside Zimbabwe and its satellites. The Zimbabwe Class 4 pottery has been accepted as being closely related to the Khami Ruins Ware, and probably ancestral to it. There can be little doubt that it belongs to a Rozwi occupation of Zimbabwe, which, if our dates are correct, must have extended from about 1450 to 1830.[1] Moreover it is to be associated with the Q style walling and the beginning of the hut platform plan as opposed to the walled hut enclosure usual in the P walling period.

The next question is whether or not there is any evidence which suggests a relationship between the Zimbabwe Classes 3 and 4? I have already expressed the opinion that the typological evidence does not indicate a complete break between these classes.[2] Taking all the evidence into consideration, it is probable that Class 3 contains some elements which went to the development of Class 4, but the latter certainly contains additional elements acquired outside the Zimbabwe sphere of influence. If this interpretation is correct then some relationship between the makers of Zimbabwe Classes 3 and 4 would appear probable. This may mean no more than that the women of Period III were taken over by the Period IV people, but the fact that the makers of the Class 4 pottery not only continued to build coursed stone walls but also improved on the original style, while their pole and daga technique, although differing in certain details from that of their predecessors, remained in all essentials very similar, may indicate some form of kinship between the two groups.

It has been stated[3] that the Mbire Rozwi dynasty had established itself at Great Zimbabwe not later than the mid-14th century, i.e. during Period III. If this is correct, then these people were responsible for the Class 3 pottery. As I have not seen the documentary evidence upon which this statement is based, I am unable to comment except to say that there appears to be nothing in the

---

[1] Summers, Robinson, Whitty, 1961, pp. 193-218.
[2] *Ibid.*, p. 216.
[3] Abraham, 1959, pp. 59-84.

archaeological evidence which forbids this possibility. Whether or not a tribal identification of the material culture at this comparatively early date is justified depends very largely upon the nature of the documentary evidence. Sicard[1] claims that two Hamitic streams entered Southern Rhodesia from the region of the Great Lakes, i.e. the Karanga *Moyo*-Rozwi and the Mbire-Shoko group of the Monomotapa. Summers[2] suggests that the people who were responsible for the first building period at Zimbabwe (P walling) were Shona immigrants. He goes on to discuss the later walling period (Q walling) which he sub-divides as follows: (*a*) structures with free-standing walls as at Zimbabwe; (*b*) hut platforms with stone built retaining walls as at Khami. The latter he connects with the Rozwi chief of the Changamire dynasty, and the former with the Monomotapa dynasty (? Mbire-Shoko). There is, however, the alternative hypotheses that the Q walling at Zimbabwe is all the work of the *Moyo* Rozwi (or done under their rule) who are alleged to stem from Changamire I, and whose descendants were responsible for Khami and related ruins. Changamire I appears to have lived c. 1494.[3] His totem was *Moyo*. The date 1494 falls within limits of error of the radiocarbon date A.D. 1450 ± 150 which marks the advent of Period IV in the Western Enclosure of the Acropolis, thus there is good reason to consider the possibility of Changamire I's influence at Zimbabwe.

To return to the earlier walling (P) at Zimbabwe, i.e. Period III. I have already stated that this period, on the evidence of the pottery, glass beads and walling, may have affinities with, (*a*) the later Leopard's Kopje sites in Matabeleland, (*b*) the culture on Mapungubwe hill (M1).

The former occupation sites are locally attributed to Sipondulu who is said to have been of the Shoko *mutupo*. It is also worth mentioning that local informants (aged Makalanga, *mutupo* Ncube) believe that the people of Sipondulu in the Matabeleland area contained a Sotho element. There is no question of cultural identity, but there is a significant resemblance between the Class 3 pottery at Zimbabwe and certain elements in that recovered from

[1] 1954, pp. 85–92.
[2] 1961, pp. 7–11.
[3] Abraham, 1959, p. 66; Stanford Smith, 1958, p. 84.

the later Leopard's Kopje sites. Moreover, the glass beads appear to support the evidence of the pottery in this respect. Radiocarbon dates for these sites are awaited with interest. It will be seen, therefore, that there is some archaeological evidence, as yet tentative, which may support the theory that Period III at Zimbabwe represents an occupation of the Acropolis by people of the Shoko *mutupo*. At present, however, there can be no certainty on this point. It seems probable that archaeology alone will fail to give a definite answer to this question of tribal identity.

Distribution of the Zimbabwe Period III culture and related sites

It has been shown that there is in Matabeleland typological and stratigraphical evidence suggesting the existence of a dominant Iron Age culture which preceded in origin the period represented by the Khami/Dhlo Dhlo type ruins, and which appears to have imposed itsel on the early inhabitants of the area (represented by the earlier Leopard's Kopje Culture sites). It is, of course, possible that this culture may have continued on during the Khami/Dhlo Dhlo period. This influence would appear to be related to that which was responsible for the occupation of Mapungubwe hill dated from A.D. 1410 ± 60 onwards, and perhaps to Period III at Zimbabwe, but this latter possibility requires more confirmation.

It is important to remember in this connection that the earlier form of the Leopard's Kopje culture has affinities with the culture at Bambandyanalo (K2), and which also occurs at the base of the deposits on Mapungubwe hill for which a radiocarbon date of A.D. 1055 ± 65 has been obtained.

At Taba Zikamambo hill (Manyanga) a fragment of a clay crucible in which gold has been smelted was recovered from a depth of 12 inches in association with typical later Leopard's Kopje pottery. This occupation, as has been shown, is overlain by a thin deposit containing band and panel type pottery, some of it polychrome. This represents the *Moyo* Rozwi occupation which was responsible for the Khami type walling. Uncoursed walling may also be noted. This hill is said to have been occupied by Sipondulu Ncube, Tumbali Pope and Mambo *Moyo*.

It is highly probable that the Umzingwane river provided an easy route between Mapungubwe and the Bulawayo area.

Exploration along this river will almost certainly produce reward-
ing results. In the Beitbridge area there are many sites which show
obvious relationship with the culture on Mapungubwe hill, one
of these located on the south bank of the Mtetengwe river has
been described.[1] The pottery from this site closely resembles the
pottery from Woolandale and related sites. The main difference
lies in the greater use of decoration in the southern area. That this
cultural influence is not confined to the south-west of Southern
Rhodesia is proved by the site located nearly halfway between the
Tokwe river and Fort Victoria on what is now known as Monte-
video Ranch, the old name was Matogani. This has been described
previously.[2] Some of the sherds from the lower levels of the
midden mound resemble material from Zimbabwe Period III
levels.[3]

In the Chibi district a certain amount of research has been done,
mainly on early Iron Age sites. Without more work it would be
rash to make a dogmatic statement, but there appears to be a
mixture of ruin building styles in the Chibi area, i.e. Zimbabwe
Period III and IV buildings, and the pottery recovered supports
this view.

An area almost completely neglected archaeologically speaking,
is that which lies south-west of Zimbabwe in the Ndanga and
Bikita districts. There are ruins, but little is known as to their
exact position in the archaeological picture. Further work is
required in this area.

Ruins in the Chipinga, Gutu, Buhera, Sabi Reserve, Mount
Darwin and Zambesi valley areas all require much more thorough
examination in order to be quite certain as to their archaeological
history.

The Belingwe Reserve contains many ruins, mainly small and
related to the Khami Ruins culture. Zumnungwe Ruin near
Masase Mission is larger and may in origin belong to Zimbabwe
Period III, but the final occupation levels contain pottery of Khami
Ruins flavour. The walling tends towards Zimbabwe P.

It will be clear from the above that more reconnaissance combined with excavation is necessary. Ruins cannot be judged simply
on the style of the walling or general plan, although both these

[1] Robinson, 1958, pp. 91-4.   [2] Op. cit., pp. 94-9.   [3] Ibid., text-figure 14.

factors are of great importance they must be checked by stratigraphical information. The map (Fig. 1) gives some idea of the
distribution of those ruin sites containing band and panel pottery
contrasted with known occurrences of the later Leopard's Kopje

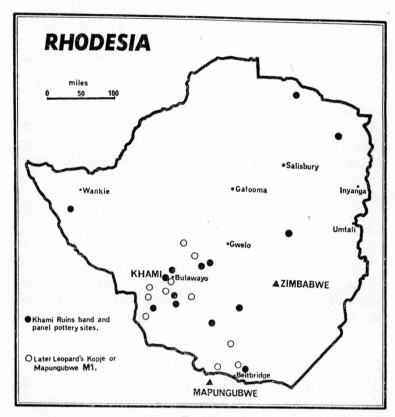

FIG. 1

Distribution of the Khami Ruins band and panel pottery compared with
that of the later Leopard's Kopje and the Mapungubwe Class M1
pottery

pottery. There are many more of the latter sites than are marked
on the map, but so far they are all located within the limits shown.

At present we cannot be certain that the chronological implications of the Zimbabwe wall classification apply outside the Zimbabwe Ruins. Moreover, up to now there is no recorded instance

of any Rhodesian ruin built with coursed stone blocks which contains pottery that can be related with some certainty to the Period III culture at Zimbabwe, but there are many containing pottery related to Zimbabwe Class 4 or the Khami Ruins Ware. This may be due largely to the fact that the earlier pottery is usually buried below later material. It is also possible that ruins which have associations with Period III at Zimbabwe are far less numerous than the later ones which are still regarded as of Rozwi origin in many instances.

Perhaps during the early walling period at Zimbabwe the coursed stone block type of building may not yet have been adopted by some of the tribal groups who may nevertheless have formed part of the same cultural and political system as that represented by Period III at Zimbabwe itself. Later on the fashion became a 'must' for any place connected with royalty or with any pretensions of an official nature.

In recent years two sites have been discovered near Mashaba where soapstone was made into dishes, bowls, phallic-like objects, etc.

Both these sites are said to have been occupied at some period by the Rozwi, and with regard to one of them the Moyo *mutupo* was mentioned. This may refer to the introduction of graphited sherds of Zimbabwe Class 4 type in the upper levels. The other site contains pottery which resembles Zimbabwe Class 3.

Distribution of the Zimbabwe Period IV culture (Fig. 2)

Mention has already been made of the main areas covered by the band and panel polychrome pottery typical of the Khami/ Dhlo Dhlo Ruins complex. Zimbabwe Class 4 pottery is almost identical with the Khami Ruins pottery but apparently without the polychrome type of decoration. The latter only occurs at Zimbabwe in small quantities in superficial positions.[1] Zimbabwe Class 4 pottery is present in some of the ruins located in the Fort Victoria, Chibi, Belingwe, Ndanga and the Sabi Reserve areas, but unfortunately no systematic work has yet been done. In 1929 Miss Caton-Thompson[2] did some investigation in the Sabi Reserve and Bikita district, but as she was more concerned with dating

[1] Caton-Thompson, 1931, p. 54.   [2] *Op. cit.*, pp. 121–62.

than any other problem the description of the pottery is somewhat sketchy. It is certain, however, that some of the pottery recovered from the Sabi sites belongs to Zimbabwe Class IV or later. Most of the walling fits into Zimbabwe Q style. The work of Wie-

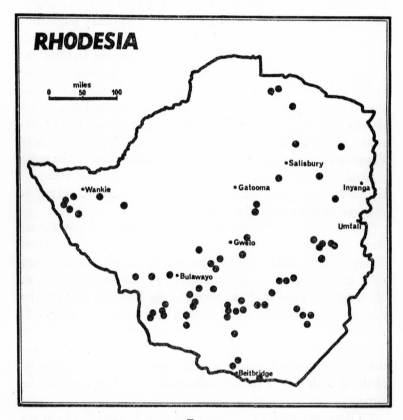

FIG. 2

Distribution of ruins belonging to the Zimbabwe tradition

schoff[1] covers Zimbabwe-type ruins in Portuguese East Africa, in the Mtoko district and in the Tati Concession. Unfortunately pottery again receives scant attention. The only pottery illustrated (not described) are some decorated sherds from the Niamara Ruins in Portuguese East Africa, not far from the Inyanga border.

[1] 1941.

Except that the designs rather resemble some of the Khami patterns it is impossible to comment.

Personal examination of the Tere Ruins, near Mtoko, traditionally regarded as the work of Makati, an early Budjga chief, and dated by Wieschoff[1] to later than the 14th or 15th century, has produced some typical Zimbabwe Class 4 pottery fragments. At Zimbabwe similar pottery is certainly post 15th century. With regard to the Tati Ruins, Schofield[2] remarks on the fact that the pottery birds from Vukwe are made in the 'well known black and red pottery of Class R1 (Khami Ruins polychrome)'. Personal investigation of the Vukwe Ruins and others in the Tati area has shown that most of the ruins belong to the Khami/Dhlo Dhlo ruin complex. The same may be said of the Mtoli Ruins near Plumtree. On the other hand there are some ruins in the same general area which may belong to the later Leopard's Kopje/Mapungubwe sphere of influence. Some careful checking is required in this part of the country.

The ruins in the Wankie district such as the Halfway House Ruin near the main Bulawayo-Victoria Falls road, the Mtoa Ruins in the Wankie Game Reserve and the ruins on the Bumbusi river are probably all much the same age and of similar origin. Well-authenticated tradition attributes the Bumbusi Ruins to the Abananzwa tribe under Chief Zankie. They are said to be an offshoot of the Rozwi during their occupation of Dhlo Dhlo or Taba Zikamambo at the beginning of the 19th century. No excavation has taken place at Bumbusi, but the pottery appears to be identical with that of Khami Ruins, and the wall style is also the same.

Of the ruins north of Salisbury and near Marandellas I can say but little as I have not done any serious work in them, but the walling and sherds recovered from some of them, suggest Zimbabwe Period IV or the Khami/Dhlo Dhlo Ruins period. Recent excavations undertaken by Miss S. Rudd for the Historical Monuments Commission at Lekker Water Ruins, Theydon, Marandellas, have produced elaborately decorated daga structures not unlike some of the daga structures which were exposed in the Western Enclosure of the Acropolis in general style. The pottery

[1] 1941, p. 62.   [2] 1948, pp. 119–22.

has proved sparse up to now, but some of it resembles Zimbabwe Class 4. The final results of this excavation may throw new light on the Rozwi period. With regard to the Zambesi valley I know the following ruins:

(a) Ruswingo we Kasekete Ruins on the Kadzi stream below the Zambesi escarpment, Sipolilo. The ruin includes a section of right-angled loopholed walling built with schist slabs and daga mortar. The remainder of the walls consist of dry stone work constructed of schist slabs, not coursed. Whether or not the loopholed wall is earlier, later or contemporaneous with the rest of the buildings is uncertain pending excavation. A certain amount of pottery has been collected from this site over the years. It all suggests the band and panel Rozwi pottery from the Matabeleland Ruins, although I do not think it is identical; this one would hardly expect. It does not suggest to me a very early date, perhaps the 16th or 17th century. It is possible, however, that there may be an earlier occupation level which is buried below later material. Surface indications, however, do not seem to promise any great depth of deposit.

(b) Ruin on Utete river. The style of walling is similar to that of Kasekete, and it forms one large enclosure. No pottery was collected nor did there seem to be any depth of cultural deposit. The pots in the sacred baobab near this ruin may very well match the pottery recovered from Kasekete.[1]

(c) Mutanda e Chiwawa, located halfway up the escarpment above Ruswingo we Kasekete. Probably later than Kasekete or contemporaneous with it.

None of the ruins mentioned above appear to have been

---

[1] Since writing I have had the opportunity of making a more detailed examination of the ruin on the Utete river after the grass had been burnt. Pot sherds were collected from old midden deposits outside the walls; no evidence of occupational deposit was noted within the enclosure. These middens appear to be thin, but it was not possible to be absolutely certain on this point in the time available. The pottery belongs without doubt to some phase of the Zimbabwe Class 4, and could be as early as 1450 if the radiocarbon dates for Zimbabwe are correct. That is to say, pottery which is typologically very similar to the material recovered at Utete was being made at Zimbabwe about that date. It may also be a good deal later, and the fact that a form of polychrome decoration occurs suggests a later date than the middle of the 15th century. Only thorough excavation can solve this and other problems.

occupied over a long period, and their importance was probably transitory. If any were the abode of the Monomotapa then his power was on the wane. This particularly applies to the Zambesi valley ruins where the walling is not even coursed. However, this latter feature may be due to a large extent to the nature of the building material available. For the time being most of the northern Mashonaland ruins must be regarded as non-proven, but at Ruswingo we Kasekete there is clear evidence in the pottery associated with the final occupation period, that Rozwi influence, perhaps emanating from central Matabeleland, was present.

The distribution of ruin sites

Only a few of our ruins have been thoroughly examined archaeologically, and it is fully admitted that unless excavation has been undertaken there can be no certainty with regard to the cultural origin or date of a building. However we do know a good deal more than was known twenty years ago about the possible implications of styles of walling and the general plan of a site. In addition, it has been possible to date pottery obtained from sealed and stratified levels. When it is clear that there is little evidence of a deep occupational deposit, and the walling appears to belong to one building period, I think one is justified in provisionally accepting the combined evidence of the building style plus any pot sherds which can be associated with the walls, providing it is recognized that any conclusions reached may have to be modified in the light of fresh archaeological evidence. Making use of this method it would appear that the longest occupied and most impressive buildings with coursed stone built walls occur in that area of Southern Rhodesia south of a line east by west drawn through Gwelo (Fig. 2). It also appears probable that the oldest ruins are also to be found in this area. Ruins north of this line tend to be smaller and more widely spaced than in the southern half of the country. Moreover they contain less evidence of prolonged occupation, while the pottery, where known, suggests a date not earlier than the 15th century. In some instances a date of the 17th or 18th century is more probable, i.e. Zimbabwe Period IV or the Khami Ruins occupation period.

The position of Zimbabwe

The Zimbabwe near Fort Victoria is the largest known ruin in Southern Africa. The buildings are the earliest of which there is any record. The first building period began about 1085 and ended about 1450, a period of over three hundred and sixty-five years. The second building period continued on for at least another three hundred years ending during the beginning of the 19th century, a total occupation period of nearly seven hundred years. This does not include the pre-walling period of occupation which when added gives a total of fifteen hundred years of occupation by Iron Age people. Thus there can be no question but that for many centuries Zimbabwe must have been a very important centre in Southern Africa. The very fact of the building of the first walls must surely indicate the advent of a power of the most compelling nature, never before experienced south of the Zambesi river. It seems possible that after building Zimbabwe and dwelling there for about three centuries, one of the Monomotapas abandoned the place and went elsewhere, while the ancestral home may have come under the care of a relation or some official. Later on Changamire 1 or one of his men took over the stewardship, perhaps by force. The Monomotapa, eventually, set up his headquarters in north Mashonaland, and established other Zimbabwes in the Zambesi valley. This is but conjecture, but the stratigraphical evidence and the dates are not. Something of the kind must have happened; the question is have we assigned the parts to the right actors? The possibility that the line of Monomotapas extends back a long way before the date usually given for the first known Monomotapa, i.e. 1445[1] may be worth consideration.

A glance at Table 1 shows that for about half a century, and perhaps longer (it is not clear whether the radiocarbon date 1370 marks the absolute base of the M1 levels on Mapungubwe hill), Period III at Zimbabwe and the occupation of Mapungubwe hill (M1) were co-existent, and the latter continued on during the Zimbabwe Period IV. That is to say, about 1370 a culture was introduced at Mapungubwe which has many features in common with the Period III culture at Zimbabwe. The resemblance between the Class M1 wares at Mapungubwe and some of

[1] Abraham 1959, p. 66; Stanford Smith, 1958, p. 84.

Caton-Thompson's Class B (now Class 3) at Zimbabwe was commented on by Schofield.[1] The rich finds of gold and the glass beads at Mapungubwe would seem to be a further cultural link with Zimbabwe. The affinities between the pottery from the later Leopard's Kopje sites and that from Mapungubwe hill and Period III Zimbabwe have already been mentioned. This all seems to point to an extension of Zimbabwe influence (? Monomotapa) southwards before the termination of Period III. The reason for this may have been the fact that both gold and copper were mined in ancient times south of the Limpopo river as well as north of it. No doubt gold was an increasingly valuable form of tribute. There is some traditional evidence suggesting that the Mono-motapa at some period went south and returned at a later date,[2] and although the traditions may not all refer to the same period or even people, they do indicate that considerable movement did occur which involved important chiefs. This fact has been stressed frequently by Sicard.[3]

The Rozwi Period

It is now time to return to the Rozwi. There have been many explanations of the word 'Rozwi', but none of these are really satisfactory. Sicard[4] has mentioned the fact that one of the Luba tribes was called Kalanga, and that the Luba kings had the title of Mulohwe, others[5] have suggested that the word may be derived from 'Waroi' meaning evildoers or wizards, or from 'rozwa' meaning despoilers. Whatever is the truth of this matter there appears to be no definite evidence of the use of the name 'Rozwi' before the 17th century.

Wall building

Period IV at Zimbabwe saw the commencement of great building activity, and the highest standard of work was attained.

[1] 1937, pp. 57–61.
[2] Abraham, 1959, pp. 59–84; Fortune, 1956, pp. 67–91; Robinson, 1957, pp. 75–87.
[3] 1954, pp. 67–92.
[4] 1954, p. 87.
[5] Bullock, 1927, p. 26; Posselt, 1935, pp. 139–40.

This activity was not confined to Zimbabwe, but occurred all over the country. Eventually there was a movement westward into what is now Matabeleland, and the period culminated in buildings such as Khami, Dhlo Dhlo and Nalatali Ruins. Whether at first this entailed a change in the centre of government or was caused by a policy of expansion designed to remove potential rivals to the chieftainship from the vicinity of Zimbabwe is not certain, but there is good traditional evidence that the ruling Mambo was living in Matabeleland towards the end of the 18th century. Until radiocarbon dates for the foundations of ruins such as Khami and Dhlo Dhlo are available there can be no certainty as to when this westerly movement began. It would appear, however, that in the kingdom of Lewanika and the Venda chieftainships there is a reflection of the Rozwi kingdom which itself was based on an earlier prototype, i.e. Zimbabwe Period III. In the western ruins the hut platform has completely replaced the hut enclosure such as may be seen in the Valley Ruins at Zimbabwe. Moreover the use of wall decoration becomes both more lavish and varied in the western area. Summers[1] has already drawn attention to this fact, and concludes that structural decoration is to be connected with chieftainship. He also points out that the check pattern only occurs in the south-west of Southern Rhodesia. These are the ruins which contain the finest of the Khami polychrome pottery. The Rozwi Mambos undoubtedly had a love of display.

Material culture

Perhaps first introduced at Zimbabwe during the Rozwi period are such objects as iron gongs, X-shaped copper ingots, and at Khami a socketed iron spearhead, cast copper spearheads and other finds which may have their origin north of the Zambesi. Another apparently exotic cultural element at Zimbabwe are the objects carved from soapstone. It has been remarked that the manufacture of dishes and bowls in this material was being practised at kraals in the Mashaba area by people whose pottery resembles Zimbabwe Class 3 (it must be borne in mind, however, that this class of pottery from sites outside Zimbabwe may not be

[1] 1958, pp. 148–53.

of the same date as the Zimbabwe Class 3 material) but pottery typical of Zimbabwe Class 4 occurred in the upper levels of one of these sites. Summers[1] records the presence of two carved bowl fragments from a sealed deposit in the Great Enclosure, Zimbabwe. The associated sherds were Class 4. Thus the only reliable evidence at present available from Zimbabwe points to a Period IV date for the soapstone bowls. Judging from the fact that they were exposed on the walls of the Acropolis when first discovered, the soapstone birds almost certainly belong to the same period, i.e. that of the Rozwi occupation. Other soapstone objects such as the 'phalli' are not yet satisfactorily placed. One thing is certain, wherever the outcrops of talc occur in the Fort Victoria district the material was utilized by the local inhabitants for many purposes. Further examination of these old kraal sites near talc outcrops may produce very interesting results. In view of the ease with which soapstone can be carved—in some ways it is a substitute for wood—its value in this respect may have been recognized over a long period by Iron Age people.

Iron and copper smelting, and subsequent forging, were known throughout the Iron Age in Southern Rhodesia (evidence of both copper and iron smelting has been dated by the radiocarbon method to A.D. 530 ± 120 at Gokomere hill). The Rozwi are traditionally said to have been skilled smiths,[2] but there is no evidence at Khami Ruins or Zimbabwe that iron smelting took place within the ruin areas.

Spinning of wild cotton has been proved at most sites of Rozwi tradition by the presence of spindle whorls made from pot sherds or stone. Clay figurines are very rare at all known Rozwi sites, but cattle figurines occasionally turn up.

An important craft was that of ivory and bone carving[3] which attained a high standard of workmanship. Bracelets made from ivory were in common use by important persons.

Gold and gold mining

The problem of the ancient mines is one of considerable difficulty, to a large extent this is due to the fact that most of the old

[1] 1961, pp. 264–8.   [2] Robinson, 1959, pp. 163–4.
[3] *Op. cit.*, pp. 155–6.

mine workings have been destroyed by modern mining activities, thus it is difficult to obtain definite archaeological evidence from a number of sites over a wide area. With regard to the Rozwi, the available evidence shows that during Period IV at Zimbabwe gold was being used for ornaments in considerable quantity, mainly in the form of beads, bangles and thin gold plate. The latter was tacked on to wooden objects such as headrests. In the western ruins, such as Khami, gold was also used, but in lessening quantities as time went on. It would appear probable that the Rozwi Mambos demanded gold as tribute from those groups who mined it as their predecessors had done for hundreds of years. In Matabeleland pottery of Leopard's Kopje type has been recovered from ancient workings.[1] This is hardly surprising as the Leopard's Kopje culture seems to have monopolized much of Matabeleland over a long period, and may have supplied the labour required by a succession of rulers.

Economy of the Rozwi

That the Rozwi were a ruling clan who, to begin with at least, kept themselves apart from the common people, has been stated by a number of writers. As such they undoubtedly extracted tribute in the form of work, agricultural produce, cattle, and perhaps at times wives, from their subjects. The stones used to build the walls of Khami Ruins are said to have been brought as tribute to Mambo, likewise the pottery is said to have been made as tribute to the royal women.[2] This may account too for the paucity of grindstones, and the little evidence of use exhibited by those present in the ruins.

Hunting was a major occupation at Khami where the middens are full of the bones of game animals. Numerous iron arrowheads have been recovered. Ivory was much valued, and perhaps used in trade. Trade with the outside world does not appear to have been large. By far the most sought after trade goods were glass beads, unless perishables such as cloth were involved. Such imports as have been excavated consist of glass beads; Chinese porcelain, and Persian, Arab and Portuguese earthenware; European silver; occasional cannon or other firearms of Portuguese origin. As

[1] Summers, 1961, p. 3.   [2] Robinson, 1959, pp. 118, 161.

Miss Caton-Thompson said,[1] 'Clearly there is nothing here to get excited about'. With the possible exception of Zimbabwe itself, imported goods do not occur in quantities in any of the ruins, and fragments are usual.

Trade there was, but the only form of trade goods which has left ample evidence of importation on a large scale are glass beads. Finally, the archaeological evidence, in my opinion, clearly indicates that the Rozwi culture as represented in Period IV Zimbabwe or in the culture of the western ruins such as Khami or Dhlo Dhlo, is directly descended from that of the early Zimbabwe wall builders who lived during Period III. Foreign influences became absorbed into the original culture as time went on and caused changes in details of the material culture, but the basic nature of the social organization appears to have remained very much the same throughout the centuries.

The reason for the long survival of this form of culture may have been largely due to the nature of the kingship. This ensured strong religious ties between the king and his people. There is ample evidence to show that there was much in common between the Monomotapas and the Rozwi chiefs. The most important elements held in common were: the divinity of the king resulting in his ritual murder when his sexual powers began to decline; the king's death kept secret; treatment of corpse; king's title which was Mambo; the feudal nature of the king's power. In addition may be added the custom of keeping the king hidden which may have applied to the Rozwi,[2] and which certainly did to the Monomotapa.[3] The above is not archaeological evidence, but is of considerable value in assessing the nature of Rozwi culture. The name 'Banyai' which is still applied to the Karanga who regard themselves as descendants of Mambo's people, originally appears to have meant 'messengers', but this may be a polite way of saying 'spies'. Mr S. Masola of Plumtree told me in 1960 that 'Banyai' means 'those who spy out and talk in secret for Netshasike'. This suggests that Mambo possessed an efficient information service.

[1] 1931, p. 92.
[2] Robinson, 1959, p. 162.
[3] Posselt, 1935, pp. 134–60; Wieschoff, 1941, pp. 95–108.

Summary of conclusions

1. It is possible that Period III at Zimbabwe represents the earliest Monomotapa period, while Changamire 1 may have been responsible for Period IV.

2. More than one ethnic group may be involved.

3. There appears to be a typological connection between the cultures of Period III, Zimbabwe, Mapungubwe hill and the later Leopard's Kopje sites in Matabeleland. This possibility is supported by some stratigraphical evidence and radiocarbon dates. This may indicate an expansion of the Monomotapa's rule southwards.

TABLE I

MATABELELAND		ZIMBABWE		MAPUNGUBWE
Culture	Date	Culture	Date	Culture
Khami Ruins	1830	Period V	1830	
—	1700	Period IV	1700	
				Culture on Hill (M1) —
? Later Leopard's Kopje[1]	1450	— Period III	1410 1370	—
				Bambandyanalo (M2)
? Earlier Leopard's Kopje[2]	1085	—	1055	—
		Period II		
—	900 (530 Gokomere)			
—	330	Period I		

Italic dates are radiocarbon tested.

4. After leaving Zimbabwe the Monomotapa probably went north to the Mount Darwin district.

5. The archaeological evidence is against a very recent arrival into Southern Rhodesia of the people now known as Rozwi, but their designation as 'Rozwi' may be comparatively recent.

[1] Later Leopard's Kopje now has a radiocarbon date of A.D. 1310 ± 90 (SR. 44).
[2] Earlier Leopard's Kopje has been dated to A.D. 840 ± 150 but this date requires further confirmation because p.E. is considered too high.

6. An examination of the ruin field suggests that the earliest and longest occupied buildings are in the southern half of the country.

7. The western ruins such as Khami or Dhlo Dhlo together with the polychrome pottery are later manifestations of the Zimbabwe culture, but with additional features obtained from unknown sources.

8. The Rozwi culture is directly descended from that represented by the first walling period at Zimbabwe. The name 'Rozwi' is of uncertain meaning and origin, and may have no ethnic significance.

9. The nature of the chieftainship may account for the lasting quality of the Rozwi culture.

10. These conclusions are subject to alteration in the light of fresh archaeological discoveries or radiocarbon dates.

BIBLIOGRAPHY

D. P. Abraham, 'The Monomotapa Dynasty', *NADA*, No. 36, 1959, pp. 59–84

C. Bullock, *The Mashona*, Juta & Co. Ltd., Cape Town, 1927.

G. Caton-Thompson, *Zimbabwe Culture*, Cambridge University Press, 1931.

G. Fortune, 'A Rozwi Text with Translation and Notes', *NADA*, No. 33, 1956.

L. Fouche, *Mapungubwe*, Cambridge University Press, 1937.

R. N. Hall, *Illustrated Guide to Khami Ruins*, Philpott & Collins, Bulawayo, 1910 (out of print).

F. W. Posselt, *Fact and Fiction*, Bulawayo, 1935 (out of print).

K. R. Robinson, 'A History of the Bikita District', *NADA*, No. 34, 1957, pp. 75–87.

K. R. Robinson, 'Four Rhodesian Iron Age Sites: A brief account of stratigraphy and finds', *Occ. Pap. Nat. Mus. S. Rhod.*, No. 22A, 1958, pp. 77–119.

K. R. Robinson, *Khami Ruins*, Cambridge University Press, 1959.

J. F. Schofield, 'The Pottery of the Mapungubwe District', *Mapungubwe*, Part III, Cambridge University Press, 1937, pp. 32–102.

J. F. Schofield, 'A Survey of the Recent Prehistory of Southern Rhodesia', *S. Afr. Sci.*, Vol. XXXVIII, 1942, pp. 81–111.

J. F. Schofield, *Primitive Pottery*, Cape Town, 1948, S.A.Arch. Gol.

H. Sicard, 'Rhodesian Sidelights on Bechuanaland History', *NADA*, No. 31, 1954, pp. 68–94.

H. Stanford Smith, 'Monomotapas: a Ring list compiled by H. Stanford Smith,' *NADA*, No. 35, 1958, pp. 84–6.

R. Summers, 'Structural Decoration on Rhodesian Ruins,' *Occ. Pap. Nat. Mus. S. Rhod.*, No. 22, 1958, pp. 148–53.

R. Summers, K. R. Robinson, A. Whitty, 'Zimbabwe Excavations', *Nat. Mus. Occ. Pap. S. Rhod.*, No. 23A, 1961, pp. 157–332.

R. Summers, 'The Southern Rhodesia Iron Age', *Journal of African History*, Vol. II, No. 1, 1962, pp. 1–13.

G. P. Lestrade, 'Some Notes on the Ethnic History of the Vhavenda and their Rhodesian Affinities', *S. Afr. G. Sci.*, Vol. XXIV, pp. 486–95.

H. A. Wieschoff, *The Zimbabwe-Monomotapa Culture in South East Africa* Geo. Banta Pub. Co., Menasha, Wis., U.S.A., 1941

2

THE ROLES OF 'CHAMINUKA' AND THE *MHONDORO*-CULTS IN SHONA POLITICAL HISTORY

by

D. P. ABRAHAM

THE basic meaning of the Shona word *mhondoro*[1] is 'lion', but the word is no longer commonly used in this sense except in the north and north-north-east of Southern Rhodesia. There is, however, a secondary meaning to it which is universally current among the Shona and broadly definable, in terms of traditional belief, as 'spirit of a deceased person of eminence held to reside in the body of a lion when not communicating from time to time with the living through an accredited human medium—and socially recognized as a source of supernatural power, authority and sanctions'.[2] Although there are certain tribes, such as the Manyika under Chief Mutasa, which have been long exposed to

---

[1] See p. 372 of M. Hannan, *Standard Shona Dictionary*, London, 1959. There is a cognate form, *mphondolo* or *mphondoro*, that I have found, in the course of field-research, to occur in chiThawara and chiNyungwe, and in the Tonga dialects spoken in Mkota S.N.A., Mtoko District, and Barwe to its south-east in Portuguese East Africa. For the Nyungwe form, see V. J. Courtois, *Diccionário Cafre-Tetense-Portuguez*, Coimbra, 1900, p. 49. I have been unable to identify a single Bantu language north of the Zambesi in which cognates of the word occur. In Portuguese documents of the 18th century onward relating to Shona *mhondoro*-spirits, the word usually appears as 'pondoro'.

[2] For material relating to the Shona *mhondoro*-cults, published post-1890, see A. Burbridge, 'In Spirit-Bound Rhodesia', *NADA*, 1924; Ch. Bullock, *The Mashona*, Cape Town, 1928; F. W. T. Posselt, *Fact and Fiction*, Bulawayo, 1935; J. F. Holleman, *Accommodating the Spirit Among Some North-East Shona Tribes*, Cape Town, 1953; M. Gelfand, *Medicine and Magic of the Mashona*, Cape Town, 1956; J. F. Holleman, *African Interlude*, Cape Town, 1958; M. Gelfand, *Shona Ritual*, Cape Town, 1959; and M. Gelfand, *Shona Religion*, Cape Town, 1962. See also Luis dos Santos, 'Apontamentos sôbre a Etnografia dos "Nhúnguès",' *Anais*, Lisbon 1949.

Portuguese influences and no longer evidence a *mhondoro*-cult,[1] and others, such as the Harava under Chief Seke, in which the institutional status of local *mhondoro*-cults is steadily diminishing[2] owing to the pervasive cultural effect of large neighbouring European centres, many Shona tribes still recognize one or more *mhondoro*-spirits. Such spirits historically equate with and socially perpetuate, in the majority of instances, the personality and status of the founder of a tribal chieftaincy and/or those of notable collaterals and descendants, both male and female. In cases where, for one reason or another, there has at no time been a *mhondoro*-spirit associated with the tribal founder, or where such spirit has been long quiescent so as no longer to constitute an active social force, the senior spirit in a tribal *mhondoro*-hierarchy usually equates historically with a brother, sister or immediate descendant of the tribal founder—and sometimes with a sister's or daughter's son.[3] Relations of authority within the hierarchy are mainly structured in conformity with the genealogical relationship that obtained between the persons whose names the *mhondoro*-spirits bear, and these spirits are believed to be in communion and to consult together on appropriate occasions. The influence, as distinct from the formal status of a tribal *mhondoro*-cult, sometimes transcends the limits of an individual tribe owing to circumstances of historically acquired prestige or owing to close historical links between one tribe and another with respect to inception or subsequent political development.

Mhondoro-spirits constitute the functionally most comprehensive sub-class of *midzimu* or ancestor-spirits—being primarily *midzimu yenyika* or territorial spirits in contra-distinction to the *midzimu yepamusha* or spirits of domestic scope and relevance.[4]

---

[1] The *mhondoro*-cults of the Manyika are referred to in the document *Discripção Corografica do Reino da Manica*, undated but assignable to the last third of the 18th century; see Arquivo Historico Ultramarino, Lisbon, Moçambique *caixa* 17. The last *mhondoro*-medium of the Manyika seems to have been Muredzwa, daughter of Mutasa Tendai, who died in 1933.

[2] Claimants to the at present vacant Seke chieftaincy have stated, for instance, that they no longer recognize their local *mhondoro*-spirits as having a say in the selection of the chief.

[3] This statement is an abstraction from numerous genealogies of Shona chieftaincies assembled by me on the basis of field-research.

[4] Cf. Gelfand, 1959, pp. 3–6.

ZP—E

In addition, they resolve into two principal status categories of political implication: a lower category of spirits at the tribal level and an upper category of supra-tribal spirits connected with the royal dynasties of Mutapa and of Togwa. The existence of institutionalized *mhondoro*-cults among the Shona is documentable from Portuguese records of the 16th century onward. The earliest reference I have been able to locate occurs in João de Barros in the context of a description of the régime of the Mutapa dynasty.[1] João dos Santos refers to the *mhondoro*-cults in the Shona principality of huTeve in his *Ethiopia Oriental* (1609).[2] Antonio Bocarro states that the subjects of the Mutapa 'believe their kings go to heaven, and when they are there, call them *muzimos* (*midzimu*) and ask them for whatever they require . . .',[3] and a letter of the same year relating to negotiations between the Portuguese and Mutapa Mavhura Filipe mentions a demand for 'cloth for his *mozimos*'.[4] Documents, including memoirs and correspondence, dating from the second half of the 18th century onward, furnish detailed information on the status and functions of the *mhondoro*-cults of the Mutapa dynasty—including data on the political activities of specific *mhondoro*-cults in what are now the Sipolilo and Mount Darwin districts,[5] and this information is materially supplemented by A. M. Pacheco in his diary of 1862 entitled *Uma Viagem de Tete ao Zumbo*.[6] The German prospector

[1] *da Asia*, 1552, Década I. See G. M. Theal, *Records of South-Eastern Africa*, Vol. VI, p. 2.   [2] Theal, *R.S.E.A.*, VII, pp. 197, 199 (and cf. p. 290).

[3] *Decada 13*, 1635. See Theal, *R.S.E.A.*, III, pp. 358–9.

[4] Letter of Antonio de Castilho de Mendonça to Francisco Figueiredo de Almeida, 25 June 1635, from Zimbabwe of Mutapa Mavhura (Torre Do Tombo, Lisbon, DRI 35, fl. 230).

[5] For instance, *doc. cit.* note 3 and *Descripção do Imperio Moanamotapa da quem do Rio Zembeze* of *c*. 1790 (Arquivo Historico Ultramarino, Moçambique *caixa* 30). Extensive references to the activity of NeBedza mediums occur in documents of this archive contained in Moçambique *caixas* 17–70 (1780–1835) and *maços* 1–32 (1827–33). Reference is also made therein to a number of other *mhondoro*-spirits associated with the Mutapa dynasty—including Samarengu, Nyamasoka and Nyamapfeka. Limited data on the activity of the NeBedza cult during the second half of the 19th century is to be found in documents included in the *Boletim Official de Moçambique* (1854 onwards).

[6] This rare bibliographic item was hand-printed on Moçambique Island in 1883. A copy has recently been acquired by the National Archives of Rhodesia and Nyasaland. The author, apparently a *mestiço*, was Captain of Zumbo during 1861–2 and killed during an uprising in the latter year.

and geologist, Carl Mauch, offers some brief material on the cult of the Budya tribal *mhondoro* NeMauyu in a diary entry of 1872, and the prestige of this cult is referred to in Portuguese documents of the 1880's.[1] F. C. Selous is the first British writer to advert to a Shona tribal *mhondoro*-cult, and the first writer of any nationality to mention the cult of Chaminuka.[2]

The historical identity of Chaminuka is uncertain. Whilst we have a wide range of Portuguese documents that enable us, in conjunction with Korekore oral tradition, to establish the identity of Mutota Nyatsimba—from whom apical *mhondoro* Mutota of the Mutapa dynasty historically derives,[3] there are apparently no Portuguese documents relating to the *mhondoro*-cults of the Rozwi. The Portuguese do not seem to have penetrated the heart of Rozwi territory north of the Central Limpopo until the 1640's, and from 1696 until 1835, when the Rozwi dynasty of Changamire was paramount over an area largely co-extensive with what is now Southern Rhodesia, their contact with it was substantially restricted, for most of the time, to the intermediacy of *vashambadzi* or itinerant trading-agents of Bantu or *mestiço* origin. Although there are two early 19th century documents of unique evidential value relating to the régime of Changamire and the contemporary Rozwi Zimbabwe,[4] neither of the two sheds

[1] National Archives of Rhodesia and Nyasaland, MA17/1/1, fol. 107, for reference by Carl Mauch; and *Boletim Official de Moçambique* 1888/11, p. 197.

[2] See, in reference to Chaminuka, F. C. Selous, *A Hunter's Wanderings in Africa*, London, 1881, p. 331 (he refers to the medium as 'Situngweesa'—by the name of Chitungwiza hill, on which he lived); also his *Travel and Adventure in South-East Africa*, London, 1893, pp. 113–17.

[3] On *mhondoro* Mutota and the historical Mutota Nyatsimba, see my 'The Monomotapa Dynasty', *NADA*, 1959; 'The Early Political History of the Kingdom of Mwene Mutapa', *Historians in Tropical Africa*, Proceedings of the Leverhulme Inter-Collegiate History Conference, September 1960, Salisbury, 1962; and the *Journal of African History*, Vol. II/2, 1961, pp. 212–13. The earliest documentary reference to *mhondoro* Mutota as distinct from the historical Mutota Nyatsimba, is one of the 1880's; see O. Martins, ed., *Diarios de Viagem de Angola a contra-costa*, Vol. II, Lisbon, 1952, p. 476.

[4] The *Discripção Corografica* contains a long section on the Changamire régime. The second document referred to is the *Acressentamento* (Additional Information) appended to *Memoria sobre a doação do Territorio Bandire* (Arquivo Historico Ultramarino, Moçambique *maço* 21, doc. of 1 June 1831). There are 18th century accounts relating purely to the military organization of the Changamire dynasty.

light on the current activity of history of the Rozwi *mhondoro*-cults; and the task of reconstructing this history is rendered still more delicate by the fact that, whilst the *mhondoro*-cults associated with the Mutapa dynasty still survive and vigorously so in the Zambesi valley sector of Southern Rhodesia and the adjoining parts of Portuguese East Africa, no single *mhondoro*-cult relating to a ruler of the dynasty of Togwa is still apparently in operation—but exclusively that of Chaminuka.[1] The fundamental reason for this state of affairs seems to be the disruption of the Rozwi polity effected by the 19th century Nguni invasions, dispersal of the Rozwi and ensuing radical injury to the cohesion of their politico-religious institutions. The Chaminuka cult did survive until 1883 as a focal point of Shona national resistance to the Ndebele,[2] but now operates in the Chiduku Reserve, Makoni District, structurally divorced from the cult of Mwari, the high deity of the Shona, and from the political system, its organic relationships with which primarily invested it with meaning and authority. Current Rozwi tradition supports the view that there was once a flourishing corporation of royal *mhondoro*-cults associated with the Togwa royal dynasty,[3] and there is no evidence that suggests this corporation differed radically in structure and function from the spiritual corporation linked to the Mutapa dynasty.

My preliminary finding, on the combined basis of documentary material, oral tradition, linguistics, archaeology, etc., is that the original, nuclear Shona were a patri-clan of designation *Soko-Mbereka* (Vervet),[4] which, known as the Mbire, and accompanied

[1] On the Chaminuka cult, see Gelfand, 1959, 1962; also his 'The Mhondoro—Chaminuka', *NADA*, 1959.

[2] In that year, according to F. C. Selous, the Chaminuka medium was killed on the orders of Lobengula, the Ndebele king (Selous's *Travel and Adventure in South-East Africa*, London, 1893, pp. 113-14). For oral tradition on the subject, see Gelfand, *NADA*, 1959, and R. M. M. Ncube, 'The True Story re Chaminuka and Lobengula', *NADA*, 1962.

[3] Rozwi informants of mine, including the recently elected *Rozwi* Mambo —Noah Washaya, Chief Marisa of Que Que District, Headman Hunina of Gwelo District, Basvi of Buhera District and Chief Chiduku of Makoni District, have referred to the following Rozwi *mhondoro*-cults: those of Dombo, Nechagadzike, Basvi, Wadyambeu, and Chirisamhuru. [Abraham considers Rozvi to be the more correct spelling. To avoid confusion with the usage of other contributors, Rozwi has been uniformly adopted by the Editors.]

[4] Muchetera, present medium of Chaminuka, belongs to this clan. The

by a number of subordinate Karanga and Nyai clans, migrated southwards over the central Zambesi under the leadership of a chief bearing the title 'NeMbire', during the first half of the 14th century. There is a tradition widely diffused amongst the Rozwi and also related by the current medium of Chaminuka, Muchetera, to the effect that the cult of Mwari, the high deity, was brought in by the Mbire from their homeland, also called Mbire, in the vicinity of Lake Tanganyika;[1] and there is a further tradition preserved in the same circles that the spirit of Chaminuka came south of the Zambesi with the group of immigrants in tutelary function.[2] The historical Chaminuka is implied to have died previously, and since, according to tradition, the medium of the Chaminuka spirit should preferably be a member of clan *Soko-Mbereka*,[3] it is possible that Chaminuka himself was an ancestor of NeMbire. Later in the 14th century, a centralized polity seems to have become firmly established with headquarters in the locality of what developed into Great Zimbabwe, and Rozwi tradition portrays the Rozwi monarchy as called into being either by Mwari or by the Chaminuka Spirit in association with Him.[4]

Muromo or official mouthpiece of Mwari, the high deity, identifiable as one and the same Chaminuka medium, also belonged to it, *NADA*, 1956, p. 55. *Mbereka* means 'female vervet-monkey carrying infant on her back'.

[1] There is a saying current among the older Rozwi, Korekore and Barwe that 'Mwari akabva Mbire' (Mwari came from Mbire). When asked where Mbire was, informants invariably refer to an area north of the Zambesi—some explicitly mentioning the vicinity of Lake Tanganyika. I deal with the matter in detail in my as yet unpublished *History of the Empire of Mutapa*.

[2] Prof. J. Vansina has informed me, in a written communication, that there is a major spirit-cult of 'Chimanuka' practised in Ruanda. Whether there is any historical basis for supposing that 'Chaminuka' and 'Chimanuka' (that which became detached from Heaven) are metathetically related forms referring to a single early historical personage remains to be investigated.

[3] According to the present Chaminuka medium, cf. note 20 above.

[4] Gelfand, *Shona Ritual*, pp. 13–14, 30–1; and *NADA*, 1959, pp. 6–7. According to what present medium of Chaminuka has told me, the first Rozwi king, Chikura Wadyambeu, was son of Senwa (Nehanda), daughter of Negupo, the latter being wife of Mutota (posthumously named 'Churuchamutapa')—of clan *Shava-Nhuka* (Eland), and daughter of NeMbire. Senwa herself is said by him to have been mysteriously impregnated—'some thought by Mwari'. Mutota, her father (not to be confused with the later Mutota Nyatsimba, who founded the Mutapa dynasty), is said to have become the first medium of Chaminuka on arrival at Zimbabwe, and to have installed Chikura, his daughter's son, as king there. Cf. the versions in Posselt, *Fact and*

Whether, in point of historical fact, the cult of Mwari and the Chaminuka spirit were simultaneously introduced by the Mbire, or whether the Mwari-cult was pre-existent in the area and later structurally syncretized with a cult of Chaminuka introduced by the Mbire, is obscure, but according to Rozwi tradition, the cult of Mwari was centred at Zimbabwe from inception of the Rozwi monarchy until the Nguni invasions of the 19th century,[1] the successive mediums of Chaminuka were stationed there until the same invasions,[2] and the monarchy at all times had its formal capital there despite occasional shifts to subsidiary *madzimbabwe*. There are references in Portuguese documents from the 16th century onward to Shona belief in a high deity,[3] and the traditional association of the Mwari-cult with Great Zimbabwe is confirmed by Carl Mauch, writing in 1871.[4] Archaeologists have already advanced the opinion that the 'Eastern Enclosure' of the 'Acropolis' served sacral functions,[5] and Leo Frobenius has published an archaic stratum of tradition relating to sacral rites performed within the 'Temple'.[6] It is within the 'Eastern Enclosure', according to certain informants of mine, that the medium of

Fiction, pp. 139–41; G. Fortune, *NADA*, 1956, pp. 81–2, note 3; and *NADA*, 1959, p. 7.

[1] Cf. J. Blake-Thompson and R. Summers, *Mlimo and Mwari*, *NADA*, 1956, p. 56, for tradition on the subject; L. Frobenius, *Erythräa*, Berlin, 1932, p. 223.

[2] According to the present medium of Chaminuka and to Hendrick Chiruka of Makuni N.P.A., Umtali District, the mother of whose maternal grandmother is stated to have been sister of the last Chaminuka medium to have presided at Zimbabwe.

[3] João de Barros 1552, *Década* I-X-I (Theal, *R.S.E.A.* VI, p. 269); António Bocarro 1635, *Década 13*, Cap. 125 (Theal, *R.S.E.A.*, pp. 358–9); Manuel de Faria e Sousa 1666–75, *Asia Portuguesa*, II-III-XV (Theal, *R.S.E.A.* I, pp. 24–5); *Descripção Corografica . . . cit.*; and *Descripção do Imperio . . . cit.*
Post-1890 material relating to Mwari and the Mwari-cult includes: Ch. Bullock, *The Mashona*, Cape Town, 1928, J. B. Richards, 'The Mlimo Belief and Practice of the Kalanga', *NADA*, 1942; H. von Sicard, 'Mwari—der Hochgott der Karanga', *Wiener Beitrage zur Kulturgeschichte und Linguistik*, No. 6, Vienna, 1944; H. von Sicard, *Ngoma Lungundu*, Uppsala, 1952; J. Blake-Thompson and R. Summers, 'Mlimo and Mwari', *NADA*, 1956; W.V. v.d. Merwe, 'The Shona Idea of God', *NADA*, 1957.

[4] R. Summers, 'Carl Mauch on Zimbabwe Ruins', *NADA*, 1952. Mauch refers to Mwari as 'mali'.

[5] K. R. Robinson, for instance, says: 'the Eastern Enclosure . . . has all the appearance of a place where sacred rites were performed' in his *Khami Ruins*, Cambridge, 1959, p. 116.   [6] See his *Erythräa*, pp. 201–5.

Chaminuka presided and, amongst other things, interpreted the squawkings of *Hungwe, Shirichena, Shiri ya Mwari*—The (Celestial) Fish-Eagle, The Bird of Bright Plumage, The Bird of Mwari, on its annual visit to the shrine, as pronouncements of the deity.[1] The soapstone birds that once stood along a partition wall of this enclosure, though differing in detail, style and execution, would seem to indicate the historical validity of this tradition,[2] and though, as yet, we have no scientifically established date for introduction of the advanced style, Q-type masonry exemplified by the outer girdle wall of the 'Temple' or 'Elliptical Enclosure',[3] it is difficult to vitiate the inference that the raison d'être of the massive Q-type structures correlates historically with the local establishment and development of the Mbire-introduced monarchy and associated Mwari-cult referred to in tradition. Had we no oral tradition at all, we would be led to hypothesize the existence of such a monarchy. In actual fact, João de Barros refers to the Zimbabwe of Torwa (Togwa) in Butua (Gunuhutwa or Guruhuswa) in 1552, and though his description is in some respects inaccurate, he rather accurately locates the site as some 170 leagues distant from Sofala—on a meridian between 20° and 21° of latitude south. He mentions 'Burrõ',[4] i.e. Boroma as the contemporary Rozwi ruler, and descendants still survive today of a Rozwi king, Boroma.[5] Togwa himself is assigned by Rozwi tradition a major role in regard to constructional activity at Zimbabwe,[6] and a Flemish document written as far back as 1502 refers

[1] My principal sources of this tradition have been: the present medium of Chaminuka, Hendrick Chiruka of Makuni N.P.A., and the present Tumbare of Buhera Reserve. According to Portuguese documents of the 18th–19th centuries and oral tradition, the post of chief executive and military officer to the Changamire para-dynasty was hereditary to the Tumbare family.

[2] With regard to the position of these Soapstone Birds, see G. Caton-Thompson, *Zimbabwe Ruins*, Oxford, 1931, pp. 90–1. At least nine of these birds are known to have been erected along the Eastern Enclosure.

[3] On Q-type masonry, see *Zimbabwe Excavations 1958* (Occasional Papers of the National Museums of Southern Rhodesia, No. 23A), pp. 289–305.

[4] Theal, R.S.E.A. VI, p. 267.

[5] The descendants of Boroma lived until recently in Selukwe District. For a reference by oral tradition to the Rozwi lineage of Boroma, see National Archives of Rhodesia and Nyasaland: N3/33/8, 'The Abelozwi (Barozwi)'.

[6] G. Caton-Thompson, *Zimbabwe Culture* . . ., Oxford, 1931, p. 177. Noah Washaya, the present nominal Rozwi *mambo*, cites the tradition in an unpublished manuscript of his.

D. P. ABRAHAM

36

to the existence of a great walled capital in the interior.[1] In the
absence, to date, of divergent oral tradition or documentary data,
I accept as *prima facie* established that the Acropolis and Great
Zimbabwe housed the Rozwi monarchy and the Mwari-Chami-
nuka cultural nexus prior to the Nguni irruptions during the
period 1828–38.

The Rozwi worshipped Mwari on certain national occasions,
revered the Chaminuka spirit as his intermediary and presented
the Rozwi kingship to their subjects as Mwari-established and
Mwari-directed. After the breakaway Mutapa dynasty established
itself in the Zambesi valley—probably early in the 15th century,[2]
the local spirit Dzivaguru seems progressively to have replaced
the Chaminuka spirit as this dynasty's immediate structural link
with Mwari, but there were certain ritual obligations that it still
continued to recognize with respect to Chaminuka.[3] In the course
of time, the historical identity of Chaminuka seems to have
become vague in the minds of the Rozwi. Mwari, according to
tradition, had no medium iof His own, and the utterances of the
Chaminuka medium funct oned as equivalent to those of Mwari.[4]
The immediate cultural association of Mwari and the Chaminuka
Spirit worked, it seems, to accelerate the process by which the
latter spirit became detached from roots in a historic personage
and apparently to separate it, into a distinct category, from that

[1] A. Lobato, *A Expansão Portuguesa de 1498 a 1530*, Lisbon, 1954, Vol. I,
pp. 62–4. The work in question is the *calcoen*, relating to the second voyage of
Vasco da Gama round the Cape and published in Antwerp in 1504.

[2] In Cap. 4 of my as yet unpublished *History of the Empire of Mutapa*, I infer
a date of *c.* 1425 for the move northwards to the Zambesi valley. A date of
c. 1450 has previously been surmised, *NADA*, 1959, p. 112, note 5.

[3] On this cult, see F. W. T. Posselt, *Fact and Fiction*, pp. 123–6; M. Gelfand,
Shona Religion, passim; also R. C. Woollacott, 'Dziwaguru—God of Rain',
NADA, 1963. The earliest reference to Dziwaguru and the status of the cult in
relation to the Mutapa dynasty occurs in a document of *c.* 1765 (*Anais*, 1954,
Vol. IX/1, Lisbon, 1956, pp. 114–15). Further information on the status of the
cult is contained in *doc. cit. c.* 1765, note 11 above. In 1862 A. M. Pacheco
retails tradition relating to Dziwaguru in his *Viagem de Tete ao Zumbo*. 'Dzivaguru' was also an epithet of Mwari! See *NADA*, 1954, p. 25; 1957, p. 44.

According to the present medium of Chaminuka, it is the traditional duty of
Makombe, ruler of Barwe, to erect the *mutoro* or cult-hut of a newly installed
medium. The first Makombe, according to tradition, was a son of Mureche,
daughter of NeBedza, the second ruler of the Mutapa dynasty.

[4] Gelfand, *Shona Ritual*, p. 14.

of the royal *mhondoro*-spirits. In fact, there is no evidence that the Chaminuka-spirit was ever formally a *mhondoro*-spirit. By the start of the 17th century, many rulers of the southern Rozwi and northern Korekore dynasties had come and gone, and the royal *mhondoro*-cults had had ample time to proliferate. Certain present-day Shona 'theologians' propound the view that the *mhondoro*-spirits owe their being to Mwari, have little or no power of their own accord and simply intercede with Him on behalf of suppli-cants;[1] and the Rozwi present the Chaminuka spirit as apical in the spirit-hierarchy[2]—directly linking Mwari with the royal and tribal *mhondoro* spirits. This concept of a pyramidal, graded spirit-structure, with Mwari, primeval, self-originated spirit at the top —Chaminuka, the idea of whose secondary spirit had become obscured in the course of time, immediately beneath him—the royal *mhondoro*-spirits, whose historical origins were still re-membered, beneath Chaminuka—and the tribal spirits, also be-neath Chaminuka, in the lowest grade, seems already to have crystallized in its essentials by the earlier 17th century; for Manuel de Faria e Sousa writes in his *Asia Portuguesa* of 1674 that the people subject to the Mutapa 'acknowledge only one God' and adds that 'they call upon the royal *Muzimos* as we the saints'.[3] Since the saints are presented in Roman Catholic theology as interceding with the Christian God, it is reasonably clear that what Faria e Sousa signified was that the royal *mhondoro*-spirits were conceived by the Shona of that time as intercessors with their deity rather than as primary sources of power authority and sanc-tions. The often stated view that Mwari was rarely if ever directly worshipped is true to the extent that, excepting at the national festivals, He only came formally into the routine life of the commonalty in terms of oath and invocation. It should be remembered, however, that the cosmological rites performed by the rulers of the Rozwi and Korekore dynasties directly expressed

[1] My most detailed exponent of this subject has been the present medium of *mhondoro* Gupo in Mukumbura-Masoso N.P.A., Mount Darwin District. The present mediums of *mhondoro* Mutota and *mhondoro* Chaminuka have expressed similar views to me; cf. Gelfand, *Shona Ritual*, pp. 13–14.

[2] Gelfand, *Shona Ritual*, p. 14.

[3] Theal, R.S.E.A. I, pp. 24–5.

institutionalized belief that their dynamism flowed from Him,[1] and that the epithets of the deity, *Nyadenga—Musikavanhu— Muvambapasi* (Lord of the Sky—Creator of Mankind—Founder of the Land) were not esoteric ones but in common circulation. Few persons can have been unaware of these epithets or of the implications underlying them, and all supplication seems ultimately to have been directed to Him.

The royal *mhondoro*-cults, taken corporately at any time, may be assumed to have functioned to maintain and perpetuate the monarchy, to regulate succession to the monarchy as between the various royal 'houses' and to decide rights of inheritance in land-estates and cattle pertaining to branches of the royal family. In other words, the royal *mhondoro*-corporation operated primarily as a conservative pressure-group in defence of the political *status quo*, was of restricted and sectional character and was not directly concerned with the interests of the people of the subject districts except insofar as rivals for the throne might seek the military support of powerful district chiefs. Whilst it was the Mwari-cult, we may suppose, that functioned at national level to mitigate such abuses as flowed from the rather narrow, ruling-class orientation of the royal *mhondoro*-cults and to create a public image of the monarchy as guided by norms of public rather than private interest—and individual kings did incur displeasure of the Mwari-cult and flee from fear of supernatural sanctions it invoked—the majority of the people lived out their existences as members of individual tribes and thought and felt at tribal level. It was to their chiefs they looked for tribal leadership and security, and, in their turn, the tribal chiefs looked for guidance and help to their tribal *mhondoro*-spirits—the spirits of their ancestors. The primary function of the intra-tribal hierarchy of *mhondoro*-spirits paralleled, at a lower political level, that of the royal *mhondoro*-spirits, and was that of perpetuating the political interests of the local patri-lineage that held the chieftaincy. There was, however, one vital distinction. The tribal chiefs were in direct, daily contact with the

[1] K. R. Robinson, *Khami Ruins*, Cambridge, 1959, p. 162, for some tradition relating to ritual performed by the rulers of the Changamire dynasty. The nature and significance of the ritual performed by the rulers of the Mutapa dynasty is treated of in detail, with full documentation, in my *History of the Empire of Mutapa*.

people they controlled and could not hope as individuals to remain long in power unless they were esteemed by them or at least seen to control the tribe with equity; and the interests of the tribal *mhondoro*-corporation, being solidarity with those of the ruling patri-lineage, it may be assumed that the corporation exerted steady influence on the chief in office of a type that would tend to secure the loyalty of the tribal populace. It was therefore fundamentally the *mhondoro*-corporations of the individual tribes that came closest to the humbler political concerns of the mass of the population and furnished them with some sort of buffer against misrule. On the other hand, the Shona kings, owing to communication problems, were not in close daily contact with their subject chiefs but commanded sufficient power to prevent them individually from directly challenging their authority on the grounds of misrule. Hence, the recourse of the tribal *mhondoro*-spirits, in case of royal oppression, was to Mwari through his intermediary, the Chaminuka spirit. The royal *mhondoro*-spirits, linked to the sectional interests of the royal family as they were, were divorced to a far greater extent from the political interests of the tribal chiefs than the tribal *mhondoro*-spirits were divorced from those of the tribal commonalties. The main, moral cement at the national political level derived from Mwari and his lieutenant, Chaminuka.

The base of the administrative pyramid, as far as the kings were concerned, was the system of districts and district-chiefs. They were not concerned with tribal internal administrative structures. The political function of the tribal *mhondoro*-spirits was not, however, simply internal (as the present day situation might suggest, in which such Shona tribes as have maintained their corporate identities have disintegrated structurally isolated political units—owing to the collapse of Shona monarchy), but correlated with the historical foundations of every tribe's existence. Reference has previously been made to founders of tribal chieftaincies, but such foundation did not occur within a political vacuum.[1] The Shona tribe was essentially a territorially delimited association

---

[1] For analyses of the Shona tribal system, see J. F. Holleman, *Shona Customary Law*, Manchester, 1952, and section by him in *Seven Tribes of British Central Africa*, 2nd ed., Manchester, 1959.

of patri-lineages of differing clan ascription—structurally unified by internal recognition of the right of one of these lineages
to local political superordination and socially homogenized by a
developing web of kinship on the basis of intermarriage. Its historical precondition of existence, however, was the availability of
a tract of territory at a given time and grant by the monarchy of
rights of occupation of the same to a specific individual of a
specific lineage in consideration of services rendered, relationship
or payment in the form of gold, ivory, livestock. weapons, hoes,
etc.[1] The grantee, by virtue of a specific political act occurring at
a specific historical time became recognized as immediate 'muridzi
wepasi' or 'owner of the soil', but overriding *huridzi* or ownership
was retained by the monarchy—subject to the final qualification
that Mwari himself was deemed 'Muvambapasi' or 'Founder of
the Land'. Subject to the continuing favour of the monarchy, a
district chieftaincy devolved on collaterals and/or descendants of
the original grantee, or, in cases that such were lacking, on a sister's
or daughter's son,[2] though in certain instances chiefs who occupied
the territory along the zone of intersection of the domains of the
Mutapa and Togwa dynasties were powerful enough to shift
their allegiance from one dynasty to the other.[3] In the course of
time, the original grantee of tribal territory or a successor became institutionalized, after death, as a *mhondoro*-spirit, and in the
further course of time, this spirit became senior spirit in the rami-
fying intra-tribal *mhondoro*-hierarchy. The senior tribal *mhondoro*,
if not historico-politically equating with the original district
grantee, became *muridzi wepasi* pro such grantee, and it was purely
temporary, contingent exercise of local *huridzi* that was conferred
on successors to the district chieftaincy. The basic *huridzi*, such as

[1] Such payments are frequently alluded to in tradition collected by me with
regard to the origins of various Shona chieftaincies. If the word 'payment' is
unacceptable, we may substitute 'valuable consideration'.
[2] In such cases the sister's or daughter's son seems sometimes to have adopted
the clan designation of his mother—to maintain formal continuity of the
chieftaincy in the hands of the original clan. This may have occurred at one
stage in the history of the Mangwende chieftaincy (Mrewa District).
[3] This can be shown to have been the case with regard to the first Chief
NeMakonde and the first Chief Zvimba (both of Sinoia District now). Portuguese documents of the 16th–19th centuries refer several times to disloyalty of
district chiefs to current Mutapas.

it was, remained perpetually vested in the senior tribal *mhondoro*, and was limited with respect to title by reservation to the monarchy of local mining rights[1] and rights of alienation of portions of the district. Such alienation appears to have occurred with some frequency in favour of individual Portuguese farmers, miners, merchants, missionaries and officials resident during the 17th century within the domain of the Mutapa dynasty.[2] The structural link that validated the existence of a tribe *qua* legally recognized territorio-political unit was furnished by the senior *mhondoros* of the individual tribe, who or which, in the symbolic status of grantee of the district, functioned vis-à-vis the monarchy as a jural corporation sole,[3] though, vis-à-vis the local chieftaincy and the tribe as a whole, he functioned as head of a spiritual corporation multiple. In other words, he was regarded by the monarchy, in terms of primary emphasis, as a basic link in the devolutionary chain of political authority.

The individual tribal *mhondoro*-corporations also served an intertribal function. Tribes, the territories of which were adjacent, tended quite naturally to contract more intimate political, economic and social relations than those at a distance from one

[1] References to prohibition of mining gold and of disclosure of gold deposits to foreigners without authority occur in Portuguese documents from the 16th century onward. The same prohibition applied to silver and other scarce minerals. From the documents, we learn gold was a valuable source of taxation-revenue to the Mutapa. The gold and golden artefacts recovered by fortune-hunters in the 1890's and by archaeologists subsequently from various Rozwi Zimbabwes would seem to indicate that gold was also a substantial source of revenue to the Togwa dynasty. The presence of gold-deposits in Rozwi territory proper and their exploitation can be documented from the early 16th century onward.

[2] Land alienation to Portuguese is mentioned in a number of 17th century Portuguese documents. In one of these, the *Informação do Estado e conquista dos Rios de Cuama* of 11 December 1667, Manuel Barreto refers to Portuguese and *Mocoques* (mestiços) who possess 'large lands or provinces they have bought from or buy every day from the King of Mocranga [the Mutapa]', see Theal, R.S.E.A. III, pp. 482–3. Since it was the rich farming lands or ones with mineral deposits the Portuguese had their eye on, district chiefs must have been wholly or partly dispossessed in many cases—accepting transfer by the Mutapa to another district or abandoning their chieftainships in favour of some form of compensation.

[3] See *American Anthropologist*, Vol. 64/2, April, 1962, pp. 313–20, for discussion by H. Befu and L. Plotnicov of economic, political and religious corporations.

another. Such relations were sometimes friendly, sometimes hostile and sometimes ones of indifference. Whenever possible, intertribal friction was reduced by negotiation between chief and chief, or failing the success of this, by negotiation between the relevant tribal *mhondoro*-corporations, for the obvious reason that, in the case of serious disorder, the monarchy would intervene. It was only in the last resort that tribes that had fallen out applied directly to the royal Zimbabwe to intervene by force or arbitration, for such force or arbitration might result in abolition of chieftaincy and bring into uncomfortable prominence the contingent aspect of the basis of local tribal authority. There is always a tendency to over-emphasize, in formal analyses, the degree of integration of the functional layers within a complex political structure. Intervention in the affairs of a local authority with a high degree of internal autonomy generally gives rise to resentment, and there were Shona tribal chiefs who adopted an assertive attitude vis-à-vis the monarchy whenever they felt strong enough to do so. The role of Chaminuka, we may assume, became especially prominent politically when major structural strains threatened the equilibrium of the Rozwi polity. During the later 17th century, the long-established Togwa dynasty of NuRozwi was relegated to purely sacral status by the Changamire para-dynasty, but Dombo, the Changamire who effected this revolution, we know from contemporary documents to have been primarily a military figure,[1] and we may suppose that his political success importantly depended on winning the support of major tribes that were discontented with the old régime. How he succeeded in gaining the spiritual support of Chaminuka we should like to know. Significant, however, is that the Chaminuka-spirit passed through this major political upheaval with unimpaired sanction to preserve the structural continuity of the Rozwi state; and when subsequently periods of interregnum occurred, it was to the Chaminuka spirit

---

[1] Changamire Dombo's seizure of power from the Togwa dynasty, his campaigning south of the Limpopo, his military clashes with the Portuguese and Mutapa Mukombwe, his support of the usurper Nyakambiru, and his destruction of the Portuguese trading-centres and attempted attack on Sena are dealt with in some detail in my *History of the Empire of Mutapa*. In the meantime, see E. Axelson, *Portuguese in South-East Africa*, Johannesburg, 1960, Cap. 12. Dombo died at the turn of 1695.

that application was made for confirmation of successors to the subject tribal chieftaincies.[1]

Underlying the systematized sanctional statuses of Mwari, Chaminuka, the royal and the tribal *mhondoro*-spirits, was a general ethic—parapolitical in that it had certain basic symmetrical relations with the total political order which operated to sustain it, and suprapolitical to the extent that the norms projected by it sometimes transcended purely political considerations in the interest of the individual. The royal *mhondoro*-cults had, by the 18th century, come to serve the important function of asyla for political refugees—the area of a shrine being considered a sacral *temenos* or enclave outside the jurisdiction of the monarchy. Royal princes, and also chiefs presumably, might reside there with impunity, but in the case of an expelled king of the Mutapa dynasty, the security of his successor was involved, and the ex-king was required either to establish himself outside the limits of the royal domain or to hang himself at a *mhondoro*-shrine under supervision of the cult. For a king to kill a predecessor, legally in office, whom he had evicted, was not permitted—the alternative solutions to the situation providing a nice compromise between ethic and political realism. The *mhondoro*-cults of the Mutapa Dynasty were also called on from time to time to adjust themselves in terms of political realism. During the 17th century, for instance, the Portuguese intervened, either by military force or threat of the same, to install rulers whom they favoured—rulers who were not always legally entitled to the throne.[2] During such periods, the royal *mhondoro*-cults had temporarily to find some formula of accommodation, but sooner or later they resumed activity behind the scenes with a view to ousting alien-installed kings in favour of their own nominees. In this aim, they were sometimes successful.[3]

[1] The first Chief Mangwende of Nohwe, an area corresponding with sections of the present Mrewa and Marandellas Districts, is related in tradition to have been confirmed by the Mwari-cult. This seems to have occurred between 1704 and 1710, when Changamire Negomo having been killed, no successor was immediately appointed owing to feud between rivals for the appointment.

[2] For instance, they evicted Kapararidze in favour of Mavhura in 1629—evicted Nyakambiru in favour of Mhande in 1694—and installed Chirimba and Nyadenga, respectively *c.* 1696 and 1699, in the face of senior claims to the Mutapa-ship.

[3] In 1702, for instance, the Portuguese-installed Mutapa, Nyadenga, was

I now come finally, in this brief survey of an intricate field, to
the matter of history and historical awareness in relation to Shona
political structures. The historical awareness diffused through the
various levels of a politically organized society is primarily social
awareness of its conceived history. This awareness is the major
factor that contributes to a sense of continuity, and such sense of
continuity tends to reinforce the stability of a political order and
the sanctions underlying it. Historical awareness *qua* form of self-
knowledge by a society also tends to permeate and shape the
activity of such a society. Hence, it operates within a given society
at a given period both as formal and as applied knowledge—
subject to the qualification that, in non-literate societies we may
assume *a priori* that historical accounts, in the process of oral transmission through time, tend to deviate increasingly from 'was
eigentlich gewesen ist' due to fallibility of memory, individual
bias, political upheaval and re-interpretation in the light of subsequent social restructuring. The distortions that progressively
occur result in modification of objective knowledge of the past,
and it is this progressively modified knowledge of the past that
functioned amongst the Shona as history for its own sake and
history of social relevance. A significant function of the *mhondoro*-
cults was the organized transmission of such knowledge, which
passed as *nekuvimbisika* (reliable) and *chokwadi* (objective) firstly,
because the Shona had no means of checking the authenticity of
information emanating from the cults by reference to documents,[1]
secondly, because the sacral status of the cults largely guaranteed
the status of such information from attack, and thirdly because
corporate association of the cults tended to 'iron out' discrepancies

---

ousted by Dehwe Samutumbu, with military aid from Changamire Negomo,
after having strenuously pressed his claims. Activity by the royal *mhondoro*-
cults, irked by alien (Portuguese) interference, probably prepared the ground
for Changamire's intervention on the scene. Previously, between 1623 and
1629, Mutapa Kapararidze was influenced by the *mhondoro*-spirits—possibly
mhondoro Mutota and *mhondoro* Samarengu—with regard to policy to be followed versus the Portuguese (*Studia*, Vol. 3, 1959, pp. 189–90).

[1] João dos Santos writes in his *Ethiopia Oriental* (1609): 'They can neither read
nor write and have no books, and all ancient history and other things they learn
by tradition acquired by them from their forbears'; see Theal, R.S.E.A. VII
p. 199.

in tradition. The royal *mhondoro*-spirits were looked to as the major, accredited sources of national history, and if satisfactory knowledge was not forthcoming from a *mhondoro*-medium in trance, his credentials as medium were assailed. Writing in 1862 of the cult of *mhondoro* NeBedza of the Mutapa dynasty, A. M. Pacheco says: 'The Unvura [i.e. *Amvura* or medium] was submitted to the most stringent tests to establish that he was the genuine medium of the *pondôro* [*mhondoro*]: which tests consist in the naming of the Monomotapas from the time of Mutota until the present ruler; in the listing of the most notable events of every reign; . . . and also in the detailing of all the public mishaps that occurred during this lengthy period.'[1]

After the death of Mutapa Nyamhandu, *c.* 1740, the Mutapa dynasty degenerated to provincial status in Thawara country west of Tete and became formally extinguished in 1902.[2] The *mhondoro*-cults associated with this dynasty did not fade away *pari passu* in the intervening period but possessed so high a degree of institutional vitality that they still function actively with respect to residual segments of the Mutapa's traditional domain—in Southern Rhodesia and Portuguese East Africa. To this fact we owe the possibility of filling in to a substantial extent gaps in the historical data furnished by Portuguese and other documents. I incline to the opinion that it is the historical function attached to these *mhondoro*-cults—a function admittedly of social relevance, that primarily accounts for their survival. Account must also be taken of their sanctional function in validating rights to political office and territory, but since such rights are now divorced from the context of the monarchy and largely affected by the policy of intrusive administrators, this function is inadequate by itself to explain their vigorous survival. The Shona appear to have been permeated by a developed degree of historical consciousness—a

[1] A. M. Pacheco, *Uma Viagem de Tete ao Zumbo*, p. 45.

[2] The last nominal Mutapa, Chioko Dambamupute, died early on during the course of the Barwe Rebellion of 1902 (João de A. Coutinho, *Relatório da Campanha do Barué, 1902,* Lisbon, 1903, p. 127). According to tradition collected by me, a number of the royal *mhondoro*-spirits of the Mutapa dynasty were active behind the scenes in preventing this anti-Portuguese revolt, including *mhondoros* Nyamhandu, Mupunzagutu, Kamota and Gupo, the cult of the last-named being established at the time in the north-east part of Mount Darwin District, Southern Rhodesia.

consciousness that has outlived to some extent its political correlates. The *mhondoro*-cults are major trace-elements precipitated
by their history, and by their institutional arrangements to perpetuate awareness of the same.

3

THE SCRAMBLE AND AFRICAN POLITICS IN GAZALAND

by

P. R. WARHURST

THE story of Lobengula, endeavouring to keep his kingdom intact against strong internal and external pressures, is paralleled in Moçambique by the reign of Gungunhana, King of the Gazas. But there is one essential difference. Lobengula's story concerns his relations with the British; but the British were not the only Europeans with whom Gungunhana had to deal. For more than fifty years before the British became actively involved in Gazaland, the Gazas had been in contact with the Portuguese. Like many other African chiefs, Gungunhana found himself caught up in international rivalry for his part of Africa.

It was Gungunhana's grandfather, Soshangane Manikusa, who had brought the tribe out of Natal in the days of Shaka. In July 1819 he had commanded the army of a Zulu-speaking tribe, the Ndwandwe, in a momentous battle against Shaka, whose young lieutenant was a certain Mzilikazi. Although he fought courageously, Soshangane was no match for the redoubtable Zulu chief and after his defeat he set out for the north.[1]

The Gazas (also known as Shangaans, Vatuas or Landeens) entered Moçambique and by 1822 had reached the coast south of Lourenço Marques. It was here that they were visited by Captain Owen, R.N., making his famous survey of the African coast, and he has left a detailed description of 'Chinchingany' (Soshangane) and his people. From here Soshangane pressed further and attacked Nxaba, an Nguni offshoot, who was already settled in the area. Retiring to the north Nxaba destroyed the Portuguese

[1] For the Natal period of Gaza history, see E. T. Bryant, *Olden Times in Zululand*, 1929.

settlement at Macequece (Vila de Manica) in 1833. In the following year (5 October 1834) Soshangane took Lourenço Marques,
killing Governor Ribeiro. He later established his kraal at Manhlagazi, near Mount Silinda, north of the Sabi. From here the
Gazas raided as far as the Zambesi,[1] and Portuguese sources reveal
that for nearly fifty years the Portuguese at Sena paid tribute to the
Gaza kings.

All the local peoples from the Zambesi to the Limpopo and
beyond were forced to accept Soshangane as their overlord and
paid tribute to him.[2] Many of them were Shona like the majority
of people in Southern Rhodesia. The Gaza settled in Ndau country, east of the Sabi, and the Ndau language, a Shona dialect,
contains a wealth of Zulu words inherited from the Shangaans.
Conquered peoples who were not Shona included the Chopi (on
the coast), the Hlengwe (between the Sabi and the Limpopo) and
the Ronga (near Lourenço Marques). The term 'Shangaan', which
properly relates to the conquerors themselves, has been loosely
used to include all of these. They contributed manpower to the
Gaza army and the Ndau lost a high proportion of their men in
this way. Gaza rule was not at all harsh provided people did not
rebel against it; any such rebellion was severely crushed. The Gaza
intermarried with the local people but failed to impose their language on them as the Ndebele were doing in Matabeleland. It is
interesting to note that influence was not a one-way traffic. Whilst
the local people learned much from the Gaza, Zulu military technique, for instance, they in turn influenced the dominant group.[3]
Ndau beliefs took on a strong hold on the Shangaans (Gazas), just
as the Ndebele took over the Mlimo concept from their Shona
vassals.

Soshangane ruled unchallenged from the Zambesi to the Limpopo, from the Sabi to the sea. When he died, in 1859, it is hardly
surprising that there should have ensued a family quarrel over this
vast inheritance. Soshangane's eldest son, Mzila, was displaced
by his half-brother, Mawewe. Mzila fled and sought refuge,

[1] J. P. R. Wallis (ed.), *The Zambesi Expedition of David Livingstone*, Vol. I,
1956, p. 54, and Bonham to Salisbury, 3 August 1888 (C. 5904/67).
[2] Wallis, Vol. II, p. 341.
[3] H. A. Junod, *The Life of a South African Tribe* (The Ronga), 1912.

possibly with the Ndebele who ruled supreme on the other side
of the Sabi. Mawewe's rule did not prove very popular with his
people. Mzila's right of inheritance as the eldest son was as
clearcut as it could be; only in exceptional cases did people deviate
from the accepted system and this was not considered a necessary
exception. They began to look to Mzila for deliverance from
Mawewe's harsh rule.

According to a Portuguese frontiersman, Dioclesian das Neves,
who was an old friend of Mzila, he was approached in November 1860 by Mzila with a request for Portuguese assistance
against his half-brother. Dioclesian promised to take the matter
up with the Governor.[1] Some time later a deputation of *indunas*
loyal to Mzila was sent to interview the Governor of Lourenço
Marques (which had been rebuilt since its destruction in 1834).
Mzila was said to have followed and to have agreed to a treaty
of friendship with Portugal, signed on 2 December 1861.[2] The
Portuguese furnished arms, ammunition and armed levies for the
forthcoming campaign and large forces gathered in August 1862
to march against Mawewe. On 17 August the opposing factions
met on the left bank of the Komati river. The engagement proved
indecisive and the final battle took place on 20 August, when
losses were high on both sides. Mawewe fled and Mzila became
king. Thus the first intervention by Portugal in Gaza politics,
some years before the Scramble for Africa, was a success. Their
ally, Mzila, had become king. What is more, the intervention had been initiated by the Gaza chief himself. The Portuguese were much too busy trying to maintain a precarious foot-
hold on the coast to interfere often in the interior. But the prospect
of friendship with the king of such a powerful people as the Gazas
was an opportunity not to be missed. They virtually regarded
Mzila as a 'Portuguese protected person'. Just how Mzila
viewed the situation is quite another matter.[3]

[1] A. Pereira de Lima, *A nossa Intervenção na Política Indigena de ha cem anos*
(Separata No. 5) Divisao do Turismo, Lourenço Marques, discusses the whole
episode.
[2] For copy of treaty, see Incl. I in Soveral to Salisbury, 4 February 1891
(C. 6495/52).
[3] See statement by Huluhulu, 27 April 1891, incl. in C.O. to F.O., 4 June
1891 (F.O. Conf. 6227/p. 312).

During the years that followed, he showed no inclination to accept Portuguese sovereignty. When he had been an exile, dependent upon Portuguese support to bring him to power, it would not be surprising for him to agree 'to remain a tributary chieftain . . . obeying all orders issued from this Government of Lourenço Marques'. But when he became ruler of the Gaza nation, he regarded himself as tributary to none. In 1870, he demonstrated his independence by sending messengers south to Natal. They appeared before Theophilus Shepstone, Secretary for Native Affairs, thereby establishing the first official contact of Gazaland with the British.[1] Their mission was threefold: to settle a dispute with the Swazi, to request a visit from a British official and to arrange trade. It is of interest to note the trade motive at this early stage. Shepstone was aware of Portuguese claims to Gazaland, and he put it to the delegation that they were Portuguese subjects. This they denied adding: 'Mzila is a king; the Portuguese are women.' Nevertheless Shepstone was cautious and, although he promised to send an emissary, he impressed upon his visitors that Britain did not wish to interfere with Portuguese rights. The emissary, St Vincent Erskine, was sent to Mzila's kraal near Mount Silinda. After avoiding the Portuguese and returning safely from a long and not very successful mission, he reported that he had found no Portuguese influence in Gazaland.[2] In 1878 Mzila's *indunas* were again in Natal, but this time only presents and no envoy were sent.[3] During the 1870's all visitors to Moçambique were warned by the Portuguese authorities that they could accept no responsibility for their safety in the interior.

After the loss of Brazil, however, Portugal began to divert her attentions to Africa. It was as well for the Portuguese that they did so, for the Scramble was to bring the British into the hinterland of their African possessions. Very soon it became clear that Britain was not prepared to accept Portugal's claim to the whole trans-African belt from Loanda to Lourenço Marques. 'Effective occu-

---

[1] S. P. Hyatt, *The Northwood Trek*, 1909, pp. 220-4, and Salisbury to Petre, 8 May 1891 (C. 6495/190).

[2] *Ibid.*, incl. 3-8.

[3] *Ibid.*, incl. 7-8.

pation' became the international demand and Portugal, with very limited financial resources, was forced to take steps to consolidate her position.

The Gazas were no longer the power they had been. Cheap spirit, imported on the coast, was demoralizing the people and though they were still able to overawe subject tribes, their fighting capacity had declined.[1] The land between the Zambesi and the Busi–Revue rivers fell to a Goanese adventurer, Manuel Antonio de Sousa (Gouveia), who ruled in the name of Portugal. In 1880 the first missionaries arrived in Gazaland. A Jesuit, Father Law, led the mission, which ended in tragedy when the leader succumbed to fever.[2] When Mzila died, he was succeeded by his eldest son, Gungunhana, the last of the kings of Gaza. In October 1885 two Gazas, claiming to represent Gungunhana, went to Lisbon and signed a treaty with Portugal.[3] There was some doubt as to the validity of their claim and accordingly the Portuguese sent an expedition to Gungunhana's kraal led by Jose de Almeida, an African, who was Secretary-General of the Province.[4] He obtained Gungunhana's approval and established a Portuguese resident there but Gungunhana later denied having accepted the treaty. It seems clear that he was playing a careful game. He had no wish to quarrel with the Portuguese, and he was equally determined not to surrender any sovereignty. When the Portuguese appeared, they were always treated with courtesy, but Gungunhana continued to exercise effective domination over the hinterland. For their part the Portuguese were quite satisfied with this arrangement. At this juncture, however, Gaza–Portuguese relations were complicated by the appearance of a third party—the British.

Spurred on by the increasing Portuguese activity, the Gazas again sent two indunas to Natal in 1887.[5] They asked for British help. By now, however, the official British view was that Gazaland was within the Portuguese sphere of influence, and

[1] D. Doyle, 'With King Gungunhana', Fortnightly Review, July 1891, p. 114.
[2] See W. T. Law, A Memoir of Father Law, 1882.
[3] For copy of the Treaty (12 October 1885), see Incl. 2 in Soveral to Salisbury, 4 February 1891 (C. 6945/52).
[4] Ibid., incl. 3.
[5] Incl. 9 in Salisbury to Petre, 8 May 1891 (C. 6495/190).

the Governor of Natal referred to the Portuguese Resident:
'The Governor trusts that any messages sent to him are sent
with the knowledge and concurrence of that official.' The
indunas returned without any promise of British help. British
concession-seekers, however, began to appear at Gungunhana's
kraal and the chief also welcomed Mr and Mrs Fels of the Amer-
can Zulu Mission. Meanwhile, friction had arisen between Gungunhana and his neighbour, Manuel Antonio, whose power had
been growing.[1] Manuel Antonio boasted that he could raise an
army of 10,000. To lessen the tension, Gungunhana decided to
move his kraal further south. In 1889, 60,000 people left Mount
Silinda and marched across country to a site near the Limpopo.
The move was a major undertaking and many people died en
route. The country over which they travelled was left bare. The
new kraal bore the same name, Manhlagazi (Manjacaze) 'power
of blood'. It was on the site of the kraal of a Portuguese vassal chief
—a grim reminder of Gaza power.[2] The Portuguese were still
continuing their efforts to strengthen relations and Almeida made
several visits to what they had designated the District of Gaza.
Gungunhana accused the Portuguese of fermenting a rebellion of
the Chopi tribe and he sent a force of 12,000 to deal with the
revolt.

It was at this juncture that Cecil Rhodes entered the Gazaland
story. He was interested in the area as an approach to the sea for
his projected settlement in Mashonaland. He wanted to eliminate
the long overland haul of 1,600 miles and provide Mashonaland
with direct access to the sea. Gungunhana claimed control over
hundreds of miles of coast-line and a treaty with him would be an
essential prerequisite for a port for Rhodesia, as Mashonaland was
to become. Aurel Schulz was sent to Manhlagazi in 1890 to
secure such a treaty.

Schulz 'squared' the other concession-seekers in the traditional
Rhodes manner and set about persuading the chief of the value of
a treaty with Rhodes' British South Africa Company. While

[1] For Gungunhana's relations with Manuel Antonio and with Mutasa of
Manica, see P. R. Warhurst, *Anglo-Portuguese Relations in South Central Africa
(1890–1900)*, 1962, Chaps. I and II.
[2] Churchill to Salisbury, 14 September 1889 (C. 5904/218).

Schulz was at the kraal, the arrival of the Pioneers at Salisbury made a short route to the sea an urgent necessity, and in October 1890 the treaty was provisionally agreed to.[1] It was not yet signed as Gungunhana wanted to see the goods delivered. The terms were very similar to those offered to Lobengula, namely, 1,000 rifles, 20,000 rounds of ammunition and an annual subsidy of £500. The Company claimed in return mineral rights and extensive privileges to go with them. The wording of the treaty, however, went further than the Rudd Concession and is of great significance. 'This Covenant', it reads, 'shall be considered in the light of a Treaty of Alliance made between the said Nation (Gazas) and the Government of Her Britannic Majesty, Queen Victoria.' Schulz had no authorization whatsoever to give this commercial treaty a political twist.[2] It seemed that Rhodes wanted to involve the British Government. But they rebuked Rhodes and informed the Portuguese Government that the unwarranted statement has been included in the treaty without their knowledge or approval.[3]

Gungunhana himself was pleased to have the British Government included in the treaty. He had, after all, been trying for years to obtain an alliance and he considered his arrangement with Schulz as an alliance with Queen Victoria. In this way he was throwing in his hand with the British and trusted them to support the Gaza against Portugal. He was not aware of the basic difference between the Chartered Company and the British Government; indeed the unauthorized statement in the treaty would seem to him to point to their mutual identification. For their part the Portuguese redoubled their efforts to ensure Gungunhana's loyalty to Portugal. They dispatched an expedition and in December 1890 several officers, forty marines and a detachment of askari arrived at Manhlagazi.[4] Gungunhana must have been duly impressed, and at a large *indaba* he was said to have confirmed his obligations to Portugal. Schulz now weighed up the situation: Gungunhana, having thrown in his lot with Britain, had suddenly

---

[1] For an account of the negotiations, see Warhurst, pp. 84–5.
[2] For a copy of the treaty, see Salisbury to Petre, 8 May 1891 (C. 6495/191).
[3] *Ibid.*, incl. 2.
[4] Incl. I in Salisbury to Petre, 13 February 1891 (F.O. 179/286 : 27).

found the Portuguese back in greater strength than ever. Schulz realized that delivery of the guns and ammunition promised in the treaty would tip this uneasy balance in the Company's favour. He reported this back to the Company office. Gungunhana himself was encouraged by the victory of his army over the Chopi rebels. His punitive expedition had burned the Chopi kraal to the ground and 7,000 of the triumphant Gaza warriors wore the death-plume to show that each had killed his man. Gungunhana now impatiently awaited the arrival of the arms and ammunition.

The Chartered Company arranged to smuggle the guns into Gazaland by running them up the Limpopo, a river over which Gungunhana claimed complete control.[1] This smuggling episode was to involve the British Government in the Company's activities in South-East Africa and provoke a showdown over Gazaland. While the Company gave general support to Gungunhana's claims over the interior, the British Government did not actually work against them. Nor, of course, did they accept them. But this non-committal attitude could not be extended to the coast. Britain had upheld Portugal's claim to the coast, from Delagoa Bay to Cape Delgado, throughout the 19th century. Recognition of Portuguese sovereignty along the coast had been essential to the success of the anti-slave trade operations and this had been established by treaty in 1817 and again in 1847. Lord Salisbury, Prime Minister and Foreign Secretary, was steadfast in his refusal to go back on these treaties.[2] To smuggle arms across the coast-line in defiance of Portugal was, in Salisbury's view, quite illegal. Portuguese sovereignty having been recognized as early as 1817 before the Gazas had even arrived in Moçambique, Salisbury accepted their prior claim. Both Gungunhana and the Chartered Company rejected this view and in February 1891 ran the guns in, on board the *Countess of Carnarvon*. As they were landing at Xai-Xai on the Limpopo they were challenged by a Portuguese official. He eventually allowed the guns through, accepting a company 'guarantee' to pay 'any just fine'. The guns were duly sent up to Manhlagazi, where they were later accidentally des-

---

[1] Harris to B.S.A. Co. London encl. in Salisbury to Petre 12 April 1891 (C. 6495/145).
[2] Grey to Rhodes, 5 June 1891 (Rhodes Papers, Oxford, 3A, 171).

troyed by fire, but the *Countess* and her crew were captured by a Portuguese customs vessel. The *Countess* was released after strong representations by the British Government.[1]

The whole Gazaland issue now became the subject of correspondence between Britain and Portugal and was eventually settled without reference to Gungunhana. In August 1890 Britain and Portugal had negotiated a draft treaty to demarcate their respective areas in South-Central Africa. The treaty gave the whole of Gazaland, that is the area from the Sabi to the sea, to Portugal, in addition to Manicaland. But Portugal having previously claimed the whole of Central Africa, Portuguese public opinion prevented ratification. Rhodes played on the non-ratification to obtain as much of the area as possible and Salisbury found it difficult to restrain his enthusiasm. For many years Britain had regarded Gazaland as being within the Portuguese sphere of influence though it was doubted how effective Portuguese occupation might be. It was only recently that the Company had begun to inform the Foreign Office of any doubts as to the validity of Portuguese claims over the Gaza chiefs. In spite of this, Salisbury did not wish to press Portugal too hard because of the European background. He pointed out to the Chartered Company that the terms of their Royal Charter presupposed Portuguese occupation, at least of the coast. The first article of the Charter defined the Company's sphere as 'the region of South Africa lying . . . to the west of the Portuguese dominions'. If they persisted in denying Portuguese sovereignty, 'they would thereby nullify their own claims to territories described as bounded by them'.[2] Having put the Chartered Company in their place, Salisbury did press their claim for a withdrawal of the Portuguese boundary further east. The final treaty was signed on 11 June 1891[3] and the Rhodesian–Portuguese border was pushed back from the Sabi. This partitioned Gungunhana's kingdom between Britain and Portugal, the former obtaining North Gazaland

[1] For the Xai-Xai affair and diplomatic repercussions, see Warhurst, p. 87 *et seq.*

[2] F.O. to B.S.A. Co., 14 May 1891, incl. in Salisbury to Petre, 14 May 1891 (C. 6495/199).

[3] C. 6370 is a copy of the Treaty.

(Chipinga–Mount Silinda) east of the Sabi, and Portugal receiving the greater part of Gazaland. Demarcation of the frontier was to be left to a delimitation commission.

Internationally this represented a final settlement. Not for the first time in the Scramble, tribal boundaries had been ignored in the interests of international expediency. Gungunhana continued to regard his territory as one whole and Rhodes, for his own motives, maintained good relations with the Gaza chief. Realizing that the undefined border presented an opportunity for further expansion, Rhodes obtained a second treaty to cover North Gazaland. This treaty, signed in November 1891, gave the Company rights to all 'waste lands' in Gazaland and Rhodes construed this as a title-deed to North Gazaland.[1] Whilst it is true that the area was sparsely populated after Gungunhana's big move, it was not made clear to the chief that he was to lose it. Two years later, when he did hear that a party of Boers were occupying North Gazaland, Gungunhana registered a strong protest through the British Consul in Lourenço Marques. Rhodes had supported the settlement scheme which had been initiated by Dunbar Moodie, a Company employee who was himself partly Scots and partly Afrikaans. Moodie led a trek of Free Staters to the area and they formed the nucleus of the Afrikaans farming community which grew up around Chipinga. Rhodes warned Moodie of possible conflict with the Portuguese in this disputed frontier district beyond the Sabi. Moodie's reply was characteristic of the man, 'I will make possession nine points of the law and be damned'.[2] In subsequent frontier incidents, he kept the Portuguese out and helped to ensure that the area was awarded to Rhodesia by the Arbitrator. The Portuguese were not the only people to contest the Moodie trek. When the Free Staters appeared in North Gazaland, they were challenged by a Shangaan (Gaza) headman. The headman, Maseka Bantu (the slayer of people), arrived with an *impi* of 400 and demanded to know by what right the Boers were entering his district. For reply, Moodie had him flogged. Gungunhana's authority was no longer recognized in North Gaza-

[1] For a copy of this Treaty, see C.O. to F.O. 23 February 1892 (F.O. Conf. 6336/36).

[2] For the Moodie trek, see S. P. Olivier, *Many Treks made Rhodesia*, 1942.

land. Rhodes did, however, keep up payments of a subsidy due
to Gungunhana under the terms of the treaty. This brought down
on Rhodes the enmity of the Portuguese; there had never been
any love lost between them, and the Portuguese accused him
of supplying arms and finance to a potential enemy of theirs.
Eventually he agreed to suspend the payments and thus prevent
further suspicion.[1]

The British Government, which had been embroiled in Gazaland affairs for two years, now began to fade out of the picture
and leave Portugal and the Gazas to come to terms. But the
dramatic British intervention left both parties with one eye on the
British. The Portuguese continued to suspect Rhodes' hand in any
new development in South–Central Africa and there was some
limited truth in their suspicions. Gungunhana, for his part, continued to feel committed to the British Government and over the
next few years tried in vain to establish relations with London.
Incensed at Gungunhana's attitude, many Portuguese proposed a
military campaign as the only way to settle the Gaza question and
events moved towards this climax.

As early as 1891 Gungunhana had sent his first deputation to
London. Rhodes arranged the visit and sent the *indunas* through,
in defiance of orders from the British Government. Salisbury and
Colonial Secretary Knutsford had made it clear that the visit
would be an embarrassment to the British Government during
their negotiations for the final treaty. They must have been very
surprised to read in *The Times* (8 May 1891) that, 'Two chiefs
have sailed in the *Roslin Castle* for England on a mission from
Gungunhana to Queen Victoria.' The Colonial Office noted the
delicacy of the situation, 'It will be difficult, if not impossible, to
make them understand that they have not been sent to England
to see the Queen, and Gungunhana will feel disappointed and
insulted if his chief *induna* is not received by Her Majesty's Government as the representatives of an independent chief.'[2]

In the event, the *indunas*, Huluhulu and Umfeti, who had previously been in the Natal mission, were accorded a good recep-

[1] Salisbury to Petre, 21 November 1894 (F.O. 179/308 : 120A).
[2] C.O. to F.O., 21 May 1891 (F.O. 179/286 : 114).

tion.[1] They went the rounds of London and were astonished at what they saw in the metropolis. Their previous experience of urban life had been confined to short visits to the small towns of Lourenço Marques and Durban. From this cordial reception, they must have gained the impression that they were being received as representatives of an independent king. Yet even while they were on their mission, the final treaty was signed partitioning their kingdom. At their audience with Queen Victoria, she told them that a communication would be made to Gungunhana and after their return this was done. It was to the effect that much of his territory was now Portuguese and he could, therefore, not be protected by Her Majesty. As a token of her friendship she sent the king a silver cup inscribed, 'To Gungunhana from Queen Victoria'. It was very much a parting gift to cover the British Government's embarrassment but to the Portuguese it was to become further evidence of Britain's perfidy.[2]

The *indunas* returned to Manhlagazi simultaneously with Will Longden, sent by Rhodes as his private emissary to deliver the subsidy to Gungunhana. Huluhulu and Umfeti had been very impressed with Britain's might and the king must have congratulated himself on backing the right horse, as he listened to their account of the visit to Britain. When Queen Victoria's letter arrived to dampen his enthusiasm, he must have been very perplexed. He had no more intention of accepting the Anglo-Portuguese Treaty as final than Rhodes had but both were playing a losing game. Rhodes' representative, Will Longden, became very popular with Gungunhana.[3] He was in an ideal position to observe at first hand an African chief caught up in the Scramble. Rejected by the British Government, hedged in by the Portuguese, the chief was confronted by forces which were too complicated and strong for him either to comprehend or resist indefinitely. Gaza manpower was sapped by an outflow of young men recruited to work on the gold-mines where the Shangaans were becoming a well-known element in the Rand labour force. Coastal tribes, beginning to break their allegiance to him, found

[1] F.O. to Goschen, 15 September 1891 (F.O. 179/287 : 200).
[2] Jose de Almada, O *Tratado de 1891*, 1947, p. 188.
[3] For Will Longden's story, see H. W. D. Longden, *Red Buffalo*, 1950.

themselves in an invidious position. The British Consul reported, 'The natives on this coast are friendly to the Portuguese but they resent having to pay the hut tax in addition to the tribute to Gungunhana'. Elsewhere the Gazas were completely powerless. Their tax-collectors going north to the Busi river area were turned away after a clash with the Portuguese.[1] Rhodes' withdrawal of Longden and suspension of his subsidy payments meant the end of an era for Gungunhana. Now he was without an ally against the Portuguese.

In 1894 Mahazul, a Ronga chief near Lourenço Marques, rose in revolt against the Portuguese over an increase in the hut tax.[2] The Portuguese sent troops to crush him. At the final engagement at Magule, Gaza *impis* were present but took no part, having orders not to kill any whites. Mahazul fled to Gungunhana, who gave him political asylum and refused Portuguese requests to deliver up the refugee. From now on it was only a matter of time before the Portuguese launched an expedition against the Gazas. An energetic royal commissioner, Antonio Enes, arrived to take charge of the province and he favoured a more forward policy. Reinforcements were brought in and Gungunhana too gathered his warriors together. An army of 25,000 men assembled at Manhlagazi or Manjacaze as it was now becoming known. Gungunhana formulated a plan of attack based on traditional Zulu strategy. The idea was to send one of three armies via Komatipoort to Swaziland where an alliance with the Swazi would be concluded. This army would proceed to exterminate the Matjolo, allies of the Portuguese, thus outflanking the latter and cutting their line of retreat. Caught between this army and a frontal attack of the other two, the Portuguese would be forced to surrender.[3] The plan was well conceived and had it gone into operation, it might well have brought the war to a different conclusion. It failed for two reasons. Firstly the subject tribes, on which the plan depended, failed to remain united and the outflanking move had to be cancelled. Then the Portuguese struck with speed.

[1] Parsonson to Kimberley, 10 November 1894 (F.O. Conf. 6066/215).
[2] Bernal to Kimberley, 1 September 1894 (F.O. Conf. 6606/99).
[3] Junod, I, Appendix 10.

The new commander-in-chief of the Portuguese expeditionary force was the most famous figure in the history of Moçambique, Mousinho de Albuquerque. A devoted imperialist, he was determined to raise the province from the low level at which it had remained for centuries. Even the new awakening since 1870 was too slow and limited for the forceful Mousinho. He wanted to extend effective administration to every district and he admitted that Portuguese occupation was very tenuous in most areas. The first move was to defeat Gungunhana. A battle was fought at Coolela (1895) where the Portuguese were victorious. They marched on Manjacaze which Gungunhana destroyed, as Lobengula had done to Bulawayo, and fled north. Similarly Mousinho pursued the Gaza king with a small patrol, but met with more success than his Rhodesian counterpart, Allan Wilson. He captured the king in a cave at Chaimite. With the swift capture of the chief, the war ended and Gungunhana was sent into exile in West Africa. He never returned to his native land.

Even at this moment when Gaza power was collapsing, Gungunhana's last mission of *indunas* was trying in vain to persuade the British authorities in South Africa of their chief's allegiance to Britain.[1] They had with them the traditional sign of submission, an elephant tusk filled with earth, but no one would accept it.

The Gaza war had another sequel. Both American missionaries and the Mission de la Suisse Romande had established themselves in Gazaland. As Protestants they were suspect to the Portuguese authorities, and after the war the Rev. Mashaba was deported to Angola. Roger Casement, at that time British Consul in Lourenço Marques, reporting on his subsequent release after British representations, commented that the only acceptable missionaries would be Trappists!

The parallel with events in Matabeleland extends further, for there was a Gaza Rebellion for reasons similar to the causes of the Matabele Rebellion. Gungunhana's royal cattle were confiscated, and this hit many people in Gazaland. They had herded the king's cattle, but for most practical purposes treated them as their own. Now they had to pay to recover them. The harvest had failed due to excessive rain and the Gazas objected to the hut tax. Like the

[1] C.O. to F.O., 27 August 1895 (F.O. Conf. 6773/130).

Shona police recruited to police Matabeleland, the 'native police'
in Gazaland used the opportunity to wreak revenge on their
former masters. Finally the question of national pride must not be
overlooked. The Gazas had always held the Portuguese in con-
tempt; now the latter had beaten them, 'by surprise' they claimed.
They looked forward to a 'revanche'. In the previous year in
Rhodesia the opportunity for the Matabele Rebellion had arisen
through the absence of troops during the Jameson Raid. In 1897
the Portuguese were likewise occupied elsewhere subduing the
Namarrāes, a tribe much further north. The Gazas rose. Their
leader, Gungunhana's commander-in-chief, Maguigana, fought
and lost the decisive battle of Macontene and fled to the Transvaal.[1] Pursued by troops, he was cornered and, according to
Portuguese sources, died a hero's death emptying his revolver into
his pursuers.

With his death ended the story of Gazaland as a separate nation.
The Gazas had conquered southern Moçambique, sweeping all
before them; now they in turn had been swept aside in the
Scramble for Africa.

BIBLIOGRAPHY

F.O. 179 (Portugal–Africa), 276–83, 286–7, 291, 308.
F.O. Confidential Prints: Correspondence respecting the Action of Portugal
in the Region South of the Zambesi, I–XVII.
Rhodes Papers (Oxford), C3, 3A.
Parliamentary Papers, C.5904, C.6495.
D. Doyle, 'With King Gungunhana', *Fortnightly Review*, July 1891.
D. Doyle, 'A Journey through Gazaland', *Proceedings of the R.G.S.*, 1891.
A. Pereira de Lima, 'A nossa intervenção na politica indigena de ha cem anos'.
Separata No. 5, Divisão do Turismo, Lourenço Marques.
J. P. M. Weale, *The Truth about the Portuguese in Africa*, 1891.

Jose de Almada, *O Tratado de 1895*, 1947.
A. T. Botelho, *Historia Militar e Politica dos Portugueses em Moçambique*, 1936.
E. T. Bryant, *Olden Times in Zululand*, 1929.
J. de A. Coutinho, *Manuel Antonio de Sousa*, 1936.
H. M. Hole, *The Making of Rhodesia*, 1926.

[1] For the military campaigns of the Gaza War and Rebellion, see A. T.
Botelho, *Historia Militar e Politica dos Portugueses en Moçambique*, II, 1936.

62   P. R. WARHURST

S. P. Hyatt, *The Northward Trek*, 1909.
H. A. Junod, *Life of a South African Tribe*, 1912.
H. W. D. Longden, *Red Buffalo*, 1950.
S. P. Olivier, *Many Treks made Rhodesia*, 1942.
J. P. R. Wallis, *The Zambezi Expedition of David Livingstone*, 1956.
P. R. Warhurst, *Anglo-Portuguese Relations in South-Central Africa (1890-1900)*, 1962.

4

ASPECTS OF THE SCRAMBLE FOR MATABELELAND

by

RICHARD BROWN

I

THE general character of the Scramble in Matabeleland was determined by the nature of the Matabele state on the one hand and by the nature of the European intrusion on the other.[1] A highly centralized and militarized society faced a powerful European advance aiming not at a mere 'paper protectorate' but at the rapid establishment of a colony of settlement. The interaction of these two factors made it highly improbable that the Matabele kingdom would survive even partly intact. Matabeleland was a key area in the whole strategy of the Scramble in southern Africa and once the imperial government had decided to give virtually free rein to the Cape Colony's expansive movement led by Rhodes a military conflict was almost inevitable.[2]

The strength of the movement which set up British South Africa Company rule north of the Limpopo is well known. The development of mining capitalism in the second half of the 19th century coupled with interests generated in over two centuries of white settlement in South Africa gave the movement exceptional determination and resources. 'I shall bring,' Rhodes informed an associate, 'what you much need in a great undertaking, the "sinews of war" both in my private fortune and my Trust Deed [i.e. of the

[1] MSS references in this paper are to material in the National Archives, Salisbury, Southern Rhodesia: HC indicates the records of the High Commissioner for South Africa; CT those of the British South Africa Company's Cape Town office; all other MSS references are to private papers in the historical manuscripts collection.

[2] For the development of British policy towards 'southern Zambesia' see R. E. Robinson, J. Gallagher, A. Denny, *Africa and the Victorians*, 1961.

63

De Beers Diamond Company] with twenty millions behind it.'[1]
Yet just because the white advance into 'southern Zambesia' was
so powerful the influence exerted on the process by the Matabele
state may be overlooked. Its ultimate failure to preserve even the
semblance of independence should not lead us to ignore the extent
to which it was an active force in the political upheavals brought
about by the Scramble. For a time at least the Matabele state
succeeded in being a considerable obstacle in the path of white
expansion, and, not unaware of much that was happening around
it, sought to manipulate the forces in play in much the same way
as any other society faced by an overwhelming external threat.
However, Matabele society was not undifferentiated and the role
that it played was deeply conditioned by its institutions and earlier
history.

In the generation before the Scramble the Matabele state was
regarded as one of the leading African powers south of the Zambesi. The colonial governments of South Africa treated it with
marked deference, and recognized that the white hunters and
traders who visited Matabeleland put themselves under the exclusive sovereignty of the king. Matabele military prowess and
discipline were famed and feared throughout southern Africa, but
too much emphasis can be placed on this aspect to the neglect of
other more significant features connected with their rapid rise to
a position of power. When Mzilikazi fled from Shaka and settled
north of the Drakensberg mountains in about 1820 he was
probably accompanied by a tribal following numbering only a
few hundred. Subsequently other fugitives from Zululand, some
with and some without previous ties to Mzilikazi, had to be incorporated, as well as thousands of Sotho and Tswana captives and
volunteers. The further move across the Limpopo in about 1838
led to the assimilation, in varying degrees, of large numbers of
former inhabitants of the Rozwi empire, while for the next half-
century the state had to absorb a steady stream of captives from
the medley of tribes periodically raided by Matabele war-bands.
It is difficult to estimate accurately the size Matabele society had
reached by the 1880's, but it was generally agreed by white

[1] Rhodes to S. Shippard, Administrator of British Bechuanaland, August
1888, RH 1/3/1.

observers that the army was from 15,000 to 20,000 strong: the total population may have been '100,000 or more'.[1] This rapid growth by incorporation rather than by natural increase obviously posed formidable problems of political and social organization.[2]

The Matabele seem to have dealt with these problems by a very high degree of centralization and by closely identifying administrative, residential and military functions. The social organization of the nation into three stratified sections based on ethnic origins between whom marriage was forbidden cut across other allegiances and also tended to reduce the effectiveness of kinship ties and to promote kingship as the primary unifying force.[3] The extensive religious and secular duties of the king in a politically centralized system helped to make his subjects dependent upon him, but although the structure was distinctly authoritarian it was not the unqualified despotism so often portrayed. If it was, it would be possible to explain Matabele actions during the Scramble period solely in terms of the ruler's interests. In fact, Lobengula's policies in the face of the white advance, as will be seen, are inexplicable except in terms of popular pressures upon him from below. Ruling the Matabele called for political qualities of a high order for unity could not come easily to a state compounded so rapidly of such diverse ethnic elements. Disintegration, such as occurred among the Ngoni, a similar Zulu off-shoot, on the death of their founder, was a constant possibility. In an area of Africa

[1] This was J. Colenbrander's estimate in 1894 after several years in Matabeleland in the service of the B.S.A. Co., C. 8130, p. 12.
[2] There are no specifically historical studies on this subject, but the anthropological writings of A. J. Hughes are useful. See his 'Reconstruction of the Ndebele Society under European Control' (typescript), no date, deposited in 1956 at the Rhodes-Livingstone Institute, and his Kin, Caste and Nation among the Rhodesian Ndebele, R.I.I. Papers, No. 25, 1956.
[3] Hughes refers to these sections as castes, but this terminology is somewhat misleading if comparisons with India are implied. The superior position was held by the section known as Abezansi, who were of Zulu origin and monopolized most of the important positions in the state. The Abenhla, of Sotho and Tswana origin, were scarcely less privileged and a wide gulf separated them from the group most commonly known as Amaholi who were formed of peoples incorporated north of the Limpopo; their position was a semi-servile one. This classification excludes those communities within the area of settlement who were under Matebele domination, such as Kalanga settlements in the south-west, but who were not fully incorporated.

which was not densely populated, where there was much unused land and many weaker peoples to prey upon, powerful subordinates had the temptation to break away from the Matabele state just as Mzilikazi had broken away from Shaka's Zululand.

Nevertheless, before the Scramble, the Matabele had overcome powerful challenges to their political integrity. The military defeats of 1837 and 1838 at the hands of Boers and Zulus did not break up the nation, though the renewed migration which followed brought about serious strains. A difficult succession followed Mzilikazi's death in 1868, but substantial unity was maintained despite a minor civil war which was still said to account a generation later for a lack of loyalty to the king in one particular region.[1]

The great dependence of the economy and social organization on continual success in war was vitally significant in determining Matabele responses to the Scramble. By the 1880's there was an evident feeling that the existing raiding grounds were more or less worked out at the same time as the increasing supply of guns to the interior had begun to make the Matabele raiding parties less invincible.[2] What would have happened if white intervention had been delayed can only be surmised, but raiding was still an integral part of the Matabele system at the time the challenge came. The economy relied heavily on cattle captured in war and large numbers were slaughtered to provide meat. Control of the cattle was nominally in the hands of the king, but they were used to reward followers, and milk from the herds placed in the charge of regimental towns was an important article of diet. The subordinate leaders, especially the younger men with a position still to win, sought captives as a means of building up their power and prestige, while the rule, apparently somewhat relaxed during Lobengula's reign, that regiments had first to win their spurs in

[1] J. S. Moffat to Sir H. B. Loch, Private, 9 December 1890, MO 1/1/5/3; also E. A. Maund in C.4643, Encl. 7 in No. 34, writing in 1885. The area concerned was Inyati, which happened to be the site of the first mission station, but this was an accidental rather than causal feature of the disloyalty. A preliminary survey of the succession dispute and its far-reaching ramifications is given in my paper in *Historians in Tropical Africa*, Proceedings of the Leverhulme Inter-Collegiate History Conference, University College of Rhodesia and Nyasaland, 1962. A fuller study is forthcoming.

[2] Reports on Matabeleland in C. 4643, encls. in No. 34.

battle before being allowed to marry also helped to make raiding self-perpetuating. Not surprisingly, therefore, it was the younger members of the two dominant sections of the people, in particular the *amatjaha* or unmarried soldiers, who were most implacably opposed to the white advance. The raiding system, Lobengula accurately claimed, 'was indispensably necessary to the preservation of his power and the political existence of his people'.[1]

II

In many parts of Africa pre-colonial contacts with whites had an important bearing on the position of African societies at the time of the partition. Among the Matabele such contacts were fairly extensive, but nonetheless not very influential. Almost without exception, the whites who came into contact with the Matabele denounced the raiding system: the traders because it led to a semi-parasitic economy which inhibited the growth of trade; the preachers because it appeared to stand in the way of conversion; the colonial governments of South Africa because its disturbances could have far reaching political repercussions and did not promote commerce or the migration of labour.[2] Hunters seem to have been the most welcome visitors at the king's kraal, but their impact on Matabele society was necessarily slight. Not surprisingly, in view of the nature of the state, the majority of the Matabele were fervent opponents of European influences. At the same time, Mzilikazi and Lobengula were well aware that it was dangerous to quarrel with whites in the circumstances of 19th century South Africa, and, indeed, it is clear that both kings followed political developments in the sub-continent as closely as they could. They saw certain advantages in limited co-operation. Lobengula shrewdly manipulated the European influences around him to gain support in his struggle to retain the throne, but, like his father, saw that the outright co-operation practised by a chief like Khama would lead to rebellion in Matabeleland. In short,

[1] Reported in Shippard to Sir H. Robinson, 22 October 1888, C. 5918, encl. in No. 32.
[2] The first labour recruiting agent, Alexander Baillie, visited Matabeleland in 1876, BA 10/2/1. By the time of the Scramble a trickle of labour was going to the Diamond Fields from Matabeleland.

Matabeleland proved highly resistant to the twin influences of Christianity and commerce which elsewhere in Africa so often smoothed the way to European control.

With some reluctance, Mzilikazi permitted the setting up of a mission in Matabeleland in 1859.[1] J. S. Moffat, one of the founders of the mission, believed that 'there is no blinking the fact that the tendency of Christianity is to overturn native governments'.[2] But he also saw clearly that the missionary impact varied greatly, depending on the type of African society involved, and that Matabeleland was a vastly different case from Bechuanaland.[3] His forebodings were justified for although the missionaries were occasionally made use of in diplomatic, technical and medical affairs, they were never allowed to gain any real influence with the people. The suggestion that a fourth member should join the mission brought a firm refusal from Mzilikazi, on the grounds that the Matabele would certainly murder a newcomer. 'He did not wish to act in opposition to the desire of his people, who had set their faces firmly against any further opening of the country to foreigners,' wrote Moffat. 'I asked how it was that he allowed the Boers to go where they pleased. He said, "Oh, they come to trade and hunt, and then go about their business. It is to people settling in the country that the Matabele object" . . . He added that some of his people were asking that we too might be sent away.'[4]

Lobengula permitted the opening of a second mission station soon after his accession in 1870, but this was almost certainly part of his policy of winning European support against a rival claimant to the throne, and hopes of a new era soon faded as Lobengula resumed his father's policy towards the missionaries. When J. S. Moffat returned to the country in 1887 after twenty-one years' absence he commented, 'I fear things are very little further than when I left. It is a remarkable case. I do not know that a similar one exists in the annals of missions; but I fear that there will be no change for the better until there has been a breaking-up of the

[1] *The Matabele Journals of Robert Moffat*, ed. J. P. R. Wallis, Vol. 2, 1945, Oppenheimer Series No 1.

[2] R. U. Moffat, *John Smith Moffat*, 1921, p. 207.

[3] J. S. Moffat to J. S. Unwin, 10 September 1859, *The Matabele Mission*, ed. J. R. P. Wallis, 1945, Oppenheimer Series No 2, pp. 70–1.

[4] Moffat to Unwin, 21 June 1862, *ibid.*, p. 180.

Matebele power and a change in the whole regime.'[1] The almost complete failure of missionary endeavour had a direct bearing on the situation during the Scramble. It made the missionaries natural, if sometimes qualified, supporters of Rhodes; their lack of success and hatred of the raiding system made them silent witnesses of measures against the Matabele which they could not approve, but would not oppose. The Matabeleland missionaries had built up none of the vested interests which turned many of the missionaries in Bechuanaland and Nyasaland into stern and sometimes influential critics of their fellow whites. The attitude of the Matabele missionaries was strikingly confirmed by their superior, the Rev. R. W. Thompson, Foreign Secretary of the London Missionary Society. On the outbreak of war in 1893 he wrote: 'I am conscious also that there is good reason for saying that the missionary interest has been on the side of the Chartered Company. The fact is, some of us who have been pretty closely connected with work in Matabeleland for many years past have been sorely troubled as to the attitude we ought to take.' He had long been convinced that a war was inevitable and that the existing Matabele system made missionary work quite impossible. Nevertheless, he deprecated talk of wiping out the Matabele altogether. 'Indeed, it would be great folly, on economic grounds, to think of such a thing. All that is needed is that the tyranny under which they live should be broken, and a different government substituted for it.'[2]

The Matabele were nearly as indifferent to the trade as to the religion brought by the whites. The activities of the hunters and traders who entered the country with increasing frequency after 1854 were also strictly controlled; in particular, the law against prospecting was almost always enforced. By the 1880's a handful of small traders had settled permanently in Matabeleland, but they were very dependent on Lobengula and their trade was precarious. They had to pay a heavy blackmail to influential figures at court, while the king frequently helped himself to their goods without payment. The traders were said to be on their last legs until Rhodes, for his own purposes, began to subsidize them.[3]

[1] *John Smith Moffat, op. cit.,* pp. 217–18.
[2] Rev J. W. Thompson to the *Daily Chronicle,* 14 November 1893, C. 7555, encl. in No. 5.
[3] Moffat to a Mr Gifford of Palapye, 1 October 1890, MO 1/1/5/3.

Mzilikazi and Lobengula did not entirely ignore the new opportunities brought about by the extension of the South African 'trading frontier' and dealt in ivory and ostrich feathers on their own account. However, the incentive to set up a trading empire like Msidi in Katanga or Kazembe on the Luapula was evidently lacking. The resources of the country were not systematically exploited, and more often than not, the articles obtained by trade, which was virtually a royal monopoly, were allowed to rot away uncared for and unused.[1] They were certainly anxious to obtain guns, but here again conservatism triumphed and Zulu military tactics remained orthodox and were employed with disastrous consequences in the 1893 war.[2]

On the eve of the Scramble, Matabele relations with the whites stretched back over a period of some sixty years. Little had been sought or granted as a result of this contact and inasfar as Mzilikazi and Lobengula had co-operated with alien influences they could still claim that the existence of their predatory state had not yet been prejudiced. It cannot be said that here was a case where the power to resist European encroachment had been undermined in advance. Indeed, the reverse was true, and the Matabele entered the dangerous world of the Scramble against a history which in a sense was too successful. Lords of the interior, they found it difficult to adapt successfully to the new era and were vitally short of allies, whether white or black. According to F. S. Arnot, sometime between 1882 and 1884 Lobengula asked Lewanika of Barotseland 'to join with the Matabele in resisting the invading white man', but the overtures were refused, Lewanika preferring to look to Khama in Bechuanaland as an ally.[3] Khama himself had a double motive in co-operating with Rhodes since he hoped to end the threat of Matabele raids and extend territorially at Matabele expense. In the Matabele hour of crisis in 1893 both Khama and Lewanika were willing to raise the sword against their old

[1] E. C. Tabler, *The Far Interior*, Cape Town, 1955, has a great deal of information on the pre-colonial activities in Matabeleland of whites from South Africa.

[2] Guns were used in a raid against a Shona-speaking group as early as 1861 (*The Matebele Mission, op. cit.*, p. 161), but their use does not appear to have become general in warfare.

[3] F. S. Arnot, *Missionary Travels in Central Africa*, Bath, 1914, p. 22.

foes. As far as the whites were concerned, all the purposes for which they came to Central Africa were thwarted by the nature of Matabele society, and since it stood in the front line of the advance, occupying a region of great strategic importance, expected mineral wealth, and known pastoral potential, it was their avowed aim to produce its downfall. It was hoped by some that it would remove north of the Zambesi, by others that it would collapse through its own internal strains, and by still others that they would have the opportunity of overthrowing it by violence. Lobengula himself, and some of his chief men, realized the great dangers threatening the Matabele kingdom, but the unjustified self-confidence of his subjects as a whole was a factor of some significance in the policies he was forced to pursue. A reconstruction of these policies, to the extent that the evidence available allows, suggests that they were essentially manœuvrings to gain time in a situation which became steadily more impossible. He clearly tried to thwart the white advance, but felt unable to check it completely. Lobengula's internal position was not so precarious that it led him as it led Lewanika to a large measure of co-operation, nor was it sufficiently strong to enable him to act decisively. In any case, to resist outright the mounting pressures from the Cape was to risk being violently overthrown by the filibustering characteristic of 19th century South Africa, while outright co-operation would provoke his overthrow from within. The elaborate legality with which the British Government wished Rhodes to proceed, but did not insist upon, gave Lobengula the opportunity to win delays and little more.

III

The era of the Scramble commenced in Matabeleland in 1885. European interest in the supposed mineral riches of Matabeleland and Mashonaland had been intermittent since the revelations of Mauch and Hartley in the 1860's, but practical difficulties, including Matabele opposition, had stood in the way of mining development. The Bechuanaland protectorate in 1885 brought imperial influence to the doorstep of Matabeleland at the same time as the

Transvaal gold discoveries stimulated renewed interest in mineral possibilities north of the Limpopo. Memoranda on the immense natural wealth and prospects of the region began to reach the office of the Administrator of British Bechuanaland in Mafeking. These reports fostered the idea that Lobengula would welcome a further extension of the protectorate to include his own dominions.[1] A military mission was dispatched to inform Lobengula of the declaration of the Bechuanaland protectorate, though the activities of the mission were not exclusively diplomatic, and long reports on the state of Matabeleland and its resources were prepared. These put forward the view that the Matabele state had reached a crisis and was on the verge of disruption, and said that Lobengula would readily reach an agreement on the boundary with Khama's country and would welcome English settlers with grants of land provided they also afforded him protection against the Boers of the Transvaal.[2]

It is important to establish exactly what the Matabele attitude to white political and commercial penetration was at this time if the Moffat treaty and the Rudd concession of 1888 are to be put into proper perspective. There is good reason to believe that there was much wishful thinking in the reports being made about Matabeleland, and they should not automatically be taken at their face value. Indeed, those who acted on these reports soon found themselves in difficulties. The 1887 expedition in search of a gold concession led by Frank Johnson and promoted by a group of prominent Cape Town businessmen provides a good example of the real feelings of the Matabele. The very full diary kept by the expedition has survived, and in it Lobengula's, and even more his *indunas'*, hostility to any attempt to exploit the gold resources in Matabeleland or those parts of Mashonaland under his sway is made clear. Lobengula evidently feared to give an outright refusal, perhaps because Johnson's party were armed with a letter of approval from Sir Sydney Shippard, Administrator of British Bechuanaland, and implied they had government backing. Instead, Lobengula's policy was to put as many practical diffi-

[1] HC 1/1/1—HC 1/1/16.
[2] Enclosures in No. 34 of C. 4643, Sir Charles Warren to Colonial Office, 26 October 1885 (Reports on Matabeleland).

culties in the way of the expedition as possible in the hope of provoking it to leave the country or transgress its laws. The king's scheme succeeded handsomely, thanks to Johnson's persistence, and the expedition ended with its members on trial for having hit a member of their escort and having improperly collected gold; and thankful to leave the country on payment of a substantial fine.[1]

Observers were no more accurate regarding Lobengula's reputed desire for British 'protection'. Europeans resident in Matabeleland, as well as visitors like Johnson, were certainly attempting to influence the king, and a deputation which waited upon him in June 1887 stressed Portuguese encroachments in the northeast, the formation of companies seeking gold concessions, and rumours of proposed Boer treks as reasons why Lobengula should request British protection.[2] The deputation, however, only succeeded in getting Lobengula to write a non-committal letter to Shippard requesting information about the dangers said to threaten him.[3]

By the end of 1887, P. J. Grobler representing the Transvaal and J. S. Moffat, Assistant Commissioner Bechuanaland Protectorate, were both in Matabeleland and the struggle for supremacy began in earnest. Lobengula talked freely about his difficulties in private, and Moffat reached the significant conclusion: 'I think his attitude towards the British or any other Government has been misrepresented by those who have written letters for him . . . I think he wants to be left alone.' Moffat also found Lobengula utterly contemptuous of Khama and quite unwilling to define a boundary with him except on the basis of a master dealing with a slave.[4] There was little sign that he was actively seeking outside support, and Lobengula indignantly denied the current rumours that he had placed himself under Transvaal protection, but when

---

[1] The Great Northern Gold Fields Exploration Company to Lobengula, 21 February 1887, JO 3/1/1; MS. diary, 14 February to 17 December 1887, JO 3/3/2; F. Johnson, *Great Days*, 1940.
[2] F. Johnson to Shippard, Confidential, 3 June 1887, HC 1/1/14; D. Carnegie (L.M.S. missionary) to R. W. Thompson, 17 June 1887, Reel 3 of L.M.S. microfilm, National Archives.
[3] Lobengula to Shippard, 4 June 1887, HC 1/1/14.
[4] Moffat to Shippard, Confidential, 12 December 1887, HC 1/1/16.

these rumours reached the Cape, fresh instructions, at Rhodes' instigation, were sent to Moffat.[1]

If there be no truth in these reports [wrote Shippard] you can point out to Lo Bengula the risk he runs of troublesome complications with foreign states through the machinations of designing persons who will not scruple to make use of forged documents to obtain possession of his country or otherwise deprive him of his rights.

You can also point out that Her Majesty's Government has no wish either to obtain possession of his country or to interfere with his sovereign rights and that if he desires to secure himself against insidious attempts or open aggression without losing his independence this result might be obtained if he could induce Her Majesty's Government to conclude with him a treaty similar to that recently entered into by Zambili a copy of which is enclosed.[2]

Zambili was Queen of the Swaziland Tongas and she bound herself not to part with any of her dominions without the previous consent of the British High Commissioner for South Africa, and the treaty Moffat obtained from Lobengula on 11 February 1888 was virtually identical. Such treaties were regarded by the Colonial Office as bringing the region in question into the British 'sphere of influence' but nothing more.

Moffat reacted somewhat pessimistically to his new instructions to obtain a non-alienation treaty from the king. 'I am doubtful,' he wrote to Shippard, 'of the expediency of pressing him under present circumstances to enter into a formal treaty or engagement, unless the way should open for it more than it does at present. He has been so worried with importunities during the last 12 months to enter into engagements, that he turns away from any approach to anything of the kind, and no wonder.'[3] But Moffat himself was probably in a stronger position than he knew, since he had previously spent the years 1859–65 in the country as a missionary before returning in 1887 as a government official. His father, Robert Moffat, had been held in high regard by the Matabele in general and Mzilikazi in particular, and the latter had only agreed to receive the missionaries on condition the son was

[1] B. Williams, *Rhodes*, 1938 edn, pp. 120–1.
[2] Shippard to Moffat, Confidential, 26 December 1887, HC 1/1/16.
[3] Moffat to Shippard, 30 January 1888, C. 5524, encl. in No. 2.

among them. However, there is very little evidence to show what Lobengula's thinking was on the subject of the treaty. That it was not obtained easily is clear from an unofficial letter from Moffat to Shippard, in which he explained that the king disliked signing any agreement 'either on superstitious grounds or from a fear of being entrapped into something more than he really agrees to'. Moreover, he found Lobengula shrewdly anxious to gauge what effect a treaty with the English was likely to have on his relations with Boers. As a result of these difficulties, Moffat admitted to having 'pressed very earnestly upon him the importance of giving us some such assurance as we are asking of him, pointing out the advisability of it from every point of view. I went further in this way than I might have done possibly had I been acting simply on my own judgement, . . .'[1] No doubt Moffat frightened the king with the extensive rights the Transvaal claimed on the basis of the treaty said to have been obtained by P. J. Grobler. Whatever Lobengula's reasons for agreeing to the Moffat treaty, it should be noted that the terms were minimal and could have appeared entirely in accord with a policy of excluding white influences since it would only come into effective operation if the king wished to give away his country, which he was clearly not intending to do. Even if Lobengula knew that in the eyes of the outside world the long-term implications of the treaty were that he had virtually reserved his dominions as a sphere of British interests— and if he did, he may have regarded this as preferable to being a sphere of Boer interests—he could not yet be aware that the future held not a mild British protectorate such as Khama was experiencing, but the full force of Rhodes' ambitious scheme for colonization.

IV

The Rudd concession was the key event in the Scramble for Matabeleland: it provided the basis for the application for a Royal Charter; led to thirty-three years of Chartered Company rule; and indelibly marked the historical development of Southern Rhodesia. For the historian of white colonization, the Moffat

[1] Moffat to Shippard, Private, 10 February 1888, HC 1/1/16.

treaty is promptly and logically followed by the concession; but
an examination of the concession through Matabele eyes shows it
to have been far from an automatic consequence. In the light of
what has been said above about the Matabele attitude to commercial penetration, the granting of such an extensive concession
as claimed by Rudd seems to mark a complete reversal of the
king's earlier policies, especially as the private reports of Moffat,
the most reliable observer in Matabeleland, show that earlier
Matabele attitudes to foreign influences were being strongly
maintained in the months before the concession was signed. It is
important, therefore, to try and discover what lay behind this
apparent shift in policy.

It has often been suggested that C. D. Rudd and his colleagues,
F. R. Thompson and R. Maguire, owed their success to the support they must have received in their negotiations from imperial
officials who were known to be closely associated with Rhodes at
a time when the Colonial Office itself still regarded him with
suspicion. Although Sir Hercules Robinson, Governor of the
Cape and High Commissioner, who was one of them, denied such
allegations soon after the concession was signed, it can be shown
fairly conclusively that the allegations were true. Robinson also
claimed that Shippard and Moffat had left the country 'before the
negotiations began'.[1] This is demonstrably false since the Rudd
party started the negotiations on 26 September 1888, Shippard
left on 23 October, Moffat three days later, while the concession
was signed on 30 October.[2] Robinson himself was urging in July
1888 Moffat's immediate return to Matabeleland, not only to
counteract Transvaal activity, but also 'to prevent Lo Bengula
from making any more promises or concessions of any kind
except such as may hereafter be expressly sanctioned by the High
Commissioner'.[3] This exactly met the wishes of Rhodes, who,

[1] Robinson to Lord Knutsford (Colonial Secretary), 11 January 1889,
African 369, No. 127. [C.O. Confidential Print.]
[2] Shippard to Moffat, Private, 30 July 1888, MO 1/1/4.
[3] On the concession negotiations see *The Concession Journey of Charles Dunell
Rudd*, an edition of his diary, ed. V. W. Hiller, in *Gold and the Gospel in
Mashonaland 1888*, 1949, Oppenheimer Series No. 4, cited hereafter as Rudd,
Diary; and F. R. Thompson, *Matabele Thompson: His Autobiography*, ed. Nancy
Rouillard, 2nd (rev.) edn., 1953, Central News Agency Ltd., South Africa.

already thinking of a Charter[1] had seen his first attempt to obtain a concession fail.[2] Rhodes informed Shippard that he was now afraid 'Lo Bengulu may give away his whole country to bogus companies who will do nothing for government and what is left of that country will not be worth our De Beers Co. while to make any offer to pay expenses of good government'. Shippard was asked to pass on to Moffat the ideas which Rhodes was evolving in the hope that Moffat might be able to prevent the king granting concessions 'to a lot of adventurers who will do nothing but tie the country up'.[3]

Moffat, who had hurried back to Matabeleland, found Lobengula alarmed by the great influx of concession-seekers, 'and there is a distinct tendency to draw in, and to concede less and less to Europeans; and to aim at a Chinese isolation from the rest of the world.'[4] A week later Moffat was able to report: 'I have put the chief in possession of the views and wishes of the Government respecting the grant of concessions. I have to be careful to avoid anything like dictating to him a line of policy. He will in all probability be unconsciously influenced by what I have said to adopt the course we desire.'[5] And the same day he wrote privately to Shippard: 'I do not think the chief has any serious intention of handing over his country to any one, and he is getting impatient of the crowd of concession-seekers and would be glad of some way of getting rid of them all. I may be able to take advantage of this state of mind, but it all requires time.'[6]

F. J. Newton, Acting Administrator of Bechuanaland in Shippard's absence, also recommended Rudd's party to Moffat and explained the hopes of Rhodes: 'You know yourself what an enthusiast Rhodes is in the matter of the extension of British influence northwards: in this case he is doubly enthusiastic, viz. politically and financially. I had a great deal of talk with him both

[1] Rhodes to Shippard, Private, 1 August 1888, RH 1/3/1.
[2] Rhodes and Beit had sent John Fry to Matabeleland early in 1888, but he became ill; 'how true it is,' Rhodes callously wrote, ' "never have anything to do with a failure".' Rhodes to Rudd, 10 September 1888, *ibid.*
[3] Rhodes to Shippard, Private, 1 August 1888, *ibid.*
[4] Moffat to Shippard, Private, 31 August 1888, MO 1/1/5/1.
[5] Moffat to Shippard, 6 September 1888, *African*, 369, encl. in No. 41.
[6] Moffat to Shippard, Private, 6 September 1888, MO 1/1/5/1.

in Kimberley and Capetown and he is I am sure prepared to do everything that Lo Bengula and those around him may wish, if the King will trust him and make an *extensive* concession. What he does not care for, is to be merely one of a number of concessionaires. . . . I confess I should like to see a thorough Imperialist and good man of business at the same time, as he undoubtedly is, get a good footing in that country. Much more can be done by private enterprise than by the lukewarm advances of the Colonial Office at home.'[1]

These advices were not lost on Moffat, who reported privately to Shippard, after Rudd's negotiations had begun, that Lobengula had gone 'very fully into the question of the plague of concession hunters and their refusal to take, No! on this I gave him advice on the lines of your letter of September 3, showing that it would be an advantage for him to act in concert with one powerful company who would simplify matters for him. I also drew his attention to the fact that your visit would give him an opportunity of talking about this question with you at first hand.'[2]

Shippard's official visit to Lobengula in October 1888 took place in the middle of Rudd's negotiations, but whether he spoke to the king on the question is not known. In his confidential report on his conversations, Shippard does not mention having dealt with the matter, except to point out that no concession hunters were official representatives of the Queen.[3] However, in view of his enthusiasm for the schemes of Rhodes it is difficult to believe that Shippard omitted the subject altogether, especially as Maguire informed Newton that 'both Shippard and Moffat did all they could for us'.[4] The backing which Rhodes received from imperial officials in South Africa is easily explained: they were much more enthusiastic than the Colonial Office for an extension of British interests north of the Limpopo and a monopoly concession in the hands of Rhodes was an effective way of forestalling

[1] Newton to Moffat, Private, 26 August 1888, MO 1/1/4.
[2] Moffat to Shippard, Private, 28 September 1888, MO 1/1/5/2. Moffat also reported this conversation to Rudd: *Diary, op. cit.*, 29 September 1888.
[3] Shippard to Robinson, Confidential, 29 October 1888, *African*, 369, encl. in No. 65.
[4] Maguire to Newton, 27 October 1888, NE 1/1/10.

the Transvaal and Portugal. Both Robinson and Shippard were delighted to hear of Rudd's success.[1]

The fact that Britain's representatives urged Lobengula to accept Rudd's proposals, though no doubt important, is not of itself a sufficient explanation of his decision. Thompson thought it was the boldness of the ammunition clause, under which Lobengula would receive 1,000 modern rifles and 100,000 rounds of ammunition, coupled with assurances that no land was sought, which had most appeal.[2] It may also have been significant that the influential *indunas* Lotje and Sekombo, who both played a prominent part in the negotiations, were offered rewards for their assistance.[3] Yet even these additional features hardly explain what seemed to be so far-reaching a step in the direction of opening the country to white enterprise. On the eve of the concession Lobengula was faced with what appeared to be two irreconcilable problems. All the information at his disposal led him to believe that his kingdom was in imminent danger of being overrun by land-hungry Boers from the Transvaal.[4] His second problem concerned the mounting influence of Europeans inside Matabeleland. Any policy which opened the country to further European penetration, which was one way of dealing with the threat from the Transvaal, heightened internal opposition. This was clear at the time of Shippard's visit in October 1888. Moffat greeted him with the news that the soldiers of one regiment had been trying to persuade Lobengula to let them massacre all the white men in Matabeleland. 'Their argument was . . . that although there are only about 30 white men here now, who, as they said, would be a mere breakfast for them, thousands may come hereafter unless the few are killed, so as to frighten the others; and they also

---

[1] Robinson actually helped to draw up the newspaper notices about the concession which were designed to conceal the armaments clauses, Rudd to Thompson and Maguire, 23 November 1888, printed in Thompson, *op. cit.*, pp. 70–1. Shippard's reaction, Rudd, *Diary*, [3 November 1888], *op. cit.*

[2] Thompson, *Autobiography, op. cit.*, pp. 65 ff.

[3] *Ibid.*, p. 66.

[4] This was very strongly stressed by Shippard in his interview with Lobengula; Shippard to Robinson, Confidential, 29 October 1888, *op. cit.* Khama, who had recently discussed the same topic with Shippard, sent Lobengula a message containing a similar warning about the Transvaal, Rudd, *Diary*, 2 October 1888, *op. cit.*

clamoured to be led against the white men's towns.' Another
regiment was asking permission to kill their present *indunas* 'who,
they said, are old women and cowards, and to elect others who
would not be afraid to lead them against white men'. Lobengula's
answer to these demands was, 'You want to drive me into the
lion's mouth'.[1]

In the light of the continuing popular outcry against all foreign
influences, it must have been clear to Lobengula that the one
course of action likely to lead to even greater internal opposition
was to co-operate with Rudd in what the Cape newspapers called
'opening his country to civilizing influences'. But was this really
what Lobengula agreed to when he signed the Rudd concession?
If it could be shown that Lobengula was deceived into signing the
concession in the belief that its implications were other than they
really were, a more adequate explanation would exist for the
striking change of Lobengula's policy implied by the terms of the
concession document.

There is an extremely revealing letter from Rhodes to Rudd
containing advice on the conduct of negotiations with Lobengula.

My advice as to Lobengulu is to take concession to work for him with
large share of profit in your name he will not understand Companies
you can apportion it afterwards. Go on the lines of becoming his Gold
Commissioner and working for him . . . I should offer a steamboat on
the Zambezi to King same as Stanley put on the Upper Congo. The
Governor writes he has no reply from Lord [Knutsford to] his confidential despatch. But my view is the matter lies more with Lo Bengula
than Knutsford as there is not even a protectorate and Lo Ben can do
what he likes with his own. Your most valuable man will be Moffat—
Newton says he is thoroughly with you. Stick to Home Rule and
Matabeleland for the Matabele I am sure it is the ticket.

Earlier in the letter, Rhodes refers to a rival having attempted 'the
"Home Rule" trick that is agreed to bring back white miners
to work for the King . . . I am sure the fellow was on the right
lines'.[2]

Rhodes's advice seems to have been followed, and the agree-

[1] Shippard to Robinson, 16 October 1888, C. 5918, encl. in No. 32.
[2] Rhodes to Rudd, 10 September 1888, RU 2/1/1. Extracts printed in Rudd,
Diary, op. cit., Appendix II, and H. A. Chilvers, *The Story of De Beers*, 1939,
pp. 88–9.

ment given a spurious attractiveness to the king. It is impossible to understand the concession from Lobengula's point of view unless certain verbal agreements entered into at the same time are taken into account. No mention of any agreements additional to the wide terms of the concession itself is made by Thompson in his autobiography, and Rudd, whose diary was dispatched in portions to his wife by the none too reliable post, merely has the tantalizing entry: 'A great deal of course passed at the *indaba* that I cannot put down, the most noteworthy being that Thompson and I, after they showed weakness, explained fully to them their own position and pointed out how they must be driven out of the country if they did not get friends and arms in to help them, and this many of them seemed to understand and looked very serious over.'[1] However, elsewhere Rudd makes the existence of verbal agreements explicit and refers to three of them: that any white miners should be bound to fight in defence of the country; that no miners or machinery should be introduced before the first instalment of rifles had been delivered, and that notices would be put in South African and English papers to keep speculators out of the country.[2] All these verbal undertakings must have helped to reassure Lobengula and his *indunas*, but the most significant undertaking of all is not mentioned by Rudd.

In March 1889, when the concession had become a matter of great controversy among the rival white groups as well as with the Matabele themselves, the Rev. C. D. Helm informed the London Missionary Society of his interpretation of the concession which includes the following important statement:

The Grantees explained to the Chief that what was deemed necessary to get out the gold was to erect dwellings for their overseers, to bring in and erect machinery & use wood and water. They promised that they would not bring more than 10 white men to work in his country, that they would not dig anywhere near towns etc. & that they & their people would abide by the laws of his country & in fact be as his people. But these promises were not put in the concession.[3]

[1] Rudd, *Diary*, 31 October 1888, *op. cit.*
[2] Rudd to G. Bower, 23 November 1888, *African*, 369, encl. in No. 89. Bower was Imperial Secretary to Robinson and a friend of Rhodes.
[3] Helm to R. W. Thompson, 29 March 1889, LO 6/1/5. Extracts printed in Rudd, *Diary*, *op. cit.*, Appendix III. Even before the concession was signed Rudd

If true, this verbal promise limiting the number of whites who
were to come into the country to ten must alter entirely the interpretation of Lobengula's motives in reaching an agreement.
Helm is hardly likely to have made this up, since he was himself closely connected with the concession. He welcomed the
plans for the concession outlined by Rudd, agreed to be the
first to put them to Lobengula unaccompanied by any of Rudd's
party, was the interpreter throughout the two day long *indaba*
which preceded the signing of the concession, and later consistently upheld its validity. Moreover, on two separate occasions
Lobengula referred to this particular promise, when refusing to
recognize the written concession, in one case actually mentioning
the figure of ten, and it seems unlikely that he could have derived
this particular idea from any other source than the one indicated
by Helm.[1] In the light of the verbal promises he must have felt
that he had gone a long way towards solving both his problems.
On the one hand he was to receive a powerful armoury which
could be used if the threats of Boer or Portuguese filibusters
materialized, on the other, at the price of only ten white men in
the country, who were to be under his authority, it was to be
sealed against further white penetration. In addition he was to
receive a handsome royalty of £100 per lunar month and a gunboat on the Zambesi or £500. It was too good to be true, but it
is not difficult to imagine that Lobengula believed that in signing
the concession he had reconciled the irreconcilable and dealt
satisfactorily with the external threat without at the same time
unduly heightening that from within. It was not unrealistic on his
part to believe that ten white men with a Matabele labour force
would be all that would be required to carry on mining. The

approached Helm with an offer of an annual retainer to act as an intermediary
between the king and the concessionaires if the negotiations proved successful.
Helm referred the matter to the L.M.S. (incidentally revealing his support for
an extensive concession to a strong company like De Beers) but nothing more
is heard of the matter and presumably it was dropped; *ibid.* Helm, the senior
missionary in the country, was also regarded by Moffat as a 'very useful and
reliable ally'; to Shippard, 24 July 1888, MO 1/1/5/1.

[1] Moffat, MS. diary, 29 November 1889, MO 1/3/1/1 (notes of a meeting
Moffat attended with Lobengula, 24 *indunas*, Jameson and other British South
Africa Company representatives); J. Colenbrander, MS. diary, 14 July 1890,
CO 4/3/1. Colenbrander was a representative of the B.S.A. Co. at the king's.

mines at Tati had been running intermittently since 1869 on that kind of scale. It is also possible that Lobengula's oft-repeated claim that he thought he was giving away rights to 'one hole' was genuine. E. A. Maund, after he had become the firm ally of Rhodes, stated: 'Everything goes to prove that the document was "*rushed*" out of him as even Helm, who backed the paper as *en règle*, admits that the king only thought he was giving away a "hole".'[1]

Whatever the exact details, there can be no doubt that there was a fundamental discrepancy between Lobengula's understanding of the concession and the use Rhodes intended to make of it. To Lobengula the concession and its verbal promises were to limit severely the activities of whites in his kingdom: to Rhodes the written concession alone was valid and was to be the key to opening both Matabeleland and Mashonaland to commercial company rule. The subsequent struggle over the concession should be seen against these strikingly opposed views. Lobengula failed to sustain his version, but his evasive tactics in the end succeeded in forcing Rhodes to concentrate solely on Mashonaland, though, as will be seen, the Matabele came perilously close to being overthrown by force of arms three years earlier than actually happened.

V

Lobengula soon became aware that he had not after all reconciled his problems when rival concession seekers pointed out to him what was being printed about the Rudd concession in the South African papers. The document itself contained, following the sole mineral rights clause, the highly ambiguous phrase 'together with full power to do all things necessary to win and procure the same'. It was capable of a restricted definition which Helm, mindful of the verbal clauses, insisted upon, or of a much more extensive interpretation, easily stimulated by the newspaper reports, such as was pressed by Rhodes's rivals and which came to be believed by a large number of Matabele *indunas* (not so incorrectly as matters turned out). The main deficiency of the written

[1] Maund to Rhodes, 25 December 1889, CT 1/13/8.

concession in the eyes of the Matabele was the impossibility of
showing categorically that it granted no rights in land.[1] Lobengula was now caught between the pressure of the concessionaires
who tried to uphold the written concession and a strong Matabele
party who refused to accept it. Direct confrontation, however,
was postponed while Rhodes negotiated for a Royal Charter. In
the meanwhile, the written concession was first suspended and
then repudiated by the king.

It has been usual to regard the great debate which raged in
Matabeleland throughout 1889 about the concession as merely
the result of the intrigues of disappointed whites. This view was
assiduously promoted by the Rhodes faction since it helped to
mask the extent to which the Matabele refused to recognize the
validity of the concession document, but the king's own role also
needs to be stressed. The notice of 18 January 1889 to the newspapers in which Lobengula announced that he was suspending all
action on the concession has been dismissed as fraudulent because
of the absence of independent witnesses.[2] Proof that it was genuine is provided by a letter from Helm to Moffat of the same
date in which Helm explained why he had refused Lobengula's
request to write an identical notice.[3] The written concession was
never properly reinstated from that day forward. Lobengula did
not deny that he had made an agreement, but he refused to recognize the concession document as accurate. His point of view was
indicated by his accepting the £100 per lunar month and rejecting
delivery of the guns: the whole matter must first be reconsidered.

Lobengula also probably took more initiative than he is usually
credited with in the attempt to get the imperial authorities in
London not to accept Rudd's version of the concession. As early
as December 1888, Moffat was writing significantly that the
king 'thinks to play the Colonial [i.e. Cape] Government off
against the Imperial. It does not need any words for me to show
how undesirable this state of mind is.'[4] A good deal of mystery
still surrounds the despatch of E. A. Maund, at this time a rival of

[1] D. Carnegie to R. W. Thompson, 15 January 1889, LO 6/1/5.
[2] E.g. P. Mason, *The Birth of a Dilemma*, 1958, pp. 129-30, following H. M.
Hole, *The Making of Rhodesia*, 1926, pp. 106-7.
[3] Helm to Moffat, 18 January 1889, MO 1/1/6.
[4] Moffat to [A.L.] Bruce, 5 December 1888, MO 1/1/5/2.

Rhodes, to England with two Matabele *indunas*, but Moffat, who began by being very suspicious, came later to believe that the king was really responsible for sending the deputation.[1] The embassy reached England on 27 February 1889 (a month before Rhodes arrived in search of a Charter) and received a message from the Colonial Office containing the clear implication that Lobengula should lessen the scope of the written concession.[2] Soon after the deputation left England—having first been treated to a display of military might—Maund was informed by Rhodes on behalf of the newly formed British South Africa Company that he must now do all in his power to uphold the concession following an amalgamation between Maund's principals (representing the Bechuanaland Exploration Company) and Rhodes.[3] This Maund did by the simple expedient of delaying his return with the *indunas* while Rhodes continued negotiations for the Charter.[4] The details of Lobengula's relations with the imperial government cannot be followed here, but it is clear that long before Maund's eventual return to Matabeleland in August 1889, Lobengula was losing the battle in London.[5] Once Lord Salisbury's administration had decided to use Rhodes and a Charter as the instrument of its southern African policies, Lobengula's freedom of manœuvre had become menacingly limited. Yet there were still three possible short-term outcomes.

Lobengula might fully recognize the written concession, allow unlimited numbers of British South Africa Company miners into the country, and delegate jurisdiction over them to the Company: this course of action was the one desired by the Company and the

[1] Moffat to Elizabeth Unwin, 21 July 1889, MO 1/1/6.
[2] Lord Knutsford to Lobengula, 26 March 1889, C. 5918, No. 70.
[3] B.S.A. Co. to Maund, Telegram, 17 May 1889, CT 1/13/8.
[4] Moffat to E. Unwin, 21 July, MO 1/1/6.
[5] A possibly authentic letter of 25 April to the Colonial Office repudiating the written concession was merely referred to Rhodes for comment and R. Maguire's disingenuous explanations accepted. C. 5918, Encl. in Nos. 101, 105, and 106 + encl. The undoubtedly genuine repudiation, Lobengula to the Queen, 10 August 1889, *ibid*., encl. in No. 130, was mysteriously delayed in transit and conveniently reached the Colonial Office 3 days after it had dispatched a letter to Lobengula advising him that the British Government had granted the Charter and now approved of the Rudd (i.e. written) concession, *ibid*., encl. in No. 129.

British Government. It was the one most unlikely to be followed, however, since Lobengula's purge of the pro-European faction, symbolized by the judicial murder of the *induna* Lotje in September 1889, was a clear indication of the continued hostility to foreign influences which the king could ignore only at his peril. Secondly, Lobengula might absolutely refuse to reinstate the concession, an action which would undoubtedly be popular with his people, but which, the king shrewdly guessed, might bring forth the agression latent in the white advance. The third and most likely outcome, since it was but the continuation of earlier policies, was that Lobengula would continue to be as evasive as possible in the hope that the white advance would be halted or diverted without the Matabele being crushed. Which of these three possibilities took place depended on how the king dealt with Rhodes's new triumvirate of Jameson, Doyle and Maxwell, who arrived in Matabeleland in October 1889 determined to reinstate the written concession.

Jameson was soon convinced that Lobengula would never agree to sign any new document which did not limit mining activities to 'one hole', nor did he believe that the king would agree to a direct ratification of the existing written document which was continually denounced by Lobengula as being Thompson's words and not his own. Jameson and his colleagues therefore sought to implement the concession indirectly by getting Lobengula's verbal agreement to begin prospecting in places selected by the king. The representatives of the British South Africa Company also had great hopes that the penetration of the Portuguese into Mashonaland would force Lobengula to accept the guns and call on the company for support. If he attempted to tackle the Portuguese alone, they believed, the Matabele were bound to be defeated. The king was therefore urged to deal with the Portuguese, but significantly the *indunas* insisted that any action must be by the Matabele alone. In the event, nothing at all was done.[1]

There appeared to be a stalemate. Jameson, who hoped for a peaceful outcome, was prepared to recommend military action if

[1] This paragraph is based on a series of letters from Jameson to Harris, October 1889–February 1890, in CT 1/13/6. See also Maund to Rhodes, 25 December 1889, CT 1/13/8, and other letters in the same series.

the 'word of mouth' policy on the concession failed. He also informed J. R. Harris, South African Secretary of the British South Africa Company: 'I have spoken freely to Helm and Carnegie [both L.M.S. missionaries] and they with Moffat are convinced that Rhodes is right in his decision that he will never be able to work peaceably alongside the natives and that the sooner the brush is over the better.'[1] Lobengula was not unaware of his position, however; Moffat had earlier informed him that the Charter would be granted,[2] thus indicating that Rhodes and the British Government now stood on common ground, and had later told him that the Charter would give Rhodes the power to raise forces.[3]

The king saw clearly that some minimal demand would have to be met, but it was still difficult to persuade his *indunas* of the wisdom of this and there were constant meetings between them and the king. One was reported to Jameson: 'all the *indunas* were against us [i.e. the British South Africa Company]; but the king told them "I am going to give the white men a hole to dig—you told me you were afraid of guns against you—the white men will bring guns and horses. If you go against me I will have to call the white men to help me—they are my friends, and if I must put kraal against kraal I must." '[4] This threat of calling in the whites to assert his authority seems to mark a new stage in the relations between Lobengula and his *indunas*. Previously, when they had challenged his decisions in relation to the white advance, he had been able to overcome their opposition by offering to let any who wished go and fight the whites at Kimberley. This is the first occasion, of which I am aware, on which Lobengula used the potential of white intervention to shore up his own position. The threat had its desired effect and the king gave a grudging recognition of the concession to Jameson, but more on his restricted version of the agreement than on Rudd's. He gave Jameson a definite permission to prospect in the south of the kingdom and

[1] Jameson to Harris, 1 November 1889; CT 1/13/6.
[2] Moffat to Shippard, 1 August 1889, MO 1/1/5/2. (This reported conversation on the Charter took place three months before it received the Queen's assent on 29 October 1889.)
[3] Jameson to Harris, 14 November 1889, CT 1/13/6.
[4] Jameson to Harris, 1 November 1889, *ibid*.

an indefinite permission to prospect, not occupy, Mashonaland if
no gold was found in the south.[1] The Company, of course, aware
that it would have much more freedom of action in Mashonaland,
had no intention of finding gold in the south. The consequences
of an outright refusal by Lobengula to treat with Jameson is
shown by what was being planned in Kimberley. Jameson's early
reports about the refusal to ratify the written concession and also
the king's letter of 10 August 1889 to the Queen repudiating it
(which Rhodes was improperly shown on its tardy journey to
England) led the South African representatives of the British
South Africa Company to plan ways and means of dispensing
with the need for Lobengula's co-operation altogether.[2]

At first it was thought that an expedition could be introduced
into Mashonaland via the Zambesi and the London Board was
requested to commence preparations.[3] Selous, however, advised
Rhodes that the scheme was unworkable[4] and a much more drastic
plan was substituted, one that has remained almost unknown, but
which is a revealing illustration of the determined nature of the
forces opposed to the Matabele. Frank Johnson and Maurice Heany,
who were still smarting from their unceremonious treatment by
Lobengula in 1887, were induced to sign a remarkable confidential agreement with Rhodes, representing the British South
Africa Company, dated 7 December 1889.[5] Johnson and Heany
agreed, in return for £150,000 and a 50,000 morgen land right,

[1] Jameson to Harris, 7 and 12 December 1889, *ibid.*
[2] Harris to Weatherley (London Secretary, B.S.A. Co.), 4 November 1889,
CT 2/11/1.
[3] Harris to Weatherley, 11, 18, 25 November 1889, *ibid.*
[4] Harris to Weatherley, 9 December 1889, *ibid.*
[5] There is a typescript copy of the agreement in Johnson's papers in the
National Archives, Salisbury (JO 3/2), the authenticity of which is vouched for
by a former Chief Archivist who saw the original when on a visit to Johnson.
It was buried during the second World War with Johnson's other papers on the
island of Jersey, and the place lost sight of on his death. Johnson included the
episode in the draft of his autobiography, *Great Days*, 1940, but it was cut out
on the advice of Sir Godfrey Huggins, later Lord Malvern, who wrote the
Foreword. Huggins, who was then Prime Minister of Southern Rhodesia, felt
that publicizing the plan would make bad propaganda among the African
population in time of war (information from the catalogue to the historical
MSS). Johnson revealed the general outlines of the agreement in an article for
the *Cape Times* of 12 September 1930, the fortieth anniversary of the occupation of Mashonaland.

to raise a European force of 500 men 'to carry by sudden assaults all the principal strongholds of the Matabele nation and generally to so break up the power of the Amandebele as to render their raids on surrounding tribes impossible, to effect the emancipation of all their slaves and further, to reduce the country to such a condition as to enable the prospecting, mining and commercial staff of the British South Africa Company to conduct their operations in Matabeleland in peace and safety'. The British South Africa Company undertook to establish immediately afterwards an 'effective civil government'. An auxiliary African force was to be obtained from Khama, whose reward was to be an extension of his boundaries into Matabele territory. The *casus belli*, Johnson later stated, was to be a manufactured incident in the disputed territory between the Shashi and Macloutsie rivers which was claimed by both Lobengula and Khama.[1]

The sequel is best told in the words J. R. Harris, the sole witness to the agreement, used to explain the postponement of the plan in a letter to J. D. Hepburn, a missionary and Khama's chief political adviser.

Heany's letters to Mr Rhodes and myself gave us full details of the conversations he had had with Khama and yourself, and especially the letter from the Chief to Heany, showed the unselfish and characteristic way in which our original plan communicated by him was viewed by you both . . . [Harris explains how Lobengula's obstructive tactics led to the formation of the plan and how news had since been received on 21 December 1889 of the king's authorization of prospecting] . . . This sudden change of front of Lobengula's made us pause and during the pause a second plan, an alternative one, suggested itself to Mr Rhodes, which has also received the approbation of the High Commissioner and of Sir Sydney Shippard. . . . An armed road making party, with Khama's consent and assistance, will commence making a wagon road . . . to Mt Hampden, . . . Permission to build this road will only be asked from Khama, in so far as it runs through his territory, but Lobengula's permission will not be asked, he will simply be informed by Mr Moffat of the fact that we start at once making it. Make it we shall and the Government authorize us, should Lobengula attack us, not only, of course, to defend ourselves but to take what measures we deem fit against him. . . . The consequences of this new and final plan are two

[1] *Cape Times*, 12 September 1930.

in number. Firstly, if Lobengula looks on in silence and does nothing, the Charter will occupy Mashonaland. . . . If, on the other hand, Lobengula attacks us, then the original plan communicated to Khama and yourself will be carried out to the very letter, as should this last attempt to deal peaceably fail, he must expect no mercy and none will be given him. . . . If he attacks us, he is doomed, if he does not, his fangs will be drawn, the pressure of civilization on all his borders will press more and more heavily upon him and the desired result, the disappearance for ever of the Matabele as a power, if delayed is yet the more certain. I trust the Chief and yourself will see that the second plan, achieving the same end as the other, is under the altered circumstances of Lobengula's attitude, even if only a passing whim of his, the more judicious of the two—it really all depends on Lobengula whether or not plan No. 1 is carried out and that is as it should be.[1]

It is clear from this letter that Lobengula had averted immediate catastrophe by a narrow margin, and that future events would depend greatly upon him.[2] The significance of the manœuvrings of late 1889 is that the British South Africa Company failed to gain full recognition of the written concession from the Matabele king and therefore abandoned the attempt for the time being to include Matabeleland within its sphere of operations: instead it concentrated its attentions on Mashonaland, where no powerful African polity stood in the way of the rapid development which a colonizing commercial company, unlike the Colonial Office, found necessary. Lobengula, by his refusal to co-operate fully with the Chartered Company without rejecting agreement altogether, had won a striking, if limited, victory. Provided he could prevent his warriors from attacking the occupation column, he had won all that the situation allowed, a breathing space. Lobengula struggled by diplomatic means to prevent the occupation of Mashonaland

[1] Harris to Hepburn, 17 January 1890, CT 2/11/1. Harris was wrong that no further consultation would take place with Lobengula: Jameson returned to the king in April for the purpose of getting permission to make the road, but Lobengula, even when threatened with force, would neither confirm nor deny that he had earlier sanctioned it; Jameson to Harris, 5 May 1890, CT 1/13/6. Mason calls this 'an unwilling half-consent', *op. cit.*, p. 140. It should be noted that Lobengula never 'sanctioned the occupation of Mashonaland', as the Company claimed.
[2] It is probable that the High Commissioner, who apparently heard rumours of the plan, also helped to thwart it, *Cape Times, op. cit.* Moffat also learnt of the plan and wrote in astonishment to Hepburn, 4 February 1890, MO 1/1/5/3.

taking place, but he stuck to his view that an armed conflict with the whites would be fatal in face of opposition from his subjects.

Moffat had been sent back to Matabeleland in July 1890 with the task of trying to keep the peace, and his reports give some idea of how Lobengula dealt with the situation. Moffat himself had generally inclined to the view that war was inevitable, but Jameson's success in leading Lobengula to promise what at one time seemed out of the question had led him to inform Rhodes in January 1890 that there was a chance Lobengula would be able to hold his 'turbulent young soldiery' and that peace could be maintained if the Company's representatives are 'wise and patient' and 'if you can afford as a company to wait for dividends long enough'.[1] Nevertheless, on his return to Matabeleland he reported that: 'The Matjaha say openly that they will listen neither to him [Lobengula] nor to the *indunas*; if the white men enter Mashonaland, they will attack them.'[2] A few days later the seriousness of the king's position with his people was indicated when two or three of his great *indunas* were overheard urging him, 'to let them have at least one slap at the Pioneers and he was urging objections. He is apparently more alive to the danger and futility than his people are of attempting an appeal to arms, but it is becoming a question of his own safety among his own people.'[3] Lobengula seems to have dealt with the situation with great skill and kept up the appearance of decisive action in the eyes of his subjects to the last.

Early in August 1890, when the occupation force was well on its way, Moffat reported: 'Nearly every kraal in the country has been up for review in turn, and now even the Makalaka are showing up after a fashion. All of course profess to be eager to assegai the white man. The chief puts them off, tells them to go home and be ready when he calls them....'[4] And a fortnight later: 'I am becoming really sanguine that the row may be thus postponed; everything looks more hopeful. The Matjaha have been fizzing for so long that their pugnacity can't keep itself going much

[1] Moffat to Rhodes, Confidential, 16 January 1890, MO 1/1/5/3.
[2] Moffat to Shippard, Private and Confidential, 12 July 1890, *ibid.*
[3] Moffat to Sir Henry Loch (High Commissioner), 15 July 1890, *ibid.*
[4] Moffat to D. Doyle, 5 August 1890, *ibid.*

longer. The chief has kept them well in play, in order to gain time.'¹ A similar motive probably underlay the despatch of messengers ordering the occupation column to withdraw. When they returned to report that it refused to turn back a large beer drink was said to have diverted attention from the matter.² Only Lobengula's political skill averted war in 1890.

As was to be expected, the older men and Lobengula himself were inclined to acquiesce in the occupation of Mashonaland once it had occurred. When talk of fighting among the *amatjaha* revived in October 1890, the older men argued that the whites in Mashonaland were doing no harm and that fighting would bring destruction on themselves. But the young men stuck to the view that Lobengula had let Mashonaland go too easily.³ Although Lobengula was induced by the trader James Dawson, on behalf of the Company, to accept a gold claim in Mashonaland in an attempt to link him to the new order,⁴ he adamantly refused to grant the Company rights of jurisdiction.⁵ This suggests he was still struggling to maintain his sovereignty intact. Indeed, as his negotiations with Lippert over the land question show, he was casting around for ways to undermine the position of the Company; and only outright duplicity on the part of Rhodes, sanctioned by the High Commissioner and aided by Moffat (against his will), enabled him to defeat Lobengula's schemes and obtain land rights for the Company.⁶

Between the occupation and the outbreak of war in 1893, relations between the Matabele and the Company were inherently unstable. The Company seems to have hoped that the Matabele system would disintegrate from within through the action of labour migration. Had Mashonaland developed economically as rapidly as the Rand goldfields this might possibly have happened. By early 1891 there was said to be a substantial leakage of people

---

¹ Moffat to Harris, Confidential, 19 August 1890, *ibid.*
² Moffat to Shippard, Telegram, 20 August 1890, *ibid.*
³ Moffat to Harris, 6 October 1890; Moffat to Loch, 5 November 1890, *ibid.*
⁴ Moffat to Colquhoun, 24 September 1890, *ibid.*; Harris to Colenbrander, 12 December 1890, CO 4/1/1.
⁵ Moffat to Harris and to Loch, series of letters on subject, October 1890–July 1891, MO 1/1/5/3 & 4.
⁶ *John Smith Moffat, op. cit.*, pp. 254–61.

of Shona origin to Mashonaland in search of work and increasing numbers were also labouring in the gold and diamond mines of South Africa.[1] But the 'second Rand' never materialized, and until such time as the new economy affected the two dominant groups of *Zansi* and *Enhla*, the Matabele state was bound to retain its essential character unimpaired. In the three years before the war, raids on Mashonaland and other areas continued and culminated in the so-called 'Victoria Incident' of July 1893. This in itself made clear the fundamental instability of the position. The Company and the settlers saw it as providing the opportunity and the justification for settling what was termed 'the Matabele question' once and for all, while for the Matabele the incident demonstrated that Lobengula no longer had full control over the actions of his subordinates. However, it was the Company which pushed the issue to a war. The end of the kingdom, direct rule by Europeans, and large-scale land appropriation followed the Matabele defeat—results which were confirmed by the outcome of the rebellion of 1896. These, together with the drawing of the former kingdom firmly into the new colonial structure that was soon to be called Southern Rhodesia, were undoubtedly the most important historical effects of the struggle between an avaricious colonizing movement and an African raiding state. Yet, the Matabele role in the events which brought about these results should not be ignored, for, as J. D. Hargreaves has pointed out, 'Once historians can begin to see African states, not just as curious museum pieces whose affairs are only intelligible to anthropologists, but as polities sharing many basic aims with governments everywhere, his whole perspective may begin to change'.[2]

[1] Moffat to Harris, Confidential, 17 February 1891, MO 1/1/5/4.
[2] 'Towards a History of the Partition of Africa', *Journal of African History* (1960), I, i, p. 109.

5

THE ROLE OF NDEBELE AND SHONA RELIGIOUS AUTHORITIES IN THE REBELLIONS OF 1896 AND 1897

by

TERENCE RANGER

THERE has recently developed a lively and fruitful interest in the traditional religious authorities of the African peoples of Southern Rhodesia. The spirit mediums of Mashonaland have attracted perhaps most attention. Thus their ritual activity has been minutely described in two studies by Dr Gelfand; their contemporary social and political significance has been examined by Dr Kingsley Garbett; and their role as the transmitters of historical tradition has been appreciated by Mr Abraham, who has thus tapped a rich store of hitherto unknown evidence for the pre-European past. The priesthood of the so-called Mwari cult has not been neglected, however, and Mr Summers has drawn our attention to the importance of traditions relating to this cult for an understanding of the history of the Zimbabwe ruins. In the course of the work of these scholars reference has been made to the past political significance of the traditional religious authorities; to their close association with pre-European state systems; and to their survival as significant centralizing factors after the collapse of those systems. It is the intention of this paper to add a little to the growing body of knowledge about the traditional religious authorities and their role in the history of the African peoples of Rhodesia, by giving an account of their involvement in the rebellions of 1896 and 1897 as it appears from the material now available in the National Archives in Salisbury.[1]

---

[1] M. Gelfand, *Shona Ritual*, 1959; *Shona Religion*, 1962; D. P. Abraham, 'The Early Political History of the Kingdom of Mwene Mutapa', *Historians in Tropical Africa*, 1962; R. Summers, *Zimbabwe, A Rhodesian Mystery*, 1963.

It is not, of course, in any sense original to assert that the religious authorities of the Ndebele and the Shona played a significant part in the rebellions. It was asserted during the rebellions by contemporary white commentators. 'We may be pretty sure that there is a witch-doctor concerned in it in one way or another', wrote the *Pall Mall Gazette* in the early days of the Ndebele rising; 'After the Matabele war short work was made with several of these gentry, but you cannot eradicate race superstition by proclamation, and the Matabele now are pretty much what they have always been, superstitious as Celts, blood-thirsty as the parent Zulu.' The Resident Magistrate of Salisbury, Marshall Hole, was of the opinion that the Shona were even more moved by superstition, which, he wrote in November 1897, 'has rendered the task of reducing the natives to submission far harder in Mashonaland than in Matabeleland, where they are more reasonable, and if prone at times to fanatical outbreaks, know at any rate when they are beaten.' And after the rebellions were over, a Native Commissioner summed up his experience of them by writing that however apparently contented an African people seemed to be it only required 'a witch-doctor, who has been fortunate in his prophecies in the past . . . to prophecy destruction of the whites, to get the majority of the tribes to rise.'[1]

Assertions such as these have rightly been received by historians, as they were by some contemporaries, with profound suspicion. They were concerned to make an allegation about the origin of the rebellions designed to clear the British South Africa Company of blame for them. The rebellions, it was claimed, were not a matter of rational reaction to bad government, but a matter of superstitious reaction to the blandishments of the 'witch-doctors'. This view in all its naïvety comes out most clearly in the account of the American scout, Burnham.

It is almost impossible for the white race to grasp, [Burnham wrote] even in a slight degree, the motives actuating the black. Under the terms of the peace made with the Matabele at the close of the first war, the natives were given generous reservations of land; also certain allotments of cattle, seed, etc., and ample employment for all who were

[1] H. M. Hole, 'Witchcraft in Rhodesia', *The African Review*, 6 November 1897; N. C. Morris to C.N.C., 25 November 1903, A 11/2/12/11.

willing to work on the farms, in the mines, or for the government. But there was one inscrutable factor in affairs that even the wisest of the officials did not take fully into account. . . . Here were people given more liberty than they had ever known before; the slaves all freed, labour paid in coin, lands held in safety, and taxes lighter by far than those levied on any white man in the empire. But let one cabalistic word be whispered in the ear of a servant by an emissary of the Mlimo and he became as a bit of grass swayed by an invisible wind. All the white man's kindnesses and the benefits of good government were swept from his mind.

As a description of the condition of the Ndebele before the rising this is, of course, absurd; and so far from being an explanation of the rising it is rather an assertion that no explanation is possible.[1]

The fact that the 'witch-doctors' were made scape-goats for the rising does not mean, of course, that the traditional religious authorities did not in reality play a significant part in them. But we must make it clear at this stage that they did *not* provoke the risings 'with one cabalistic word'. The Ndebele 'high priest', the Rozwi priest of Mwari, the Shona spirit medium did not stand in that kind of relationship with their societies; they did not command or persuade men to perform actions which they were otherwise unready to perform, but rather they embodied and set the seal of ritual approval on the decision of the community as a whole. Their general involvement in the risings was in itself an indication of the total commitment of most of traditional society to them. This paper is not concerned, then, with the traditional religious authorities as agitators; indeed it is not primarily concerned with the *cause* of the rebellions at all. It is concerned with the organization of the rebellions and with the traditional religious authorities as co-ordinators.

There are three problems of organization which must be examined by any student of the rebellions. Given a general readiness or desire to resist, how did the Ndebele, scattered after the 1893 war, succeed in organizing a more or less simultaneous outbreak in most areas of Matabeleland; how did the Shona, who had not enjoyed centralized political authority since the collapse of the Rozwi confederation in the 1830's, achieve the same feat in

[1] Burnham, *Scouting on Two Continents*, 1934.

most areas of Mashonaland; and how was there established any kind of working co-operation between the two sets of rebels? This chapter does not set out to provide a full answer to these questions, which would involve a consideration also of the part played by secular authorities, but sets out to see how far a study of the part played by the religious authorities helps to answer them.

Let us look first of all at the outbreak of the Ndebele rising—or more exactly, the rising in Matabeleland. Less than three years before the rising the Ndebele had been organized into one of the most centralized 'state' systems of sub-Saharan Africa, with one of the clearest structures of authority. And despite the defeats of 1893 the old regiments still felt a corporate loyalty and recognized the authority of their old commanders. It was this which made the Ndebele rising so formidable. Nevertheless, there were problems of organization in 1896. King Lobengula, who had been so much the effective centre of the Ndebele system, was dead and despite various efforts made in 1894 and 1895 no successor to him had been chosen. The sons born to him while he was king, from among whom a successor would properly have been chosen, had been sent to school in South Africa by Rhodes. Moreover, in the 1890's there was no generally recognized regent, as there had been on Mzilikazi's death, when the *induna* Nombate had played a decisive role in Lobengula's accession. The senior *indunas* were much divided among themselves. In these circumstances it was not surprising that the regimental commanders and the members of the royal family should have looked for an initiative to the chief religious authority of the Ndebele nation, who symbolized its unity more effectively than any other man alive in 1896.[1]

The fullest account of this chief religious authority is given by T. M. Thomas, a missionary who was present in Matabeleland between the death of Mzilikazi and the accession of Lobengula. Thomas tells us that quite separate from the witch-finders and diviners and doctors and non-Ndebele rain-makers, there was a 'high priest of the tribe', or rather a family responsible for the conduct of the great annual Dance and ceremony of First Fruits,

[1] For Nombate, see R. Brown, 'The Ndebele Succession Crisis, 1868–1877', *Historians in Tropical Africa*, 1962.

whose senior member Thomas calls the 'high priest'. The Great
Dance was an annual demonstration of Ndebele unity and
demonstrated in itself the tightness of the Ndebele state as opposed
to the far-flung confederation of the Rozwi which it had succeeded.
The Ndebele state required no elaborate and numerous priestly
hierarchy, but on great national occasions the 'high priest' and
his family had a central role. Thomas tells us that when Mzilikazi
died it was the 'high priest', Umtamjana, who performed the
rituals of burial, sacrificing cattle and commending the dead king
to his ancestors 'in the highest terms'. Umtamjana also played a
part in the selection of Lobengula; it was he who 'by instructions,
ceremonies and charms' prepared the young king for his installation; and it was he who on 17 March 1870 'in the presence of
about six thousand people . . . gave the king a charge, in which he
dwelt upon the laws and customs of the tribe, and the responsibilities and difficulties of the present government of the country.'[1]

Thomas' evidence gives us some idea of the role played by the
'high priest' during the crisis of the Ndebele system which followed Mzilikazi's death. In the much more profound crisis which
followed the death of Lobengula the 'high priest' once again
played a part of great importance. By the 1890's Umtamjana had
been succeeded by Umlugulu, whom various witnesses described
in 1896 as 'the head of the family who had charge of the rites';
'the representative of the priestly family of the Matabili tribe, who
during the great war dance . . . had control of the whole people
and rule of the country'; 'the head dance doctor'; and 'the king
maker'. Early in 1894, just before the king's death, Lobengula
sent Umlugulu a commission 'to the effect that if ever he had the
power he was to re-institute the Great Dance and with it the rites
of the Matabele kingdom'. This commission, and the absence of
any recognized regent, made Umlugulu the central figure in the
movement for the establishment of a successor to Lobengula in
1894 and 1895.[2]

The missionary Carnegie, who had spent many years among

[1] T. M. Thomas, *Eleven Years in Central Africa*, 1872.

[2] Carnegie, Memorandum on the Rebellion, 29 March 1896; HO 1/3/4;
Carnegie, Evidence submitted to Sir Richard Martin, June 1896, C. 8547,
pp. 31–3; Report of Acting Administrator, 3 April 1896, A 10/12/2.

the Ndebele, described this movement in a memorandum written in June 1896. 'Ever since the late king's death, the natives have been, as they say, "longing for a fire at which to warm themselves"; in other words, they wanted a king with whom they could be more in touch than they found themselves with the white government. One abortive attempt was made to accomplish this, but failed; later on the government suggested appointing a Native who should be the intermediary between the Natives and the government, but their nominee was unacceptable.' Meetings held by the Ndebele *indunas* to discuss the kingship issue alarmed the administration; one of Lobengula's close relatives was banished from Southern Rhodesia; another took his followers away to the northwards, to try to re-establish Ndebele institutions outside the boundaries of Company authority. Umlugulu, in common with many others, began to despair of the possibility of achieving a restoration of the monarchy within the framework of Company rule and to plan for its restoration by force.[1]

Selous, who was a neighbour of Umlugulu before the rebellion, and who describes him as 'a very gentle mannered savage, always courteous and polite', believed that Umlugulu was confirmed in his decision that the time had come to defy the Company by the news of the failure of the Jameson Raid. Before the raid, Selous tells us, Umlugulu had often complained of various aspects of the Company régime—the abuses of the police, the seizure of cattle, and so on—but had been concerned rather to evade than to resist. But after the news that 'the whole of the police force of Matabeleland, together with the artillery, munitions of war, etc. . . . had been captured by the Boers', Umlugulu made no more attempts to persuade his white neighbour to protect his cattle by running them with his own herd, though, Selous tells us, 'he often came to see me and always questioned me very closely as to what had actually happened in the Transvaal.'[2]

By the end of 1895, then, Umlugulu was at the centre of a group of senior *indunas*—Sekombo, Babyaan, Somabulana, etc.,—who were planning an armed rising and the restoration of the kingship. Messages were sent out to other *indunas* and early in

[1] Carnegie, Evidence submitted to Sir Richard Martin.
[2] F. C. Selous, *Sunshine and Storm in Rhodesia*, 1896.

1896 meetings were held in the hills near Umlugulu's home, where, it was reported to a disbelieving administration, 'they are massing with a view to raiding Bulawayo, stating that in consequence of the capture of Dr Jameson's force the town is unprotected'. The accounts we have attribute the initiative to Umlugulu through-out; it was he, we are told, who 'induced chiefs in other districts to join in the movement'; he who was the 'chief instigator' or the 'main-spring' of the rising. However this may be, it was certainly he who was to play the main role in the ceremony which was planned to initiate the rising. It was the intention of the rebels, so the *indunas* Gambo and Mjaan later declared, to hold a Great Dance at full moon on the night of 26 March, 'on the borders of the Filabusi mining district'. At this dance Umlugulu was to 'go through the ceremonies'; proclaim a member of the royal house, Umfezela, as the new king, 'and inaugurate, in spite of the present government, a new régime'. Thus the rising would from the start possess a directive centre.[1]

This dance was never held. Carnegie explained this in terms of police and military activity in the chosen area, and the premature murders of Ndebele police which set the whole movement of insurrection in motion before the new king could be proclaimed. But in view of the fact that the rebels found it impossible, once the revolt had begun, to agree upon a candidate for the kingship, and that a centre command was never established, we may guess that the failure to hold the dance had something to do with the opposition to Umfezela's candidature on the part of the 'young bloods'. Umfezela had the support of Umlugulu and the older *indunas*; the younger men wanted Lobengula's eldest son, Nya-manda; and the difference involved different attitudes towards the rising and how it should be conducted. These differences were not resolved and throughout the rising the Ndebele aristoc-racy was divided into two rough factions, whose fortunes, as we shall see, varied widely. Thus Umlugulu's influence was not enough to unite the whole of the Ndebele aristocracy behind a single authority, though it did play a significant part in bringing

[1] Report by the Chief Native Commissioner, 19 June 1896, PO 1/2/2; Acting Administrator to Secretary, Cape Town, 13 February 1896, LO 5/2/47; Carnegie Memorandum, 29 March 1896, HO 1/3/4.

together the senior *indunas* and in mobilizing the regiments which they commanded.[1]

To bring the Ndebele aristocracy into rebellion, moreover, no longer automatically involved bringing the Ndebele nation into it as a whole. The problem which faced Umlugulu and other rebel leaders was not merely that the superior Ndebele castes were divided into two rough parties, but also that the third and largest caste, the Holi or Lozwi, showed considerable reluctance to enter a rising under the command of their former masters. It is hard to estimate the extent to which the overthrow of the Ndebele state in 1893 had meant a break-away by members of the Holi caste.[2] It was commonly assumed by whites at the time that nearly all of them had seized their opportunity of 'freedom' and made off into Mashonaland with Ndebele cattle; the High Commissioner went so far as to approve the inadequate Reserves recommended in 1894 by the Land Commission on the grounds that the numbers of the Ndebele had been so drastically reduced by these defections that the land provided would be amply sufficient. This assumption was based more on the white belief that the Holi were oppressed slaves who hated the Ndebele system than on any actual observation. In fact, as Hughes has shown, the great majority of the Holi continued to regard themselves as Ndebele and as superior, in their own estimation, to the Shona; the prestige of the Ndebele state long outlasted its conquest. But it does seem that in the 1890's there was real anxiety among the Ndebele aristocracy about the newly independent attitudes of the Holi. As Umlugulu himself complained, 'Our great grievance is that we have no one now to work for us. The Maholi do not recognize us any longer; they say "We belong to the white men as well as you" '.[3]

Then there was the problem of the Kalanga, Rozwi and other groups who lived in the north, north-east and south-west of Matabeleland, but outside the limits of the Ndebele homeland proper. While the Ndebele state flourished these people recognized its authority and paid tribute to it. But if we are to trust

[1] Carnegie, Evidence submitted to Sir Richard Martin.

[2] A class originating in people captured or otherwise incorporated into the Ndebele State in contrast to descendants of the original break-away Zulu group from South Africa.

[3] *The Bulawayo Chronicle*, 26 June 1897.

the evidence of the missionary, Elliott, writing in 1894, there was continuing resentment of Ndebele rule, particularly among the scattered Rozwi groups, whom he depicts as mourning 'the departed glories of their race'. 'How can we pray', he reports the Rozwi of the north-east as complaining, 'now that the Ndebele have conquered us? We are afraid to go *pa dzimbabwe* but offer our little offerings in our villages and houses. Our oppressors have taken all we had.' With the collapse of the Ndebele state in 1893 these peoples no longer responded to the authority of the Ndebele *indunas*; yet it was important to bring them into the rebellion. We get a glimpse of the Ndebele desire to do this and the difficulties encountered from Selous' report of the situation in the Fig Tree area. Umfezela, the senior *indunas*' candidate for the kingship himself, had sent messages to the Kalanga of Fig Tree by his son, urging them to make common cause against the whites who were 'killing all the black men they can catch'. A rising of the south-western Kalanga would have blocked the road between Bulawayo and the south and seriously threatened the security of the town. But the Kalanga chief merely replied that the 'people don't wish to fight; they wish to sit still'. And sit still they did.[1]

How were the Holi to be securely gained for the revolt and how could an effective appeal be made to the Kalanga tribes of Matabeleland? A partial answer was found in the priesthood of the Mwari, or Mlimo, cult, a religious authority of much greater antiquity and complexity than that represented by Umlugulu. There is no place in this paper for any elaborate history of the cult, or account of its organization, but its role in the rebellions of 1896 and 1897 was so important that some discussion of it is necessary. Mwari, or Mlimo as the Ndebele called him, was the Kalanga concept of deity; an omnipresent and omnipotent High God; all-powerful but not remote; controlling especially the seasons and the harvests; and accessible to invocation or appeal. Mwari was worshipped in different ways over the whole of what is now Southern Rhodesia and in adjacent territories, but the Mwari cult as such, in the sense of a complex and hierarchic organization of priests and messengers through whom direct

---

[1] Elliott, 'The Ma-Shuna', in Carnegie, *Among the Matebele*, 1894; Selous, *Sunshine and Storm in Rhodesia*, p. 112.

approach was made to Mwari, existed only in Matabeleland and western Mashonaland, though its reputation extended further afield. In Central and Eastern Mashonaland, as we shall see, Mwari was approached rather through the spirits of dead rulers or tribal founders, whose living vehicles were the senior spirit mediums. The Mwari cult had become closely identified with the Rozwi confederacy. The cult headquarters appears to have been at, or adjacent to, the *Zimbabwe* of the Rozwi *Mambo*—at Great Zimbabwe itself; at Khami, or in the last days of Rozwi rule at Taba zi ka Mambo. The cult organization, as Messrs Summers and Blake Thompson have pointed out, was 'identical with that of the courts of important African chiefs. . . . The addressing of petitions to one official, the issuing of edicts by another, a secret intelligence service and a numerous court were common form.' The Rozwi controlled especially the 'secret intelligence service', while other offices in the cult were held by representatives of older peoples. This intelligence service was provided by regular visits to the central shrine of the intermediaries variously called the Children of Mwari, the *Wosana*, or the *Manyusa*, from the various districts of the Rozwi confederation. These also provided a machinery for the transmission of advice and instructions from the cult centre to scattered worshippers. Some authors have felt the Rozwi control of the cult to have been so important that they refer to the Rozwi hegemony as 'a sort of spiritual domination', and if this perhaps underestimates Rozwi administrative and military ability, there seems no doubt that the support of the cult was a significant source of power and prestige.[1]

When the Rozwi confederacy was broken up in the 1830's, and the Rozwi aristocracy scattered, the cult survived in something like its old elaboration. At first, indeed, it seemed as if the new Ndebele rulers might come to the same sort of working arrangement with the cult which the Rozwi had so successfully established. 'On arriving in their land, about forty years ago', T. M. Thomas wrote in 1872, 'Umzilikazi found several Ama-Kalanga doctors and wizards there, and for a time, on account of

[1] Summers and J. Blake Thompson, 'Mlimo and Mwari', *NADA*, 1956; Devlin, 'The Mashona and the Portuguese' and 'The Mashona and the British', *The Shield*, May and June 1961. See also, H. Franklin, 'Manyusa', *NADA*, 1932.

their influence over the chiefs of their own tribes, and knowledge of the country, they were of much use to him as newsmongers and leaders of his troops on their raids into different parts of the interior.' But the Ndebele state was built on different principles from the Rozwi confederacy. While the Rozwi had built up a diffused system of supremacy stretched out over a wide area, the Ndebele concentrated their power in a relatively small area, outside which they were content to raid, to levy tribute, and so on. Within the highly centralized Ndebele state itself there was no place for the Mwari priesthood as a co-ordinating agency. Thus Thomas tells us that once the priests 'failed to discover any more AmaKalanga or AmaSwina cattle they were despatched.'[1]

This certainly gives altogether too dramatic an idea of the fate of the Mwari priesthood. They were certainly not exterminated; it was merely that the cult was no longer used for continuous political purposes at the centre and that it was closely watched and controlled. Its shrines in the Matopos were allowed to operate. After all, the Ndebele felt the need, which Father Devlin tells us was common to all conquerors in Rhodesia before the Europeans, to be 'at peace with the land', and Mwari was pre-eminently the god of fertility and harvest. It seems that at all times under the Ndebele kingship the dispatch of gifts to the chief Mwari shrines was permitted, and that it was even the responsibility of the Ndebele king to send such gifts on behalf of the nation. If Mr Hughes is right the Mwari priesthood were also formally represented each year in a special compound at the Great Dance and feast of the First Fruits.[2]

But at the same time there was the feeling, as Thomas puts it, that the 'fame and influence' of the cult 'were inconsistent with those of the Amandebele king'. Thus our evidence suggests that it was only at times when the power of the Ndebele monarchy was for one reason or another at an ebb that the cult was able to manifest its old vigour and its emissaries able to travel freely through the whole area of its influence. Thomas tells us, for instance, that 'the mountain god's' representatives did not begin

[1] Thomas, op. cit.
[2] A. J. B. Hughes, 'The re-construction of the Ndebele state under European control', unpublished thesis in the Rhodes Livingstone Institute Library, Lusaka.

to go round the towns and villages 'until Mzilikazi had become old and feeble'; that they rapidly built up great influence, becoming in each town they entered 'the real lord of the place'; that the cult centre was even consulted after the death of Mzilikazi on the choice of a successor; but that almost immediately after the accession of the new king 'this underground mysterious being was denounced and his representatives roughly handled'.[1]

In the same way, after Lobengula's death, there was a similar expansion of the cult's activities. The Ndebele *mahaja*, Nganganyoni Mhlope, who was one of those sentenced after the rising for the murder of whites at its commencement, gave a full account of his participation in the rising in a confidential interview in 1938. Mhlope had this to say of the Mwari messengers. 'The Wosana were rain-bringers. They used to come in a group and say that they were sent by the Mlimo to make rain. They would dance at a kraal and the people would give them presents. In the time of Lobengula they were not allowed to go round the kraals and dance. Lobengula used to send a few men to Njelele with black oxen and they would find Wosana there and the Wosana would dance to make rain. When the white people came into the country then the Wosana started to go round from kraal to kraal.' Mhlope also commented upon the prestige of the local representative of Mwari. 'There was a man who was delivering the message. His name was Mkwati . . . Mkwati was the messenger of the Mlimo. . . . He was just like an Nkosi. He was not an Nkosi but we took him as an Nkosi because he was sent by the Mlimo.'[2]

With this renewed vitality the cult offered considerable possibilities of co-ordination. 'The Mlimo', wrote General Carrington on the basis of army intelligence reports, 'is a Makalaka institution which has been adopted with great fervour by the Matabele. For special occasions the people appear to travel enormous distances in order to consult the Mlimo and his orders fly about from one end of the country to another with great rapidity.' Here Carrington was almost certainly over-estimating the centralization, as well as the authoritarianism of the cult. Whatever may have been the case during the Rozwi confederacy, there was no single cult

[1] Thomas, *op. cit.*
[2] Statement by Nganganyoni Mhlope, 20 November 1938, WI 8/1/3.

centre, no one recognized senior representative of Mwari, in 1896, nor had there been for many years. In 1879, for instance, the missionary, Joseph Cockin, wrote from Hope Fountain describing the Mwari centres. 'To the East amongst the Amatoppo Mountains there is a town named Ematjetjeni, to the South is another named Enjeleli and to the South-West is a third, named Umkombo. These belong to a man [sic] called Ungwali, a god in whom the Matabili have great faith. . . . Not very far from Ehmlangeni—Inyati Mission station—there dwells another God named Ujugwa.' It is clear that these cult centres were still active in 1896, though Baden-Powell and other reporters tended to run the various shrines in the Matopos into one, and to describe a three-fold division into the Matopos shrine, the south-western shrine and the Inyati centre.[1]

Even this picture is undoubtedly an over-simplification. There was one major shrine outside the borders of Matabeleland, in the Transvaal, and there were local oracular caves in the various districts of Matabeleland and western Mashonaland. These shrines stood in no simple relationship or hierarchy; nevertheless there was, as we shall see, a centralizing connection between them. We may perhaps accept for the time being Baden-Powell's concept of the triple division and imagine a situation in which the Matopos shrines exercised influence in central Matabeleland and enjoyed a reputation far beyond it; the south-western shrine exercised influence over the Kalanga of the south-west; and the Inyati shrine exercised influence over the various peoples to the north and north-east of Bulawayo. This, or something like this, seems to have been in operation in 1896. Not all of these cult centres were brought into the rising. The Matopos shrines supported it; so did the Inyati shrine. But the south-western cult centre refused to join in the rising, used its influence to keep the Kalanga quiet, took an active part in warning local whites, including missionaries, of their danger, and generally played an important role in keeping the southern road from Bulawayo open. By an irony when Native Commissioner Armstrong and Scout Burnham tried to end the whole rising in June 1896 by 'shooting the Mlimo', they shot

[1] Carrington to Goodenough, 25 July 1896, BA 2/1/1; Cockin to Mullins, May 1829, LO 6/1/4. I am obliged to Mr Richard Brown for this last reference.

this 'loyal' south-western priest and imprisoned his family and associates—with the result that the south-western Kalanga very nearly joined in the rising after all![1]

But if the Mwari cult was not unanimously committed to the rising there is no doubt of the importance of the commitment of the Matopos and Inyati shrines. As in the 1830's, the officers of these shrines could contribute 'influence over the chiefs of their own tribes and knowledge of the country.' They also, as some of the evidence already cited has shown, exercised a not inconsiderable influence over the Ndebele themselves. Finally, as we shall see, they exercised influence outside the borders of Matabeleland which proved to be very important in relating the Shona to the Ndebele rising.

To indicate the role played by the Mwari officers let us take one example—the chief officer of the Inyati shrine, Mwkati, whom we have already seen acquiring the reputation of an *Nkosi* in the evidence of Nganganyoni Mhlope. Mkwati was an ex-slave of the Leya tribe, captured near the Zambesi during Lobengula's reign by an Ndebele raid. Before 1893 he had lived in the great military kraal at Jingen, and acted as one of the delegates sent with gifts to Mwari from the Inyati area. After 1893 he moved to a cave on Taba zi ka Mambo which rapidly became an important oracular shrine. As we have seen his prestige grew equally rapidly, and it was assisted by his control of two remarkable associates. One of these was the woman Tenkela, known to the Kalanga as the Mother or Wife of Mwari, and to the Ndebele as Usalugazana. 'After the white people came', Mhlope tells us, 'Mkwati came back from Njelele with a woman—a tall woman with a light complexion; her name was Tengela. And he told the people that she was the Inkosikazi of the Mlimo.' 'The Mlimo has one wife', an African prisoner testified in August 1896, 'and three children. Umkwati is the father of these children.'[2]

Now this figure—the Mother or Wife of Mwari—certainly plays an important, if as yet mysterious, part in the cult. For

[1] Reed to Duncan, 4 April 1896, A 10/1/1; Burnham to Grey, 8 July 1896, LO 5/6/2; Correspondence relating to feared rising of the Kalanga, Confidential Prints, African (South), No. 520, pp. 294–7.
[2] Mhlope, *op. cit.*, Malima's statement, August 1896, LO 5/6/2.

instance, in 1913 messages were sent from one of the Mwari shrines to the people of Chibi Reserve instructing them to observe certain rest days, the first of which was 'to propitiate the Mwali's mother, who is the *imbuya* or grandmother of all the natives.' Hughes and van Velsen tell us that in Matabeleland belief in Usalunganzana amounts almost to 'a parallel cult'. At any rate, Tenkela was clearly regarded as a personage of importance in 1896, and evidence suggests that she as well as Mkwati was consulted by elements among the rebel leaders. 'It has been reported to me', wrote Father Prestage in April 1896, 'that Umpotshana . . . went at the beginning of the last hoeing to consult Usalukazana (mother of Mlimo). She advised that the Amandebele should kill the white men in the country outside Bulawayo, undertaking to send a bolt of fire to destroy Bulawayo with its inhabitants at the time of rain.'[1]

Mkwati's other remarkable ally was Siginyamatshe, the 'stone-swallower'. Siginyamatshe, whose real name was Siminya, was a well known Child of Mwari, who lived in the neighbourhood of Bulawayo, at the Ntembeni kraal. He had a considerable reputation as a wonder worker. At his trial in 1898 one witness testified, according to the obviously hostile and slanted report of the magazine *Rhodesia*, that Siginyamatshe 'would go down on his hands and knees and imitate animals. On one occasion he butted with his head a big stone on which they ground their corn and broke the stone in halves. The people on that occasion were quite convinced he was supernatural and went forth to murder the whites with cheerful ardour.' At the trial also one Matafeni, who had been a subordinate official at the Inyati shrine, was reported as saying that 'messengers were sent round to the people to invite them to come and see the prisoner, who was described as the wonderful Child of the Mlimo. When a number of them arrived, the prisoner would be found talking to Mkwati. Mkwati would then mysteriously disappear. As a matter of fact, he would slink round the hill and get into a cave and between the two of them they would deceive the people and induce them to murder the whites.'[2]

---

[1] Prestage to C.N.C., 24 April 1896, A 10/1/2; N. C. Chibi to Superintendent of Natives, Victoria, 19 July 1913, N 3/33/12.

[2] 'How the Rebellion was worked', *Rhodesia*, 7 May 1898.

We should perhaps interject here a warning that it is as well to bear in mind when reading the reports and statements of 1896 and 1897, all uniformly hostile to the Mwari cult and all uniformly assuming that it was nothing more than a clever swindle, that this is far from being an accurate picture. We should remember, for instance, that Elliott was told by the peoples around Inyati that they recognized a man as a genuine Child of Mwari not only because of his entry into a state of trance, or his supernatural abilities, but because of his moral character. 'If he honours others and is upright and good, we know he is sent from Mngwali.' Recent commentators have emphasized that the Mwari cult possessed 'a genuine conception of deity', and a developed religious sense. In short we shall not understand the part played by men like Mkwati and Siginyamatshe if we regard them merely as unscrupulous 'witch-doctors'. They were, in fact, highly respected representatives of a religion which played a profound part in the lives of the people.[1]

But the contemporary sources, however distorted, serve to show us the leading role of the two men. Thus they show us Mkwati moving from Taba zi ka Mambo to Jingen and around the kraals north of Bulawayo in the days before the rising; consulting with Ndebele regimental commanders; and assuming a sort of directing role in the attack on the whites in the Inyati area. Mhlope, whose evidence does not share the same hostility towards the Mwari officers but possibly overstates their importance as a sort of alibi, described the outbreak in Inyati as follows:

The first place where we started to fight was Inyati ... We had news from the Matopos that Mlimo was going to help us. We had no grievance against these people. We killed them simply because they were white people. We were going to kill all white people because we had news that the Mlimo was going to help us ... Mkwati brought back the message from Mlimo. ... We did not touch anything in the store [at Taba zi ka Mambo, where Mhlope participated in the killing of three whites] because we had been told that we were not to touch anything belonging to the white people. We were told that the Mlimo would come and take them. There was a man who was delivering the message. His name was Mkwati and he came round collecting all the

[1] Elliott, 'The Mashuna', op. cit.

things . . . when we killed the three white people it took some time and Mkwati came and stayed at the store and told us all to bring everything there. He was just like an Nkosi.[1]

The sources show us Siginyamatshe similarly engaged in the kraals to the south of Bulawayo. 'Umgalu, *induna* of the Elibeni kraal', runs a report of Siginyamatshe's trial, 'said that the accused came to his kraal just before the fighting. He came with a lot of girls in front, who were jumping and dancing and clapping their hands. He said he came from the Mlimo. . . . He said "You must close up the road and if any white men come you must kill them". They covered the road as they were told.' 'Had it not been for the accused', concluded the judge, 'many of the natives around Bulawayo would not have arisen.'[2]

Interestingly enough these specific examples show us the influence of the cult officers among the Ndebele themselves. In more general terms the sources agree that their influence was particularly important, and perhaps decisive, in bringing the Holi into the rising, and in mobilizing the Kalanga and Rozwi of the north and north-east. Mkwati, though not himself a Rozwi, had married a daughter of the Rozwi chief Uwini, one of the old Rozwi chieftaincies allowed to survive by Lobengula, and a key figure in the rebellion in his area. Moreover, by basing himself at Taba zi ka Mambo, the site of the last Zimbabwe of the Mambos, Mkwati was appealing to memories of the old confederacy. At any rate some of his most militant supporters, the men indeed who formed his personal body-guard, were Rozwis of the Inyati area. In this way Mkwati and his fellows helped to hold together the different elements of the rising.

What was the relationship of Mkwati and the other Mwari officers to Umlugulu and the Ndebele aristocracy? Many authorities have asserted that the Mwari cult was 'an instrument employed by the actual leaders of the insurrection' and that 'the subservience of the cult to the Matabele was made abundantly clear in 1896'. Selous thought that 'the Umlimo was made use of for the purposes of the present rebellion by Umlugulu', while other writers stressed a particular connection between Umlugulu and Siginyamatshe. But on a closer examination the thesis that Mkwati and Siginya-

[1] Mhlope, *op. cit.*   [2] *Rhodesia*, 9 July 1898.

matshe were tools of the Ndebele 'high priest' begins to look very improbable. For one thing their closest links with the Ndebele aristocracy were not with Umlugulu and the senior *indunas* at all, but with the young men of Nyamanda's party, led by the intransigent Mpotshwana. Mpotshwana was described as Mkwati's 'military adviser'; after the last and decisive fight on the Umgusa which broke the rebel ring around Bulawayo, Mpotshwana and the younger men retreated north to Taba zi ka Mambo, while Umlugulu and the older men and their followers fell back into the Matopos hills. For another thing, the accounts already quoted, and a great deal of other evidence, reveals Mkwati and Siginyamatshe as directing rather than directed by Ndebele *indunas*, kraal heads and regimental commanders. But more important than either of these considerations was the fact that Mkwati and his fellows were appealing to groups whose interests were different from those of the Ndebele; groups which responded to Mkwati's influence not because he was the ally of Umlugulu or Mpotshwana but because he spoke to their memories of the pre-Ndebele past.[1]

As the rebellion proceeded this divergence of interests became clearer. In October 1896, indeed, Native Commissioner Fynn went so far as to suggest that the whole rising was a Rozwi plot to bring about the discomfiture of the Ndebele!

Uwinya was a chieftain of the AbaLozwi tribe, tributary to Lobengula and lived at the Madwaleni mouth of the Shangani. He consulted with Mkwati . . . and these two having laid their heads together and having in common a bitter personal and tribal feeling against the Matabele and having probably been approached by the chiefs of the latter with a request for aid in the rebellion, . . . made a deep scheme for the destruction and complete humiliation of their hereditary foes, the Matabele. The scheme was as follows: Mkwati was to concede the requests of the chiefs and prophesy the extinction of the whites and the success of the rebels, thus strengthening the hands of the chiefs, as without the divine aid of the Mlimo the common people could not have been persuaded to rise. The far-seeing Mkwati had no doubt that the ultimate success would be with the whites, and then Uwinya

[1] Selous, *op. cit.*; Hole, *The Making of Rhodesia*; F. Sykes, *With Plumer in Matabeleland*, 1892; Summers and Blake Thompson, *op. cit.*

would play his part. The part of the country occupied by him is one which would from its position be naturally used as a place to flee to, and there the Matabele went upon their forces being broken up by the whites in the southern parts of the country. There also went Mkwati, who had allied himself to Uwinya by marrying his daughter. Uwinya then laid himself out to discourage by every means in his power the surrender of the Matabele and for that purpose he established a force which he called 'Police', whose work was to kill all natives who showed any intention of surrendering.

Uwini's police, according to Fynn, fell on the Ndebele refugees, killing them and carrying off their women and children, thus taking their revenge for the overthrow of the Rozwi confederacy. The idea that Mkwati plotted the downfall of the Ndebele from the beginning is, of course, absurdly improbable, but Fynn's account could only have been given in the context of a bitter divergence of interests between Mkwati and his former allies.[1]

Some of these points emerge more clearly from an examination of the role of Mkwati and Siginyamatshe once the rising had begun. At first, no difference of interest was discernible. Mkwati used his influence, as Umlugulu his, to bring the various rebel forces together around Bulawayo. Siginyamatshe represented Mkwati in the field; Mkwati gave moral support and directions from Taba zi ka Mambo. A witness at Siginyamatshe's trial told how he had seen the accused before the first fight on the Umgusa 'calling out the natives and saying he was the Child of the Mlimo; he was in command of an *impi*'. The witness heard him 'calling out: "I am collecting this *impi*, I am the Child of the Mlimo, the *impi* must fight".'[2]

Mkwati's role emerges from the evidence of the boy, Malema, who was taken prisoner in August 1896. Malema testified that after each set-back or significant development messengers were sent from the armies around Bulawayo to seek the advice of Mwari at the Taba zi ka Mambo shrine. In May 1896, for example, Malema was sent

to report to the Mlimo the defeat we had sustained. On a former occasion I had accompanied Siginyamatshe, the Child of the Mlimo,

[1] N. C. Fynn to Baden Powell, 1 October 1896, PO 1/1/1.
[2] *Rhodesia*, 9 July 1898.

to report our leaving the Umgusa for Ntabayesinduna. On this occasion I was the message bearer. . . . The Mlimo was at Ntaba zi ka Mambo, having removed there from the Zingeni. When I got to the Ntaba zi ka Mambo I saw the people of the Mlimo, to wit, Umkwati of the Zingeni, Zenkele, Undabambi, and others. . . . We came to the approach of the cave, which was curtained with grass. Zenkele and Undabambi were there during my interview with the Mlimo but Umkwati had disappeared and we did not see him again until the interview was over and the Mlimo had bid us farewell. I told the Mlimo the message I had been given by the *indunas* and told him that the whites had gone on towards the Shangani. The Mlimo, who was invisible, spoke from the cave and told me to return to the *impi* and tell them to follow the white men as far as the Shangani.

After a clash on the Shangani Malema was again sent to the oracular cave. 'As before the Mlimo told me to return . . . and to tell them to go again to the Umgusa. They did so. I accompanied them.'[1]

This return to the Umgusa was both the high point of Mwari cult influence on the conduct of the rising and the key military moment. In June the rebel forces were crushingly defeated. 'This fight was followed by the best effects', a military commentator later wrote, 'owing to the fact that the rebel *impi* consisted of carefully selected men from eight different regiments who had been chosen to take part in this venture, the success of which had been guaranteed by the Mlimo. After this engagement the rebels could never be persuaded to fight until they were by the pressure compelled to do so.' The Ndebele *impis* broke up, some retreating on Mkwati's stronghold at Taba zi ka Mambo; others retiring into the Matopos.[2]

The Umgusa fight was followed in early July by Plumer's successful storming of Taba zi ka Mambo and the break up of the forces gathered round Mkwati. Some of the heaviest fighting of the rebellion took place in this engagement. Rebel losses were heavy and the Mlimo's cave, filled with European loot, was taken. De Vere Stent has left us a vivid account of the operation, of Rhodes's part in it, and of the return of the victorious column. 'First the screen of scouts, riding in careless mood . . . then a great

[1] Malema's report, August 1896, LO 5/6/2.   [2] Staff Studies, PA 1/1/2.

mob of cattle—ten thousand head, they said; they seemed to cover
the veld for miles . . . then tramping in rough formation, the
prisoners and the women and children.' The defeat marked the
end of the Ndebele faction grouped around Mkwati as a formidable military force and undermined the prestige of Mkwati himself. He had in fact left Taba zi ka Mambo just before the attack.
'When the white forces were advancing on Ntaba zi ka Mambo',
an African witness tells us, 'the Mlimo said he was going to
examine and inspect the land in the Somabula forest and on
the night before the fight Umkwati followed him.'[1]

The crisis of the rebellion in Matabeleland had now come. The
white forces turned their attention to the senior *indunas* in the
Matopos and a bloody stalemate now developed. Umlugulu and
the senior *indunas* began to think in terms of saving the Ndebele
system from complete destruction and making the best bargain
they could for themselves through a negotiated peace. The leaders
of the young bloods, however, scattered as they were in the north-
east, and unlikely to share in whatever advantages peace might
bring, favoured continuing the war. And the Mwari officers, both
in the Matopos and in the north-east, bitterly opposed the idea of
negotiation or surrender. As representatives of the older peoples
of the Rozwi confederation they had no interest in a peace based
on the advantage of the Ndebele aristocracy.

By July there was already friction between Mwari officers and
Ndebele *indunas* in the Matopos, with the priests vainly trying to
check the drift to peace by 'deposing' various Ndebele commanders. By August it was clear that the Ndebele leadership had
decided to treat. 'Mlimo now has nothing to do with the revolt',
declared an Ndebele captive to military intelligence on 9 August.
'He does not like the Matabele and talks of clearing out of the
Matopos. Before they had determined to surrender the Mlimo
had ordered them on no account to leave the hills. The Matabele
are now fighting in self-defence. If a chance had been left to them
of coming in, they would have done so.' 'The Mlimo has had a
dispute with the three chief generals of the Matabele', *The Times*
reported a few days later, 'with the result that the Mlimo left the

[1] H. de Vere Stent, *A personal record of some incidents in the Life of Cecil
Rhodes*, 1924; Malema's report.

Matopos taking all his people with him.' One of the three 'generals' named in the report was Umlugulu. Umlugulu was also present at the famous first *indaba* with Rhodes, at which Sekombo was the main spokesman. 'We are the ears and eyes and the mouth of the Matabele nation', Somabulana is reported as saying at the end of the meeting. 'What we speak is law. Dhliso is here; I am here; Nyanda is here; Umlugulu and Sikombo are here. It is peace; you have our word.' By September the local Mwari representatives gave up the struggle against the negotiations. 'The man whom we considered would fight to the last, namely Unthwani', wrote Rhodes to Lord Grey on 21 September, 'is here and sleeps here tonight. You must remember that Unthwani is the Mlimo's mouth-piece and it speaks volumes that he has come out. In fact we may say that the matter is over as far as the hills are concerned.'[1]

In the north-east, however, the balance of power was different. There Mkwati was surrounded by faithful 'Makalakas', by his Rozwi bodyguard, and by the men of his father-in-law, Uwini. Those Ndebele in the north-east who wished to surrender found things very different indeed from the Matopos. On 3 August the Native Commissioner, Inyati, explained the situation in his own area. He reported that Mkwati was supported by some Ndebele, particularly those from Jingen kraal, but that his main support came from

the Maholi who have also armed and declared that they will fight for the Mlimo. . . . My informant also says that the Mlimo has instituted a 'police force' of his own and is doing his utmost to prevent the Matabele coming in to surrender. Any messenger found with a pass, unless he goes straight to the Mlimo with it, is killed; any people speaking of the Mlimo as a fraud are dealt with in like manner. I have here an *umfaan* who managed to escape when his people were killed by an *impi* acting under the orders of Incomo because the head man, named Somapunga, talked of going in to surrender. In other cases people who are suspected of disloyalty to the Mlimo are surprised by the 'police' and disarmed, their guns, etc., being given to the Maholi who have declared heart and soul for the Mlimo.[2]

[1] Staff diary entry, 9 August 1896, LO 5/6/3; *The Times*, 11 August 1896; Sykes, *op. cit.*; Rhodes to Grey, 21 September 1896, LO 5/6/4.
[2] N.C. Gielgud to C.N.C., 3 August 1896, BA 2/9/2.

On 6 August the Native Commissioner wrote again:

A few more men have come in to surrender. They all tell the same
story of intimidation and violence on the part of the *indunas* of the
Mlimo. The Mlimo's faction has established picquets on all the roads
and tracks who stop families going south to surrender, often killing
the men and sending back the women. The Mlimo has instructed the
Maholis to kill all the Matabele they may find returning to the white
people or carrying messages calling on the people to surrender.

And on 10 August another Native Commissioner reported that
'the Makalakas are the strongest today in that district and prevent
the Matabeles from coming in to surrender.'[1]

The Native Commissioners besought the administration to
launch an attack on the Somabula forest. 'The fact that they were
not followed after the Thabas zika Mambo fight has given them
time to regain their confidence in themselves and in the Mlimo.'
Three hundred troops could disperse 'the fighting remnant of
Matabele and armed Maholi . . . the Maholi would have been
driven from their homes and had all the fight knocked out of
them.' In fact no force was sent until early September, for fear of
compromising the surrender negotiations in the Matopos. But
then Baden–Powell's patrols dispersed the rebel forces on the
Somabula, harrying Mkwati's party out of the forest, breaking
up his 'police', capturing and executing Uwini, and freeing the
Ndebele to surrender. 'I asked the natives now on the Battlefield
block what was their opinion of the death of Uwinya', wrote
N.C. Fynn on 1 October, 'and they replied that they were glad
that the Government had now opened the way for the surrender
of the Matable.'[2]

In this way the rising in Matabeleland came to an end. The
fortunes of the two religious leaders we have been examining
were very different. Umlugulu was appointed as salaried *induna* of
the Gwanda district as a part of the bargain with the Ndebele
aristocracy. Siginyamatshe was captured in September 1897 and
sentenced to twelve years hard labour in July 1898. As for Mkwati,
he fled from Matabeleland at the end of 1896, his co-operation

---

[1] N.C. Gielgud to C.N.C., 6 August 1896, LP 5/6/2; N.C. Fynn to C.N.C.,
10 August 1896, BA 2/9/2.
[2] Fynn to Baden–Powell, 1 October 1896, PO 1/1/1.

with the Ndebele aristocracy ended in mutual hatred. 'The Matabele followers,' a Rozwi Child of Mlimo tells us, 'who had suffered very much from hunger and sickness, began to lose faith in the Mlimo's high priest, saying they were being humbugged and made a plot to kill him. They took myself and Matafen into their confidence, but Matafen gave the priest, Mukwati, the tip and both Mukwati and Matafen cleared that night, and the Matabeles being disgusted began to trek back.' Mkwati, having escaped this plot, arrived at the main base of the rebellion in Western Mashonaland some time in October, where he announced that 'Mlimo will kill all natives who made peace and that we were going to fight again'. In other words the Ndebele phase of the rising was over—but the rising in Mashonaland continued.[1]

It is to the rebellion in Mashonaland that we must now turn. Contemporary white opinion was astonished that a rising had been organized in Mashonaland at all. 'The Mashona race has always been regarded', wrote the Resident Magistrate, Salisbury, in October 1896, 'as composed of disintegrated groups of natives, having no common organization and owing allegiance to no single authority, cowed by a series of raids from Matabeleland into a condition of abject pusillanimity and incapable of planning any combined or premeditated action.' The Native Department in Mashonaland believed that Shona chiefs were virtually power-less: 'they have not the smallest authority', wrote the Native Com-missioner, Hartley, in December 1895. 'They are defied even in their own kraals.' It was held also that the Shona were recent comers to the country, without any sense of tradition or of their past—'Unlike the Zulu', wrote the Native Commissioner, Salis-bury, 'the Mashonas have no folk lore and are content to enjoy today and think nothing of yesterday, or tomorrow either for that matter.' How, then, did a co-ordinated rising take place in Western and Central Mashonaland?[2]

A full answer to this question would involve us in a detailed exposure of the fallacies of contemporary white beliefs about the Shona; would involve some narrative of the Shona past as it is

[1] Tshiwa's statement, 10 January 1897, LO 5/4/1.
[2] Hole, Report of 29 October 1896, A 1/12/25; Half-yearly report, Hartley, December 1895, N 1/1/3; Monthly report, Salisbury, January 1896, N 1/1/9.

now being recovered; some discussion of the position of the Shona paramounts, so different from the Zulu and Ndebele authorities with whom the whites were accustomed to deal; some statement of the deep and resilient attachment of the peoples of Mashonaland over centuries to their secular and religious institutions. The failure of the Native Department to understand the Shona situation arose largely from their ignorance of all this. 'We had underrated the Mashona native', admitted one of the early Native Commissioners after the rebellion. 'We knew nothing of their past history, who they were or where they came from, and although many of the Native Commissioners had a working knowledge of their language, none of us really understood the people or could follow their line of thought ... We were without a sufficient knowledge', he concluded specifically, 'of their belief in the Mondoro or Mwari.'[1]

This conclusion reminds us that although a full answer to our questions would involve a long discussion of the secular authorities and of the history of 'state' systems in Mashonaland, it is the purpose of this chapter to examine only the role of the traditional religious authorities. This role was particularly important in Mashonaland, though the subsequent discussion of it does not imply that the religious authorities of the Shona provided the only co-ordinating factor in 1896 and 1897.

From the religious point of view Mashonaland, in the sense in which that term was used in 1896, has to be seen not as a single unit but as an area in which two different, though related, religious systems operated. One system was, of course, the Mwari cult. We must say a little more about the cult in Mashonaland since the extent and nature of its influence there has been imperfectly appreciated. After the rebellions the Rhodesian administration naturally kept a close watch on the Mwari officers and as a result a considerable body of evidence exists on cult activities in Mashonaland between the late 1890's and the 1920's. From this it is plain that the cult existed in fully organized form in a great crescent of Mashonaland, lying immediately to the east of the Matabeleland border. There were recognized *Wosana* or *Manyusa* and local oracular caves, dispatch of gifts to the chief Mwari shrines and

[1] Reminiscences of 'Wiri' Edwards, ED 6/1/1.

receipt of messages from them, recorded in the Belingwe, Charter, Chibi, Gutu, Hartley, Ndanga and Victoria native districts. In this part of Mashonaland in 1896 the cult was in full operation and in constant contact with its Matabeleland centres.[1]

Outside this area I have come across no references to continuous cult activity. But it is important to note that the prestige of the cult, inextricably bound up with the prestige of the Rozwi, extended throughout Mashonaland. The early Native Commissioners in Central and Eastern Mashonaland when asked to report on religious customs all returned somewhat garbled accounts of the special relationship of the Rozwi with Mwari and of the operation of the cult. Thus the N.C. Salisbury was told by the Shona peoples of his area that 'every MaRaswi is supposed to have a familiar spirit' which 'answers all questions asked of it by its owner . . . from the sky, the tops of trees or out in the veldt'. The Native Commissioner, Makoni, reported that in his area 'they speak of the VaRosi . . . as God's chosen people and have great respect for them, the VaRosi being looked upon as priests'. The Native Commissioner, Umtali, gave the fullest account.

The natives of Manicaland [he reported] worship a supreme being known as Morimo, Mali, or Murunga. They believe he is omnipresent but that he only speaks to them from one place, viz. Matjamahopli near Bulawayo, and then he will only speak to a chosen few. . . . The generality of the people don't presume to pray to the Morimo personally but address Muzimo, the spirits of their ancestors and ask them to intercede for them. . . . Before the Matabele came the whole of the country was tributary to the BaRozi. Then they used to build huts in which to pray to the spirits, but this is seldom done now. They say the BaRozi are more holy than they and Morimo always listens and speaks to them.

This continuing prestige of the Mwari cult and of the Rozwi was a factor of some importance in co-ordinating the rebellion in Mashonaland.[2]

The other religious system, which overlapped with the Mwari

---

[1] See A 3/18/2; A 11/2/12/11; N 3/14/5; N 3/31/1; N 3/31/3; N 3/33/12; N 3/32/1; LO 5/7/1 to 5; LO 5/5/3 to 33.
[2] N.C. Campbell's report, January 1896, N 1/1/9; N.C. Meredith's report, December 1894, A 15/1/1; N.C. Nesbitt's report, 1896, N 1/1/11.

cult in the Charter and Hartley districts especially, and which was dominant in Central and Eastern Mashonaland, was the system of the spirit mediums, through whom the people addressed 'Muzimo, the spirits of their ancestors and ask them to intercede for them'. Whatever the original relationship of the spirit mediums with the Mwari cult there seems no doubt that in 1896 the two systems were distinct in theology, in organization, and largely in geographical area. The system of the spirit mediums is so much better known than the Mwari cult and has been so minutely described by Dr Gelfand that there is no need to give any full account of it in this paper. But one important point must be made. Dr Gelfand in his first study, *Shona Ritual*, postulated a spirit hierarchy, operative over all Mashonaland, in which the mediums of the less important ancestor figures were junior to those of the more important, and these junior to the spirits of dead kings, and all subordinate to the spirit of Chaminuka, so that the recognized Chaminuka medium at any one time would be at the apex of the whole system. In *Shona Religion*, however, Dr Gelfand's study of the north-eastern area of Mashonaland convinced him that this picture would not do; one had to postulate at least two distinct hierarchies—the Chaminuka-Nehanda hierarchy, operative in central and western Mashonaland, and the Mutota-Dzivaguru hierarchy, operative in north-eastern and eastern Mashonaland. We shall discuss later whether such a picture is not in itself an over-simplification, but we need note here only that, whatever other modifications have to be made, the division between these two areas, between the Chaminuka-Nehanda hierarchy and the Mutota-Dzivaguru hierarchy, seems to be of particular significance. It derives, no doubt, from the past history of Mashonaland and in particular from the fact that the north-east and east was the nuclear area of the Mwene Mutapa confederacy. At any rate in 1896 and 1897 the western and central areas were generally involved in the rebellion, and the KoreKore and Tavara of the north-east were not, a fact which Father Devlin has explained partly in terms of this religious division. Thus in our account of the role of the traditional religious authorities in the rising in Mashonaland we must deal with the Mwari cult and with what we have loosely called the Chaminuka-Nehanda hierarchy of mediums, but not with the mediums of the Mutota-Dzivaguru hierarchy.[1]

Let us look first at the activities of the Mwari cult in western Mashonaland. The representative of the cult in that area who played the most active part in the rising was one Bonda, a headman in a Rozwi group which lived under Musarurwa in the Range-Charter district, 'the nursery of the Mashona rebellion', as the official report on the disturbances later described it. Some time in April 1896 Mkwati sent a Rozwi Child of Mwari, Tshiwa, to summon Bonda and other representatives from the western Mashonaland area to his headquarters at Taba zi ka Mambo. Bonda went there in May, and with him went emissaries from paramount chief Mashiangombi of the Hartley district. 'I hear from one of my spies', wrote the Native Commissioner, Hartley, on 24 May, 'that Mashayingombi himself is in communication with someone in Matabeleland and has lately sent some young men down. I taxed Mashayingombi with this but he informed me that he had only sent to the Matabele Umlimo for some medicines to prevent the locusts from eating his crops next year. This spy also told me that it had been proposed by the Matabele and Maholi inhabitants to rise and first kill all my police . . . and then try Hartley. . . . I attach no importance whatsoever to the above', concluded this tragically complacent officer. 'I find the natives very quiet and civil when I go to their kraals to collect tax. But I am just complying with your instructions to report all I hear.'[2]

Within two weeks the Native Commissioner was dead, killed near Mashiangombi's kraal in the first out-break of rebellion in Mashonaland. This outbreak was stimulated by the return from Taba zi ka Mambo early in June of Tshiwa, Bonda and Mashiangombi's emissaries, bringing with them 'the Mangoba regiment . . . to incite the Mashonas into rebellion'. Most of the Ndebele impi remained at Mashiangombi's kraal, which became the centre of the rebellion in western Mashonaland. Tshiwa and Bonda went on to carry the rising further afield. We get a glimpse of Tshiwa at work in the vivid reminiscences of Native Commissioner Weale.

[1] Gelfand, op. cit.; C. Devlin, 'The Mashona and the Portuguese', The Shield, May 1961.
[2] N.C. Hartley, to C.N.C., 24 May 1896, N 1/1/3.

I sent messengers out into Ndema's country to spy out the land [he tells us of the period just after the outbreak] and the police boys brought back word to say that the whole of the country ahead was disaffected and that a Mondoro of the Mlimo, a MaRozwi named 'Tshiwa', was doctoring the rivers so that the white man and his horse's feet would burn up when they stepped into the water, and stated that he had arranged it that our bullets would be as harmless as water, but what was more to the point was that they had distributed among them some Matabele braves to help and urge them on to fight.

Weale describes how the loyalist chief Chilimanzi took a party of his men, together with white police, and 'stepped into the river dividing Banga's country from his own' in order to demonstrate the falsity of Tshiwa's promises. But Chilimanzi was very much the exception; his rival, Banga, and many other chiefs answered Tshiwa's call and joined the rebellion.[1]

Bonda had equal success to the south, in his home area. In July 1896 Colonel Beal collected evidence in the Charter district which showed what had happened in some detail. According to his informants, Bonda had returned to his own kraal, accompanied by six Ndebele. He had then sent out the men of his kraal as messengers of Mwari, to carry instructions to the smaller kraals in the neighbourhood, while he himself went to the kraals of chiefs Umtigesa, Meromo and Msango. 'They went to Meromo's', deposed one witness. 'When they came there they said they were sent by Umlimo and they were the Umlimo's people. Meromo said he also was one of Umlimo's people; he joined hands with them.' The other chiefs in the district reacted in the same way, and soon the local whites were being attacked and killed.[2]

We may here legitimately draw on some later evidence to demonstrate the sort of prestige that men like Tshiwa and Bonda enjoyed in western Mashonaland, and the way in which the Mwari cult could be used for the transmission of messages. In 1904 one Manyanga, a representative of the south-western Mwari shrine, travelled through Chilimanzi, Gutu and Ndema and eventually came to the kraal of the Njanja paramount, Gambiza,

[1] Tshiwa's statement, 10 January 1897, LO 5/4/1; Weales' reminiscences, WE 3/2/6.
[2] Evidence taken by Col. Beal, July 1896, A 1/12/11.

in the Hartley district. He 'told Gambiza to give him meat and shelter . . . then told Gambiza to send for all his people. Gambiza did so and on their assembling told them that the prisoner had come from . . . the Gods.' Gambiza, though paramount, gave up his own hut to the messenger of Mwari; he and his headmen squatted on the floor in an adjacent hut, speaking with Manyanga through an intermediary because 'he represented himself to be a big man and would not speak directly to us'. Manyanga was then escorted about the surrounding kraals by the paramount's messenger, announcing that 'he lived on beer, milk and meat and not on the ordinary food of natives and that if he got plenty of the former he would drive the white man from the land'. The only chief who refused to receive him was the cautious Gwenda, who testified that 'what alarmed me about the accused coming to the kraal in the manner he did was that a man came in a similar manner just before the last rebellion and I compared him with that man.'[1]

Considerably later, in 1915, Mwari messages were being passed from kraal to kraal in Gutu, Chilimanzi, Charter, Victoria and Ndanga districts. In Charter, for instance, 'six young men and five young women wearing fantastic head-dresses made of limbo and drawing people around them by their talk, singing and tom-tom playing . . . were telling the people that they were sent by Mwari to convey his tidings to the people.' In other areas the message was carried from village to village, chain letter fashion; 'they all say they got the message from adjoining kraals; people came singing and dancing and saying that they had received a message from Mwari that they were to visit six kraals, dance and sing and demand a fowl', and to tell the people of those six kraals to do the same. The Native Police in Charter thought 'that the movement is a mischievous one and similar to that which took place prior to the rebellion of 1896'.[2]

In this sort of way we may imagine the message of rebellion being sent out in western Mashonaland in 1896. In some places

[1] Preliminary examination into charges against Manyanga, A 11/2/12/11. Thomas in 1872 wrote that a Mwari messenger entering a village, 'finding he has become the real lord of the place, does as he likes—commands, orders, sends or calls whomsoever he pleases and even eats their food without scruple'.

[2] Reports on Mwari messengers, 1915, N 3/14/5.

Tshiwa or Bonda or some other important Child of Mwari carrying the message himself and being received with instant respect; elsewhere the message being passed on from kraal to kraal until it had spread through the whole area. Nor did the importance of men like Bonda end when the rising had begun. We catch constant glimpses of him in the next few months, carrying messages from Mashiangombi's kraal to the south and east, leading *impis* on raids on loyalists, and generally playing a most significant role in keeping western Mashonaland mobilized behind the rising.[1]

In October Bonda's influence was reinforced by that of Mkwati himself, who arrived at Mashiangombi's kraal in that month and at once set to work to prevent the example of the Ndebele surrender being followed in Mashonaland. We get some idea of the atmosphere of Mkwati's régime at Mashiangombi's from a statement made by the Rozwi Child of Mwari, Tshiwa, who was captured by Native Commissioner Weale in January 1897. Tshiwa had been used as an emissary between Mashiangombi's and Mkwati while the latter was at Taba zi ka Mambo.

I returned with the Mlimo to Mashiangombi's when the soldiers drove us away from Ntabazika Mambo . . . Mashiangombi sent over and his people carried the Mlimo's loot and placed it in his kraal and we all went and lived there. All the loot which was taken was supposed to be given to the Mlimo and the Mlimo would divide some of it out among his followers. I was given three rifles and a revolver, two wives and a lot of blankets and coats. As I had a wife whom I had not seen since the rebellion, I wished to find her, so I told Mkwati I would go back. He then accused me of wishing to go back to make peace with the whites, and would have killed me had his wife Tenkela not interfered. I was at last allowed to go but had to leave all presents I received with the exception of one rifle and a revolver. . . . There were no whites taken prisoner—all were killed. Mkwati was told that Mlimo will kill all natives who make peace and that we were going to fight again.

There is no doubt that at the end of 1896, when the Company were making serious attempts to negotiate with the Shona paramounts and so end the rising in Mashonaland as they had ended

[1] See especially, N 1/1/3.

that in Matabeleland, Mkwati's intransigent influence was a major factor in determining the rebel leaders to prepare to take the field again in the next dry season.[1]

This, then, was in brief, the role of the Mwari cult in western Mashonaland; to help to link the rising there to the Ndebele rising, to help co-ordinate the rising within the area itself, and to help to keep it alive there when the Ndebele had come to terms. We must now examine the role of the spirit mediums of western and central Mashonaland.

We have for convenience sake referred above to them as the Chaminuka–Nehanda hierarchy to mark their division from the mediums of the north-east and east. We must now ask how far in fact they did form a regular and effective hierarchy and how far an effective principle of centralization. The answer is that the system of the spirit mediums was even more complex than that of the Mwari cult and the relations of the mediums to each other within the system even less susceptible to definition. No one senior medium enjoyed a determining influence over the whole area of the Shona rising, nor did the mediums as a whole unanimously agree to support it. Thus, for instance, chief Kunzwi-Nyandoro's own medium, Ganyere, was against participation in the rising, but her advice was rejected in favour of that of the medium of the Nehanda spirit. Nevertheless when these qualifications are made, it remains true that the influence of the senior mediums was much more extensive than that of any secular authority. Once again we have later evidence which we can use to demonstrate the range of influence of an accepted Chaminuka or Nehanda medium. In 1903 a new Chaminuka medium emerged in the Hartley area and the following chiefs either sent gifts or went in person to pay their respects—paramounts Mashiangombi, Mashaba and Tumbare of Hartley district; paramounts Mashanganyika, Chinamora, Nyandoro, Seki, Makumbi, Chiota, Mangwende and Zwimba of central Mashonaland. They heard, or so it was alleged, the medium pronounce: 'I am Chaminuka. I know everything. I am all powerful. I caused the downfall of the BaRozwi and the Matabele and I will cause the white man to leave the country.' In 1906 a Nehanda medium arose, claiming to have

[1] Tshiwa's statement, 10 January 1897, LO 5/4/1.

come 'to take care of all the Mashonas again'. She was visited by
Wata, Chiweshe, Chinamora, Seki, Chikwakwa, Masembura and
Gutu. These lists, coming from a period when it was almost
dangerous to visit or send gifts to a senior medium, do not bear
out, certainly, a claim to represent 'all the Mashonas' but they
do show an impressive range of influence.[1]

In fact Mr Ogot's recent summary of the 19th century situation
in Central Nyanza might be applied to central Mashonaland.
'No political superstructure, such as a federation or a confederation, existed. But many of the famous prophets, who acted as
counsellors to the chiefs, and whose main function was to look
after the spiritual well-being of the tribe, and to prescribe moral
standards against which the policies of individual chiefs had to be
judged, were known and consulted all over Luoland.' The chiefs
whom we have seen sending gifts to the mediums of Chaminuka
and Nehanda had been in the early 1890's on terms of rivalry, or
even open enmity with each other. That they combined in the
rebellion was partly due to the principle of unity embodied in the
senior mediums and in them alone.[2]

Let us look at the part played by one of these senior mediums—
the medium of Nehanda. Before the rising it was believed in
official circles that her influence was no longer significant. 'Great
belief was also formerly placed in the Mandoras or Lion Gods',
wrote the Native Commissioner, Salisbury, in January 1896, 'and
especially in one called Nianda ... but as Mr Selous puts it, "since
the arrival of the white man the Mashonas have lost belief in their
Mandoras and the Mandoras have lost belief in themselves".' Two
years later the same official was writing in very different vein.
'Nianda has been constantly spoken of in my hearing ever since
I came to Mashonaland in 1890 by the Mashonas. At the present
moment Nianda is the most powerful wizard in Mashonaland and
has the power of ordering all the people who rose lately and her
orders would in every case be obeyed.' Behind this change of
opinion lay two years of activity on the part of the Nehanda

[1] Correspondence on the Chaminuka medium, 1903, A 11/2/12/11; on the
Nehanda medium, 1906 and 1915, N 3/31/4 and N 3/14/5.
[2] B. A. Ogot, 'British Administration in the Central Nyanza District',
Journal of African History, Vol. IV, No. 2.

medium in mobilizing and sustaining the rising in central
Mashonaland.[1]

She was directly responsible for the death of Pollard, the Native
Commissioner of the Mazoe area, at the outbreak of the rising.
'They took him to Nianda', one of Pollard's messengers later
testified; 'she said "Bring him here". Then she came and knelt
down and spoke with Pollard. . . . I heard Nianda say to Wata,
"Kill Pollard . . .", so they took him off. Wata said "Nianda sent
me". Then he took his axe and chopped him behind the head.'
Her influence was dominant on the rising in the Mazoe area
generally. 'Nehanda is responsible for rain and sometimes fighting', we are told by an old man living in the Chiweshe reserve;
'she was behind the rebellion right from the start. Her great
injunction was that the African people should touch nothing that
belonged to the white man. The defeat of the Africans was the
result of the violation of this great order. During the rebellion the
power of the spirits rendered the white bullets useless and in-
effective. Not many Africans were killed in the actual fighting.'
Encouraged by such spiritual protection the people of Mazoe and
Chiweshe rose against the whites, and obeying the orders of the
mediums they carried the goods captured to Nehanda's kraal, just
as in Matabeleland such goods were carried to Mkwati's cave at
Taba zi ka Mambo. 'She received a very large share of the loot
obtained by the natives', reported the Chief Native Commissioner.
'Among other things obtained from Nianda's kraal have been
numerous rifles and over £140 in gold. I know that she still has
concealed some £700, but because of the spirit she possesses the
natives are afraid of giving any information there-on.'[2]

In this way the Nehanda medium and many others helped to
bring central Mashonaland into the rising in June 1896, just as
Bonda and Tshiwa and the rest were raising western Mashonaland. How was this co-ordination established? One answer to this
is that the mediums of central Mashonaland were in contact with
those of the Hartley and Charter districts, and that these latter

[1] January report, Salisbury, 1896, N 1/1/9; N.C. Salisbury to C.N.C.,
3 March 1898, N 1/1/9.
[2] Gutsa's Evidence, 12 January 1898, HC/M, No. 252; Interview with Bob
Nyatsunga, 20 January 1963; C.N.C.'s report, 4 March 1898, LO 5/4/8.

mediums were working in an area where the Mwari cult also existed in organized form. Thus we have seen how the Children of Mwari carried the message to the chiefs in Hartley and Charter, how Mashiangombi was in touch with Mkwati and how his kraal later became the main Mwari centre in Mashonaland. But at the same time, and with no sense of incongruity, the chiefs consulted the mediums of the area; Mashiangombi had his own special medium, his half-brother Dekwende, who appears in the sources as helping to raise the country in June 1896, and so on. After all, the great Chaminuka mediums of the 19th century had lived in the Hartley area, and although in 1896 there was no generally recognized medium of Chaminuka, other important mediums of the hierarchy were active. One such was the female medium of the Vachikare spirit, whom Dr Gelfand describes as 'important' and as 'in touch with Chaminuka'; she participated in the 1896 rebellion, fled from Hartley early in 1897, and was arrested in Lomagundi in December of that year. The co-operation of Bonda and Dekwende, who are reported on one occasion as jointly leading a raiding party from Mashiangombi's kraal, demonstrated in general that there were no obstacles to the co-operation of the Mwari cult and the central Mashona mediums.[1]

But more specific steps were taken to ensure co-ordination. One of the spirit mediums operative around Salisbury was the medium of the Kagubi spirit. This man had lived originally in the Hartley area and was a member of the chiefly family of Chiveru; he was well known to paramount chief Mashiangombi. In April 1896 when Mashiangombi received messages from Mkwati, offering assistance to a rising in Mashonaland if one could be organized, he sent in turn for the Kagubi medium. When Mashiangombi's messengers accompanied Tshiwa and Bonda back to Taba zi ka Mambo, some of 'Kagubi's' people went with them. According to a report written in 1897 by the Native Commissioner, Mazoe, 'Umquarti told them that he himself was a God and could kill all the whites and was doing so at that time in Matabeleland and that Kargubi would be given the same power as he, Umquarti, had and was to start at once killing the whites in Mashonaland.

[1] For Dekwende, see *Rhodesia*, 4 June 1898, N 1/1/3. For Vachikare see *Rhodesia Herald*, 12 January 1898. For the Chaminuka mediums see N 3/33/8.

Immediately on receipt of these messages Mashiangombi started killing the whites and Kargubi then sent orders to all the paramounts and people of any influence to start killing the whites and that he would help them as he was a God.' However we may interpret this report, there is no doubt that the Kagubi medium based himself at Mashiangombi's kraal from April 1896 until the end of the year and that from there he sent out messengers to central Mashonaland who played the same role in mobilizing the rising there that Tshiwa and Bonda were playing in the west.[1]

We can follow this process in some detail from the records of scores of preliminary examinations into charges of murder of whites held in Mashonaland in 1897 and 1898. It appears that at the end of May or the beginning of June 1896 the Kagubi medium summoned representatives of all the central Shona paramounts to his new headquarters. 'I remember the recent rebellion', testified a witness in 1898. 'I was then living near Mashiangombi's kraal. I remember the people assembling at Mashiangombi's kraal to get medicine for the locusts.' It was a distinguished assembly—or rather series of assemblies. The central Mashona chiefs sent trusted headmen or close relatives, in many cases their sons. Chief Chiquaqua, for instance, sent Zhanta, his best warrior and commander of his *impis* before 1890 and now again in 1896; chief Zwimba sent his son; chief M'Sonthi sent his younger brother. These we know to have been there; others, in view of their later close collaboration with the Kagubi medium, we may guess to have been there: men like Panashe, bandit son of chief Kunzwi-Nyandoro, or like Mchemwa, son of chief Mangwende.[2]

At these meetings news of the progress of the Ndebele rising and of the intended western Shona revolt was given, and the Kagubi medium urged the central Shona peoples to join the movement against the whites. His leading part emerges clearly, perhaps indeed with too great emphasis, from all reports. 'On the occasion of any great gathering', runs one hostile report, 'Kagubi and Dekwende arrayed themselves in striking feather caps and fastened horns upon their heads. . . . These two worthies would then rush into the centre of the people, who were sitting in a

---

[1] N.C. Mazoe to C.N.C. Mashonaland, 20 October 1897, N 1/1/6.
[2] Evidence of Marowa, 7 December 1898, HC/M, No. 391.

circle. . . . Then, feigning to fall into a trance, Kagubi pretended
to be possessed by the Mulenga . . . and in that condition gave
orders for the destruction of anybody obnoxious to him and his
fellow conspirator.' 'Kagubi sent two messengers to Mashon-
ganyika's', testified the old warrior, Zhanta, in October 1897.
'They went to Gonta's and told the people they were to come to
Kagubi's at once. I went with them. I thought he would give us
something to kill the locusts. When I got there he ordered me to
kill the white men. He said he had orders from the gods.' 'What
can I say?' asked Zawara, son of chief Garamombe in November
1897. 'All this occurred through Kagubi. He said all whites must
die this year. . . . He gathered us to his kraal and said I am the
God.'[1]

From these gatherings word was swiftly carried back to central
Mashonaland. 'Zhanta was Kagubi's post-man', testified a witness
in 1897. 'He brought a message that the Mashonas must kill all
whites. I heard him deliver the message to Chiquaqua.' 'The
murders were committed by order of Kagubi', testified a Lomagundi witness. 'Zwimba's son brought us the message Kagubi
sent to Zwimba.' According to the evidence given at the trials
Kagubi's 'orders' were accepted as law: 'I am not guilty. It is the
law which was given by the God', said one accused. 'They said
it was Kagubi's order to hit the white man, so I did', said another.
'I lived all right with Mr Campbell in my kraal but Kagubi said
all white men must be killed', said a third. A woman servant
testified that she had seen four men enter her master's house and
heard them cry out, 'The will of God'. 'That is why I looked
inside. I expected to find the white man dead; that is Kagubi's
law.[2]'

No doubt this testimony overstates both the Kagubi medium's
authority as against other mediums and the chiefs themselves, and
also his powers to command. We should rather imagine a general

[1] *Rhodesia*, 4 June 1898; evidence of Zhanta, 7 October 1897; evidence of
Zawara, 23 November 1897; HC/M, Nos. 213 and 215.
[2] Evidence of Wampi, 7 December 1897, HC/M, No. 213; evidence of
Tinani, 4 January 1898, HC/M, No. 258; evidence of Mabidza and Gamanya,
30 December 1897, HC/M, No. 258; evidence of Masenda, 8 February 1898,
HC/M, No. 261; evidence of chief Mashanganyika, 15 January 1898, HC/M,
No. 255; evidence of Chinende, January 1898, HC/M, No. 243.

response to his initiative in which the Nehanda medium played a particularly important part. But there can be no doubt of the importance of his role in co-ordinating the central Shona rising with events in the west, so that at much the same time that Bonda was bringing out the chiefs in Charter whites were attacked around Salisbury and in the Mazoe Valley.

Once the rising had broken out the Kagubi medium continued to play a leading role in it, apparently particularly taking the initiative in the punishment of Africans who had served the whites. His influence was especially important at the end of 1896 when, as we have seen, the Company administration sought to come to terms with the Shona chiefs. The Kagubi medium then joined with Mkwati to frustrate these overtures. 'When Kunzwi and Chiquaqua were visited by Major Jenner', wrote Native Commissioner Armstrong in February 1897, 'they both sent to Gargoobi and were told not to give up their guns. . . . The Mashonas still implicitly obey Gargoobi.' The Shona, reported Father Richartz in January 1897

still believe that the white men will be done away with, but they much hope in an extraordinary intervention of that extraordinary power of their chief Mondoros, as they did in the beginning of the rising. . . . Our boys always asked me whether the Mulenka or Witch Doctor at Mashiangombi's had given in, and assured me that the war would be over and the people would come into work at once, as soon as he allows them to approach the white people and gives orders to stop hostilities.[1]

So far from giving in the Kagubi medium was, in fact, joining with Mkwati in a last desperate attempt to keep the rising going in some effective and co-ordinated way. The Ndebele military system had come to terms with the whites; some of the Shona paramounts were tempted by peace offers. In these circumstances the two religious leaders decided to try to revive the old Rozwi paramountcy and so give some back-bone to the rising in Mashonaland.

The story of this remarkable effort can only be briefly told here. We have already seen Mkwati's alliance with Rozwi interests in

[1] N.C. Armstrong to C.N.C., 20 February 1897; Richartz, Intelligence report, 10 January 1897, LO 5/4/1 and 2.

Matabeleland; his residence at Taba zi ka Mambo; his control of
the Rozwi *manyusa* Tshiwa and Bonda. We have seen the prestige
of the Rozwi extending far into Mashonaland. We must now add
three other pieces of information to complete the picture. The
first is that the Rozwi enjoyed a continuing military prestige as
well as a spiritual one. In October 1897, for instance, a Karanga
witness, explaining why he had paid tribute to a Mwari messenger,
testified that he had done so 'because he was a MuRozi, belonging
to the BaRosi country. The BaRosi are the big people of the
country. We are afraid of the BaRosi because they sometimes
attack with us an *impi* like the Matabele and kill us.' Clearly the
Rozwi paramountcy did not seem an impossibly remote authority
in the 1890's.[1]

The second point is that not only were the days of the Mambos
remembered but there were also various scattered Rozwi chiefs,
living among the Shona tribes, who could claim direct descent
from the last Mambo. One of these, Mudzinganyama Jiri Mteveri,
living in 1896 in the Ndanga district, was widely acknowledged
to have an especially good claim. In 1901, some years after the
events to be described below, the Native Commissioner, Belingwe,
met him travelling through his district. 'He informed me, *inter
alia*, that he was the eldest male descendant of the Mambos and
therefore should be king of Rhodesia. He appears to be an
intelligent native and is feared and respected by the local natives'.[2]

Finally we must realize that there were small Rozwi groups
living throughout central Mashonaland and exercising an influence out of proportion to their numbers. In or near the Makoni
district, for example, lived the holder of the Rozwi title Chiduku,
who himself claimed descent from the royal house and whose
presence was necessary at the installation of the Mangwende paramount; the holder of the Rozwi title, Tandi, whose presence was
necessary at the installation of the Makoni paramount; and the
holder of the Rozwi title, Mavudzi, a man of considerable spiritual
power, who appears in Rozwi tradition as a 'priest' at the court of

[1] Evidence of Umqueba, October 1897, HC/M, No. 306.
[2] Report for Belingwe, April 1901, LO 5/7/6. Mr Nengubo, who carried
out research on my behalf in February 1963 in the Bikita Reserve tells me that
it is claimed there that Mudzinganyama was the great-grandson of Mambo
Gumbo-Remvura and the great nephew of Mambo Dlembeu.

Mambo and 'even now is the great rain-maker of the VaRozwi and indeed of all the tribes in this district'.[1]

There seems little doubt that these men played an important part in the rising in the Makoni area. There is evidence that both Tshiwa and Bonda paid visits to them; a recent Rozwi informant holds that Mavudzi is the recognized intermediary between the Mwari cult and the Nehanda medium; we possibly have in these men and their continuing influence one of the co-ordinating links between the rebellion in Makoni and the risings of Western and central Mashonaland. Certainly they were in rebellion. 'I have been astounded by the number of WaRosi rebels', wrote Native Commissioner Armstrong, 'and believe the WaRosi were the main support of the rising in every district and our bitterest enemies.'[2]

Given all these circumstances the scheme devised by Mkwati and Kagubi does not seem quite so far-fetched. The plan was to have Mudzinganyama Jiri Mteveri recognized by the other Rozwi chiefs as the Mambo and then to gather together under his leadership Rozwi groups from all over western and central Mashonaland to take the field in the dry season 1897 in a campaign in the country north of Salisbury. Bonda was the go-between used to broach this project to the Rozwi chiefs, and late in 1896 and early in 1897 he made many journeys from Mashiangombi's to the Sabi, to Wedza and to Makoni, where he consulted with Chiduku, Tandi, Mavudzi and Mbava. Perhaps surprisingly the Rozwi were more ready to agree to recognize Mudzinganyama as Mambo than the Ndebele had been to recognize any claimant as King. In December 1896 an impressive delegation waited upon Mudzinganyama to invite him to assume the Mamboship. The delegation consisted of Bonda and 'several of the Mlimo's messengers'; of the Rozwi chiefs, Chiduku, Mbava and Mavudsi; and of the Njanja chief Gambiza's son, with others of his people. 'I learnt', wrote the Native Commissioner, Ndanga, reporting this in March 1897, 'that Mtebera', his corruption of Mteveri, 'was the

---

[1] See Marodzi, 'The BaRozwi', *NADA*, 1924; E. M. S. Lloyd, 'Mbava', *NADA*, 1925; S. Muglanga, 'Mbava and others', *NADA*, 1926; Abraham, 'The principality of Maungwe', *NADA*, 1951.

[2] N.C. Armstrong, 26 May 1897, N 1/1/7; interview with Chihiya, a Mwari cult officer, Bikita, February 1963.

head of all the VaRozwi and that he had taken the title of Mambo.
. . . Why after all these years should the name Mambo be revived
now?'[1]

The scheme appeared to be working. Mudzinganyama had been
recognized as Mambo and was waiting in a temporary kraal on
the Sabi River for his followers to assemble. The Rozwi everywhere were being told that 'all WaRosi killed by white men were
to come to life again'. In February Mkwati followed the Kagubi
medium away from Mashiangombi's kraal to a new headquarters
north-east of Salisbury, where together with the Nehanda medium
they awaited the arrival of the Rozwi forces for the dry season
campaign. But the authorities were aware of what was being
planned. The reports of the Native Commissioner, Ndanga,
alerted them to the danger. In March 1897 Native Commissioners
were instructed to keep an eye on the Rozwi in their areas and to
report particularly on Bonda's movements. 'The Mlimo has sent
one Bonda to incite the AbaRosi to rise', reported the Native
Commissioner, Charter, adding that he had sent police to arrest
Bonda. 'The Mlimo has sent Bonda to incite the AboRosi to
rebellion', reported the Native Commissioner, Victoria, adding
that he 'had placed spies among the AboRosi to watch for the
advent of the messengers.' These precautions were not successful
in apprehending Bonda but they did result, almost accidentally,
in the arrest of Mudzinganyama and his detention for the rest of
1897 at the office of the Native Commissioner, Charter.[2]

With the arrest of Mudzinganyama the scheme for the revival
of the Mamboship collapsed even though many Rozwi did gather
as planned and took a leading part in the 1897 fighting. Despite
the failure of their plan the traditional religious authorities remained at the centre of the rising while it lasted. As a result of the
move away from the regions of organized Mwari cult activity
and into the home country of the Kagubi and Nehanda mediums,
the influence of Mkwati and Tenkela declined, but that of the
Nehanda, and especially of the Kagubi medium was as great as

---

[1] N.C. Ndanga to C.N.C., 2 and 24 March 1897, N 1/1/8; N.C. Armstrong
to C.N.C., 20 February 1897, LO 5/4/2.
[2] N.C. Charter to C.N.C., 9 March 1897, N 1/1/2; summary of work done
in week ending 19 March 1897, LO 5/4/2.

ever. Gradually the authorities came to realize, and then no doubt to over-estimate their importance. In June 1897, for instance, the Native Commissioner, Salisbury, gave impressive testimony to the central role of the Kagubi medium.

I read in one of the local papers a short time ago that there was no head to the Mashona rebellion [he wrote] and that each kraal was its own empire, hence the difficulty of subduing it. But there can be no greater mistake. The Mashona war has as clearly a defined a head as the last Zulu war; catch Kagubi and it will mean the same thing as it meant when Cetewayo was caught with regard to the Zulu war. . . . Mashiangombi's was the centre of the rebellion last year because Kagubi was there. The centre of the rebellion is now the hills around the Umvumi River, 35 miles N.E. of Salisbury. If we capture Kagubi the war is over. If not, unless there is a famine among the natives, or we get a few thousand troops up, it may drag on for several years.[1]

In the same way the missionaries came to revise their original estimates of Shona religious feeling. 'Amongst the Mashonas', Father Hartmann of Chishawasha had reported in 1894, 'there are only very faint traces of a religion . . . they have hardly any idea of a supreme being . . . The Mashonas are united as a Commonwealth by nothing except the unity of their language. They are broken into many tribes and clans without a uniting centre.' By 1897 the Chishawasha fathers knew better. Their own station attacked by their own flock at the instigation of the Kagubi medium, they had come to see the rebellion as a war between religions. 'Their conduct is controlled by religion', wrote Lord Grey of the Shona after a visit to Chishawasha, 'which is more than can be said for many of us whites. We are at present engaged in the most difficult of operations, the bursting up of their faith by chevying their witch-doctor from point to point and proving him to be a liar.'[2]

Lord Grey's endeavours to 'burst up' the faith of the Shona make a fascinating story, and incidentally demonstrate that in addition to the use made of the 'witch-doctors' to excuse the Company in public propaganda, the men on the spot so firmly believed in their central importance that they based their strategy

[1] N.C. Salisbury to C.N.C., 15 June 1897, N 1/1/9.
[2] Appendix by Father Hartmann, B.S.A. Co. *Report on the Administration of Rhodesia*, 1892-4; Grey to Lady Grey, 23 January 1897, GR 1/1/1.

upon it. The story—of how the Kagubi medium escaped patrol after patrol, how he tried to carry the rising to Portuguese East Africa, how he was at last arrested, and in the final gruesome combat of the two religions converted to Catholicism almost literally on the scaffold—cannot be told here. In the end the mediums and their Mwari cult allies were bound to be captured; the rising was bound to fail. There was no mercy for these religious leaders. Mkwati died some time in 1897, killed it was thought by the disillusioned Shona themselves; the Kagubi and Nehanda mediums were put on trial for murder and both hanged in May 1898. Both were 'buried in a secret place, so that no natives could take away their bodies and claim that their spirits had descended to any other prophetess or witch-doctor'.[1]

This last precaution shows how far the Rhodesian authorities still were from understanding Shona religious belief. The arrest and trial and secret burial of the two mediums discredited neither them nor the belief which they represented. If the Ndebele rising had ended with friction between the military and the religious leaders it was not so in Mashonaland. The spirit mediums remained as a powerful and respected influence there, however chivied by the authorities. In the north-east, in the old Mwene Mutapa country, they were able in the so-called Mapondera rising to repeat something of the role of the Kagubi and Nehanda mediums; elsewhere they remained a focus of less outright opposition to colonial government. But in a way the failure of the risings did begin to 'burst up' the traditional systems; the missions all found themselves presented with an unexpected opportunity to break through the previous barrier of passive resistance on the part of the Shona. This, too, is another story, but we should note in ending this account of the role of the traditional religious authorities in the 1896 and 1897 risings, that their failure marked the end of a successful resistance to Christian penetration by the Shona peoples over a period of centuries, and the beginning of a new age which was, in the end, to produce the very different religious and political leadership of the separatist church founder and the African parson.

[1] Notes by A. H. Holland, September 1949, HO 7/4/2; Richartz, 'The end of Kagubi', *Zambesi Mission Record*, November 1898.

6

RELIGIOUS ASPECTS OF POLITICAL SUCCESSION AMONG THE VALLEY KOREKORE (N. SHONA)

by

G. KINGSLEY GARBETT

A CONSIDERABLE amount of attention has been given to the religious significance of spirit mediums (*svikiro*; pl., *ma-*) among the Shona-speaking peoples but their political role has tended to be overlooked. In this chapter I examine the political role of the spirit mediums in succession disputes among the Valley Korekore, a northern Shona people. Formerly mediums appear to have had the sole prerogative to install a chief's successor. The rules of succession are such that after a chief's death a number of candidates, all with more or less equal claims, compete with one another for the succession. Succession disputes appear to be a characteristic feature of the Korekore political system. The mediums perform an important function in eventually conferring spiritual legitimacy upon one of the candidates and installing him as the one, true, chief. In addition the rules of succession operate so that chiefs are generally old when they succeed and do not rule for very long. Spirit mediums, who are often young men when they are first 'possessed' by a spirit, may be called upon to install several chiefs during their lifetime. Their political role is thus of considerable importance. However, in recent years, the political activities of the mediums have been affected by the fact that the District Commissioner now makes the final appointment of a chief's successor. In this chapter whilst I concentrate upon the activities of the mediums I also consider the District Commissioner as part of a total system which consists of both the traditional political, and the modern administrative, systems. I attempt to assess, in relation to succession disputes, in what respects the role of the District Commissioner is similar to, or different from, that of the mediums.

I begin by outlining the principal ecological and sociological features of the area in which the material was collected.[1] I then describe briefly the various components of the total politico-religious system in which the spirit mediums are involved and how they are interconnected, before turning to a fuller examination of the mediums and their role in succession disputes.

The Korekore identify themselves by their language and their custom, though all the people who speak Korekore, or follow Korekore custom, do not form a nation or a tribal unit. There are probably some 300,000 Korekore-speakers who occupy an area stretching south from the Zambesi between longitude 28° and longitude 33° East. The majority live in Southern Rhodesia, though some live in Mozambique. In this chapter I deal mainly with the Valley Korekore who differ, in a number of ways, from the Korekore who live on the plateau along the edge of the Zambesi escarpment.

The name 'Korekore' appears to have been given by Tonga and Tavara to a band of Karanga who invaded the valley from the south in the distant past, probably in the 15th century.[2] Abraham claims to have identified Mutota, the 'father' of the Korekore and the leader of the Karanga invasion, as a 'Monomotapa'.[3] Many Korekore chiefs in the Urungwe, Sipolilo and Darwin Administrative Districts of Southern Rhodesia claim that they are patrilineal descendants of Mutota, or of one of his 'brothers'. Though they acknowledge their common origin, the chiefs do not all belong to one 'clan', nor do they all share a common praise name (*mutupo* and *chidao*). The lineal descendants of the Karanga invaders

---

[1] The fieldwork on which this chapter is based was made possible by the award of a Fellowship by the International African Institute, to whose trustees, and to Professor C. Daryll Forde, its Director, I make grateful acknowledgements. I must also acknowledge the help I received from Mr B. J. Foggin of the Office of the Secretary of State for Native Affairs, Southern Rhodesia, who, after I left the field, compiled from widely scattered sources a skeleton history of the chieftainships which I discuss here. I thank Dr A. L. Epstein, Professor M. Gluckman and Dr J. van Velsen for their valuable comments on the arguments which I advance here.

[2] D. P. Abraham, 'The Monomotapa Dynasty', *NADA*, 1959, p. 62.

[3] *Ibid.*, p. 71.

claim that they are the only 'true' Korekore. In this chapter the term Korekore is used more widely to refer to people who speak Korekore and follow Korekore custom.

Nothing now remains of the kingdom established by the 'Monomotapa' save for a few stone ruins and the myths and legends related by the leaders and the spirit mediums, though it does appear that the extensive organization associated with the cult of the spirit mediums is in some way related to the ancient kingdom.

The material presented in this chapter was collected mainly in and around Muzarabanhi[1] Reserve which forms part of the Administrative District of Mt Darwin. The reserve lies largely in the Zambesi valley and the major portion of it is isolated from the plateau to the south by a range of mountains. Due to its isolation, poor climate, and relative lack of natural resources, the region is sparsely populated and economically undeveloped. In some areas the density of population is as low as 3 per square mile whilst in other areas it rises to 18 per square mile. People still practise a form of shifting cultivation which entails the periodic movement of hamlets to new sites.

Politically the Korekore are organized into small chiefdoms, though these are only loosely structured and chieftainship is not a highly developed institution. The chief has an informal council drawn from important commoner elders and this meets irregularly. There is little distinction in dress or behaviour between commoners and royals (the agnates of the chief). For administrative purposes, a number of chiefdoms have been grouped together under a senior chief, but this was not a feature of Korekore political organization in the recent past. In Muzarabanhi Reserve, for example, Chiefs Chiweshe and Muzarabanhi have been placed under Chief Kasekete, the Senior Chief. All three chiefs receive a small salary, though Kasekete's is the largest (£88 p.a.).

In the past chiefdoms appear to have fragmented as groups moved away and established new ones. Because of the establishment of the reserves and the enforcement of the Land Apportionment Act this process can no longer occur. This is one of the

[1] The anglicized form, 'Mzarabani', is used by the administration. Since there is a Chief *Muzarabanhi*, I have used the Korekore form for both the name of the Reserve and the chieftainship within it.

factors which appears to have exacerbated succession disputes in recent years since royals now have only a limited number of positions of authority for which they can compete. They cannot found new chiefdoms.

Within a chiefdom people live in small hamlets, usually containing a patrilineally extended family (of a man plus his wife or wives, his unmarried children, and his sons and their wives), which are scattered alongside the major rivers where perennial water and the better alluvial soils are found. Hamlets are short-lived and periodically shed off some of their members who may then move away and found new hamlets. Individual mobility is high and this is partly associated with the initial period of uxori-local marriage[1] which tends to disperse the male members of a family over a large area. Moreover, because Korekore lack strong attachment to particular plots of land, and there are few cattle[2] or other goods around which economic interests can develop, descent groups are shallow and dispersed. Only royal descent groups have some internal cohesion and these provide, as it were, the framework of the chiefdom to which commoner headmen are attached by a complex network of kinship ties. Royals and commoners live intermingled throughout a chiefdom and co-operate socially, ritually and economically, though the chief has no ritual functions.

The Valley Korekore have a complex political system on to which a modern administrative superstructure has been imposed. This imposition has modified the traditional political system, and has added a new dimension to it. Alongside the modern administrative system large parts of the traditional political system continue to function intact.

The traditional system has two major components: one is the political organization of the chiefdoms, the other the politico-religious system associated with the cult of the spirit mediums. Though each component is associated with its own sphere of activity, they intersect at certain points. The component in which the spirit mediums are involved has two aspects, a lineal (or genealogical) and a territorial. Whilst I give in outline the general

[1] In which a man lives after marriage at his wife's hamlet.
[2] Until recently this area was infested by tsetse fly.

features of the territorial aspect and its connection with the lineal one, I shall be concerned here largely with the latter.

The territorial aspect

The general features of the system are as follows. All land, whether now occupied or not, is divided into areas of varying size, each of which is associated with, and often named after, one of the original Karanga invaders, or a descendant of one of the invaders, or occasionally an autochthon. The spirits of these men are believed to protect the fertility of the earth and control rainfall. I term them spirit guardians and the area of land with which each is associated I call a spirit province. Korekore term the spirit guardians *varidzi vepasi* ('the owners of the earth'), and the spirit provinces *nyika* ('regions' or 'provinces'). The spirit provinces have definite boundaries which are usually hills, streams, rivers and other natural features. Some are several hundred square miles in extent, others only a few hundred acres. The spirit guardians are said to have been related to one another, and this is explained by reference to a long genealogy. Some of the spirit guardians are represented by living mediums who are identified with them, and called by their names. The mediums are ranked in a hierarchy according to the genealogical seniority of the spirit guardians whom they represent. At the apex of the system is a medium representing the 'founding ancestor', often also believed to be the first occupier, or first user of the land, and I call this medium the senior spirit medium. He is considered to have authority over the other spirit mediums and should confirm their appointment. The total area over which the senior spirit medium has influence, through his authority over lesser mediums, I term a spirit realm. Spirit realms are very large and may embrace an area of several thousand square miles, and may include chiefdoms.

Consider for a moment Fig. 4 which represents a hypothetical spirit realm divided into spirit provinces of various sizes. The figure should be read in conjunction with Fig. 3. The founding ancestor 'a' has two sons, 'b' and 'c' who in turn have further descendants, 'd', 'e', 'f', etc. Each of 'a's' descendants to the fourth descending generation has a spirit province named after him and is represented in Fig. 4, in which he is considered to be the guardian. Assuming that each spirit guardian is represented by a medium then the mediums will be ranked according to the positions that the spirit guardians whom they represent occupy in Fig. 3; viz.: the medium of 'h' will be inferior to the medium of 'd', since 'd' was father of 'h'. Similarly the medium of 'd' will be considered inferior to the medium of 'b'. All mediums are inferior to the medium of 'a', the senior spirit medium representing

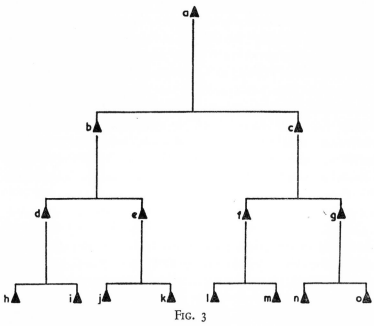

FIG. 3

Hypothetical genealogy to show relationship among spirit guardians

the founding ancestor. In the case of mediums representing brothers such as 'b' and 'c' the medium representing the elder is considered senior. A spirit realm thus consists of a series of spirit provinces articulated into a total system by the genealogical connections believed to have existed between the spirit guardians.

Spirit realms are also linked into a wider system, for the founding ancestors of the various realms are believed to have been related to one another agnatically, cognatically, or affinally, and the senior spirit mediums regulate their behaviour towards one another according to how the spirit guardians whom they represent are related. In the past these links appear to have extended to embrace large sections of the Shona-speaking peoples and it was the senior spirit mediums who played a large part in uniting groups of Shona during the rebellion of 1896[1] by threatening that the rains would fail and the cattle die if the Europeans were not driven from the land.

Within each spirit province there are a number of land shrines, usually baobab trees, at which people gather to make ritual offerings to the spirit guardian to ensure that he brings rain and a good

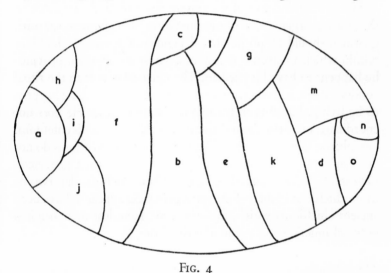

FIG. 4

Hypothetical spirit realms divided into spirit provinces

harvest. I term clusters of hamlets which habitually associate together to perform this ritual a land shrine neighbourhood. The land shrine neighbourhood is the basic unit of the territorial aspect of the organization in which the spirit mediums are involved. If the rains fail within a particular land shrine neighbourhood, or there is pestilence and disease, then senior elders are sent to approach the spirit medium representing the spirit guardian of the province in which the land shrine is situated. The medium, becoming 'possessed', will then inform them in what ways they have

---

[1] C. Bullock, *The Mashona*, Juta, Cape Town, 1928, p. 125; B.S.A. Co., *Reports on the Administration of Rhodesia*, 1898, pp. 55, 69, 79.

offended the spirit guardian and what they must do to atone. If they are not satisfied with what the medium says, or his instructions fail to produce any improvement, representatives will then be sent to the senior spirit medium. In the case of the hypothetical example (Fig. 4) this would mean that if the land shrine was situated in the spirit province of 'h' then elders would approach the medium of 'h', and from him they might proceed to the senior medium representing 'a'. They would not approach the intervening mediums representing 'd' and 'b'.

The territorial aspect of the system functions independently of the political organization of the chiefdoms. Which particular spirit guardian should be propitiated depends not upon the chiefdom within which a person is living, but within which spirit province he happens to have his gardens. The chief takes part in the ritual conducted at the land shrine in the province in which he happens to be living, but only in his role as a hamlet head. He does not coordinate, or initiate land shrine rituals throughout his chiefdom. I emphasize that the territorial boundaries of the chiefdoms do not necessarily coincide with the boundaries of the spirit provinces. One spirit province may have boundaries which overlap two or more chiefdoms. Some of the spirit provinces appear to have been ancient chiefdoms which, in some way, have lost their original political function and acquired a ritual one.

The lineal aspect

In the lineal aspect of the system, in contrast to the territorial, the chiefs are linked directly to the cult of the spirit mediums. Many spirit guardians are also royal ancestors; in addition to their responsibility for maintaining the ritual well-being of the spirit province with which they are associated, they are also believed to be interested in the activities of their living descendants *wheresoever they may be*. In the hypothetical spirit realm (Fig. 4) I assumed that all the spirit provinces are associated with the guardians who can be represented on a genealogy. This is not always so. In the case of guardians believed to have been autochthons the exact genealogical connections will not be known. Usually they are classed as 'sisters' sons' (*vazukuru*) of the founding ancestor and, in the cases which I examined, were not credited with any living descendants. Nor do all royal ancestors have direct living descendants. In the lineal aspect of the system we are only concerned with those spirit guardians who are royal ancestors, who have living patrilineal descendants, and who are represented by mediums.

Spirit mediums representing such ancestors give advice to the latters' descendants on such matters as the inheritance of wives and family titles, but their most important function is to determine, from a number of rival candidates, which one shall succeed a dead chief and to confer spiritual legitimacy upon him. As I have noted, the spirit mediums are ranked into a hierarchy according to the genealogical position of the spirit guardians/ancestors whom they represent. In the lineal, in contrast to the territorial aspect of the system, the hierarchy of mediums is utilized. Whereas in the hypothetical spirit realm (Figs. 4 and 3) the people living within the spirit province of 'h' would consult the medium representing him, and then proceed to the senior spirit medium representing 'a', the patrilineal descendants of 'h' would consult his medium, and then if they did not receive satisfaction proceed directly to the medium of 'd', then perhaps to the medium of 'b', and finally to the medium of 'a'. Thus people proceed for lineal purposes from an inferior medium to one more senior, until the senior spirit medium is reached. His decision, in theory, is final. I stress that in the lineal aspect of the system when people are consulting a medium as the representative of an ancestor, they come to consult him from wherever they may be living. It does not matter in which chiefdom, spirit province, or spirit realm they live. It is possible, therefore, for people to be involved with two different mediums: one whom they consult as a spirit guardian about the ritual well-being of the spirit province in which they live, and the other whom they consult as representing an ancestor. It is also possible for a chiefdom to be part of one spirit realm whilst its chief and royals are lineal descendants of the founding ancestor of another spirit realm. The royals would thus be involved with two separate hierarchies of mediums; one which they utilized for territorial, the other for lineal matters. Political and ritual affiliations thus tend to cut across each other. However, it would take us beyond the scope of this paper to consider the full implications of this. Suffice it to say that there is some evidence which suggests that spirit mediums may have had some influence, because of these various cross-cutting affiliations, in regulating political activities between neighbouring chiefs. It may be that each politically independent Shona chiefdom was brought into a wider system of political relations by these means.

The spirit mediums

Korekore believe that before a spirit guardian died, he ate special medicines to ensure that his spirit (*mudzimu*, pl., mi-)[1] would return and speak through a medium (*svikiro*, pl., ma-). After his death Korekore believe that his spirit sought out a lion host (*mhondoro*[2]). Some say that the spirit appeared from the grave in the form of a tiny lion cub; others that it sought out a lion in the forest. After a period of dwelling in the lion host and wandering through the forest, the spirit guardian became restless and wanted to speak through a human host. He left his lion host and travelled to a distant land seeking a devout man who had led a blameless life. When the spirit guardian found such a man he caused him to be troubled by dreams and to act strangely, making him wander through the forest and eat raw meat like an animal. Eventually the spirit guardian is supposed to have guided the man to his spirit province. Here the man became established as the medium of the spirit guardian. Korekore believe that when a medium dies the spirit guardian returns to a lion host for a period before seeking out another medium. They stress that a man chosen as a medium ought not to be a patrilineal descendant of the spirit guardian, nor ought he to have been previously associated with the spirit province in which he becomes a medium.

A man who arrives in a spirit province and claims to be the medium of its guardian is not immediately accepted. He has to answer questions put to him by senior elders in the area about the genealogy which connects the spirit guardian to the founding ancestor and to relate the myths and legends associated with the activities of the spirit guardian when he was alive. In the past new

---

[1] The honorific plural *vadzimu* is used usually for the spirit of a personal ancestor such as one's father's father's spirit.

[2] The term *mhondoro* is also applied to a spirit guardian and to his human medium.

mediums were also tested by the senior spirit medium, though I was unable to establish if this is still the practice. Not all men claiming to be mediums are accepted and occasionally mediums are also discredited after they have been installed. Korekore believe that anyone who falsely claims to be a medium will be killed or inflicted with madness by the spirit guardian. Once accepted the medium's whole life becomes surrounded by elaborate ritual prohibitions with regard to his dress, the food and drink he consumes, and his personal hygiene.

When a medium has been installed he selects a number of acolytes (*nechombo*). Usually there are both male and female acolytes, the latter being old women past the menopause. The medium chooses one of the male acolytes to be his principal assistant. His duties are to meet visitors coming to consult the medium and to act as a spokesman for them, to arrange the séances, and to accept the gifts and the consultation fee on behalf of the medium. The other male acolytes serve as a congregation when the medium falls possessed whilst the female acolytes prepare beer used on ritual occasions and clean and tidy the spirit hut (*dendemaro*) in which possession occurs. When a medium dies the spirit hut is destroyed and a new one built by the male acolytes. The female acolytes keep it clean and in repair and make sure that no one enters it or tampers with the articles and relics it contains until a new medium appears.

Mediums are great showmen and, dressed in their black (or white)[1] cloths, with their long unkempt hair falling onto their necks, their carved ritual staffs (*mangato*) and elaborate necklaces, they are readily identifiable figures who immediately inspire in Korekore awe and respect. When a séance has been arranged the principal acolyte shepherds the visitors into the presence of the medium after 'possession' has occurred, and then puts the questions which they want to ask him. Séances are conducted with considerable dramatic feeling, the medium's pronouncements, delivered in a distorted voice, being punctuated by the rhythmical handclaps of the congregation and by occasional roars and screams from the medium himself. When a medium has heard the questions

[1] The particular cloth which a medium wears does not signify his status as it appears to do among the Zezuru. (Cf. Gelfand, *Shona Ritual*, 1959, p. 25.)

'he' may reply immediately, or 'he' may order beer to be brewed and say that 'he' (i.e. the spirit guardian/ancestor) will go away and consult with the 'other spirits' and deliver his answer at some future time. This procedure appears to be a means by which a medium can delay making a difficult decision, and I think it gives him time to sound out public feeling on the matter. In the succession disputes which I investigated I found that the mediums involved had been consulted a number of times before they had made their choice of candidate. In the case of a succession dispute the medium appears to wait until public opinion has crystallized in favour of one or two candidates before delivering his pronouncement.

When a medium dies Korekore told me that another medium does not appear for about five years. During this period, as I have explained, the female acolytes maintain the spirit hut in repair. However, they do not occupy hereditary offices and should a new medium not appear during their lifetime the spirit hut falls into decay; since most of those I met were quite old this sets a limit of, at the most, ten years. Nor does the office of principal acolyte appear to be hereditary. I recorded only one case where an acolyte's father had held the position before him. Korekore assured me that this was only because he was the most suitable candidate available and had learnt from his father how to perform the various duties connected with the medium. From my observations I conclude that the continuity of the system is not maintained by the acolytes.

Spirit mediums have esoteric knowledge, particularly of tribal history and genealogies which is not known in its entirety by any one elder. The extent of a medium's knowledge appears to vary with his position in the structure but it is always considerable. The more senior mediums know more about the upper levels of the genealogy which relates the various spirit guardians to one another whilst the junior mediums have a more detailed knowledge of the lower levels of this genealogy down to living descendants. I have stated that Korekore say that a medium ought to be a stranger who appears from a distant land and who has no previous connection with the area. How then do they acquire their esoteric knowledge? In an attempt to answer this question I investigated the back-

grounds of five mediums. In the case of two mediums I established that they had fallen 'possessed' whilst living in the hamlet
of a senior medium. This senior medium's paternal grandfather
had also been a senior medium before him. In addition, I established that all these three mediums were personally related by
various bonds of kinship. In one case (though I stress that this
appears to be exceptional) a medium claiming to represent a royal
ancestor was himself a royal. In the case of the other two mediums
I was able to establish that they had been in contact previously
with people agnatically related to the royals of the area in which
they were living though I was unable to determine the exact
circumstances of their appearance. These two mediums were also
living in hamlets in which, during my stay in the area, two new
mediums were supposed to be emerging. In the case of all the
mediums, save one, they were living in spirit provinces which
were some distance from their natal hamlets.

Though this evidence is not wholly adequate and I have to do
more research on this point, it seems highly likely that potential
mediums acquire their special knowledge by being associated with
other mediums. However, it appears that a man does not succeed
to the medium from whom he acquired his knowledge but moves
to some more distant spirit province where his connection with
the medium is not generally known. Whether a new medium is
actually taught in a formal way, or whether he picks up his knowledge by constant attendance at séances in an informal manner, I
have not yet established.

Spirit mediums do not appear to occur haphazard throughout
the system. In the case of the lineal aspect of the system all royal
ancestors who founded chieftainships, with very few exceptions,
are represented by mediums. The reason for the appearance of the
mediums at these points appears to be connected with their role in
the selection of chiefs. Considering the territorial aspect, Korekore
say that in the past each spirit province had its medium. This is
not so today. Only about a third of the spirit provinces have
mediums. In the territorial aspect the rather haphazard way in
which some spirit provinces have mediums whilst others do not
may be due simply to changes in the processes by which the
mediums are recruited and replaced. I suspect that the determining

factors are probably the size of the spirit provinces in relation to their population densities in conjunction with modern factors which may be restricting the recruitment of mediums. My impression is that the few mediums that now exist are distributed over the larger and more densely populated spirit provinces.

It seems significant that in the area in which I worked the founding ancestor of the spirit realm, and the founding ancestors of two adjacent spirit realms were each represented by mediums. This reflects the importance of the senior spirit medium for the articulation of the total system. His position is important for, in terms of the total organization, it lies at the point where the territorial and lineal aspects intersect. As one ascends the hierarchy of mediums, corresponding to the genealogical hierarchy, the more senior the medium, the greater the number of people who may consult him. But only when the senior medium is reached do the two aspects, the lineal and the territorial, completely merge, since he alone may be consulted not only by all the descendants of the founding ancestor, but also by all the people living in the various spirit provinces which make up his spirit realm. I feel that were it without a senior medium for very long the whole complex structure would fall apart.

In the past it appears that in some spirit realms a medium representing the son of the founding ancestor made the final selection from among a number of candidates for a chieftainship after some preliminary selection by junior mediums, and then installed the new chief in office.[1] Senior mediums in the past do not appear to have become directly involved in succession disputes. However, in the succession disputes which I observed in Muzarabanhi Reserve this did happen, possibly because there was at that time no medium who represented the son of the founding ancestor. The tradition that a medium representing the son of the founding ancestor should make the final selection of a chief appears to have served to keep the senior spirit medium out of the arena of local politics and away from the bitterness and recrimination which are sometimes the result of succession disputes. This further emphasizes the importance of his position in the total politico-religious organization.

[1] Cf. Gelfand, *Shona Religion*, 1962, p. 23.

The sanctions which maintain the system

Korekore often likened the senior spirit medium to a king, who had his Governor, his Chief Commissioner, his Provincial Commissioners, his District Commissioners, and his little messengers. However, they readily distinguish between the secular authority of the chief and the religious authority of the mediums. Chiefs have their territories in which they are responsible for maintaining law and order but the mediums are seen as being concerned with the moral order of the universe and the relation of people to the earth. Their duties are to act as intermediaries between the great spirits who control the fertility of the earth and the people who live upon it. The spirit guardians are believed to observe the activities of people upon the earth and to punish them for offences which pollute the earth, the most important of which are incest and homicide. Since the mediums become identified with the spirit guardians whom they represent, their pronouncements during a séance are treated with great respect. To fail to obey the order of a medium is to run the risk of being killed by a lion or struck down by lightning. Though the influence of the mediums appears to be waning they still have considerable authority which is supported by the belief in the effectiveness of the mystical sanctions. Every time the crop fails, the rains are late, lightning strikes, or a lion attacks a man, this provides proof that the spirit guardians are still actively concerned with the behaviour of men upon the earth.

The spirit mediums must be seen, therefore, as part of a total organization. Mediums do not appear randomly to represent just any spirit guardian and ancestor but occupy positions which can be related to other aspects of the religious and political systems of the Korekore. Furthermore, I have suggested that mediums are trained, either formally or informally, for the positions that they occupy. In this way they acquire their special knowledge which is important for their function. Though for purposes of analysis I have separated the lineal and territorial aspects of the organization in which the spirit mediums are involved, and have separated the mediums' religious from their political functions, Korekore do not make such rigid distinctions. Korekore see the mediums primarily as religious figures. My argument is that it is the religious activities of the mediums, and the belief in the effectiveness of the mystical sanctions, which give great weight to the pronouncements of the mediums when these have political significance. The insistence of the people themselves upon the religious significance of the mediums has misled earlier writers into underestimating or even ignoring their political importance.

The role of spirit mediums in succession disputes

I have stated that in the lineal aspect of the system in which the spirit mediums are involved, all royal ancestors who founded chieftainships which are still in existence, with very few exceptions, are represented by mediums. I stated that this appeared to be connected with the important role that mediums play in selecting a chief's successor. When a chief dies, a considerable number of candidates, all with more or less equal claims, may make some bid to succeed him. The reason why a large number of candidates may come forward to press their claims is because of the way in which the rules of succession operate among the Korekore.

When a man who has established a chiefdom dies, each of his sons, provided that he is not incapacitated by mental or physical infirmities, ought to succeed in turn. On the death of the last of the filial generation, the eldest son of the founder's first son ought to succeed, followed by the eldest surviving son of the founder's second son, and so on. After all the eligible men of this generation have succeeded, the title ought then to drop a generation and rotate in the same way among the descent groups established by each of the founder's sons in order of seniority. Once the title has passed to the second descending generation there is a definite rule that no man should succeed his own father immediately as chief, though it is accepted that the son who succeeds to the personal estate of his father should act as regent during the interregnum.

Assuming that senior sons marry and have children before their younger brothers and given the fact that with polygyny there may be a considerable difference in age between them, the difficulties that arise within only three generations of the establishment of a title are considerable. Consider Fig. 5, which is a simplified version of an actual royal genealogy. After A1's death the title

passed to each of his surviving sons, B1 to B6, in turn. We will
suppose that the difference in age between B1 and B6, the eldest
and youngest of A1's sons is in the region of 30 years, which is not
unusual in polygynous households. B1, we shall suppose, died

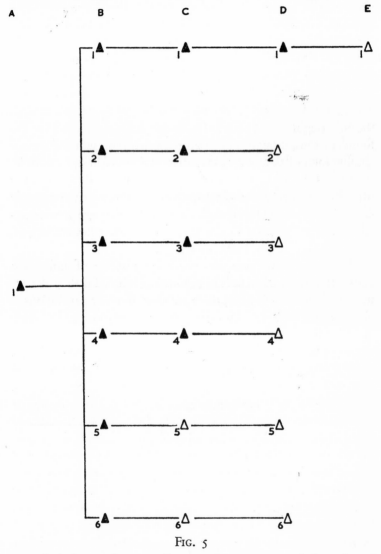

FIG. 5

Hypothetical genealogy to illustrate the operation of the rules of
succession

when he was 60 and had his first son when he was about 20. His son C1, therefore, would be 40 years old when he died, whilst B6, B1's youngest brother, would be only 30. Suppose that B6 succeeds to the chieftainship in his late fifties and rules until he is sixty, or thereabouts. It is highly probable that C1 will be dead before he gets a chance to succeed. If these same factors operate for a generation or so, we arrive at a position in which the surviving men of the senior branch are as old as, if not older than, men in the junior branches, but a generation, or even two generations junior to them. In the case I have in mind C6 was about the same age as E1, D2 and D3. According to the rules of succession, though the title ought to rotate among the branches established by the founder's sons, it ought not to drop a generation whilst there are eligible men of the senior generation still alive. In our example, E1, though he belongs to the senior branch which did not get the title again because of C1's death, cannot, in theory, succeed while C5, C6, and D2 to D6, are still alive because they are genealogically senior to him. Gradually therefore, if the rules are strictly adhered to, the senior branches are excluded.

The rules of succession thus produce a number of difficulties: firstly, the senior branches are gradually excluded if the rules are strictly observed; secondly, there are men of junior generations as old as, or older than, men of the senior generation; and thirdly, the most likely candidates are going to be old men.

It is customary for a chief's successor not to be appointed until about a year after his death. However, the records of the Administration relating to succession to titles in the area, together with oral traditions, reveal that interregna have been frequently longer than this: often two years, occasionally three or four. In addition, this evidence reveals that though a few chiefs ruled for a considerable number of years, many ruled for only a year or two, and in one chiefdom, three men succeeded each other as chief in the space of about ten years. My own view of the situation is that succession disputes have always been a characteristic feature of the Korekore political system, though this tendency has undoubtedly been exacerbated by the interference of the Administration in the appointment of chiefs, and by the present inability of the royals to secede and create new positions of authority. If this is a valid

view, then the importance of the spirit mediums in finally establishing and legitimizing one of the candidates as the one true chief,
can be seen. Given the traditional belief in the ability of the ancestors and spirit guardians to exact vengeance if their decisions
are questioned, we can appreciate that the medium's nominee was
in a very strong position.

However, as far as I could judge, the mediums do not just
choose any candidate they feel might be suitable but they assess
the general public feeling and appear to choose finally the candidate who has most support. Support for a particular candidate does
not appear immediately he presses his claim. It develops slowly as
people weigh up the attributes of the various candidates, looking for the qualities traditionally ascribed to chiefs, such as wisdom,
leadership and the ability to handle cases, and for qualities such as
the ability to handle Europeans, which is considered an important
asset in the modern political situation. As I have pointed out,
mediums delay making their choice by saying that they must have
time to consult with 'other spirits'. They may do this a number of
times but if a junior medium continues to procrastinate, people
will by-pass him and go to a more senior one.

In a succession dispute which I observed one group of royals
visited a medium three times before he made a choice and declared
one candidate chief. Administrative records show that in 1937,
during another succession dispute in the same area, a medium
representing the son of the founding ancestor was consulted at
least four times before he came to a decision. We must see
mediums, therefore, not as powerful authoritarian figures, who
pronounce in favour of one candidate or another, but as men who
are swayed and guided in their decisions by public opinion. When
this has not had time to crystallize, they delay making their choice
(which is, in reality, the choice of the people) for as long as
possible.

Nowadays the medium's nomination, though it is still earnestly
sought after, does not necessarily bring a succession dispute to its
conclusion because the District Commissioner makes the final
appointment and all royals know this. The Commissioner, too,
considers public opinion when making his final choice. Often
he employs a form of election by getting administrative headmen

to line up behind the candidates they support. This may be done several times until there is a substantial majority in favour of one candidate. I did not observe this process but Mr Beale, the present District Commissioner at Mt Darwin, wrote a letter to me after I left the area in which he describes his attempt to bring one of the succession disputes, concerned with the senior chieftainship of Kasekete, to a conclusion. He called a meeting of the administrative headmen and told them to bring suitable candidates with them. He described how, at the first meeting he held, there was considerable disagreement and he eventually asked the headmen to line up behind the two candidates they had produced. The two candidates received almost equal support so he sent them off to consult the spirit mediums, hoping that they would be able to resolve the difficulty. At a second meeting held some six weeks later one of the candidates present at the previous meeting appeared again, though his rival on that occasion appears to have lost favour in the meantime and was replaced by another. Mr Beale writes that at the second meeting, though he found that the various candidates had consulted the spirit mediums, no decision had been reached. The administrative headmen asked him to make the final choice. The Commissioner asked the headmen to line up again behind the candidates whom they supported, and this time the one who had appeared at both meetings gained a clear majority and was installed as chief. This particular dispute had been in progress for two years, from September 1959 until October 1961. In 1938 in a dispute over the same senior title the then Native Commissioner appears to have acted in a similar fashion. In this case the dispute had gone on for three and a half years. In a letter to the Chief Native Commissioner (21 October 1938) the Native Commissioner wrote that 'representatives of the tribe appeared and stated that they had failed to reach an agreement on the question of nominating a successor and asked me to select one'. He goes on to describe how he selected the man that he considered 'most suitable' from one of the royal descent groups as it was the 'turn' of this group to provide a successor.

A succession dispute in Muzarabanhi Reserve

So far I have considered in general terms the total system in which the spirit mediums are involved, their traditional role in succession disputes and how this has been affected by modern factors. I now consider briefly aspects of a succession dispute which I observed in Muzarabanhi Reserve for the title 'Muzarabanhi'.

There are three chiefdoms in the Reserve, Kasekete which is the largest, Muzarabanhi, and Chiweshe, which is very small and lies beyond the mountains on the edge of the plateau. While all three chiefdoms bear some relation to traditional political units, they are largely administrative creations. Similarly, the titles of the three chieftainships have their origin in administrative decrees, though one, *Kasekete*, appears to have been in use before the Administration was established. The Kaseketeship is recognized by the Administration as the senior chieftainship and carries more formal administrative authority than the other two. Despite the fact that the titles, by and large, were instituted by the Administration, people act as if they are traditional titles which should be awarded according to traditional rules. However, there is some dispute as to which of the three titles ought to be recognized as administratively senior. The arguments are based upon various conflicting interpretations of the history of the establishment of the European administration in the area. We need not concern ourselves with this problem here, except to say that the royals of Chiweshe and Muzarabanhi both argue that their own titles ought to be recognized by the Administration as the senior.

Originally the title *Kasekete* rotated among the royal descent groups founded by the sons of Chihwahwa (K1) (Fig. 6). It no longer does so because the Administration will not consider as candidates for the Kaseketeship royals from descent groups which hold other administrative sub-chieftainships. This excludes the descendants of Kavai (L4), Mudzengarere (L5), and Chuzu (M1). The title *Chiweshe* rotates among the descendants of Kavai (L4) whilst the title *Muzarabanhi* rotates among the descendants of Chuzu (M1).

When I arrived in the area the three chieftainships of Kasekete, Muzarabanhi and Chiweshe were vacant. In the three chiefdoms succession disputes were in progress. In addition there was a dispute about which title ought to be recognized as senior by the

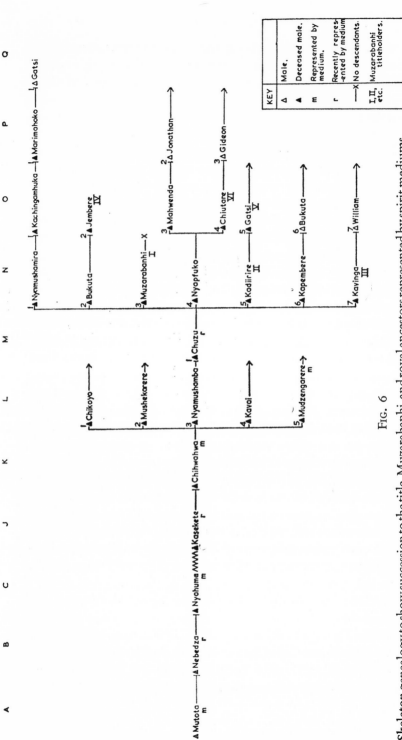

KEY

△	Male.
▲	Deceased male.
m	Represented by medium.
r	Recently represented by medium
──X	No descendants.
I, II, etc.	Muzarabanhi titleholders.

FIG. 6

Skeleton genealogy to show succession to the title, Muzarabanhi, and royal ancestors represented by spirit mediums

Administration. The four separate issues tended on occasions to get intertwined. In this chapter I have based my generalizations about Korekore succession disputes, and the involvement of the mediums in them, upon my observations of these disputes. However, the separate disputes are of such a complexity that I have decided to consider only one here, that for the title *Muzarabanhi*. I give only the barest outline of the dispute, concentrating mainly upon incidents in which spirit mediums are involved.

Aspects of the dispute for the Muzarabanhi title

I begin my consideration of certain aspects of the Muzarabanhi succession dispute with the death of Gatsi (*c.* 1930?), Muzarabanhi V (O5). Up to that time the title *Muzarabanhi* appears to have been awarded by the Administration with little or no recourse to the spirit mediums. None of the chiefs preceding Gatsi ruled for long and Gatsi himself died only a few years after his appointment.

When Gatsi became chief there was no medium representing Chuzu (M1). Some time after the last of Chuzu's sons had died a Nsenga woman from the northern side of the Zambesi appeared, claiming to represent Chuzu (M1). She was soon discredited. It is unusual for a woman to represent an ancestor and elders told me that they did not like clapping to the medium as if she were a man. I do not know if there was another reason for her being discredited.

During Gatsi's reign another medium appeared claiming to represent Chuzu. The circumstances surrounding the appearance of this medium have some significance and I now consider them.

The senior spirit medium in the area represents Mutota (A1), the 'father' of the Korekore, and the man who is supposed to have led the original Karanga invasion. The senior medium is Zezuru by tribe and originally lived at Gota, a region which lies southwest of Muzarabanhi Reserve, on the plateau, near Sipolilo. In this area lies Mutota's spirit province. To the senior medium's hamlet came two royals from Muzarabanhi in search of wives, Mahwenda (O3) and Chiutare (O4). Chiutare married the sister of the wife of the senior medium. Whilst he was living in the hamlet, Chiutare became 'possessed' by the spirit of Chuzu (M1).

He then returned to Chuzu's spirit province which lies on the western edge of Muzarabanhi Reserve. I have no evidence as to what took place during Chiutare's stay in the senior medium's hamlet, but his emergence as a medium in this hamlet appears significant, particularly in view of the fact that a few years later another young man was also 'possessed' here, and later came to live in the valley as the medium of Chihwahwa (K1).

After Gatsi's death (c. 1930?) a great séance was held at which the senior medium representing Mutota (A1), and the mediums of Nyahuma (C1), Chihwahwa (K1) and Chuzu (M1) (represented by Chiutare), were present. At the séance the royals, who seemed to have been concerned at the way in which the chiefs were dying in fairly rapid succession, asked the mediums why this was. The mediums attributed it to the fact that the title *Muzarabanhi* was being awarded by the Administration instead of by themselves.

I was told that at the séance, which continued through the whole of one night, Chiutare, speaking as Chuzu (M1), said that he (Chiutare) ought to be made chief. The senior medium said that this could not be, since a medium ought not to become a chief. However, it would appear that Chiutare eventually had his way and was installed as Muzarabanhi VI.

Everyone to whom I spoke about this said that it was quite wrong not only for a royal to be a medium of a spirit from whom he was patrilineally descended, but also quite wrong for a medium to become a chief. Some said that the long and painful illness which Chiutare subsequently suffered was due to the anger of Chuzu's spirit when Chiutare took the chieftainship. However, despite all these protestations, Chiutare appears to have been accepted as a genuine medium. His case is unusual and the only one of which I heard where a royal and a chief was also a medium. Considering the circumstances of his appearance as a medium, and the events surrounding his installation as a chief, it certainly appears as if there was an element of collusion between Chiutare and the senior spirit medium which also may have involved the other mediums.

Up to Gatsi's death, as I have stated, the title *Muzarabanhi* was awarded by the Administration. With Chiutare's appearance as the medium of Chuzu there appears to have been a concerted effort by the mediums to establish their right to award the title, as if it were a traditional one. Chiutare's motives in accepting the title himself, even though he was a medium, are obscure. Nevertheless, from that time on, the spirit mediums have had some influence over the succession to the title.

Chiutare died in September 1959, some ten months before I arrived in the area. No new medium representing Chuzu had appeared meanwhile, and in the succession dispute which ensued for the title *Muzarabanhi* only the medium of Chihwahwa (K1) and the senior spirit medium representing Mutota were involved. The medium of Nyahuma (C1), a very old man through whom Korekore say 'the spirit no longer speaks strongly', was by-passed in the hierarchy.

Bukuta (O6), the principal candidate for the Muzarabanhiship, had already consulted the medium of Chihwahwa (K1) a number of times before my arrival. Bukuta was supported in his claim by a number of senior headmen, some of them commoners, several of whom lived in his neighbourhood. His claim was opposed by William (O7) a man of about fifty and some ten years or so junior to Bukuta, and by men of the junior generation, among them Jonathan (P2) and Gideon (P3). The men of the junior generation opposed Bukuta's claim on the grounds that he was too old, slightly crippled and a little deaf. They wanted a younger man, able to travel to the Administrative headquarters and make representations there on their behalf.

At a séance which occurred a few weeks before I entered the area, the medium of Chihwahwa awarded the title *Muzarabanhi* to Bukuta. Many of the senior headmen in the chiefdom accepted this decision, but the younger headmen, including both commoners and royals, were not at all happy about it. They then put forward the argument that the title was an Administrative creation and that it could only be awarded by the Native Commissioner.[1] One of the younger headmen, Gideon (P3) the son of the last chief, who had acted as regent during the interregnum and had some designs on the chieftainship himself, went to Mt Darwin on a number of occasions, ostensibly to see the

[1] In 1962 the title 'Native Commissioner' was changed to 'District Commissioner'.

Commissioner about the vacant chieftainship. As far as I am aware,
he did not always see the Commissioner on these visits about this
issue. On one occasion he came back with the story that the Commissioner would not accept Bukuta as an administrative chief
since he was too old. This precipitated something of a crisis among
Bukuta's supporters and they resolved to see the medium of
Chihwahwa again. I accompanied them on this visit. At the
séance they put the problem to the medium raised by the supposed
refusal of the Commissioner to accept Bukuta. Chihwahwa's
medium refused to take back the title and said that the people
would have to sort the matter out for themselves. He had given
them their rightful chief. If the Europeans did not approve of his
choice and appointed another chief, then he would not recognize
that man. He threatened that any man who took the title without
his permission would soon die, killed by his (i.e. Chihwahwa's)
ancestral wrath. Chihwawha's medium thus once again asserted
the right of the mediums to award the title as if it were a traditional one.

When Bukuta and his supporters returned from the séance they
decided that Bukuta would remain the 'traditional' chief, whilst
they would find someone to act as his 'legs', i.e. as administrative
chief. They decided to push forward Gatsi (Q1) of the senior
branch descended from Nyamushamira (N1). Gatsi was about
fifty years old, but two generations junior to Bukuta. In terms of
the rules of succession he was no threat[1] to Bukuta's position as
'traditional' chief and he also had a weak personality. I think that
Bukuta had in mind that Gatsi would be passive and do what he
was told. Some of the other headmen refused to accept Gatsi. They
argued that Gatsi was dull-witted, afraid of Europeans, and a
'child' to them. Bukuta and his supporters then dropped this idea.
Eventually, some of the younger headmen put pressure upon
Bukuta to get him to go to see the Commissioner. He kept on
prevaricating for a while, arranging meetings with administrative
headmen at Mt Darwin then failing to arrive for them. Eventually
one of the more forthright administrative headmen, exasperated
by Bukuta's behaviour, wheeled him to Mt Darwin on the back
of his bicycle and more or less compelled him to see the Com-

[1] A chief fears the sorcery of his close rivals.

missioner. The Commissioner noted Bukuta's claim and told him to go and consult Acting Chief *Kasekete*, who also had to confirm Bukuta's appointment. However, Bukuta came back loudly proclaiming that he had received official recognition. When I left the area the dispute was still unresolved.

In the contemporary dispute for the *Muzarabanhi* title only the medium of Chihwahwa was mainly concerned. In this particular hierarchy of mediums at the present time there are only three mediums active, those of Chihwahwa (K1), Nyahuma (C1) and Mutota (A1). Nyahuma's medium, for the reasons I have given, was by-passed. This leaves only one medium, Chihwahwa's, who, traditionally, would have been concerned with a succession dispute. The senior medium's position as I indicated earlier appears to have been protected by the convention that a medium representing a son of the founding ancestor made the final selection of a chief. In the recent past there was a medium representing Nebedza (B1) who appears to have performed this function and there were also mediums representing Kasekete (J1) and Chuzu (M1). Informants stated that in the past they would have been involved in the dispute.

Though Chihwahwa's medium was mainly concerned in the contemporary dispute one candidate attempted to involve the senior spirit medium. He was Jonathan (P2), son of Mahwenda (O3), the man who had accompanied Chiutare, the last medium of Chuzu, to the senior medium's hamlet when he was a young man. Jonathan made a number of 'secret' visits to see the senior medium and people said that he was trying to bribe the senior medium to give him the title, though this story was probably invented to discredit him. Jonathan was making use of the known antipathy between the mediums of Mutota and Chihwahwa. This had arisen because the medium of Mutota, the senior medium, had been forced by the Administration to leave the spirit province of Mutota on the plateau. This region has been reallocated recently under the terms of the Land Apportionment Act. Mutota's medium came into the valley and took up residence near to the hamlet of Chihwahwa's medium and in Chihwahwa's spirit province. This annoyed Chihwahwa's medium because it exposed him to a mystical danger (two mediums are not supposed to live in the same spirit province) and also because the senior medium overshadowed his position as the most important medium in this part of the valley. When I spoke to Mutota's medium he said that Chihwahwa's medium had no right to make the final decision on the *Muzarabanhi* title without first consulting him. Chihwahwa's medium, on the other hand, argued that in the absence of mediums representing Chuzu (M1) and Nebedza (B1) he had the right to award the title and the senior medium had no right to intervene. He was stressing here the convention that the senior spirit medium should not be involved in succession disputes. It would appear, therefore, that the personal relations which exist between mediums also affect the operation of the system.

As I have shown the *Muzarabanhi* title was originally instituted by the Administration. However, we observe that the spirit mediums made a concerted effort to establish their right to award the title as if it were a traditional one. The mediums utilized the belief in the effectiveness of the mystical sanctions which support their authority to account for the fact that the chiefs installed by the Administration had died after ruling for only a few years. The medium of Chihwahwa, in the contemporary dispute, invoked similar sanctions and reaffirmed the mediums' right to award the title. We see here, therefore, a successful attempt by the mediums to incorporate into the traditional system an institution, that of administrative chief, which, when it was first instituted, was outside their influence.

The role of the District Commissioner in succession disputes

Because the District Commissioner may be called upon by the various parties to a succession dispute to act as an arbitrator we can see that in these situations his role is similar to that of the spirit mediums. Unlike the mediums, however, the Commissioner has the power to enforce an arbitrary settlement but he is reluctant to use it. The reason for this stems from the important position of the chief in the local administration. Despite various protestations about 'direct rule' in Southern Rhodesia the Administration does make use of its chiefs and sub-chiefs to disseminate information, to implement certain of its policies and to maintain law and order at the local level. The chiefs also provide a vehicle for the expression of public opinion within their territories and keep the Commissioners informed about local problems and people's aspirations. While the chief has lost certain of his traditional powers he has come to occupy a new and important position as an intermediary between the people and the Administration. If the Commissioner makes a wrong choice when appointing a chief then the new chief will receive little support from his subjects. This may lead to constant friction within the chiefdom as people grow discontented, and friction may result ultimately in the implementation of Administrative policies being brought to a halt. Consequently the District Commissioner endeavours to avoid making the final choice as long as he possibly can. Like the mediums, he waits until public opinion has crystallized before intervening, and as far as possible allows the people to choose their own chief. As one Native Commissioner of the Darwin District put it, in reply to a letter from a Korekore advocating the appointment of an 'educated' chief, 'I cannot recommend the appointment of a man unless he is the right choice according to native custom. Native custom is recognized and followed very meticulously in the very important matter of the appointment of a chief, otherwise all sorts of complications might arise.'[1] However, unlike the mediums, the Commissioner is not prepared to allow a succession dispute to drag on interminably. Whilst an acting chief may be appointed during an interregnum, he does not command the support of the people in the same way as a properly appointed chief, particularly when it comes to important matters. If the acting chief speaks on behalf of the Administration and asks people to carry out certain instructions then often his orders will be disobeyed on the grounds that he is not a full chief. This happened on a number of occasions whilst I was in Muzarabanhi Reserve particularly in connection with the maintenance of roads and Administrative camping sites. An acting chief may also be reluctant to press forward any complaints which the local population may have. Consequently during an interregnum communication between the Commissioner and the people of the chiefdom tends to break down. Ultimately the District Commissioner is forced to act both because of the exigencies

[1] Native Commissioner to Katapura, 9 March 1959.

of the situation itself and also because other administrative officers, such as the Pasture and Land Development Officers who find their work hampered, may urge the Commissioner, both formally and informally, to use his authority. In the past some Commissioners have acted precipitately and this has tended to exacerbate subsequent succession disputes.

Mediums and District Commissioners as 'strangers' or 'outsiders'

In recent years sociologists have devoted much attention to the role of 'strangers' or 'outsiders' in acting as intermediaries between disputing parties. Frankenberg[1] distinguishes between the 'stranger' and the 'outsider'. The 'stranger', he argues, 'is merely removed from the informal conflicts which, with his help, may be resolved without awakening open hostilities.' The 'stranger' is not necessarily outside the community in which he acts; he may be a 'stranger' in one social situation but not in another. In Africa, as Frankenberg points out, whilst similar principles operate they may be expressed in a mystical idiom. 'The stranger ... whether human or spirit, acts through mystical sanctions to prevent divisions inherent in a formal structure from breaking into open conflict.'[2] The spirit mediums fall into this category of 'strangers'. Their pronouncements are supported by the belief in the ability of the ancestors and spirit guardians to bring disaster to any individual or community incurring their displeasure. Korekore emphasize that mediums ought to be men from distant places who have no knowledge of local affairs. In reality, this rarely appears to be so. Nevertheless, when mediums speak as, and are identified with, ancestors who are removed from the affairs of men, they are 'strangers' in the contemporary system of social relations. This device by which men can on one occasion be part of a system and on another be translated to a higher level 'outside' it, resolves one of the difficulties ever present in the role of the 'stranger', which is that after the passage of time, the 'stranger' himself may become absorbed into the system and therefore lose his value as an 'unbiased' intermediary or arbitrator. I suspect that some of the

[1] R. Frankenberg, *Village on the Border*, Cohen & West, London, 1957, p. 155 ff.
[2] *Ibid.*, p. 156.

mediums who are discredited are those who have too obviously sided with one or another of the disputing parties.

District Commissioners, on the other hand, in certain situations, fall into Frankenberg's category of 'outsiders': 'strangers' who are excluded from all informal social contacts. The 'outsider' not only lacks kinship ties with the community 'but is also excluded both as a participant and as a subject from the gossip and back-biting of the community'.[1] The District Commissioner stands aloof from the manœuvring, backbiting and recriminations which are part of a succession dispute. Whilst in his administrative capacity he has formal contacts with the people of his district he is not part of the tightly-knit network of social relations within their communities. Whilst he has the power to act arbitrarily, I have pointed out that there are factors which usually restrain him from doing so, except as a last resort. He is an 'outsider' to the system and this appears to be one of the reasons why people ultimately thrust upon him the task of choosing between rival candidates for a chiefly title.

I have argued that recurrent succession disputes are a charac-teristic feature of Korekore political organization. I have said that since the establishment of the Administration secession and the founding of new chiefdoms giving new positions of authority has not been possible. This has added to the intensity of the disputes. In addition, I have stated that chiefs have acquired a new im-portance as intermediaries between the people and the Admini-stration. The chief has also acquired new powers, in that his decisions, if they accord with the Administration's view of justice, will be supported by the police force of the Colony. Chiefs also receive salaries. Whilst these are not large (Acting Chief Kasekete received £88 p.a. in 1960), in this poverty-stricken area where even migrant labourers seldom earn more than £5 per month, undoubtedly they have some attraction. Chiefly office is therefore attractive and men are willing to compete for it earnestly.

All these factors, in addition to occasional arbitrary interference by the Administration in the choice of chiefs, have tended to intensify succession disputes. Furthermore, new conflicts of in-terest have emerged. Men of the younger generation want a

[1] *Ibid.*, p. 156.

young chief who is active and 'progressive': a man who will negotiate with the Administration for schools, clinics, roads, stores and the like, even if this does mean passing over the candidate most acceptable according to the traditional rules. The older generation view 'progress' with some suspicion and would prefer a chief with more traditional qualities: an old man, wise and well versed in customary law. In this new situation the spirit mediums may have difficulty in exercising their traditional role in that the disputes are of such intensity, and the contradictory interests so radically opposed, that these cannot be resolved easily in terms of the 'traditional' processes. Spirit mediums may delay making their 'choice', waiting for public opinion to turn in favour of one or two candidates, in the way that I have explained, but when there are many candidates, and such divergent views as to the attributes a chief should have, clear favourites for a chieftaincy may not emerge for a very long time, if at all.

In the succession disputes which I observed in Muzarabanhi Reserve the situation was further complicated because some of the mediums had begun to support particular candidates and even the senior spirit medium had become involved in local politics. This may have occurred to some extent before the establishment of the Administration. I cannot say. Certainly the ideal is that the mediums should remain aloof from local politics and should not side with one particular candidate. However, people accuse certain mediums of taking bribes from some of the candidates, though I have no evidence that they do so.[1] Many of these stories, of course, are invented to discredit particular candidates and mediums.

We see, therefore, that a new situation has developed. Because secession has become impossible, there are many candidates for a vacant chieftainship. Also, the chieftainships have acquired a new importance which has intensified competition for them. In addition, the spirit mediums who are supposed to remain impartial, have begun siding with particular candidates, or are suspected of doing so. In this new situation it appears that people turn to the District Commissioner as an 'outsider' to help settle the matter for them. In Muzarabanhi, during the succession dispute, several

---

[1] Sgt. Harvey of the B.S.A. Police, Sipolilo Division, told me that some years ago a medium in the Sipolilo Reserve was prosecuted for accepting bribes.

headmen stressed to me the difficulty of approaching the Administration on any matter when there was no administratively recognized chief. These were the men who urged the various candidates
to go to the Commissioner and get the matter sorted out.

I have argued that spirit mediums are organized into a system
and that their emergence at particular points within it is not haphazard but can be related to other aspects of Korekore social
organization. I have analysed the system into two aspects, a lineal
and a territorial. The lineal aspect concerns mainly political activities, the territorial mainly religious ones. Spirit mediums who
represent both spirit guardians and royal ancestors are involved
in both aspects of the system. The mystical sanctions which support
their religious activities in the territorial aspect of the system also
serve to support their pronouncements which have a political
character. I have confined myself mainly to discussing the significance of mediums in the lineal aspect of the system where one of
their most important functions is to select and install a chief's
successor. I related this function to the rules of succession among
the Korekore which tend to operate to produce a large number of
candidates. I indicated that sociologically the mediums can be
seen as 'strangers' in the system, since because they speak as
ancestors, they are translated to a higher level 'outside' it. Since
the establishment of the Administration, I stated that there were a
number of factors which appeared to have intensified succession
disputes and made their resolution by traditional processes more
difficult. In this situation I considered the District Commissioner
as an 'outsider' to whom people turn to help them resolve their
disputes. My main concern has been to show how the mediums,
viewed primarily as religious figures by the Korekore themselves,
perform an important political function.

My analysis has been based upon data collected in a relatively
small area by the intensive observation of the activities of a few
mediums. However, I presented my analysis of the political
activities of the mediums against the background of the system of
which they are a part. The principles which underlie the structure
of this system have a wider relevance. The Shona-speaking peoples
were fragmented into many tribes and many autonomous chiefdoms. However, I have shown how spirit realms, which may

include a number of chiefdoms within them, are linked together by the 'fictions' of kinship which exist among the senior spirit mediums. Also, I pointed out that because ritual affiliations tend to cut across political affiliations this may serve to regulate political relations among neighbouring chiefs. It would appear, therefore, that what were apparently politically autonomous chiefdoms, were involved in a wider system of social relations based upon the ritual connections which exist between various hierarchies of mediums. Though further research remains to be done on this problem, it is becoming clearer that the spirit mediums were part of a system which linked certain Shona tribes and chiefdoms into a wider polity.

7

TRADITIONAL AUTHORITIES AND THE RISE OF MODERN POLITICS IN SOUTHERN RHODESIA, 1898–1930

by

TERENCE RANGER

IN her recent study of the South African National Congress, Mary Benson shows how that movement began in an 'alliance of solid middle class urban men with chiefs and tribesmen from rural areas'. She describes the first meeting of the Congress in January 1912; summoned by the young African lawyers, Seme, Mangena, Msimang and Montsioa; opened with prayer by the Ethiopian Church leader, Reverend Ngcayaya, and supported by other ministers, like Reverend John Langalibalele Dube, who became the first President; attended by the Regent of Swaziland and representatives of the Paramounts of Basutoland and Bechuanaland. She shows how this alliance of the new and of the old élite was much more than merely a matter of convenience, and how the Oxford educated lawyer, Seme, married into the Zulu royal house and came to be more concerned with his work as adviser to the Swazi royal family than with the Congress movement as a whole, or how Reverend Dube was 'first and foremost a Zulu patriot, related to the royal house and adviser to the Paramount Chief.' It is interesting to inquire whether the earliest political movements organized by Africans in Southern Rhodesia arose from a similar alliance of traditional leadership with the young educated or semi-educated. As we shall see, such an inquiry shows that in Rhodesia, despite the overthrow of the Matabele monarchy in 1893, the House of Lobengula played a significant part in early African political movements. It also shows that many of the men responsible for the formation of the South African National Congress interested themselves in Rhodesian affairs, and attempted to extend their movement of opposition to Rhodesia.[1]

It should be said at this point that the political movements described in this paper arose in Matabeleland rather than in Mashonaland; their urban strength resided in Bulawayo; their rural strength among the Matabele on European farms or in the Reserves. By the end of our period there were certainly some manifestations of opposition to the colonial administrative or ecclesiastical régime in Mashonaland. In the late 1920's there was a vigorous Salisbury branch of the Industrial and Commercial Workers' Union. At the same time the Watch Tower movement, which had hitherto been virtually restricted to Nyasa and Northern Rhodesian labour, was spreading into the Mashonaland Reserves. And in the towns, African school teachers, ministers and clerks were being drawn into the Government-approved Welfare Associations. Even in the earlier period there were some interesting, if isolated, movements of Mashona opposition—like Matthew Zwimba's Church of the White Bird, which counted those killed in the Zwimba Reserve during the 1896-7 rising as its martyrs and intercessors. But there can be no doubt that, for a variety of reasons, 'modern' political or proto-political activity developed much sooner and on a much wider scale in Matabeleland and that before 1930, it is there we have to look for anything resembling South African developments.

There are a variety of factors which in combination do something to explain this fact. Bulawayo developed much more rapidly than Salisbury as an industrial centre, for instance, and was the natural home of developing urban politics. Moreover in the early years there seems to have been a greater flow of migrant labour from Matabeleland and back again than from Mashonaland. And Matabele migrant labour came into intimate contact with the vigorous development of Zulu independent churches and political associations. Again, the Matabele felt from the beginning one overriding grievance which the Mashona experienced much less sharply—shortage of land and particularly of land in their ancestral areas. But in addition to these factors, there can be no doubt that the surviving institutions and memories of the tradi-

[1] M. Benson, *The African Patriots*, Chapters 1-3.

tional political structure of the Matabele provided a base for 'modern' politics which was lacking in Mashonaland.

To begin with, most of the leaders of the Matabele rebels of 1896, as well as the leaders of the Matabele 'loyalists', had been recognized as salaried *indunas* by the Government after the rebellion ended. These men continued to exercise a widespread influence and authority over their people—in contrast to the Mashona chiefs, many of whom were newly installed by the Government as a reward for service against their rebel predecessors. But in addition, the evidence suggests that the Matabele *indunas* were also more willing and able to exploit the opportunities offered by new conditions than were the Mashona chiefs. Thus in Native Department correspondence a contrast was regularly drawn between the enthusiasm with which the *indunas* sent their sons to school, sometimes to school in the Union of South Africa, and the low level of education among the probable successors to Mashona chieftainships. By the 1920's, as we shall see, educated and travelled heirs to Matabele indunaships were beginning to play their part in African politics.

Then there were the memories of the past. Despite tensions both before and after conquest, the Matabele did possess a concept of themselves as a 'nation' in a way which was certainly not true of the peoples of Mashonaland. Even in Mashonaland it was possible for the first medium of the Nehanda spirit to arise after the rebellion to claim that she had returned to speak to the Government on behalf of all the Mashona people. But this was something very different from the Matabele sense of 'nationhood', which readily produced such concepts as that of the Matabele National Home, and such associations as the Loyal Amandebele Society, the Matabele Home Society, and the rest.

Above all, there was the memory of the institution which had been essential to the idea of Matabele nationhood—the kingship. The kingship was never formally revived after 1893 but it remained a factor of major importance in Matabele thought. 'They regard their particular type of chieftainship or kingship as a thing radically different from the type of chieftainship found among neighbouring peoples, and as a thing which marked them off sharply from these other peoples', Hughes tells us. 'From the point of view of the Ndebele it is a fact of paramount importance that they once had a king. The kingship and the state organization welded together the diverse elements, the peoples of various different tribal origins and the members of different castes, into a single political unit, and from the political unit of the past has sprung the degree of social unity which exists today.' [1] Thus, as far as at least the two superior castes of Matabele society were concerned everyone was always in favour of the restoration of the monarchy, even if a majority failed to agree upon any one candidate at any one time. And thus, also, all major discontents within the Matabele nation inevitably tended to find expression after 1896 in terms of the claim of one or other of the contestants for the kingship. In this way the suppressed kingship of the Matabele played something of the same role in the emergence of 'modern' politics in Rhodesia as did the existing paramountcies of South Africa in the development of politics there.

In Rhodesia, as in South Africa, the royal family commanded the support not only of traditionalists but also of members of the new urban and educated élite. The idea of a restoration of the monarchy certainly did command the support of traditionalists. It was expressed clearly, for instance, by both rebel and loyalist leaders at the third *indaba* between Rhodes and the Matabele *indunas* in October 1896 when there was unanimous demand for 'one head, not half a dozen heads'. From that time on until the 1930's—and indeed beyond—the campaign for the restoration of the monarchy was a constant factor of Matabele politics. In the early years it was led by a group of the salaried *indunas*, among whom the most prominent was Umlugulu, one of the main Matabele leaders in 1896 and the very embodiment of Matabele tradition. In later years, when leadership had largely passed to town-based associations like the Matabele Home Society, the campaign remained closely associated with a desire to defend the Matabele 'way of life'; with expressions of regret at the blurring of caste distinctions, the invasion of the towns by 'foreign' Africans,

[1] A. J. B. Hughes, *Kin, Caste and Nation Among the Rhodesian Ndebele*, Rhodes-Livingstone Paper 25, 1956, pp. 65–6. An extended treatment of the topics raised in Hughes' paper is contained in his 'The Reconstruction of the Ndebele Society under European Control', a draft thesis of which a copy may be found in the Rhodes-Livingstone Institute Library, Lusaka.

the alleged immorality of Matabele women in marrying these foreigners, and so on.[1]

But such expressions of regret were not, of course, incompatible with acceptance or exploitation of the new opportunities of the towns and of education. And the agitation for particular candidates for the Matabele kingship was supported by representatives of the new elements in Matabele society from the beginning; by the school teachers, the clerks, the pastors. It was even supported at various times by 'foreign' Africans themselves. Such support was made easier because the Matabele kingship, unlike Mashona religious institutions, was essentially of a kind which could be detached from the support of traditional and ritual sanction and make alliance with new forces, this being precisely what it had done in the past; and also because the recognized heirs of Lobengula were themselves the most highly educated and 'westernized' of all Matabele in the early 20th century.

Njube, the generally accepted heir, was a student at the premier South African secondary school for Africans. His brother, Nguboyena, was even more academically gifted—indeed, he nearly came to combine in his own person that alliance between traditional royalty and new legal skills which Miss Benson has shown operating in early South African politics. His tutors reported that his work was 'quite up to European standards' and that he was 'essentially a student'; they thought him 'well worth sending to the university'. In 1908 Nguboyena began to prepare for the English Bar, much to the alarm of the British South Africa Company which did not like the prospect of Lobengula's son becoming the first African advocate. 'I explained to him that in the very distant future it might be possible for members of the coloured races to take up the learned professions', wrote the Secretary of the Company's London Office, 'but that at present he must take the word of those wiser and more experienced than himself that it could not be'. In the end Nguboyena became a victim of the transition from one world to another, withdrew

[1] The atmosphere of these urban associations comes out clearly from the following files on the Loyal Mandabele Society and the Matebele Home Society; N 3/21/1, S 84/A/261 and 262. These and subsequent references to documentary sources refer to public records located in the National Archives, Salisbury.

from his law course and relapsed into sullen insanity under guard in Cape Town. But the potentialities of his career demonstrate something of the possibilities of the Lobengula family's claim to the kingship as a focus of Matabele politics.[1]

In the case of both Njube and Nguboyena we can see the mixture of old and new in their support. When Njube was allowed to visit Bulawayo in 1900 old Umlugulu was the first to come to do him honour, but the visit had been arranged by young men who had come down to Cape Town to arrange matters and been in touch with Matabele migrant labour there. If the analysis of the Native Department was correct, Njube's support was derived from one section of the Matabele people.

They are divided as far as their own 'internal affairs' are concerned. A very large section would view with grave concern the return to the country of the late Lobengula's son. . . . They have accepted their position and recognize that under this administration they have absolute security of property, *irrespective of status*, which was not the case during the régime of Lobengula. There is, however, a certain section of the Matabele who . . . do not favour the policy of 'equal rights' for all natives in so far as the acquisition of wealth in the form of cattle is concerned. It is this particular section who keep in constant communication with Njube and who advocate his return.

In 1904 when Njube was refused permission to make another visit to Bulawayo, it was said that his supporters were 'those who rebelled in 1896 . . . while the "loyal" portion of the nation does not desire his return'. Whether these analyses were true or not, Njube's support was certainly not derived exclusively from the traditional as distinct from the modern. In 1905, for instance, he applied for and was given permission 'for Natives of known good character . . . to collect money on his behalf'; this collection was organized by educated Matabele living in Bulawayo. Njube's protest against his continued exclusion from Rhodesia, made in November 1909, is in some ways the earliest document of modern political agitation in Southern Rhodesia. 'I observe from reports of His Excellency's speech in Rhodesia', he wrote to the High Commissioner's secretary, 'that I am not to be allowed to return to my own country. What the cause of this decision may be I know

[1] Nguboyena's story can be found in A 11/2/12/8; A 3/18/2.

not and can only assume it is a fresh "colour bar" on the eve of Union. I am a peaceable man', he continued, 'who has done no harm to my King or my country yet I am hounded from my own home while members of parliament in England, like Mr. Victor Grayson and Mr Keir Hardie, Mr Lloyd George and Mr Winston Churchill, all publicly avowed anti-Monarchists and consequently, I assume, rebels are permitted to continue their propaganda unmolested.' 'This letter', minuted the High Commissioner, 'will require to be carefully answered.' [1]

The same sort of picture emerges from Nguboyena's visit to Bulawayo in 1908. This was greeted by the chief *indunas*—'We rejoice greatly that the child has come back to the country to settle . . . and that his bones will eventually be left here'—but also by another element. 'Nguboyena does undoubtedly receive sympathy from the educated natives (Matabele and others) in Bulawayo', wrote the Chief Native Commissioner, 'and it is from this direction that he is likely to obtain support in the event of his wishing to give trouble.' The Chief Native Commissioner was dismayed by the uses to which Nguboyena appeared to be putting his English education and his English contacts. 'Nguboyena is an extremely intelligent youth', he wrote, 'He is at present studying the conditions of native life in this country, and has asked for varied information regarding the Native Reserves, the terms on which the natives reside thereon and has applied for a map showing the Reserves . . . He has shown an inclination to act independently of my wishes, his object being apparently to provoke the Government into taking steps which might be misunderstood by his "friends" in England, and gain him the sympathy of the natives here.' [2]

It is interesting to speculate what might have occurred, and how far the growth of modern political methods in Matabeleland might have been accelerated, if Njube and Nguboyena—with their education, their friends in England, their interest in the explosive land issue—had survived as effective influences into the period of real Matabele discontent which we shall survey later.

[1] For Njube see A 3/18/1; LO 5/7/2 and 4; LO 5/5/29; AM 2/1/7.
[2] C.N.C. to Secretary, Administrator, 9, 16 September, 10 November 1908; A 11/2/12/8.

In fact the influence of both was soon removed. Njube died in 1910; Nguboyena withdrew into his sullen silence in the same year, and although his partisans later aspired to cure him of his melancholy, he was never again a serious candidate for the kingship or for Matabele leadership. Neither had done more than to indicate the possibilities. The Administration drew a breath of relief. 'Through his death', wrote the Chief Native Commissioner about Njube in 1910, 'the natives realize that the last connecting link with the royal house of Kumalo has been severed.' The agitation for the revival of the kingship would now, he thought, die down.[1]

This was not an unreasonable assumption. There was no longer any obvious candidate for the position of Lobengula's heir. Njube's sons, Rhodes and Albert, were theoretically disqualified because their mother had been a Fingo woman, married without the approval of the Matabele *indunas*. Lobengula's eldest son, Nyamanda, who was a salaried *induna* in Matabeleland and who after 1910 began to put forward claims to the kingship, was theoretically disqualified because he had been born before Lobengula himself became king. The Chief Native Commissioner kept on insisting that under these circumstances the Matabele would never recognize any of them as heirs; but the Matabele, in need of leadership, refused to behave as he expected. There were parties who supported Nyamanda; there were parties who supported Rhodes and Albert. And because of various changes in the situation in Matabeleland and outside it these doubtful heirs became the focus of movements of opposition much more organized and formidable that those which had been grouped around Njube and Nguboyena.[2]

The first change—or rather development—which we must notice was the increasing dissatisfaction of the Matabele generally with the land settlement in Matabeleland. The best account of Matabele grievances concerning land is that given by the Superintendent of Natives, Bulawayo, in a letter of June 1920, when Nyamanda's campaign was at its height.

The formerly dominant tribe of this Territory, through whom the

[1] C.N.C.'s Annual Report, 1910.
[2] C.N.C. to Secretary, Administrator, 20 October 1910; A 3/18/2.

first titles to the Territory were secured by whites, [he wrote] are, of all tribes, now in the worst position in respect of land. . . . It is an unfortunate fact that the premier native race whose organizing power and gift for government enabled them to impose their will on the minor tribes, and whose inherent character must inevitably establish their major influence for good or bad in the future development and happiness of our natives, should now suffer from an ever-increasing sense of dissatisfaction with the provision made for them in this regard. Their misfortune was in the first place their national predilection for the red and black loams . . . within a few months of the European occupation practically the whole of their most valued region ceased to be their patrimony and passed into the private estate of individuals and the commercial property of companies. The whole of what the term '*nga pakati kew lizwe*' (the midst of the land) conveyed became metamorphosed, although they did not early realize it, into alien soil, and passed out of the direct control even of the Government. (Not so the tribes of Mashonaland who were for the most part left in uncoveted possession of the granite soil preferred by them to all other.) In the native concept Government and Ownership of land are indivisible. That land on which people live, and have lived for generations, can be purchased for money is a matter hard to be understood. White men of varied origin and race become in a day their landlords, their over-lords, with power to dispossess and drive forth. To an aristocratic race the delegation of such power has appeared unseemly in many cases. The word '*amaplazi*' . . . meaning 'farms', stands, it may be said, for all that is most distasteful in our rule. Almost it stands for helotage and servitude to a chance-made master.

The superintendent went on to show that the Reserves in Matabeleland did not offer an adequate answer to the problem and asserted that 'well founded and growing discontent by an important section of the community cannot justly or safely be ignored'. 'We have already seen attempts by agitators to make the natives discontented with their lot', he concluded. 'It can be forseen that as the land difficulty becomes more acute Nyamanda's policy of constantly harping upon it is certain to augment his following with the effect of consolidating native opinion in an undesirable manner.'[1]

Although, as the Superintendent of Natives said, 'the harm had

[1] S/N, Bulawayo, to C.N.C., 1 June 1920; N 3/16/9.

been done . . . within a short while after the occupation', realization of what was involved came to the Matabele only gradually, as owners of farms began to clear and develop them, as rents were demanded and as Matabele communities were forcibly ejected from private land. By the outbreak of the First World War, however, the Matabele generally felt an acute sense of grievance over the land question. By that time, also, another significant, though very much smaller, group of Africans had come to feel an equal sense of grievance over another aspect of land policy—the practical denial of the theoretical right of Africans to buy land anywhere outside the Reserves. The idea of buying land occurred to some of the wealthier Matabele, Nyamanda among them, as a way out of their difficulties with private land-owners. It also occurred to various native immigrants of South African origin, and especially to the Fingo community, who wished to consolidate their 'progressive' status by the achievement of individual title to land. The rejection by the administration of both groups as acceptable land purchasers served to throw them together, with important political results.

The Fingo community in Rhodesia, though small, came to play, as we shall see, a leading role in the development of 'modern' political tactics in that country. Articulate and educated, it formed a small African 'middle class', though at first, one which was very conscious of its difference from and superiority to the Matabele. In 1909, for instance, the Fingo community petitioned the High Commissioner for exemption from the pass laws, for permission to carry guns, and other privileges. They expressed themselves as astonished by the disrespect with which the Matabele had treated the High Commissioner and by Matabele recalcitrance generally. 'We Fingoes are not in the same spirit as them', the petition continued. 'The Fingoes are in very small number in this country and also are unfriendly to the people of the country although they have never been in quarrel with us. Our only friend is the British Government who kept our grand-fathers and now is still looking upon us, and he serves us with his good hands and his mouth is full of love to his children under his power.'[1]

The Fingos did not get special concessions. 'The Fingos should

[1] Fingo petition, 3 December 1909; A 3/18/1.

remember', ran the reply, 'that they have been under civilized rule for a very much longer period than the Matabele and it is consequently their duty to show that they have benefitted thereby, by adopting an amicable demeanour towards those who have not enjoyed the same advantage.' The same refusal met all other Fingo attempts to stabilize and develop their 'middle class' status. The history of the development of Government attitudes towards native land purchase, for instance, could be written in terms of Fingo applications for land and their refusal from the first application of the Fingo minister, John N'Gono, in 1904 onwards. In 1904 when N'Gono's application was turned down, the Chief Native Commissioner minuted that it was 'a matter of paramount importance to prevent these people from contaminating the indigenous population with that spirit of vain-glorious truculence to which some of them are prone, being carried away by the spectacle of their own slight accomplishments in the first acquisition of civilization.' By the late 1910's, the Fingo community, and especially its most prosperous families like the Hlazos and the Sojinis, were becoming so discontented with Government refusal to lease or sell land, that they turned to the Matabele leadership rather than to the British Government and began to 'contaminate' the indigenous population with their own sophisticated ideas of political pressures and tactics. And not the least important aspect of this alliance between an alien 'middle class' group and the Lobengula party was the fact of contact between the Fingos and African political leadership in the Union of South Africa.[1]

In addition to the increasing Matabele resentment over land and the stimulus of the Fingo alliance, we should note that by the late 1910's some sort of indigenous 'middle class' had also grown up. We shall see members of this new grouping—teachers, clerks, ministers—participating in the movements described below.

In the decade that followed Njube's death and Nguboyena's illness, then, a situation developed which offered considerable potential for the creation of a widespread movement of political opposition in Matabeleland. In 1918 Lobengula's eldest son,

[1] C.N.C. to Chief Secretary, Salisbury, 26 October 1904; A 3/18/24. John N'Gono's application and correspondence relating to it is in L 2/1/175; Garner Sojini's application is in N 3/10/5. See also N 3/7/2/; A 3/18/24.

Nyamanda, put himself forward as leader of such a movement and as claimant to the Matabele kingship. In many ways it was surprising that Nyamanda should have been the man to head the first considerable 'modern' African political movement in Southern Rhodesia. His young nephews, Albert and Rhodes, who were students at Lovedale College and competing with the sons of other chiefs for places in the school cricket eleven, might have seemed much more part of the new world than Nyamanda, who had taken an active part in the rebellion and been included in the administration's list of proscribed ring-leaders. But Nyamanda turned out to be a not unsuitable leader for the sort of movement which developed. Precisely because of his past experience he was better able to speak to the Matabele *indunas* and their people than his nephews could have been—'It is a shocking shame to realize', wrote young Rhodes, 'that since we were born we never saw our home'. Nyamanda, moreover, felt the general Matabele grievance over land with a personal sharpness. He had occupied land on a farm in the Insiza area; had moved from there when the owner began to develop it; had then settled in the Bubi area and been told 'to remove by the Company owning the land'. But while he could speak to the Matabele mass from out of their common experience, Nyamanda was not altogether isolated from new men and new forces. He was on friendly terms, for instance, with the Reverend D. P. Maghatho, leader of the Ethiopian movement in Southern Rhodesia, and sent his son to an Ethiopian school in South Africa recommended by Maghatho. He was also acquainted with the Fingo leaders. Let us see how all these elements worked out.[1]

It was the land grievance that first turned Nyamanda to 'political' activity. From the first to the last he was motivated by a sense of personal resentment, which gradually broadened out into a sense of the wrongs of the Matabele as a whole. In 1915, for instance, he expressed his feelings in a way hardly calculated to appeal very widely. 'I see my father's dogs in enjoyment of his herds of cattle', he complained, 'while I have nothing.' Later he told a Native Commissioner that he would never have commenced agitation or allied himself to foreigners had it not been

[1] For Albert and Rhodes see N 3/19/1. For Nyamanda's land see A 3/18/10; A 3/18/18/6.

for his treatment over land. 'He said that being landless and at the
mercy of any purchaser of land was a different position and a
bitter pill for a man of his standing to swallow and that he felt
that the Government had no sympathy or regard for his difficulties or troubles.' But gradually he came to see the problem as
one affecting the Matabele people generally and by 1919 he was
acting as their spokesman. 'They made it clear', wrote the Superintendent of Natives, Bulawayo, about Nyamanda and his uncle,
Joyi, 'that they consider themselves entitled to voice the desires of
the tribe. They base their claim on the fact that Nyamanda is the
son of the late Lobengula.' In this role as spokesman for the nation,
Nyamanda put forward a demand for a consolidated Matabele
National Home. 'All we want is for the Government to say "This
is a tract of land for Lobengula's people".' The land he asked for
ran 'from Thabas Induna to Mwala Kopjes, thence to Passe
Passe, thence to the Magokweni Drift on the Khami River, thence
down the railway line, including all land watered by the rivers
flowing into the Zambesi'. 'I know that some of the land within
these boundaries is already occupied', he told the Chief Native
Commissioner in 1920. 'It is for Your Honour to decide how I am
to acquire it. We will find the money.' Nyamanda's policy was
summed up by a Native Commissioner: 'I think he simply feels
that all the best land in the country has been taken by the whites
and they have none to themselves. He dreams of segregation
of the natives—with local option—or perhaps even Responsible
Government!'[1]

Nyamanda's stand on this issue enjoyed wide support from the
old men of influence among the Matabele.'We are all contributing
to the purchase of land', said his uncle Joyi. 'The whole nation is
doing it; it is not Nyamanda only.' 'We as earnestly desire this
tract of land as our nephew Nyamanda', said his uncle Bidi. 'We
don't want to be always troubling the Government; we are being
chased from farm to farm.' In addition to this support from members of the Lobengula family, Nyamanda canvassed other powerful
indunas in 1919. 'I write this paper of mine to you, all Chiefs of

[1] Interview between Nyamanda and Administrator, 11 October 1915; N.C.
Inyati to S/N/Byo., 16 March 1920; S/N Byo. to C.N.C., 21 April 1920;
A 3/18/18/6.

the Regiments', runs one of his letters. 'I say to you, all nations that have been conquered by the English, the Government gave them Chiefs to whom they pay their tax. Look at Khama! He has his country, and Lewanika, he has his plot. His country is settled well, and Mosheshe he has his land. Also the son of Dinizula has his country. All natives have their bit of ground where they pay their taxes. They pay taxes they know and are not like you who pay for what you know not. You do not know what is done with your money. It is like money that is lost because you pay so greatly and do not know what your money does. At the same time you undergo tribulation.' 'I want to hear your word', ran another. 'We remain in a scattered state all the time. Even if people have been conquered may they not abide in one place? For myself I ask of you, ye owners of the territory, inasmuch as you are the nation. I do not say it is war, my compatriots, I only inquire. You also know that all black tribes in great numbers were over come by white people, but they have their piece of land to stay on happily. We, forsooth, pay only for staying on white men's farms, and for what reason?' These letters to the *indunas* achieved a much wider response that the administration at first imagined or cared to admit.[1]

But Nyamanda's campaign, as well as appealing to all the traditional elements of the Matabele nation, was essentially modern in concept. The *indunas* were not being called to war but to contribute money to pay Nyamanda's expenses 'so that I can essay across the Ocean and go to the King over the Water in England and go and talk with the Big King George. I say to you, O People! A child who does not cry out dies at labour.' Nor, when the child cried out, was it in the homely imagery of Nyamanda's letters to the *indunas*. The various petitions produced during the campaign were, on the contrary, the fruit of considerable political sophistication and a wide knowledge of developments in South Africa.[2]

It is time to turn to Nyamanda's contacts with the Fingos, with the urban Matabele, and with the leaders of the South African

[1] Interview between Nyamanda and C.N.C., 9 April 1920; A 3/18/10; Nyamanda's letters are translated in A 3/18/18/6; N 3/19/4.
[2] Nyamanda's letter, 10 August 1919; N 3/19/4.

National Congress. Before we do so, however, we must note that the first recruitment of South African politicians to further a Rhodesian cause was made not by Nyamanda but by European missionaries. In 1914, when the Privy Council began its hearings of the case concerning the ownership of land in Southern Rhodesia, the Reverend A. S. Cripps and other missionaries, in conjunction with the Aborigines Protection Society, were anxious to have legal representation on behalf of the Africans of the Colony. They therefore turned to a delegation of the South African Native National Congress, who were in Britain to protest against the Native Lands Act of 1913. In April 1914 these South African leaders joined with the missionaries in a petition to the Privy Council setting out the claim of Rhodesian Africans to ownership of the land. The African signatories of the petition were the Reverend John Langalibalele Dube, President of the South African Native National Congress; Reverend Walter Rubusana, Sol Plaatje, and other leading Congress members; and Saul Msane, the editor of the Congress newspaper, *Abantu-Batho*, and described in the petition as 'a nephew of a former Queen of the Matabele'. Dube, so the authorities were informed, intended to visit Rhodesia with the intention of commencing 'enquiries among the natives of Southern Rhodesia in order to ascertain whether any of them wish to prefer a claim to the unalienated land on behalf of the natives, in their collective or tribal capacity, or even to ascertain whether any of the natives, who from their position as *indunas* of the late Lobengula or otherwise can be regarded as representative of the natives of the territory can be persuaded to take such action.' Dube was not allowed to enter Rhodesia, but this petition was clearly the fore-runner of the co-operation between Nyamanda and leading members of the South African Native National Congress which is described below.[1]

This co-operation began in 1918. In that year the Hlazo and Sojini families called Alfred Mangena up from Johannesburg to help them set out their case on land. Mangena was the first African barrister to practise in South Africa and had run offices in Johannesburg and Pretoria since 1909; he had also been one of

[1] Petition of 17 April 1914; Assistant Secretary, B.S.A. Co., London, to Under Secretary of State, Colonial Office, 12 August 1914; N 3/16/3.

the conveners of the inaugural meeting of the South African Native National Congress in 1912. In 1918 he did not hold any leading Congress office but he was still in touch with the movement. When he arrived in Rhodesia, his Fingo clients suggested that he approach the Lobengula family with offers of assistance, and he was ready enough to do so. 'I have visited the royal family of Lobengula', he wrote to Jeremia Hlazo in September 1918. 'I saw Nyamanda, who received me with open arms.' Nyamanda himself later described how 'the Fingos had approached him and told him that they were in a position to make representations that would lead to the country being divided between himself, as representing the Matabele nation, and the white inhabitants of the country'. But before any course of action could be arranged, the Rhodesian authorities became alarmed at Mangena's activity among the Matabele and deported him.[1]

This was not the end of the new alliance, however. Mangena deputed Nyamanda's legal representation to his friend, Richard Msimang. Msimang was the son of the founder of the Independent Methodist Church of South Africa, had qualified as a solicitor in England, and was another of the conveners of the inaugural meeting of Congress. He had been appointed chairman of the committee set up to draft the constitution of Congress, and was admirably qualified to act as Nyamanda's constitutional adviser. Mangena also recruited the Congress chaplain, Rev. H. C. Ngcayaya, leader of the Ethiopian Church of South Africa. Ngcayaya was a suitable person to represent Nyamanda's interests for two reasons. In the first place he was in contact with ministers of the Ethiopian Church in Southern Rhodesia, particularly with Nyamanda's friend, Maghatho, and with Reverend Radasi of Bembesi, who was an ally of the Fingo leaders. His visit to Rhodesia in February 1919 was made ostensibly to visit these men. But Ngcayaya had also been chosen to go to Europe as one of the Congress deputation to Versailles and London. While there he would be able to present a petition on behalf of Nyamanda, the Lobengula family and the Matabele people.[2]

[1] Mangena to Hlazo, 12 September 1918; N 3/19/4; N.C. Inyati to S/N/Bulawayo, 16 March 1920; A 3/18/18/6.
[2] For Mangena, Msimang and Ngcayaya, see Benson, *op. cit.*

On 10 March 1919 a number of men met at the house of a Matabele Wesleyan catechist in Bulawayo. They were Nyamanda and his Matabele allies, Joyi and Madhloli; the Fingo John Hlazo; and Rev. Ngcayaya. Reverend Ngcayaya presented to the meeting the form of a petition, which he had very probably brought with him ready drawn from South Africa. Nyamanda and his associates approved and signed the petition; Ngcayaya hurriedly left Bulawayo and carried it back to South Africa. On 19 March he and other members of his church, together with Stephen Hlazo, waited on the High Commissioner in Cape Town to give notice that he 'would be leaving for England with the native deputation from the Union in the course of the next two days.' A copy of the petition was presented to the High Commissioner; the original was taken to England.[1]

This petition of 10 March 1919 is a document of very considerable interest to the historian of African politics in Southern Rhodesia. It was addressed to the king in the name of the Lobengula family and of 'the President, Ministers, Members and Adherences of the Ethiopian Church of South Africa, representing over twenty thousand members and adherences in South Africa . . . the aboriginal inhabitants'. It was an informed and pertinent document; however little Southern Rhodesian Africans were responsible for its drafting it stated the essentials of their position with clarity and accuracy. Its theme was two-fold. It referred to the agitation among the whites of Southern Rhodesia for Responsible Government and asked that there be instead direct Imperial control of African affairs. It referred also to the recent Privy Council decision on the ownership of land and asked that Britain use her newly acquired powers of ownership for the benefit of the African people.

Referring to Native laws and treatment, [the petition ran], Your Petitioners have experienced with great regret that High Commissioners and Governors General, who are the true representatives of Your Majesty, have merely acted as disinterested spectators whilst Responsible Government parties of various names and associations are interpreting the Laws in class legislation to suit their purpose. Your

[1] S/N, Bulawayo, minute of 1 April 1919; A 3/18/18/6.

Petitioners pray that in case Rhodesia is granted any form of Government the Imperial Government take over the Administration of Native Affairs in that Country in the same manner as is the case with regard to British Basutoland, British Bechuanaland and Swaziland. Your Petitioners are further aware that the Judicial Committee of Your Majesty's Privy Council has found that the so-called unalienated land belongs to the Crown by reason of an alleged right of conquest and the de-thronement of the late King Lobengula. The right of justification of that alleged conquest Your Petitioners do not seek to discuss here; but in the interest of right and justice, and in pursuance of the fact that the right of conquest . . . is now repudiated by the civilized world, Your Petitioners pray that Your Majesty be pleased to hand back the so-called unalienated land to the family of the late King Lobengula in trust for the tribe according to Bantu custom, and the right of chieftainship therein to be restored and acknowledged.[1]

In London Ngcayaya was received by Amery at the Colonial Office and lobbied Lloyd George—'You have the sympathy of your nation, the Welsh people.' The petition was published in the English press and a certain amount of sympathy achieved. In Rhodesia meanwhile Msimang had gone up to advise Nyamanda in the further pressing of his case; funds were being collected to send him to England to make a personal appeal to the King; and support was being shown by both Matabele *indunas* and by the new educated. The character of Nyamanda's Rhodesian support was fairly, though somewhat feverishly, indicated by a European farmer who informed the authorities that Nyamanda and Madhloli were planning 'a black king and presumably a blacker kingdom'; that they were proposing to call out the regiments and march on Bulawayo; and that a local Matabele school-teacher and preacher was calling for 'Africa for the black' and announcing that 'we should have our own king from our own people, and our own laws'.[2]

It would be tedious to trace in detail the course of the campaign during the next two years. It attained another petitionary highpoint in August 1921 in an appeal to the High Commissioner. 'We learn', said the petitioners, 'that a welcome change of Government in this Territory of Southern Rhodesia is about to take

---

[1] Petition to the King, 10 March 1919; A 3/18/18/6.
[2] Wallston to the High Commissioner, 16 October 1921; A 3/18/11.

place and in regard thereto we would most respectfully request Your Royal Highness as High Commissioner to make representations on our behalf to His Majesty's Government, that the Natives of the country be given an opportunity to express their wishes in the Rights and forms of Government they would prefer and on the Safe Guards that might be made in their welfare and protection.'[1]

But, needless to say, the campaign failed either to achieve a Matabele National Home and the revival of the kingship or to avert Responsible Government in Southern Rhodesia. The South African Native National Congress could no more save Rhodesian Africans than it had been able to save itself from being handed over to local white rule. The Colonial Office was polite but firm; the Rhodesian administration was firm and not particularly polite in calling to account those *indunas* who had shown support for Nyamanda. Funds dried up; Msimang's bill remained unpaid; Reverend Ngcayaya found himself stranded in London and dependent upon the charity of the British South Africa Company for a passage home. The alliance of the Lobengula family and South African politicians ended with some recriminations on both sides.

With the failure of Nyamanda's campaign and the establishment of Responsible Government in 1923, a new era opened for the infant African politics of Southern Rhodesia. The tactics of direct appeal to London had failed; there no longer seemed much point in making demands which whites on the spot would clearly never grant. As a philosopher of the change, Abraham Twala put it: 'Experience has taught us that our salvation does not lie in Downing Street. I strongly advise our native fledglings in Southern Rhodesia, indulging in politics, to find out and make their friends in Southern Rhodesia. When this has been done we shall see what the harvest shall be.' Since the problem of the ownership of land was now clearly a closed issue, there were no further appeals for the grant of land to the Lobengula family as of right— the attempt was rather to persuade the new Government to agree to a just Native Purchase policy. Since it was clear that there was no possibility of the new régime agreeing to the restoration of the

[1] Petition to the High Commissioner, 13 August 1921; A 3/18/10.

Matabele kingship, at any rate in the context of a sort of Matabele
Bantustan, this issue ceased to be central to Rhodesian African
politics, though it remained of great importance to those who
were essentially Matabele patriots. In other words African politics entered a period in which the alleged rights of the Lobengula
family were no longer useful and in which the claims of that
family could no longer play the same nuclear role.[1]

From this time on it would be possible to distinguish a division
between the Matabele patriotic associations which were exclusively concerned with the restoration of the kingship and the safeguarding of the Matabele way of life, and the new political associations which sprang up, largely under Fingo leadership, to meet
the new conditions. Nevertheless, it would be a mistake to make
too sharp a distinction. Nyamanda was no longer the leading
figure—but his support for the new associations was valuable to
them. The creation of a Matabele National Home was no longer
in the foreground, but the land hunger of Matabele *indunas* still
provided the new movements with something of their dynamism.
Thus Nyamanda attended a meeting of the Rhodesian Bantu
Voters' Association in July 1924 and 'extended his sympathy to
the Association', which was headed by his old ally, Garner Sojini.
Later both he and Madhloli became paid-up members. Thus the
militant Southern Rhodesian Native Welfare Association, which
flourished in the Gwelo district, attracted the support of many
Matabele *indunas*, especially the 'young chiefs who have attained
to some degree of education'. One such young chief was Gwebu,
induna of Inyati, who was for a time president of the Association;
'he has a small smattering of education and worked in Cape Town
for some time before his appointment as chief was made', wrote
the Chief Native Commissioner. 'I think there are some grounds
for suspecting that while in Cape Town he came under the influence of the I.C.U.'[2]

Indeed, though they were different in many ways from the
loose coalition of interests which had gathered around Nyamanda

[1] Letter from Abraham Twala, 31 March 1922, *Rhodesia Herald*.
[2] For the Rhodesian Bantu Voters' Association see S 84/A/260; S 84/A/300;
S 84/A/261. For the Southern Rhodesian Native Welfare Association see
S 84/A/260 and 261.

in 1919 it is not unreasonable to claim that these new associations owed a good deal to the experience of that earlier attempt at political pressure. Many of the same men were involved, for instance; the Hlazos and the Sojinis; old Rev. D. P. Maghatho's son, Zacharia, who became Treasurer of the Rhodesian Bantu Voters' Association and a member of the Southern Rhodesian Native Welfare Association Executive. These new associations were also based almost exclusively in Matabeleland; in this, too, they were the heirs of the kingship agitation. And when, with the passing of the Land Apportionment Act in 1930, the failure of the new policy was as clearly apparent as the failure of the old, they reverted to something essentially similar to Nyamanda's position. These new associations had hoped, by mobilizing African voters, by making African views articulate to whites of good will, by working with such bodies as the Southern Rhodesian Missionary Conference, to persuade the new Government to make a generous settlement of the land question. The leaders of the new associations were primarily interested in the question of land purchase; but the interests of their followers drove them also to demand the creation of new reserves. They greeted the news of the appointment of the Carter Commission of Inquiry into Native Land Purchase with great satisfaction; some of them, indeed, claiming that it had been appointed due to their pressure. But the recommendations of the Commission, and the Act of 1930, seemed to them to be grossly inadequate; it was not the principle of partition to which they objected but the amount allocated to the African people.

In July 1929, while the Land Apportionment Act was before the Assembly, a general meeting of these new associations was called in Bulawayo. It expressed its complete rejection of the Bill and spoke instead for something like Nyamanda's old policy of 'segregation of the natives—with local option'.

'You all know', said Wesley Sojini, for the Rhodesian Bantu Voters' Association, 'that from 1925 it was suggested that the land be proportioned into land for the black man and land for the white man . . . This Bill does not show any security for the native land. This is against our evidence. The evidence given by the natives was that the land should be halved; the black man to have one half and the white man the other half.' 'Let us tell the Government that this Bill is wrong', said Masola, on behalf of the Industrial and Commercial Workers' Union. 'The Bill is no good. It is all for the white man. Rhodesia is big. Let them cut the land in half and let us live on one side and the white man on the other.'[1]

So politically concious Rhodesian Africans entered the 1930's in a state of disillusionment and bewilderment. Many different political expedients lay ahead. Nor was the Matabele kingship movement dead. But from this time onwards it became less and less important both as a part of African politics generally and as a focus for the aspirations of the Matabele. Even in its hey-day, which I have attempted to describe in this chapter, the kingship movement never had any chance of success. 'Our steadfast policy has been', wrote the Chief Native Commissioner in 1929, 'to oppose the building up of a unity among the Matabele which would have been a danger; the policy of *divide et impera* was, in effect, adopted; and because of our more or less direst rule and scattered Reserves, we were able to avoid the evils which followed the Zulu-land settlement.' The administration never had any intention of restoring the kingship; no claimant ever succeeded in mobilizing behind him the whole force of Matabele opinion. But despite this, the kingship movement did play a significant role in the emergence of African politics in Southern Rhodesia, as I hope this chapter has shown.[2]

Note: In a study of this sort reference should probably be made to the founder of the first Congress movement for Rhodesia, even although it was not a success. The man concerned was a Matabele migrant, living in Johannesburg, the Rev. P. S. Ngwenya. Ngwenya had learnt his politics in the Zulu independency movement. He first founded his own church, the African Mission Home Church, which had ministers at work in Rhodesia in 1914. He then founded the Matabele Rhodesian Society, to act as a focal point for Matabele exiles in South Africa. Finally, in 1919, he founded the Rhodesian Native National Congress. In a manifesto

[1] Speeches by Sojini and Masola, reported by Detective Inspector Watt, 14 July 1929; S 84/A/261.
[2] C.N.C. to Minister for Native Affairs, 18 November 1929; S 84/A/262.

issued in that year he called upon all black Rhodesians to send delegates and funds to Johannesburg. 'From 1893 until 1919 the Government has been bad towards the brown man of Rhodesia,' ran his manifesto. 'Even if I had killed a man, after such a lapse of time I would be forgiven for having done so. If I have not been forgiven what am I to do? It is good that you should contribute money and ask others to do so, money being a sword and buckler, for without money you can do nothing and you cannot open your mouth. You chiefs, too, of Rhodesia, listen to this word which is spoken, our chiefs. Help us and we will fight for you. Contribute money so that we can speak to the Rhodesian Government as to the rule under which we are ruled. It is right that you should help us, your people, in this thing we want to do.' The time was certainly not ripe for Matabele chiefs to accept the leadership of an exile like Ngwenya—even though, as we have seen, it was ripe for Matabele 'royals' to accept the help of men of his sort. Ngwenya's project gained no support. But he may stand as an excellent example of the 'modern' Matabele. (N 3/5/8; N 3/5/3.)

PART TWO

NORTHERN ZAMBESIA

8

TOWARDS A HISTORY OF THE BEMBA FROM ORAL TRADITION[1]

by

ANN TWEEDIE

BEMBA history is still by no means complete, partly because oral tradition has not yet been fully collected and partly because oral tradition appears not to be satisfactory for some periods.[1] Assuming that the band of immigrants from Luba who became the Bemba royal clan arrived on the banks of the Kalungu in what is now central Lubemba at the end of the 17th or very beginning of the 18th century,[2] the history of the Bemba area may be divided as follows: the period before the arrival of the immigrants from Luba; the period *c.* 1680 or 1700 to *c.* 1770 during which the immigrants established themselves over the central area of Chitimukulu, Mwamba, Nkolemfumu, Nkweto and Nkula; the period *c.* 1770–*c.* 1850 during which further expansion took place and the first chieftainship of 'sons of chiefs', the Makasaship, was established; and the period *c.* 1850–1898,[3] when the Bemba area was enormously extended to north, south, east and west, many new chieftainships were established, the power of the chiefs was entrenched by their trade in ivory and slaves for guns and cloth with the Arabs, and the Bemba were welded into a unity by the wars against the Ngoni. Towards the end of the period this unity seems to have diminished, though raiding activities were intensified, with finally, at the greatest

---

[1] The work for this chapter was done while the author was in receipt of a grant from the Colonial Social Science Research Council, for which assistance she is grateful.
[2] See discussion of dates below.
[3] 1850 (following Brelsford) is taken somewhat arbitrarily to indicate the date that Chileshe Chepela usurped the throne. This is not a firm date, and some of the evidence suggests that he became Chitimukulu considerably earlier.

extent of their territory, the Bemba submitted to the rule of the British South Africa Company.

The sources of oral traditions

As might be expected, the quantity and quality of oral tradition for these periods vary. The account of the last period is the most full and detailed, that of the first two very scant. Oral tradition also includes another 'period'—the departure of the royal clan with their followers from Luba, and their journey to the Bemba area—which is fairly full, although the accounts of the journey are not always consistent with each other.

There are at present both primary and secondary sources of oral tradition which are now considered in turn.[1]

Amongst primary sources there are, first, the living representatives of historic or ancient titles.[2] Most of these are headmen, though some are not. They, together with other senior members of their families—or in the case of chiefs, their councillors—are the keepers of the traditions with regard to their titles. There are many such titles going back to the time of the immigration from Luba, some go back even earlier. The types of traditions vary with the age and type of title: the title may be of a *kabilo* (councillor), *shimapepo* (priest), *cingo* (burier of chief), *mushika* (captain), *shimwalule* (keeper of a burial grove), descendant of men who were formerly chiefs, or simply an ordinary headman. The *shimapepo*, besides the history of his own name and of his village and the area around can usually tell something of the *mipashi* (dead ancestors) to whom he prays; the keeper of a burial grove besides the history of his own family can usually name who has been buried in that grove; and so on. The villages of descendants of men who were formerly chiefs are of particular interest to the historian.

Besides those men and their families (for the most knowledgeable man is not always the holder of the title) who keep the traditions of their own titles and their own traditional duties, there are also a few men who by virtue of their position close to the

---

[1] See bibliography.
[2] Cf. I. G. Cunnison, *The Luapula Peoples* and *History on the Luapula*, where a similar system of succession to titles is described.

courts of chiefs, their interest in history, and their intelligence and memory, hold a position very like that of professional historian. Such positions are not hereditary but achieved (usually by a hereditary councillor) and there are very few such men indeed in the whole area. These men are the most authoritative keepers of the tradition of the chieftainships where they live.

It is not sufficient, however, simply to question such men on the history of their names, their duties and the chieftainship, but it is also necessary to employ the methods of historical geography. Many place-names are of historical significance, as are the names of the spirits in an area, and also there are many historical sites: of battles, of old chiefs' villages, of boundaries, of places where people died or are buried. Unless these are investigated important clues which could be obtained are very likely to be overlooked. It is as well to visit the sites concerned, especially in the case of important old villages, to see how big they are, whether they were ditched, etc.

Another source is the praise-names (*amalumbo*) of chiefs and others and the poems (*imishikakulo*) recited before chiefs. I believe that a careful collection and comparison of the praise-names of the Chitimukulus would considerably elucidate the history of the very obscure period from the settlement on the banks of the Kalungu to the end of the 18th century. These praise-names would have to be collected independently from the greatest number of authorities possible, in order to establish which phrases referred to which chief. Praise-names, though liable to mention certain qualities generally desired, do also usually enshrine some memorable incident or some outstanding characteristic in the life of the man praised. They also often mention the name(s) of his chief wife (wives). Even the collection of old songs may be of value: different informants differed for instance on whether the Chitimukulu whom Chileshe Chepela drove from the throne was Chinchinta or Susula, and whether these were the names of two distinct Chitimukulus, but an old song was quoted which mentions them as one and the same.

A further important source for Bemba history, which is not yet available to historians, is the contents of the relic-houses (*nganda ya babenye*.) In these are the relics of the chiefs: bows, stools, spears and other things, and while they would not contribute much to the post-1850 period, for the earlier periods they might well help to establish important points. It is not only Chitimukulu and other leading chiefs who have relic-houses, but also many *bakabilo* and descendants of men who were formerly chiefs. These relics, however, are not likely to be available for inspection. It is not the relics themselves that would in most cases be interesting, but the evidence they would give for the existence of particular chiefs. A knowledge of the organization of the priests and the relic-houses ritual at Chitimukulu would also throw light on historical matters.

A word needs to be said on Bemba attitudes to history. Chiefs vary very much in their knowledge of history. They are, of course, themselves in an excellent position to become specialist historians of the kind described above and there are some who might be so described. Many chiefs, however, have very little interest in or knowledge of historical matters. As for their subjects, they themselves make an important distinction between young and old. The old may or may not know but the young couldn't possibly. The answer to a question '*Tekuti njishibe pantu ndi mwaice kano fye abakalamba*' ('It is impossible that I should know as I am a young man: only older people could know') is only too familiar to the researcher from people of any age. If one further enquires as to who the *bakalamba* are, one is either given answers leading along the chain to the specialist historians or to the representatives of titles referred to above, or one is told that so and so (now deceased) really did know about the things of the past, but alas he is dead; indeed on consideration, all the *bakalamba* are dead: there are none left now ('*bakalamba bonse balifwa, tapaba nomba*')—another very familiar phrase. This sense of history dying with the bearers of it is very real, but accepted as inevitable. A living keeper of tradition rarely—with the exception of the very few specialist historians, some of whom are very widely known—seems to others or to himself to know anything at all, in comparison with the ones who have died. There does not seem to be a general interest in history (though the knowledge of a few events such as the coming from Luba is widespread), and the incidental historical discussions at chiefs' courts are 'occasional' rather than 'constant'.[1] Nevertheless certain historical events are enshrined in ritual and in 'perpetual behaviour' and the traditions connected with titles are kept by the holders of the titles. Part of the prestige of inheriting an important title lies in the knowledge, part of it often secret, that goes with it. Historical knowledge is not generally considered to be secret, but the incentive for its preservation is the prestige of the title. Thus the hierarchical nature of the society and the chieftainship which gives, through secular or ritual duties, so many of the holders of the titles their places in the hierarchy, helps to preserve history. Nevertheless, one has the strong impression that the Bemba are not as interested in their history as, for instance, the Lunda-Kazembe.

Here one should perhaps note that oral tradition, and especially the conflicts in oral tradition, do reflect aspects of the social structure. However, far from this being necessarily a disadvantage, or resulting in the historian's being perpetually faced with several different traditions between which he cannot choose, his knowledge of social organization should enable him to disentangle such conflicts: an example of this is my attempt below to sort out the conflicting traditions about the early Chitimukulus partly with the aid of traditions from titles other than those of the dominant lineage of chief.

Let us turn now to secondary sources of oral tradition. There are several published and unpublished recorded accounts of oral history. Although none of them give a full enough story, and they all contain inaccuracies at points, only from the few specialist historians would it be possible to get as coherent accounts of Bemba history as a whole. Two of these accounts, largely based on the same sources, have been published: *Ifyabukaya: Fourth Bemba Reader* (White Fathers, Chilubula, n.d. but in fact 1932) and Fr. F. Tanguy, *Imilandu ya BaBemba* (1946). These have been used as school readers for many years, and so any Bemba under the age of about forty-seven who has had some primary education may well have read then. The general Bemba history which such people know seems to be the version given in these books which have acquired a considerable authority although it is known that

[1] This differs from the position amongst the Lunda-Kazembe, and also possibly from the position as it used to be among the Bemba.

they are not entirely accurate. I do not think, however, that their inaccuracies or wrong emphases have yet corrupted the springs of the tradition. There are still specialist historians, such as Chief Mwamba, BaMilambo, and BaShiMulamba, who are old enough to have learnt entirely from oral souces, and even if later they might have got to know the contents of these books, they by then knew their own version too well to be affected. And the histories attached to the inheritance of titles are too particular to be corrupted by such books.

I myself have spent a total of about six weeks in field investigations into Bemba history.[1] This together with a study of already recorded oral tradition for the Bemba and surrounding tribes enables one to sort out to some extent the general pattern of Bemba history and to contribute here and there some new material, to see what the main problems yet to be solved are, and to be aware of the kind of investigations that could lead to the most definitive history possible from oral tradition, but it is not a long enough time to enable one to write such a history now.

The versions of Bemba history that the secondary sources give us are mainly those of the dominant group, and they tend to streamline the course of events and to skip lightly and in confusion over the period when this group was not perhaps so gloriously dominant. In the rest of this paper I shall examine what the available sources have to offer for each period, and shall show where further research could perhaps complete the picture. I shall particularly concentrate on the period 1700–1850 which is at present so very obscure, and I shall deal only very briefly with the period 1850–1900, where the central oral sources are still quite rich, and, what is more, seem to give a fairly complete and coherent picture. Finally I shall make a few general remarks about the problems still remaining to be solved.

The content of oral tradition

The texts on general Bemba history, both those embodied in the written records and those recorded by me, deal in lesser or greater detail of incident, some with nearly all, some with a few, of a definite group of subjects: the departure from Luba, the

[1] In 1962 and 1963.

journey to Lubemba, the *bashimatongwa* (the 'original inhabitants') of Lubemba; the early Chitimukulus, the later Chitimukulus (from Chileshe Chepela onwards); the wars with the Lungu, with the Bisa, with the Ngoni, with the Mambwe, with the Bena Mwanga; other aspects of the reigns of the later Chitimukulus. Some of the texts on general Bemba history also carry sections on the Mwamba- and Nkolemfumuships and on the chiefs in Icinga (to the east of the Chambeshi), but these are on the whole scanty.

The departure from Luba and the journey to Lubemba

All accounts agree that Chiti Mukulu or Muluba and Nkole wa Mapembwe (Nkole being the elder brother though only chief after Chiti died), the sons of Mukulumpe and Mumbi Mukasa (of the *Ngandu* clan), together with their sister named variously Bwalya Chabala or Chilufya Mulenga[1] and with Kazembe and Chimba, other sons of Mukulumpe by other wives, and a great company, left Luba and crossed the Luapula where Kazembe was left, the others going on, giving chiefs to the Lala and Lamba and splitting with the Bisa before finally settling in Lubemba. Most sources add that Kazembe had an elder brother (same mother, same father) named Mwati ya mfwa. Katenda says that the reason why Kazembe's people call themselves Lunda and the Bemba say they came from Luba is that Mukulumpe married a Lunda wife. If this gives the generic relationship between the origin of the Bemba and that of the Lunda-Kazembe, rather than a physical one, then one might, as a hypothesis, identify Mukulumpe with Chibinda Ilunga the Luban who married Makwe Luweji the Lunda princess.[2] The Lunda-Kazembe tradition does not mention the Bemba as such until after the Lunda were already settled in the Luapula Valley,[3] but it does mention that Chibinda Ilunga treated

[1] The White Fathers—Tanguy, *Ifyabukaya* and Hering (after Labrecque)— say Chilufya Mulenga, most of the others Bwalya Chabala. The latter name seems more likely therefore; also Chabala is a name connected in the traditions of other tribes with the migrations.

[2] It is interesting that the name Mukulumpe occurs in the praise-name of Ng'anga Bilonga, the first Kazembe (see Chiwale, *Royal Praises and Praise-Names of the Lunda-Kazembe*).

[3] I. G. Cunnison, (trans.), *Historial Traditions of the Eastern Lunda*, p. 49. Kazembe here says that there were friendly relations between Mwamba Mubanga Kashampupo and Mwata Ilunga I Kazembe III (d. 1805) and goes on,

the Luba who had come with him harshly, and 'set them to work on various tasks, clearing the ground and the roads', and that they fled and crossed the Luapula. 'This was perhaps in 1635.' Kazembe left Lunda considerably after this.[1] Bemba tradition states that as a result of some project of Chiti and Nkole, people were killed and Mukulumpe made his sons do menial punishments, such as sweeping the royal yard. When further tasks of cleaning the shrines were given Chiti refused and his men killed the men his father sent to beat him. They and their people then left, but with their father's blessing. If we may thus read the Lunda and the Bemba traditions together[2] and identify Chiti and Nkole and their followers with the Lubans who fled in about 1635, it looks as if, although there is a close relationship between the Bemba and the Lunda-Kazembe, the Bemba crossed the Luapula some time before the Lunda did. This is also supported by inference from Bemba tradition, since the Kazembe's crossing of the Luapula has been fairly reliably stated at *c.* 1740,[3] Brelsford gives *c.* 1850? as the date of the usurpation of the Bemba throne by Chileshe Chepela, and it is hard to believe that the period 1740–1850 gives enough time for the slow movement towards Nsenga country, the return towards Lubemba, and the great number of Chitimukulus before Chileshe Chepela. Also, if *c.* 1635 is a possible date for leaving Luba, since tradition is definite that

---

'Long ago when the Lunda came they had not heard of Chitimukulu and at that time they had only heard of Mwamba who had sent them men'.

[1] *Ibid.*, p. 7. See also E. Verhulpen, *BaLuba et BaLubaises du Katanga*, Anvers, 1936.

[2] But it is possible that the Lunda tradition of the departure of the Luban followers of Chibinda Ilunga is in fact a fitting into the Lunda history of the Bemba tradition of the punishment of his sons by Mukulumpe, since Father Labrecque who had already recorded Bemba tradition was present at the sessions when the Lunda history was written, and also the Lunda themselves must have had some knowledge of the Bemba tradition. Also many consider Kazembe's book extremely unreliable, and written with a political bias—to make the Kazembeship seem more important than it is and to belittle the importance of the Bemba. While this is just one more example of the well-known influence of social structure on oral tradition, Bemba informants universally insist that Kazembe came at the same time as the Bemba and crossed the Luapala with them.

[3] See I. G. Cunnison, *The Luapula Peoples*, pp. 38–40, and the references given there.

Chiti and Nkole were the leaders of the migration from when it left Luba until Chiti died in Nsenga country and Nkole at Mulambalala on the banks of the Katongo stream near Milemba (Shi Mwalule) and they are not mentioned as being aged when they died, the settlement in Lubemba (after both Chiti and Nkole had died) could not have been much after 1680. However, these datings are by no means clear and since the earlier part of Bemba history is itself so very confused, I shall take it that the Bena Ngandu chiefs settled on the banks of the Kalungu in Central Lubemba somewhere between about 1680 and 1710.

The Lunda-Kazembe, the Bisa (of the *Ngona* clan) and the Lala chiefs (of the *Nyendwa* clan) were not the only groups in the area besides the Bemba (of the *Ngandu* clan) which came from Luba. There were also the Aushi chiefs, of the *Ngulube* clan, and the chiefs of the Unga, Chishinga, Ngumbo and Mukulu, all of the *Ngoma* clan, besides chiefs of the *Mumba* (Chief Matanda) and *Mbeba* (Chief Mupeta) clans. Although the Aushi tradition[1] is that they came with the Bemba, there is nothing in the Bemba tradition to indicate this, and the Bena Ngoma tradition[2] is that they were there before the Bemba. There may even have been groups in Lubemba itself which had come from Luba under an earlier migration than that of Chiti and Nkole.[3] Kazembe says that the Lunda *found* the Chishinga, Aushi and Mukulu already there when they arrived on the Luapula. So, all considered, it seems likely that they were pre-Bemba. The general picture is of several migrations from the Luba/Lunda clans, which, having a more efficient organization than the people already in the area, were able to establish themselves as chiefs over the latter, or, in sparsely populated places, simply to settle as independent groups.

The sources are agreed that after crossing the Luapula at Kashengeneke the Luba migration made a village at *Isandulula fyalo* (increase of territory), and then at *Keleka* and at *Chulungoma*

[1] As recorded by Barnabas Chimba.

[2] As recorded in *History of the Bena Ng'oma* by African Elders assisted by Father Labrecque.

[3] Only the White Father texts on Bemba history mention them, though *History of the Bena Ng'oma* also does so. Father Labrecque's influence may tell here.

(which is also called *Chisaka*). But after this they differ, the White Father version saying that after building another village on the Lwena, *Mushitu* or *Kashi ka Lwena*, they crossed the Chambeshi at Safwa and then went to Ilala before proceeding to Mwase's Nsenga country, another version[1] giving a quite different route and naming other village sites. The sources are agreed, however, that at one point, the White Fathers say Isandulula, Luchele Nganga divined the journey, and Chiti and Nkole sent Kapasa their half-brother with others to fetch their sister Bwalya Chabala who Mukulumpe had refused to allow to go with them, and that Kapasa committed incest with her on the way back; also that at another point, the White Fathers say on the Luchindashi to the south of the Chambeshi, the Bemba divided from the Bisa, but in friendly fashion, Chitimukulu planting a *mutaba* barkcloth tree for them. The sources are agreed that the Bemba then went to Mwase's Nsenga country and built *Chitabata* and *Chibambo*. Probably at the latter Chiti died, scraped by a poisoned arrow of Mwase's when the latter was removing his wife Chilimbulu who had been seduced by Chiti. The group, now led by Nkole, then built *Chanjikile Ipunga* ('We have met with misfortune') near the Kaunga stream, and then *Mungu wa Mbuto ni Lesa abika* ('The squash full of seeds which God has saved') on the other side of the Kaunga. From here revenge was taken on Mwase, and his body and that of his wife were burnt to kill his spirit at *Mulambalala* on the banks of the Katonga.[2] The smoke from the fire made Nkole ill, and he died soon after the Fipa had been raided for cattle to provide ox-hide in which to bury Chitimukulu. After burying Chiti and Nkole at Milemba they crossed the Chambeshi at Chikulu and settled on the banks of the Kalungu where the Milando joins it at *Ngwena*.

Further research on this section of the tradition could probably discover the exact route taken, and the position of all the village sites, including those not named here.

The early Chitimukulus (Pre-Chileshe Chepela) c. 1700–1850

This period of Bemba history is extremely obscure, far more obscure than any period of Lunda-Kazembe history or Aushi or

[1] Mushindo.   [2] Mushindo gives the names of other villages as well.

Bena Ng'oma history. We do not even know who the Chitimukulus were. I have seen eight lists of those between Nkole and
Chileshe Chepela, and the numbers quoted vary from 4 to 23,
most being in the 17–23 range. (Since 1850 there have been 9.) As
Ifyabukaya says of its list, the order is not at all certain, it is not at
all clear if all these were Chitimukulus or if some are duplicated,
some names being perhaps part of the praise-names of others. It
is not clear how the Chitimukulus were related and no-one has
yet been able to produce a convincing genealogy. Indeed, says
F. M. Thomas,[1] 'The Bemba have a list of 24 chiefs . . . The Bisa,
however, discount this and say that the Bemba often quote as
chiefs the names of claimants.' It is not clear either how the
chieftainships of Mwamba, Nkolemfumu or Nkula began or
what the relationships of the Mwambas and Nkolemfumus to the
Chitimukulus were. The clue to this obscurity is I think to be
found in the tremendous expansion of Bembaland in the second
half of the 19th century associated with the rise and final complete
dominance of the 'Miti' branch of the royal clan. The political
pattern as it became fixed during this late period has acted as a
screen for the period before, and the dominant branch's pre-
occupation with itself has led to the earlier history being neglected.
Nevertheless the period from the late 18th century to 1850 is
considerably less obscure than that from *c.* 1700–70, which we
shall chiefly concentrate on.

The earlier Chitimukulus did not belong to the 'Miti' branch of
the royal clan, and one method of investigating this period would
be to interview such people as Chewe, Mwaba wa Nkulungwe,
Mumena, Nkweto, Mutale Mukulu, Chileshe Mukulu, Chimbola—all members of the Ngandu clan who claim to be 'chiefs'.

The obscurity begins in the names of those sons of Mukulumpe
who left Luba.[2] While Chiti and Nkole are mentioned by all, a

[1] F. M. Thomas, *Historical Notes on the Bisa Tribe*, p. 4.
[2] The following account of the early Chitimukulus is based on all the texts
plus a list of Chitimukulus given to Mr Lloyd, N.C., at an 'Assembly of the
BaBemba' at Chitimukulu in 1924. (*Kasama District Notebook.*) In the following
discussion where I say 'mentioned by all sources' I omit Milambo who mentioned only four Chitimukulus for this period. For convenience I give at the end
a 'List of Early Chitimukulus based on a Comparison of Sources'. The names
mentioned in this discussion which are included in that list appear in capital s.

third brother is also often mentioned, sometimes Katongo, sometimes Kapampa Mubanshi. Kapampa Mubanshi was a leper; he is buried at the source of the Nsofu and his relics (bows) are in Munuka's village. His true history could probably be obtained from this village. It is not clear whether he actually was a Chitimukulu. Katongo is said in some accounts to have been the eldest of the three brothers and to have had his eyes put out by Mukulumpe. Although one or two sources say that he came on the journey from Luba, this seems unlikely, and it is more probable, as Katenda in fact says, that the well-authenticated Chitimukulu Katongo was quite a separate person. He may have been a sister's daughter's son of Chiti and Nkole. (ShiMulamba says he was the son of Chilufya Mulenga and was much younger than Chilufya ca mata yabili.) CHILUFYA CA MATA YABILI was the third Chitimukulu, and a son of Bwalya Chabala. He succeeded after a regency by Chimba, half-brother of Chiti and Nkole. ShiMulamba says that Katongo succeeded next, after another regency by Chimba. Chilufya ca mata yabili did, however, have an elder own brother MULENGA POKILI. Milambo says that he did not succeed and that since he was the elder brother he refused to give tribute to his younger brother Chilufya, but that he camped separately and threw all his tribute into the river Kalungu. But most sources say that he became the next Chitimukulu after Chilufya. Others whose names are mentioned are:

SALALA BANA BONKE ('Let the children suckle'). He is mentioned by all sources, but in his praise-name are also mentioned Chimpolonge and Chimanga wa Nkalwe, who are by some said to be separate chiefs.

CHIBENGELE: His praise-name indicated that his was a time in which the tribe grew. He is mentioned by all sources except *Ifyabukaya* which gives his name as part of the praise-name of Chileshe Chepela.

KASANSU: Mentioned by most sources. A very old man when he succeeded.

CHIFUNDA CA BUSOSHI: Mentioned by most sources, but Chimbola gives this name as that of one of the women to hold the Chandaweyayaship.

Chipasha wa Makani: Mentioned only by the White Fathers. Milambo says that he was chief in the present area of Mwamba and ShiMulamba confirms that this village was in the Ituna area. He does not seem to have been a Chitimukulu.

KAYULA WA NSEKO or *Kayula Milyango:* Mentioned by all sources including Milambo. His name indicates that he was well-liked.

KATONGO: All sources mention him. He came from the east of the Chambeshi to the Chitimukuluship, and a later Chitimukulu, Chimpolonge, is known to have been his sister's son.

Ntamba Lukuta: Is only mentioned by Labrecque, and by Hering who is based on Labrecque. Was probably not a Chitimukulu.

Ndubwila: Mentioned by two sources, but I suspect he is not a separate individual.

LWIPA: 'Cacila mabyala'. Mentioned by most sources. His name indicates that he was more junior than his rivals when he succeeded.

CHIMPOLONGE: Is mentioned only by a minority, but there is sufficient evidence to include him amongst the Chitimukulus. He was sister's son of Katongo and came from the east of the Chambeshi. Chimbola and Milambo mention him in the praise-name of Salala. He may well be the same person.

CHIMANGA WA NKALWE: He is not mentioned by most sources. His name is included in the praise-name of Salala.

MUTALE WA MUNKOBWE: Mentioned by most sources. His praise-name indicates that he would laugh with people but had other things in his heart.

Kanabesa: Mentioned by most sources but *not*, interestingly, by the 'Assembly of the Babemba'. I doubt if he was a Chitimukulu and he is discussed below.

CHIBAMBA WA MANSHI: Mentioned by most sources. Was the victor of the fight with Chisoka (and possibly Chishisa), below, for the throne.

CHISOKA CA BAKATA: 'Nshiwile, napyatapo fye' ('I have not fallen, I have only touched the ground'). Mentioned by all sources. Died hardly a month after his accession.

CHISHISA: This may be the Ndubwila (see above). But he is mentioned only by the interconnected White Father sources, and, of them, not by Tanguy. Had a very short reign.

Kabemba: Mentioned only by the White Father sources. Was
  probably not a Chitimukulu.
MUKUKA WA MALEKANO: Mentioned by all sources.
CHILYAMAFWA: Mentioned by all sources.
CHINCHINTA SUSULA: Mentioned by all sources. Milambo—he is
  unique in this—says that Susula Mpapa and Chinchinta are two
  distinct chiefs with Kayula Milyango in between.

There are also eight other names which are mentioned by one
source only in each case, and about which no information is
given. I therefore omit them.

After this process of sorting we are, then, left with 18 names
of possible Chitimukulus.[1] Of these it is quite possible that Salala
bana bonke, Chimanga wa Nkalwe and Chimpolonge are in fact
one person: Chimpolonge the sister's son of Katongo, and that
Chibengele is merely part of the praise-name of Chileshe Chepela.
Certainly very little is known about Salala, Chimanga or Chibengele. (Oger gives Salala and Chibengele as part of the praise-
names of Chilyamafwa.) Of those that remain Kasansu had only a
very short reign as did Chisoka ca Bakata and Chishisa. This
leaves possibly twelve chiefs who had more than a month or two
on the throne, or if we include Salala, Chibengele and Chimanga,
fifteen, to cover the period c. 1700–1850.

The Luba immigrants who settled at Ngwena on the banks of
the Kalungu did not find the country empty. The original inhabitants were various. In Lubemba itself there is some mention
of people called Bemba, who had been part of an earlier migration
from Luba, living along the Bwambi stream. They seem to have
been mixed with the Musukwa under the chiefs Mulopwe and
Kalelelya. The Musukwa were iron-workers, cultivated mounds
in grassy plains and chewed barkcloth with their teeth. The Luba
immigrants abolished their chieftainships; some of them fled, it is
said to Lake Mweru, others remained. There were also Sukuma
(i.e. Fipa) in some areas. The Nkondo were settled under Ntacim-
bwa at Ntasu to the north of the Myaba near the Iyaya Hills.
These had come from further north. They were fierce fighters

[1] Thus we now omit the names of: Kapampa Mubanshi, Chipasha wa
Makani, Ntamba Lukuta, Ndubwila, Kanabesa, Kabemba.

and although the Bemba used to raid into their area from time to time, it appears that they did not overcome the Nkondo (also called Mambwe) until the first half of the 19th century.[1] In Bulombwa there were the Beba under Kafwimbi who fled with their cattle, at the approach of the immigrants, to the Isoka hills. Oger says that there were also some Lungu iron-smelters and blacksmiths in Mpanda. ShiMulamba says that there were Sukuma in Ituna but that there was no-one at all in Miti.[2] There is no direct information as to who were the original inhabitants of the area east of the Chambeshi at the time of the arrival of the Luba immigrants.

Having settled on the banks of the Kalungu at Ngwena the Luba immigrants first took possession of the area between the Chambeshi, Luchindashi and Chibile on the western side of the Chambeshi leaving Nkweto on the eastern side in Chilinda. Chilufya ca mata yabili (?) sent Mukoma to subdue the Bena Mwanga, which he did, sending back tribute to Chitimukulu. Pokili Mulenga fought the Langashi who were called by the Fipa to punish the Bemba for having robbed the Fipa cattle to get ox-hide to bury Chitimukulu in. Later, possibly after the death of Mulenga Pokili, the Mambwe invaded with chiefs Kanga Bakali, Lupando, Makumba and Nyola, but were defeated by Shula Malindi, a claimant to the throne.

Thus at the beginning of the period there was a considerable amount of fighting by the immigrants in order to become established, but after this, apart from the sporadic raids against the Nkondo in Mpanda, no more external wars are mentioned until at the end of the 18th century, when Mubanga Kashampupo held the chieftainship in Ituna, and Chilyamafwa that in Lubemba, there was a war in which the Lungu were utilized by one side in an internal dispute. It is very difficult to say anything definite about the Chitimukuluship during this time of comparative peace. There seem to have been one or more succession disputes. Names mentioned in connection with these are Shula Malindi (who, after hoping to gain the throne by defeating the Mambwe,

[1] See Oger.
[2] This conflicts with Mushindo who has a unique account of the origin of the Mwambaship and Nkolemfumuships.

was killed for his pains by his rivals), Lwipa, whose praise-name
indicates that he succeeded over the heads of those senior to him,
Chibamba wa Manshi (a scion of the Nkulungwe family), noted
for his single combat with Chisoka ca Bakata (and possibly
Chishisa Ndubwila) who (both of them, possibly) succeeded
him. These succession disputes will be further discussed when we
deal with the name Kanabesa.

There are three well-authenticated Chitimukulus of whom we
know nothing except a few personal characteristics embodied in
their names: Mutale ma Munkobwe, Chifunda ca Busoshi and
Kayula wa Nseko. Milambo attributes to Kayula some actions
with respect to Chileshe Chepela that other sources attribute to
Chilyamafwa.

This leaves us with several Chitimukulus of this period about
whom something definite can be said and a rough chronology
given.

KATONGO seems to have been a close matrilineal relative of Chiti
and Nkole. He must have reigned before Chimpolonge, his
sister's son, and Chimpolonge must have reigned before Chilyamafwa because Chilyamafwa was succeeded by Susula-Chin-
chinta who in turn was ousted by Chileshe Chepela (c. 1850).
Chilyamafwa is said in the texts to have been at least partly contemporaneous with Mubanga Kashampupo, who was chief in
Ituna, and the latter had dealings with a Kazembe who died in
1805, Mwata Ilunga I, Kazembe III, at the beginning of the
Kazembe's reign, possibly about 1770. The reign in Ichinga of
Nkulu Chewe, a sister's son (?) of Chimpolonge, who succeeded
when young and who was made to flee when an old man by
Chileshe Chepela after the latter had seized the Chitimukuluship,
probably began in the time of Mubanga. It is thus possible to
make out a rough chronological table for some of the chiefs of
this period (see Fig. 7). Katongo came from Ichinga where he
had been chief. He must have significance since the relic-houses
(with their attendant priests) at Chitimukulu are called Chitimukulu, Nkole, Katongo and Kanabesa, but it is unfortunately
not clear to me what this significance is.

CHIMPOLONGE was also from Ichinga and a sister's son of
Katongo.

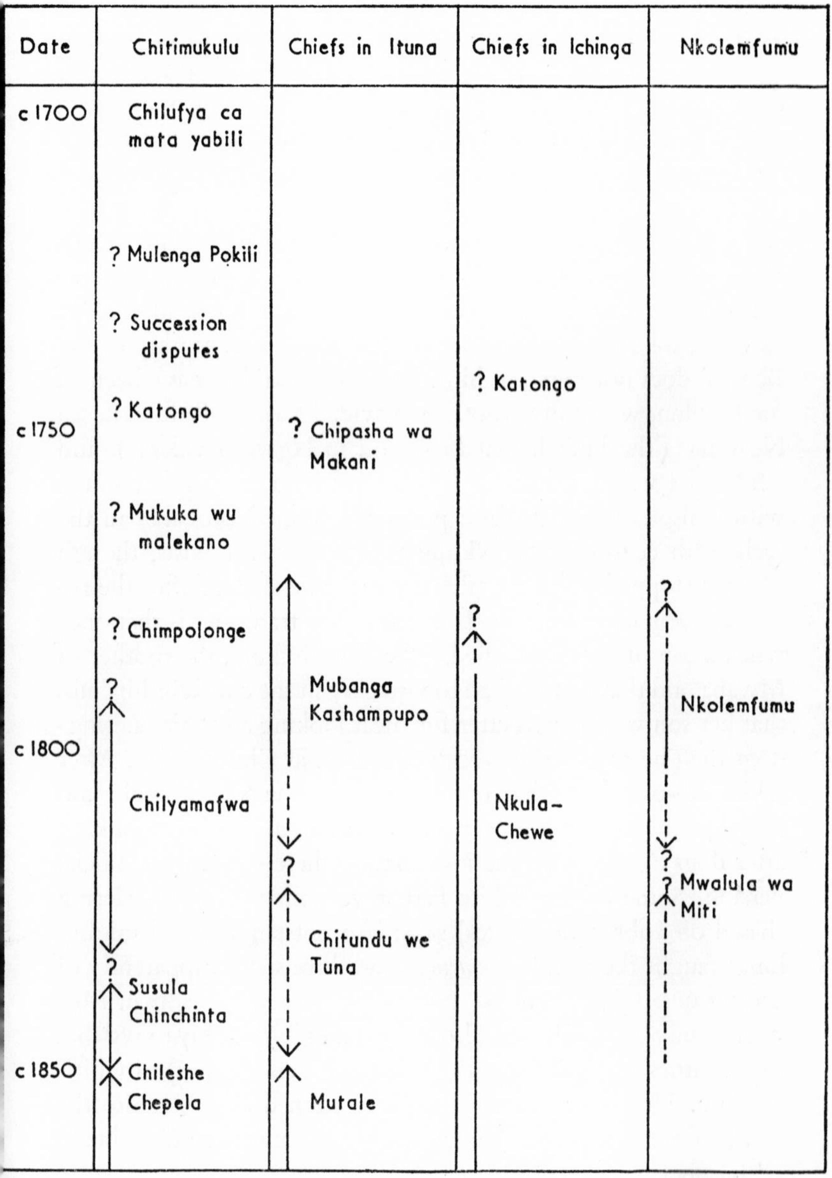

Date	Chitimukulu	Chiefs in Ituna	Chiefs in Ichinga	Nkolemfumu
c 1700	Chilufya ca mata yabili			
	? Mulenga Pokili			
	? Succession disputes		? Katongo	
c 1750	? Katongo	? Chipasha wa Makani		
	? Mukuka wu malekano			
	? Chimpolonge		?	?
	?	Mubanga Kashampupo		Nkolemfumu
c 1800	Chilyamafwa		Nkula–Chewe	
		?		? Mwalula wa Miti
	? Susula Chinchinta	Chitundu we Tuna		
c 1850	Chileshe Chepela	Mutale		

FIG. 7

Rough chronological table c. 1700–1850

MUKUKA WA MALEKANO. The White Fathers' accounts say that he has the name 'wa malekano' ('of the separations') because he separated the country, giving Ituna to his brother Chitundu. This does not agree with Milambo's account of the chiefs in Ituna, which, because he is the Ituna specialist, I am more inclined to accept.

At the end of the 18th century CHILYAMAFWA was on the throne and external wars began again. He was succeeded by CHINCHINTA SUSULA who in turn was ousted by Chileshe Chepela (*c.* 1850).

Kanabesa. This name is included amongst those in the list of Chitimukulus by most sources, but Lloyd's 'Assembly of the Bemba' does not mention him. Kanabesa is said to have been of the Nkulungwe family who also provided Kasansu Kafunikile ku Ngwena' ('the branch that broke off in Ngwena village'), and Chibamba wa Manshi who fought and won the single combat with Chisoka Nshiwile (and possibly Chishisa) probably in the early 18th century. The Nkulungwe family still exists, though Mwaba stopped being an officially recognized chief after the re-organization of Bemba chiefs in 1944. The tradition[1] is that once when a son of hers was called to be Chitimukulu, the mother of Mwaba said that people died too quickly in the chieftainship, and that her son was doing better for meat looking after his hunting-dogs than he would if he received tribute as Chitimukulu. After which no-one from that family ever became Chitimukulu and they became known as *mfumu sha mulelambwa*, 'chiefs for looking after dogs'.[2] That is all the information there is from the official version. Some of the White Father versions add more. Hering (based on Labrecque's notes) says: 'An outstanding and mighty king; taught the people *citemene*.[3] Had three statues apparently of European origin. There are two more statues in headman Mumena's village. There are also two books.' *Ifyabukaya* says that these statues are in the *nganda ya babenye* (relic-houses) of Chitimukulu. The name Kanabesa, as I mentioned above, is also the name of one of the relic houses at Chitimukulu, the others being

[1] Brelsford, *Succession of Bemba Chiefs.*

[2] Note that Chiwele, the *cingo* (burial official) of Chewe is of the *Mbwa* (dog) clan.

[3] *Citemene*: the method of millet cultivation by lopping the branches of trees, piling them and burning them, and sowing millet in the ash-bed.

Chiti, Nkole and Katongo. Nowadays the word is widely used as a term of respect when speaking to chiefs—just as Mulopwe sometimes is—or even in a friendly fashion when speaking to friends. Milambo denied that it was anything more or that there ever was a Chitimukulu called Kanabesa.

As I mentioned earlier there are still several *Bena Ngandu* (royal crocodile clan) families scattered around the older areas, such as Chewe Kalubila, Mwaba wa Nkulungwe, Mutale Mukulu, Chileshe Mukulu, Mumena, Nkweto, Chimbola, Mulenga wa Chibungu, Kabungo (in Ichinga). It has been usual to assume, after Brelsford, that these are relics of earlier paramount lineages which either because they were ousted, or because they were descendants of junior princesses, do not succeed to the main chieftainships.[1] But it seems that at least in the case of Chewe Kalubila and Mwaba wa Nkulungwe, there is more to it than that.

When I interviewed Chewe and his elders he told me that *the Chewes did not come from Kola* (i.e. Luba). Neither did Kapolyo Mfumu their sister. *They were here before Chiti and Nkole came and were the Bakanabesa* (Kanabesas). The name Chewe originated from the man who would have succeeded to the chieftainship but whose sister[2] refused. It was the name the heir had before succeeding. (It was not clear from the conversation whether the chieftainship which the sister refused to let her brother go to was the Chitimukuluship or the Kanabesaship. I asked what the names of the one who succeeded instead of him to the Chitimukuluship were, and Chewe's elders said that that story belonged to the

[1] Brelsford, *The Succession of Bemba Chiefs* (2nd edn. 1948) says, p. 37, 'Scattered throughout Bemba area are several chieftainships held by men of royal blood but who are only vaguely connected with the present reigning families. These are Chimbola, Mfungo, Nkweto and Mwaba. In the past there were many more, all descended from young royal sisters but none of them, for various reasons discussed earlier, being allowed to enter into the main succession.' By saying 'in the past' he is presumably referring to the fact that these 'chieftainships', whose representatives are still village headmen, were not recognized by the Government, and were entirely subordinate to the reigning 'Miti' lineage. There is no empirical evidence for his statement that they are 'all descended from young royal sisters'. They may well be descended from senior sisters or even be biologically unrelated to the reigning lineage, as in the case of Kanabesa.

[2] Not mother as Brelsford said.

family of Mutale Mukulu, and I should have to ask him. I then
asked what the relationship between the Chewes and Chiti and
Nkole or their descendants was, and it was then that I was told
that there was none, and that the Luba immigrants were in one
part of the country while the Kanabesas were in another. Nor
were they able to give me the name of the chief whom the Chewe
whose sister refused the chieftainship was to have succeeded.)
Chewe further said that Mwaba of Nkulungwe was also of the
house of Kapolyo Mukulu. Chewe was unable to explain how it
was that he should be of the *Bena Ngandu* clan although he did not
come from Luba.

There is not a hint of any of this in any of the main texts on
Bemba history, yet the main point, that the Chewes did not come
from Luba, was rapidly confirmed from several reliable and
independent sources.[1] Also, ShiMulamba said that the Chewes
came to their present home in Chitondo in Chitimukulu area
from the eastern side of the Chambeshi; ShiTantameni also says
this and that it was the one whose sister refused to let him go to the
chieftainship who came to Chitondo.[2]

What are we to make of this? It does at least seem clear that
there was a chieftainship of Kanabesa on the eastern side of the
Chambeshi which existed before the Luba immigrants arrived. I
think it might be possible by further field research[3] to elucidate
the precise relationship between the Luba immigrants and their
chieftainship of Chitimukulu, and the Kanabesas. But on any of

[1] ShiTantameni, Chief Munkonge, Chimbola and his councillors.

[2] Although I am certain that the information given me by Chewe is the
tradition for that title, I am fairly sure that he and his elders might, at a later
date, be able to give me a fuller account of that tradition. ShiTantameni had
made a few notes on the Chewe tradition which he kindly let me have. He
says that Katumba is the 'mother' of Chewes and Mwabas. She had two sons,
Chibende and Chikangwa. It was this Chikangwa who did not take up his
appointment as Chief and came to Chitondo. Kalubila, who was the son of a
junior sister ('*Kalubila e ba munganda inono*'), succeeded Chikangwa. And
Kalubila's younger brother Chewe was appointed to the Luchindashi and
died there. There still is a close connection between Chewes and Mwaba for in
1946 the present Chewe was appointed to be Mwaba wa Nkulungwe but did
not take it up.

[3] Especially at Mwaba wa Nkulungwe, Chileshe Mukulu and Mutale
Mukulu, and Chitimukulu's court. I regret that I have so far not interviewed
Mwaba or done research in Ichinga.

the possible interpretations the implications for this early period of Bemba history are revolutionary. For it seems either that in the names of such supposed Chitimukulus as Kasansu and Chibamba wa Manshi, we have in fact not the names of Chitimukulus at all, but holders of an earlier chieftainship, the Kanabesaship, or that some members of a family which did not even come from Luba became Chitimukulus. It is not yet possible to decide this question, but the latter possibility seems the more likely. It may be significant that Chibamba wa Manshi is said to have succeeded to the Chitimukuluship as the victor of a succession dispute possibly after the death of Mulenga Pokili. It is possible that a non-Luban Kanabesa forced his way into the Chitimukuluship. For Hering records that though the fight between Chibamba wa Manshi and Chisoka Nshiwile began as a single combat, after Chisoka had refused to admit defeat their respective followers joined in and so fierce was the fight that the forest (*mushitu*) of Pandwe was completely destroyed in the process, being chopped down for the making of fortifications.

If this latter interpretation is correct (but only further field research will show whether it is) it does provide a possible explanation for the obscurity of this early period of Bemba history. If the Chitimukuluship was usurped for a time by a non-Luban 'who taught the people *citemene*' this is not a fact creditable to the *Ngandu* clan of Luban extraction, who seem to have at a later date got the Chitimukuluship back.[1]

At any rate this discussion of the name Kanabesa has disrupted the picture given of this early period by the published texts on Bemba history, and it has shown that even now it may be possible as a result of further field investigations to build up a much clearer picture of this period.

The origins of the Mwambaship and the Nkolemfumaship

The last quarter of the 18th century marks a division in the pre-1850 period. By this last quarter there were established chieftain-

[1] This statement is based on the fact that Katongo we Chinga who was related to Chiti and Nkole (Brelsford, ShiMulamba) became Chitimukulu, as did Katongo's sister's son, Chimpolonge; and on the possibility that the Chibamba wa Manshi and Chisoka combat occurred on Mulenga Polili's death. (Tanguy and the process of elimination above.)

ships in Ituna and Miti and oral tradition becomes much more definite. The way in which these chieftainships were established is less definite. Milambo says that Chikuku Mwela was the oldest remembered name in Ituna.[1] And after him came Chipasha wa Makani, who is a definite enough figure to have a deserted village site on the Milenge stream, and from whom Milambo is able to give a named genealogy containing all the later Ituna chiefs. ShiMulamba says that Nkole wa mapembwe (*not* the Nkole wa mapembwe who was the elder brother of Chiti and came from Luba) had a village at the source of the Miyongolo stream. He says 'Chipasha wa makani and Nkole wa mapembwe were close

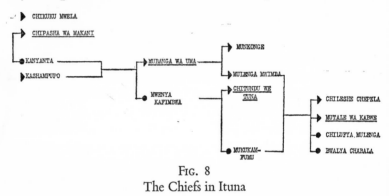

FIG. 8
The Chiefs in Ituna

to one another by birth. Chipasha lived in one part of Ituna and Nkole in another. The ancestress of Chitunda we Tuna was also the ancestress of Chipasha and Nkole.' This seems to point to a fairly flexible chiefly organization at that period. Later, Nkolemfumu started a chieftainship in Miti but as ShiMulamba frankly said: 'I can tell you the names of the Nkolemfumus and what they did, but how the chieftainship started I do not know, except that there is a connection with Nkole the brother of Chiti.'

The final period 1850–1900[2]

This is the period of the third great expansion of the Bemba area. The first expansion took place slowly during the 18th century, and resulted in the formation, besides the Chitimukuluship

[1] Milambo's words were: 'Chikuku Mwela e mukalamba mu calo cino.'
[2] I do not propose to go into this period in detail as there is not sufficient space to do so and it is far less obscure than earlier periods.

and the Nkwetoship, of the three royal clan chieftainships in Ichinga, Ituna and Miti. The second expansion took place during the reign of Chilyamafwa at the end of the 18th century (at the expense of the Lungu) and in the early part of the 19th (at the expense of the Mambwe in Mpanda). This resulted in the establishment of the Makasaship, the first chieftainship for a 'son of a chief'. The origin of the third great expansion was in the first half of the 19th century when Chileshe Chepela, before he came to the throne, fought and conquered Chisopa wa Mapampa, a Bisa chief who had 'extended his sphere of influence to the Chinama region along the left bank of the Chambeshi' (Hering). This is the region of the salt pans, and the war may have been started for these. After this battle the Arab slave traders appeared for the first time and captives were sold for cloth. Later after Chileshe came to the throne (c. 1850) and the Lungu attacked the Bemba, the Bemba conquered them and again the captives were sold to the Arabs. The Arab slave trade seems to have played an important role in the Bemba expansion and to have greatly increased the wealth, and thus the power, as well as the military resources of the chiefs. During this period also the Bemba were gravely threatened by the Ngoni, and were only able to finally overcome them, when some Bemba chiefs had already submitted, by complete unity under the leadership of Chitimukulu. At the end of the century, the British South Africa Company arrived, and in the context of a changed situation in East and Central Africa, and by utilizing a succession dispute and the inroads already made by the White Fathers, gained dominance in the country by their superior force of arms.

Further problems

Besides the problems still remaining in Bemba history that are obvious from the above discussion particularly of the period of the early Chitimukulus, there are several other aspects which also need to be covered.

A large gap in the records is the oral tradition for the area east of the Chambeshi. Brelsford has something[1] on this, and Mushindo has more, but these still barely touch what there must be to

---

[1] Especially in *Aspects of Bemba Chieftainship*.

find out. Such an investigation could throw light on all the periods of Bemba history.

The period *c.* 1770–1850 shines in a kind of half-light. The names of the chiefs seem to be known, and something of what they did, but the relationships between them are very obscure. Chimbola is supposed, by Brelsford, to have some connection with the Chitimukulu whom Chileshe Chepela deposed, but on interviewing Chimbola, I could find this Chitimukulu nowhere on his genealogy, although Chimbola obviously is connected with the family whom Chileshe Chepela ousted, since some of the names occurring in the Chimbola genealogy also occur in connection with earlier chiefs in other areas.

LIST OF EARLY CHITIMUKULUS
BASED ON A COMPARISON OF SOURCES

1. Chilufya ca Mata Yabili.	10. Chimpolonge.
2. Mulenga Pokili.	* 11. Chimanga wa Nkalwe.
* 3. Salala bana Bonke.	12. Mutale wa Munkobwe.
* 4. Chibengele.	13. Chibamba wa Manshi.
s 5. Kasansu.	s 14. Chisoka ca Bakata.
6. Chifunda ca Bushoshi.	s 15. Chishisa.
7. Kayula wa Nseko.	16. Mukuka wa Malekano.
8. Katongo.	17. Chilyamafwa.
9. Lwipa.	18. Chinchinta Susula.

Notes: *—a name which may be a duplicate (inference from praise-names);
            s—very short reign.

This list begins after the death of Chiti and Nkole and ends with the Chitimukulu whose throne Chileshe Chepela usurped. Those of the Chitimukulus who can be dated (even roughly) or put in chronological order have been entered on the Rough Chronological Table.

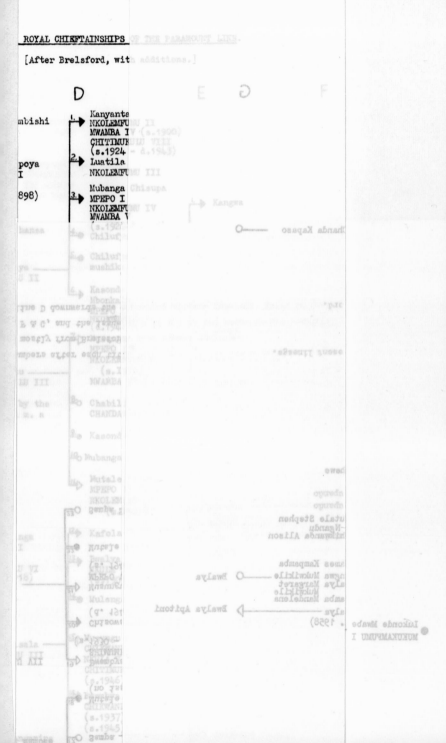

ROYAL CHIEFTAINSHIPS OF THE PARAMOUNT LINE.

[After Brelsford, with additions.]

A   B   C

                                          → Chanda Bali
                                            (d.)

                                          → Mubanga Chi
     → Chitenda   MOCOLOMOFUMU
       (no issue)   MWAMBA III
                                            (d.1887 - d.1

BIBLIOGRAPHY

A. *The surrounding tribes*

There is a certain amount of recorded oral tradition, both published and unpublished, relevant to the history of the Bemba-speaking peoples. The oral tradition relating to the Lunda-Kazembe is the best documented, both for their origins and since the arrival in the Luapula country.

I. G. Cunnison, 'History on the Luapula', *R.L. Paper* 21, 1951.

I. G. Cunnison, *The Luapula Peoples of Northern Rhodesia*, Manchester University Press for *R.L.I.*, 1959.

J. C. Chiwale, *Royal Praises and Praise Names of the Lunda Kazembe of Northern Rhodesia*, Central Bantu Historical Texts III, R.L. Communication No. 25, 1962.

Mwata Kazembe assisted by Fr. E. Labrecque, *Ifikolwe Fyandi na Bantu Bandi*, Macmillan & Co., 1958 (in Chibemba); and a translation into English of this work:

I. G. Cunnison (trans.), *Historical traditions of the Eastern Lunda*, Central Bantu Historical Texts II, R.L. Communication No. 23, 1962.

V. W. Turner, 'A Lunda Love Story and its Consequences: Selected Texts from Traditions collected by Henrique Dias de Cavalho at the Court of Mwati-Amvwa in 1887', *R.L. Journal*, xix, 1955, pp. 1–26.

For other tribes the recorded oral traditions is less full.

B. Chimba, *A History of the Baushi*, Oxford University Press, 1943, 2nd ed. 1956 (in Chibemba). This gives a connected and vivid account of the main Aushi chieftainships and wars with other tribes, though it does not name its sources.

African Elders assisted by Fr. E. Labrecque: *History of the Bena Ng'oma (Ba Chungu wa Mukulu)*, Macmillan, London, 1949 (in Chibemba). This book is less clear than the one on the Aushi, and does not deal in equal detail with all the branches of the Bena Ng'oma people. But the information comes from Chief Chungu Mulonda, and Elders, some of whom are named.

W. V. Brelsford, 'Fisherman of the Bangweulu Swamps: A Study of the Fishing Activities of the Unga Tribe', *R.L. Paper* 12, 1946. Some of the Unga chiefs are Bena Ng'oma and this book should be read together with the previous one. The accounts do not entirely coincide. Brelsford got his information from Chief Kaoma and Headman Kasopa of Matongo Island in 1942–4.

F. M. Thomas, *Historical Notes on the Bisa Tribe of Northern Rhodesia*, R.L. Communication No. 8, 1958.

J. T. Munday, *Kankomba*, Central Bantu Historical Texts, R.L. Communication No. 22, 1961.

Thus there is a certain amount of recorded oral tradition of varying quality for some of the Bemba-speaking tribes of Northern Rhodesia, but a great deal remains to be recorded: for example, the oral traditions of the Mukulo, lesser

Aushi chiefs, Bena Chishinga, Bena Ngumbo, Bena Kabende, the Bisa of Luwingu and Chinsali Districts, other Mukulu chiefs, Lungu, and Tabwa.

As for the non-Bemba-speaking tribes in the area there is some information on the Mambwe in:

W. Watson, *Tribal Cohesion in a Money Economy* (Manchester University Press for R.L.I., 1958).

But (unless W. Watson has unpublished material) the traditions of the Lungu and the tribes in Isoka still need to be recorded.

Some information on tribes for which histories have not been published will be found in the various well-known general accounts: Moffat Thompson; Coxhead; *Ethnographic Survey of Africa*, Brelsford.

B. *The Bemba*

As for the Bemba themselves there are the following published works in which oral tradition is recorded.

W. V. Brelsford, 'Shimwalule: A Study of a Bemba Chief and Priest', *African Studies*, i, 3 September 1942.

W. V. Brelsford, *Aspects of Bemba Chieftainship*, R.L. Communication No 2, 1944. Gives some account of the early history of the Nkulaship.

W. V. Brelsford, *The Succession of Bemba Chiefs*, Government Printer, Lusaka, 1948, 2nd ed.

Ifyabukaya, Fourth Bemba Reader, White Fathers, Chilubula, n.d. but 1932 (in Chibemba).

E. D. Labrecque, 'Le Tribu des Babemba I. Les Origines des Babemba', *Anthropos*, Band XXVIII, 1933.

S. A. Mpashi, *Abapatili bafika ku Babemba*, Oxford University Press, 1956 (in Chibemba).

G. Robertson, 'Kasembe and the Bemba Nation', *Journal of the African Society*, x, January 1904.

A. I. Richards, 'The Life of Bwembya, a Native of Northern Rhodesia', in M. Perham (ed.), *Ten Africans*, Faber & Faber, London, 1936.

F. Tanguy, *Imilandu ya Babemba*, Oxford University Press, 1948 (in Chibemba).

A little-known work which is based on contemporary sources and deals with the coming of the White Fathers to Bembaland, is:

Henry Pineau, *Évèque Roi des Brigands*, Les Pères Blancs, Quebec and Montreal, 1944.

I have also seen the following manuscripts which record oral tradition and for which I am grateful to their authors:

Fr. L. Oger, *Calo ca Mpanda: Calo ca kwa Makasa* (in Chibemba), (cyclostyled MS. in Fr. Oger's possession at Kasama).

Fr. Joseph Hering (W.F.), *History of the Bemba Tribe* (unpublished MS in Fr. Hering's possession at Chilubula, P.O. Kasama. Based on Fr. Labrecque's notes).

Rev. P. B. Mushindo, *A Short History of the Bemba* (unpublished MS in Mr. Mushindo's possession at Lubwa, P.O. Chinsali).

Fr. E. Labrecque, *History of the Babemba* (in Chibemba) (unpublished MS in Fr. Oger's possession, White Fathers, Kasama). I am grateful to Fr. Oger for lending me this MS which is apparently Labrecque's original work. It is notable for the number of praise-names which it records.

The White Father Sources—*Ifyabukaya*, Tanguy, Labrecque, Hering—are not entirely independent. Labrecque did important work *c.* 1924–6 and his chief informant was Dismas Musabandesa from Kangwa wa Mpumpa. He was the old catechist referred to in Labrecque's Anthropos article. Hering's manuscript is based on Labrecque's work. *Ifyabukaya*, with which Father van Sambeek was connected is also probably based on Labrecque's work, but I was told that local teachers also contributed. Tanguy's work was based on what had been done before and he was helped by Joseph Muma, at that time a catechist, and now Headman Chikunga and a hereditary councillor of Chitimukulu.

Paul Mushindo is closely related to several of the leading councillors and has been in a good position to record the tradition. He spent six years in collecting material for his manuscript. It will be of very great value when it is published.

Father Labrecque's Bemba work was done before he started on Lunda Kasembe and Bena Ngoma history. One cannot be completely sure whether one has influenced the other.

In my own investigations in 1962 and 1963 I have been trying to fill in some of the gaps in the written records, particularly for the pre-1850 period. Amongst my informants have been:

1. *Milambo.* He is the chief councillor on traditional matters to the present chief Mwamba and must be well on in his eighties. He has been close to Chief Mwamba all his life and in an excellent position to learn the tradition. Since the death of Chitikafula in 1962, he seems to be generally considered the greatest living authority on the past in Kasama District. Mwamba Mutale wa Kabwe was his mother's father. The interviews with Milambo were tape-recorded.

2. *ShiMulamba.* The ex-chief councillor of Chief Nkolemfumu. He must be at least in his seventies: he has grandchildren in their mid-twenties. The ShiMulambas were some of the first headmen in Miti, Nkolemfumu's country.

3. *Chimba.* An important priest. He acts as regent between the death of one Chitimukulu and the installation of the next. He gave me his own history.

4. *Katenda.* A hereditary councillor of Chitimukulu, who, while probably not a leading historian, did have some interesting comments to make on historical matters.

5. *Chewe and his elders.* A headman of the royal clan, who has the title of *mfumu* (chief) and is addressed as such.

6. *ShiTantameni.* Court assessor of Chief Tungati, comes from Kanyanta village near Chewe.

7. *Chief Munkonge.* Considered to be well-informed on traditional matters.

8. *Chimbola and his councillors.* A chief of the royal clan but not of the paramount line. He was able to give some information on the royal lineage which was ousted by Chileshe Chepela.

9. *ShiMumbi and his councillors.* A chief of the royal clan and the paramount line. He gave the history of his chieftainship and some information on the royal lineage which was ousted by Chileshe Chepela.

10. *Tungati and his councillors.* A 'Son of a Chief'. Gave information on the history of the Tungatiship.

A NOTE ON THE MAP

The Map of the Expansion of Lubemba is illustrative rather than exact. In default of more exact data the boundaries of the present-day chiefdoms have been taken and marked according to the date when it seems that a permanent Bemba chieftainship was established in that area. In cases where it is known that not all of a present-day chief's area was established at one time, this is indicated; though again the exact boundaries at particular times are not always known.

A. C. P. Gamitto in 1831–2 went through what is now the SW part of the Bemba country which had then been recently conquered by the Bemba. Gamitto's book was not available to me when the map was drawn. A continuous chieftainship was not however established in the Chinama area until considerably later. See A. C. P. Gamitto (trans. Ian Cunnison), *King Kazembe* (Junta de Inuestigacoes do Ultramar, Centro de Estudos Politicos & Sociais, Lisbon, 1960)

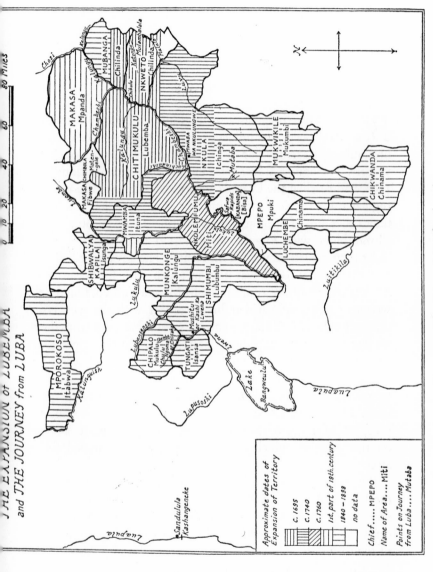

THE EXPANSION of LUBEMBA
and THE JOURNEY from LUBA

0 10 20 40 60 80 Miles

Approximate dates of
Expansion of Territory

c. 1695
c. 1740
c. 1760
1st. part of 19th. century
1840—1898
no data

Chief.....MPEPO
Name of Area....Miti
Points on Journey
from Luba....Mutaba

FIG. 10   The Expansion of Lubemba

9

KAZEMBE AND THE ARABS TO 1870

by

IAN CUNNISON

BEFORE the time, towards the middle of the 19th century, that Arabs began to influence directly the course of events in his country, Kazembe had already had experience of non-Bantu visitors. Portuguese from Tete, in two major expeditions since 1798, had reached the Luapula Valley and attempted to establish regular trade relations with him; but they had failed in this, and their other aim of opening a trans-continental trade route to link Mozambique with Angola was thwarted by Kazembe's refusal to let them penetrate west of his capital. The advantage had been all to Kazembe: fo h e was now in touch with Europeans from the east coast and hre could boast to Mwata Yamvo, king of the western Lunda, who had indirect contact with the west coast, that he too had his white men and the goods that came from them. By the time of the expedition of 1831–2 Kazembe appeared to have a clear policy of retaining in Lunda hands the caravan route which linked him with Mwata Yamvo, a route across which the two kings exchanged gifts, and trade goods went in large quantities. This Portuguese expedition was so badly received and the prospects of trades were so remote, that its leaders wrote a report on the situation which could hardly have encouraged future attempts.[1]

But during subsequent decades coastal Arabs penetrated past the lakes and traded in Kazembe's area, while the Yeke, an offshoot of the Nyamwezi tribe of Lake Victoria, succeeded in carving out of the western portion of Kazembe's empire a state of their own, which was based on successful trade. Together the effect of the Arabs and the Yeke was to alter Kazembe's foreign

[1] Cunnison, 'Kazembe and the Portuguese, 1798-1832', *Journal of African History*, II, 1, discussed the period and policies.

relations, and the size and structure of his state. Previously he had used his soldiers to expand territorially and to hold what he gained; now he had to use them in defence against militant foreigners, while the area under his control began to shrink and the old Kazembe/Mwata Yamvo axis was cut. Internally, armed rebellions of princes successfully began.

While in this chapter I deal mainly with the Arabs it will be realized that the effect of the Yeke was also important, but their main impact was later. The period in which the influence of these two invaders was felt began about 1840 and ended about 1890 with the almost simultaneous arrival of British and Belgian official expeditions, the end of the Yeke kingdom and the Arab caravans, the eclipse of Mwata Yamvo under pressure from the Chokwe, and the beginnings of European rule. I consider here the period up to about 1870 when Arab influence predominated.

The Arab penetration of the interior from Zanzibar appears to have started during the reign and under the stimulus of Sultan Seyyid Seyd, when he transferred his court from Oman to Zanzibar.[1] According to Coupland, 'after 1840 there was evidently a great increase in Arab enterprise; the routes extended further inland and carried far more caravans than ever before'.[2] He saw the Arab movement as 'more than an invasion. In a very limited and localized sense it was occupation too.' Because of the distances involved, and difficulties in travel during the rains, 'the long-range Arab merchants and their dependents were accustomed to settle down somewhere up-country during the wet weather and to stay away from their homes on the coast or at Zanzibar for two years or sometimes more. Here and there, accordingly, little Arab "colonies" grew up along the inland trade routes.'[3]

It seems likely, however, that besides the Bisa middlemen who had long been plying the trade, a few Arabs had penetrated to Kazembe before these dates and had traded directly with the coast. Evidence for this comes from three sources of varying

[1] Sir R. Coupland, *East Africa and its Invaders*, London, 1938, pp. 295, 303–5; H. Brode, *Tippoo Tib*, London, 1907, p. 9. The date of the transfer was 1840 but Brode claims the sultan made an effective stimulus on the trade from 1832, when he was already spending much of his time in East Africa.

[2] Coupland, *op. cit.*, p. 306.

[3] *Ibid.*, p. 309.

reliability. Livingstone was told, when he was at Kazembe in
1867, that at the time of the Lacerda expedition (1798–9) there
were some 'Ujijians' (who might well have been Arabs) with
Kazembe. 'The Portuguese and the Ujijians began to fight, but
Casembe said to them and the Portuguese, "You are all my guests,
why should you fight and kill each other?" He then gave Lacerda
ten slaves, and men to live with him and work . . . He made
similar presents to the Ujijians, which quieted them.'[1] However,
the Portuguese expedition diary has no reference to these. Again
in 1831 Gamitto came across two 'Moors' who were accustomed
to take their goods to the mainland opposite Zanzibar; and he
made the general statement that 'the nations of the eastern part of
Africa which frequent Cazembe are the Bisa and the Impoanes,
the name given to the Arabs of the Zanzibar coast'.[2] Moreover,
according to Livingstone again, an Arab whom he met had himself been at Kazembe at the time of the 1831 expedition. This was
Muhammad bin Saleh[3] who is known to have been long in the
interior and whose father, also according to Livingstone, 'was the
first to open this country to trade with the Arabs'.[4]

But by general accord it was after 1840 when Arabs began to
invade in large numbers. Coupland writes that in the course of
fifteen years from 1840 'the field of commercial exploitation had
been extended westwards beyond all the three great lakes';[5] and
Verbeken affirms that 'it was at this period, 1840–5, that the first
Arab traders reached the regions to the north and east of the
Katanga'.[6] Verbeken was of the opinion that it was the discovery

[1] D. Livingstone, *Last Journals*, London, 1874, Vol. I, p. 246.
[2] A. C. P. Gamitto, *O Muata Cazembe*, Lisbon, 1854 and 1937, p. 360 (references are to the 1854 edition). This travel diary was translated as *King Kazembe*,
Lisbon, 1961 (two vols.). *Pwani* is Swahili for 'coast'.
[3] Livingstone, *op. cit.*, p. 294. Gamitto did not mention him.
[4] *Ibid.*, p. 277.
[5] Coupland, *op. cit.*, p. 307.
[6] E. Verbeken, *Msiri Roi du Garanganze*, Brussels, 1956, p. 29. Also, in 1861
Livingstone met, at Lake Nyasa, men who had been fourteen years in Katanga:
'we were satisfied that the Arabs must be driving a good trade'. *The Zambesi
and its Tributaries*, London, 1865, p. 389. It is conceivable that the Arab penetration at this period was a result of a lessening contribution by the Bisa to the
trade of the interior. Much of Bisa country had been attacked and conquered
by Bemba in the early 1830s and their activities were diminished. This warfare
and some of its effects are extensively described in Gamitto, *op. cit.*

of Katanga copper by Arabs, with Nyamwezi carriers in their caravan, which gave to Msidi's father the idea of trading there himself.[1] In the published Lunda history the first mention of 'Balungwana', a term the Lunda use to describe Arab and Yeke merchants and sometimes soldiers, occurs in the reign of Kazembe VI (1854–62); although at this point they are mentioned simply as the people through whom the Yeke traded their exports.[2]

The latest authority to publish on the Yeke is Verbeken whose book gives the result of his researches into the origin of the kingdom. According to these, the pioneer of Yeke penetration into South-East Katanga was a Nyamwezi chief called Kalasa-Muzwiri, of the Usambwa group of Nyamwezi centred some hundred miles north-west of Tabora. This tribe 'had in fact monopolized transport and regularly carried to the coast; there were no other professional carriers in this part of Africa'.[3] Like many men of his tribe, Kalasa-Muzwiri had seen service with Arab traders, but started to organize caravans on his own account, seeking ivory and slaves which he then sold to the Arabs of Zanzibar. He heard of copper in Katanga, made brotherhood with a number of chiefs there, and for his second expedition to the region went accompanied by his son, aged twenty, who later became Msidi: this youth had also seen service with Arabs. On his earlier travels Kalasa-Muzwiri had neglected Kazembe, but the young Msidi now formed his own caravans and visited him because the part of Katanga to which he was going was in Kazembe's hands.

According to the account written by his descendant, Mukanda-Bantu, he arrived at the court of Chinyanta (Kazembe VI)[4] who welcomed him. When he desired to cross the Luapula to Katanga another Yeke said to him: 'Chief, don't let this Msidi cross; don't let him go to Katanga.' But Kazembe allowed the Yeke to go and trade as they wanted. Another version states[5] that Kazembe, on

[1] Verbeken, op. cit., p. 40.
[2] Mwata Kazembe XIV, Ifikolwe fyandi na Bantu bandi, London, 1950, p. 85 (translated in Rhodes-Livingstone Communication No. 23; all references to Bemba text).
[3] Verbeken, op. cit., p. 31, citing R. F. Burton.
[4] Ibid., p. 40. In the translation of this document in G. E. Tilsley, Dan Crawford of Central Africa, London, 1929, p. 137, the name of Chinyama—who was chief of the Aushi further south—is given instead.
[5] Verbeken, op. cit., p. 47.

receipt of some small-pox medicine and a musical instrument, gave Msidi the permission he sought, as well as two women of whom one was to bear Msidi's eldest son and successor. This is not borne out by Lunda testimony. What the Lunda say[1] is that Kazembe replied to Msidi, 'The place you are going to is my land, I do not want you to do anything bad in it, for the copper there is my copper and the people there are my people'. Msidi agreed to this and Kazembe gave him guides to cross the river. The date of the crossing was probably during the 1850s and before 1862, the year in which Kazembe VI died.[2]

Msidi lived peaceably enough, plying his trade, for some time— one source states six years[3]—and then appears to have gained control, by diplomacy and force, of Chief Katanga (Lamba tribe) and Chief Mpande (Sanga tribe) who had been tributaries of Kazembe. At the same time, in order not outwardly to provoke a breach, he allowed Kazembe's representative in South-East Katanga, Kashiba, to remain unmolested.

It is impossible to say now why Kazembe should have allowed the Yeke to trade where he had disallowed the Portuguese. Perhaps the most likely explanation is that the Yeke started on a small scale, small enough to be almost indistinguishable from the Arab and other individual traders who so far had caused little trouble. Whatever the reason, Kazembe was soon disillusioned; conflict which was to last on and off for thirty years broke out. The immediate cause was the killing by Msidi of two 'nephews'[4] of Kazembe on their westward journey to Mwata Yamvo. When Kazembe heard this news he resolved to kill all the 'Balungwana' he could, thinking that they and Msidi's people were the same. From this point, the fortunes of the Yeke, the trafficking Arabs, and the Lunda became closely intertwined.

[1] Mwata Kazembe, op. cit., p. 85.

[2] My article 'The reigns of the Kazembes', Northern Rhodesia Journal, III, 2, 1956, discusses problems involved in dating the reigns.

[3] Verbeken, op. cit., p. 51, quoting E. Verdick.

[4] Holders of the hereditary office of 'nephew to Kazembe'. In Mwata Kazembe, op. cit., p. 91, we read that they were fleeing from Kazembe; but in Verbeken, op. cit., pp. 63-4, that they were being sent officially to Mwata Yamvo; they thought that Kashiba, by his quiescence, was in Msidi's pay, and so they disregarded him; in revenge for the slight, Kashiba gave their presence away to Msidi.

In contrast with the Arabs and Yeke, the Portuguese of the Lacerda and Monteiro-Gamitto expeditions had not involved themselves in local politics, and had not attempted to settle down in the area. The only Portuguese establishment in the whole of their 'interior'—the Marambo settlement in the Luangwa valley— had collapsed partly through bad organization and partly through bad luck.[1] Although the members of these expeditions would attend audiences and ceremonies on invitation, they remained essentially aloof, and nowhere in the reading of their diaries does one get the impression that they entered with any degree of interest, sympathy, cameraderie, understanding or intensity into the life of the interior. In contrast with later invaders they refused to take wives from the people.[2] Some individual members of the expeditions intrigued with Kazembe or his officers to get their own petty benefits[3] but intrigue was not used as a conscious policy for gaining political ends. Moreover, confronted with some of the cruelties of Kazembe's treatment of prisoners and captives, the Portuguese would raise objections which, understandable though they might appear, could hardly have been expected to further their material aims. Neither Arabs nor Yeke were missionaries in this sense. From Gamitto one has the impression that the leaders of that expedition suffered, in their formal dealings with Kazembe and other Lunda, from their inability to relax an overbearing sense of military honour and personal dignity, and from a grudge that their aims, which they felt to be so laudable, were continually thwarted by men who, to them, were mere barbarians.[4] The Portuguese, although well armed, were remote from their base over unfrequented roads, and their lack of security made them desire nothing better than to scurry back to Tete. The Arabs carried their homes with them, established big households in the country, and were sufficiently well organized to remain for long periods

[1] Gamitto, op. cit., pp. 137–8.

[2] The Arabs did intermarry; see, for example, Livingstone, Last Journals, Vol. I, p. 231; the trader Hamees married the daughter of chief Nsama to seal a peace. The Yeke would have had no difficulty in marrying with Lunda; nowadays there is much intermarriage between them.

[3] See Pinto's diary in Travessia da Africa, Lisbon, 1937. Pinto took Lacerda's place on the latter's death during the 1798 expedition.

[4] That Gamitto had humanitarian sympathies is evident from his diary, but they seem not to have affected his outward conduct as an officer.

away from their bases. There were many simultaneous Arab groups going to the interior, and their communications were accordingly better than those of the Portuguese, who were in the interior alone. The Arabs were more ready to use force in order to subsist. Their leaders had a very fair prospect of dazzling personal wealth, whereas the Portuguese expeditions were acting in the service of the Crown and breaking the way for others to amass wealth by commerce; and such honours of service as came to the expeditions would be confined to their leaders.

While the expedition of 1831-2 ended in a political rout, the Arabs seem to have achieved success in the sphere in which they sought it. They entered local politics: some natives, with the wealth of their land, and some Arabs, with the force at their disposal, found that they could be mutually advantageous. Interested groups of natives entered shifting short-term alliances with various of these Arab traders. While they often suffered at Arab hands, they could still use the Arabs in furtherance of their political aspirations, and the Arabs were quick to respond if they saw mercantile benefit in doing so.

Two generalized descriptions exist of the way in which the Arabs established themselves. Campbell knew personally, rather later, many of the North-East Rhodesian Arab traders who survived, and suggested their method of gaining local power in the following passage:

The Arabs usually settled down beside some . . . chief, and made a trading centre. There they traded, and when ivory and slaves were sufficient they sent off caravans to the coast, which brought back guns and powder and other trade goods. After a time of peaceful penetration, having ingratiated themselves with the people, and having built a walled village, the armed Arabs one peaceful morning would attack their erstwhile hosts and friends, killing their men and carrying off women and children. Other villages around, seeing the futility of fighting such strong foes, would . . . carry ivory and slaves to them and obtain whatever peace terms the Arabs cared to impose. It had to be peace at any price. From then on raids in the more distant villages were the order of the day, while the locals, turned into Arab servants, shared the plunder. Thus mushroom Arab kingdoms were brought into being and built up through Central Africa.[1]

[1] D. Campbell, *In the Heart of Bantuland*, London, 1922, p. 258.

Livingstone said that Arabs would make their first approaches with substantial gifts to 'smooth the way';[1] and that they would use their position as legitimate merchants to condemn any attack on them as a 'breach of public law'.[2]

It was probably by methods such as these that Arabs established some strong points on the periphery of Kazembe's country. The capital of Nsama seems to have become one such place, but there were many others in the neighbourhood at the time of Livingstone's arrival in 1867.

Livingstone reached Kazembe from the north-east; from there he turned north to make for Lake Tanganyika and Ujiji, but failing in this he returned through Kazembe again in 1868 on his way south to Lake Bangweulu. Thence he turned north towards Ujiji, this time omitting Kazembe's capital. His observations on the disposition and activities of traders are of great value.

The extent of foreign penetration is well shown by his encounters. Kazembe was virtually ringed about by Arab and Nyamwezi traders, and by the Yeke kingdom which was now well established. From Livingstone we learn of the presence of Tippoo Tib, the Arab, who had just entered Lungu country and was having trouble with Nsama of the Tabwa. Here there was an Arab force of six hundred.[3] Syde bin Habib, an Arab, had a house at Mpweto at the north end of Lake Mweru.[4] 'Hamees Wodim Tagh', an Arab, was at Chitimba in Lungu country[5] with at least three hundred followers.[6] At Kabakwa, north of Lake Mweru, lived an Arab, a son of Muhammad bin Saleh who was then a prisoner at Kazembe, with a number of Nyamwezi.[7] Inside the

[1] Livingstone, *op. cit.*, pp. 210, 215.
[2] *Ibid.*, p. 217.
[3] H. Brode took down Tippoo Tib's autobiography and published it in German. This was translated into English (bibliographical reference above) 'Tippoo Tib' was a nickname for Hamid bin Muhammad bin Juma Burajib. At pp. 29–30 of the English translation we read: 'Tippoo Tib resolved to go to Itahua [Itabwa] a country which then bore a very bad reputation. A sultan ruled there called Nsama, a powerful and most bloodthirsty chief, of whom all Arabs who had hitherto entered the territory had had a bad experience'. Nsama had blocked any Arab advance in force to Kazembe. And see Livingstone, *op. cit.*, p. 257.
[4] Livingstone, *op. cit.*, p. 282.
[5] *Ibid.*, p. 210.
[6] *Ibid.*, p. 214.   [7] *Ibid.*, p. 216.

northern boundary of Kazembe's country was a village of the
Nyamwezi trader known as Fungafunga.[1] Juma Merikano and
Seide be Umale, Arabs, were near Kazembe.[2] Muhammad Bog-
harib, an Arab, was at Kazembe for seven months during 1867-8.[3]
At Chikumbi, a big trading centre south-east of Kazembe, was a
Nyamwezi stockade.[4] Many of these traders were travelling frequently into Katanga, Lamba country, and 'Rua', the country to
the west of Lake Mweru. When he returned to these parts in 1873
Livingstone found that Kawende's territory north of Lake Bangweulu was 'overrun by Nyamwezi who now inhabit that country'.[5] He noticed also how much the horizons of ordinary people
had been widened; at the village of Mwinempanda, one of
Kazembe's officers, he heard songs: 'I have been to Syde [the
Sultan of Zanzibar]; I have been to Meereput [Portuguese
governor]; I have been to the sea.'[6] He found also that a letter
which he carried from the Sultan of Zanzibar made a great impression on Kazembe.[7]

Many of these traders had settled in country which was directly
Kazembe's or was tributary to him. Kazembe was powerful but
his control was less on the outskirts of his country than it was in
the centre. Away from the centre he had district representatives
whose main job was to see to the forwarding of tribute; they were
perhaps neither permanently in their positions, nor very efficient
at political control. The Arabs had not tried to attack Kazembe
yet, but they had managed to control Nsama who was a lesser
chief. Kazembe, who reserved for himself a monopoly in the
trade of ivory, and who alone disposed of slaves, would probably
see benefit in the presence of small numbers of Arabs who would
not contest his sovereignty. At the same time he must have seen
the threat their growing numbers implied. The years after about
1867 were specially difficult: his supply of ivory appears to have
become short,[8] and this would, no doubt, affect adversely his
relationship with the Arabs.

Tippoo Tib had left the area after defeating Nsama, but returned

---

[1] Livingstone, *op. cit.*, p. 291.   [2] *Ibid.*, p. 215.
[3] *Ibid.*, p. 296.   [4] *Ibid.*, p. 311.
[5] *Ibid.*, Vol. II, p. 282.   [6] *Ibid.*, Vol. I, p. 305.
[7] *Ibid.*, p. 276.   [8] *Ibid.*, pp. 260, 296, 299.

about two years later to the same place.[1] When previously he had
defeated Nsama, 'Casembe had issued strict orders to his people
not to allow the Arabs who fought Nsama to enter his territory'.[2]
Now Tippoo Tib came forward, reached the Kalungwisi River
and 'was attacked by the Walunda, who took a quantity of
merchandise and muskets. ... Our traveller [Tippoo Tib] resolved, before retaliating, to inquire into the causes of this unexpected hostility. He was haughtily answered that the Walunda
had attacked the Arab followers quite deliberately for they [the
Arabs] had boasted that they had defeated Nsama, and now they,
Kazembe's men, would show them that they were something
different and had determined to strike down the intruder into
their country.' Tippoo Tib got more troops from Itabwa 'and in
a few months all Lunda was subjugated. The Kasembe—Tippoo
Tib did not remember his name[3]—was driven from the country,
and a new chief named Mabote set up in his place. This man had
been Kasembe once before, but had been deposed because he
refused to submit to circumcision.'[4] Soon after this Tippoo Tib
left the area for good to begin his greater adventures in the north.

Lunda country was 'subjugated' in the words of Tippoo Tib, to
the extent that a new Lunda king was installed with the force of
Arab arms. The episode has confirmation from Lunda history.
This relates that when Lukwesa Mpanga ('Mabote') had been
elected earlier (he would then have been Kazembe VII if he had
actually reigned), he alienated the Lunda by his behaviour in the
circumcision lodge; he had made various threats of dire punishment for Lunda of all ranks. He was driven out, and he went into
exile in Itabwa. There, together with Chief Nsama he raided and
killed a Lunda governor on the Kalungwisi River. The man who
actually became Kazembe VII sent a punitive expedition against
Nsama, and Lukwesa Mpanga fled to Mpweto. Now Lukwesa
made an alliance with Arabs in the locality with such effect that
he got the throne. As the Lunda account puts it:

[1] Length of time easily deduced from Brode, *op. cit.*, Chap. IV.

[2] Livingstone, *op. cit.*, p. 260.

[3] It was presumably Kazembe VIII, Chinkonkole, who in Lunda tradition
preceded 'Mabote', the name by which Kazembe IX, Lukwesa Mpanga, is
frequently known.

[4] Brode, *op cit.*, pp. 69–70.

One day Pembamoto[1] found Lukwesa Mpanga at Mpweto and said
to him: 'I hear the Lunda are mentioning you and saying you are now
to be Mwata Kazembe.' Lukwesa Mpanga answered: 'True enough,
the Lunda cannot forget me.' Pembamoto said: 'Don't worry, we'll go
together, I'll take you; I've heard with my own ears it's you they
want.' When Pembamoto had finished his work at Mpweto he went
to Mofwe with Lukwesa Mpanga. Before they arrived a citizen told
Kazembe: 'The enemy are on the way, let us gather here.' Chinkonkole
[Kazembe VIII] asked who the enemy were. The man said: 'It's that
Arab who killed Mwinempanda[2] . . . and he's with Lukwesa Mpanga.'
Fear then came upon Chinkonkole . . . and he ran away. . . . The people
did not like him [Lukwesa] but they were afraid that Pembamoto
might kill them.[3]

Although there are discrepancies between the Lunda history
and that of Tippoo Tib[4] the point I want to make is, I think,
established: there was a fruitful alliance between a prince, Lukwesa
Mpanga, and an Arab with force behind him, fruitful enough
for the prince, whom the Lunda had previously rejected, to win
the throne as Kazembe IX. This episode not only shows Arab
methods of penetration, but also is a very significant one for
Lunda history. Previously no prince as candidate for the throne
had managed to muster enough force within Lunda country itself
to raise a successful rebellion against a reigning king. Now the
presence of armed merchants gave a prince the opportunity. This
started a whole new pattern of political behaviour. In order to
drive out the unpopular Kazembe IX, the prince Kanyembo
Ntemena went and sought military help from another foreign
group, the Bemba; he was successful in turn; and the deposed
Lukwesa Mpanga then went and sought help from the Yeke. He

[1] I think that Pembamoto is a name given in Lunda history to more than one
Arab merchant, including Tippoo Tib. Here, however, when taken together
with Tippoo Tib's story, it almost certainly refers to him.
[2] A Lunda aristocrat, second in rank, who had been killed in the battle on
the Kalungwisi.
[3] Mwata Kazembe, op. cit., pp. 94-5.
[4] For example Lukwesa Mpanga is said to have had 'Pembamoto' killed
shortly afterwards; the Bena Ng'oma also claim to have killed him in a campaign by Chikumbi in alliance with a fellow-chief, Chungu; see History of the
Bena Ng'oma, London, 1949, pp. 60-1.

was soon killed but his mother's kin kept going a conflict between Lunda and Yeke for twenty years.

The Arabs were thus the first strangers to enter with efficacy into the political affairs of the Lunda. From previous experience the reigning king had been always wary of attempts by rivals to the kingship to gain the throne by guile or force, and had taken steps to forestall them. An early Kazembe had an ambitious prince killed by his own men during a war.[1] Later, Gamitto reported that princes were made to live under the eye of the king in a street of the capital, and although they were occasionally sent out to command troops, the troops were not their own but those of aristocrats who could not claim the kingship.[2] After these episodes described above, Kazembe X gave a strong rival brother most of the trappings and some of the powers of kingship, and a palace of his own in the capital. Without a willing external force, like that of the Arabs, no Lunda prince gained kingship by rebellion.

While the destructive aspects of Arab dealings in the last century have long been recognized the positive influence which they exerted on states and dynasties needs much more examination. For Kazembe's Lunda I have been able to find little material on this subject: the only episode which I could take is not well documented, and doubtful in details. Yet it is suggestive: it suggests that Arab dealings brought changes of great consequence. These changes have a special interest, since they must be largely responsible for the situation in many tribes which British administrators later found, and which they accepted as a basis for the organization of local government.

[1] Mwata Kazembe, *op. cit.*, p. 45.
[2] Gamitto, *op. cit.*, shows the 'street of the princes' on his map of the capital.

10

THE ORIGIN OF THE LOZI:
SOME ORAL TRADITIONS

by

MUTUMBA MAINGA

O NE of the most interesting problems of pre-European Lozi history is that of the origin of the Lozi state. The Lozi kingdom is a characteristic 'sudanic' type divine monarchy. As in all states of this type, the central figure is a sacred king who is the head of both the state and the theocracy. The king is surrounded by mystery, ritualism and magic. It is believed that he holds his power as much by the consent of his dead predecessors as by that of his living subjects. The dead kings continue to wield their power among the living through the institution of the royal graves. The dead kings are still consulted and given all the respects due to monarchs; they are even deemed more powerful than the living. The Queen Mother and Queen Sister offices which are so prominent in the Lozi state are a common feature of all states of the divine kingship type. On the whole, royal institutions are regarded as the foundations upon which men must build for safety against famine, drought, foes and all sorts of disasters that may befall a nation. In *Garenganze West and East* F. S. Arnot writes of Lewanika: 'The Barotse had great faith in his power to bring rain, and to protect his people from the lightning. When a severe thunderstorm broke over the town, all came into the King's enclosures.'

In Southern Africa, the two clearly established centres of such ideas are Luba-Lunda in the present Congo, and Karanga-Rozwi in the present Southern Rhodesia. The Luba-Lunda centre, as has been established by archaeologists, was in existence as early as the 8th and 9th centuries. On the other hand, Al Masudi of Baghdad as early as A.D. 922 talks of a large African state in the present Southern Rhodesia. From later descriptions by Portuguese traders and travellers it is clear that this state had most typical features of sudanic divine kingship.[1]

We have plenty of evidence of other sudanic states in Southern and Central Africa that have originated from one or the other of the two old centres. For example, it has been clearly established that the Lovedu state of the Rain Queen in North-Eastern Transvaal had its origins in the Karanga-Rozwi centre.[2] The Lovedu kingdom was founded early in the 17th century by a break-away group from Monomotapa's empire. Lovedu tradition has it that the leader of the group, a princess, daughter of one of the Mambos, carried with her rain charms and the sacred beads. This tradition is a way of accounting for the origin of the Lovedu institutions, which of course have since absorbed into their original culture many diverse elements from tribes in the south.

A Rhodesian 'state' which can be traced back to the Luba-Lunda centre in the Congo is that of the Lunda of Kazembe in the Luapula area. It has now been clearly established that the Lunda of Kazembe came from the empire of Mwata Yamvo establishing themselves in the Luapala area in the first half of the 18th century.[3]

Among the Kazembe Lunda, as with the Lozi, the king radiates power and is feared as a reservoir of power. His movements and public appearances are restricted. The institution of the royal graves is equally strong. Dr Lacerda like Coillard in Barotseland was asked to offer sacrifice to the dead kings.[4] The king, it is believed, is always in contact with the spirits of his dead fathers. Dr Lacerda, observing this reverence for the dead among the Lunda of Kazembe, wrote in his diary, '. . . these exceedingly superstitious Caffres hold their dead to be gods . . .'

It seems rather unreasonable to suppose an independent origin of these ideas in Barotseland or to postulate it as a third old nucleus. Lozi institutions are likely to have been derived either

[1] R. Oliver and J. D. Fage, *A Short History of Africa*, Pelican, 1962, pp. 47, 48.
[2] E. J. Krige and J. D. Krige, *The Realm of a Rain Queen*, 1943.
[3] I. G. Cunnison, *The Luapula Peoples of Northern Rhodesia*, M.U.P., 1959, p. 39. Also C. N. White, 'The Ethno-History of the Upper Zambesi', *African Studies*, Vol. XXI, No. 1, 1962, p. 11.
[4] R. F. Burton ed., *The Lands of Cazembe*, 1873, p. 162:
'I was also directed to leave at the burial place of the royal ancestors a blue cotton (Ardian), 4 fathoms of cotton cloth, and a small quantity of white and coloured stoneware beads'—entry from Dr Lacerda's diary.

from the Luba-Lunda or the Karanga-Rozwi centres. Indeed outside Barotseland various authorities have in the past argued for
either a Rozwi or Lunda origin, and both Rozwi and Lunda oral
traditions claim credit for the origin of the Lozi state.

Lunda oral tradition has it that a brother of one of the Mwati-
yamvwas, named Mutanda Yembeyembe who was the first leader
of the Lunda of Kazembe when they settled in the Luapula area,
discovered deposits of salt which he hid from the king. When the
matter became known, Mutanda fled south where he founded the
dynasty of Lozi chiefs on the Upper Zambesi. This would place
the founding of the Lozi dynasty in the late 17th or early 18th
century.[1]

Rozwi oral tradition on the other hand, holds that as the empire
of Monomotapa became disintegrated and was divided among
the various sons of the king, one of the great princesses fled the
country taking with her a large following. They argue it was this
queen who became the founder of the Lozi dynasty. They claim
this queen carried with her what today forms the Lozi regalia.
They also argue that the word 'Lozi' is a corrupted form of the
word 'Rozwi'. They even claim that the name 'Lewanika' is
derived from the Shona word 'Ruwanyika' or 'Ruwananyika'.
Certain authorities have used these claims to account for similarities of patterns found around the Zimbabwe ruins and those
found among the Lozi; they have also pointed out the identical
plan of the ruins and that of the 'Mileneni' (royal capitals or
palaces) in Barotseland.[2] If these hypotheses were accepted it
would place the founding of the Lozi state somewhere in the
late 17th or early 18th century.

However, up to now no evidence has been found in Barotseland itself to support either of these claims. On the contrary, to all
the early writers, chief of whom is Jalla, the Lozi gave an 'official'
version aimed at emphasizing Lozi uniqueness and primacy. The
version given to Jalla stresses a directly divine origin and does not
admit the pre-existence of other people in the present Lozi area.[3]

[1] *Historical Traditions of the Eastern Lunda*, Mwata Kazembe XIV, Rhodes-
Livingstone Communication No. 23.
[2] J. D. Clark, *Pre-History of Southern Africa*, Pelican, 1959, p. 29 and fig. 64.
[3] A. D. Jalla, *History, Traditions and Legends of the Barotse Nation*, C.O.
African No. 1179.

As a result Lozi tradition has been described by historians as strangely unsatisfactory and mythical, C. N. White, for example, contrasting it unfavourably with Lunda tradition.[1]

One achievement of the University College research project[2] in Barotseland has been to prove that there is a second layer of Lozi oral tradition which is very different from the official version and which is comparable to Lunda or other traditions in giving an account of the arrival of the Lozi, their origins and the people they displaced or conquered. Strangely enough, the two theories of Lunda and Rozwi origin still appear simultaneously even within Lozi oral tradition, although the Lunda origin emerges more strongly than the other.

The fullest story, given by Mr Neo Zaza of Mule Village, offered an account of both the Rozwi and Lunda relationships as well as how the various Lozi groups came to settle in the particular parts of Bulozi.[3] This version has it that the Lozi are a branch of the Rozwi of Mambo who lived in Bunyai. When the empire of Mambo began to collapse, one group of the Rozwi under the leadership of a woman named Akatata, left Bunyai followed by her sister Akatoka. Akatata is the Lozi ancestor. She was accompanied by her two brothers, Isimwaa and Imenda. They entered the present Bulozi from the south. From Bunyai they passed through Tongaland before they reached Sesheke. After Sesheke they began moving in the direction of north-north-east.

Isimwaa, Akatata's brother, soon got tired of wandering and

---

[1] White, *op. cit.*

[2] Refers to Rockefeller Ethno-History grant to the University College, Salisbury.

[3] Informant Mr Neo Songa Zaza of Mule Village in Sinumuyambi sub-district. Interviewed 19 November 1962. 52 years old. Self-employed—general dealer and speculates in raw materials like timber, hides and fibres. Quite a well-known man. From 1954 to 1958 member of the Barotse Advisory Council. Also served on District Local Education Authority; Barotse Special Juvenile Court; Zambesi River Transport Board of Control.

Mr N. Zaza and his brothers, in the 50's, were outspoken critics of the Lozi administrative system as it had then developed. The Litunga threatened the whole village of the Zazas with banishment but public opinion which was very much for the Zazas prevented him from carrying out his intentions.

Mr Zaza is very much interested in Lozi history, and has collected information on the Lozi past which he intends to publish in book form.

when they got to Mutungi, he decided to remain there.[1] Imenda his brother went on for some time, but he too, when they reached Lukulu, decided to break off from the main group and settle there. Akatata died before they reached Lukulu where Imenda remained. Akatata's place as leader of the group was taken by her daughter Mwambwa. Mwambwa was not very pleased when Imenda decided to stay at Lukulu. She told him he would starve and live on mushrooms—'Mutamba ku lya mbowe'. However, she gave him a few seeds so that his people could cultivate fields and grow their own food.

Mwambwa and the rest of the group went on till they came in touch with the Lunda whose great king was called Mwata Yamvo. In order to establish friendly relationship, Mwambwa gave her daughter, Mbuyu, to Mwata Yamvo as hostage and wife. However, Mwambwa's people were not very happy here and she decided to go back to where her uncles had remained (i.e. in the present Bulozi). Mbuyu remained as hostage and wife to Mwata Yamvo, but did not live long. She died without having any children.

Mwambwa's people came south beyond Lukulu and settled at Mutindi. Mwambwa bore another daughter whom she named 'Mbuyu' after her first daughter who had remained in Mwata Yamvo's country. It was this Mbuyu who succeeded Mwambwa and became the mother to Mboo the first king of the Lozi.

Bulozi, or Ngulu as it was known then, was inhabited by a people called Manatwa or Manyantwa. These lived in Bulozi proper and were great hunters. It was these people who nick-named the invading Lozi, 'Aluyi' or 'Aluyana' which meant 'foreigners'.[2] The other people found in the country by the

---

[1] In the version given to Jalla, Isimwaa is mentioned in connection with the plot to transfer from female to male rulers.

I was also informed the present grave keeper is also a 'mukwa Nasimaa'. Makono is a very important place in Lozi kingship in that it is where all kings go for their coronation rituals.

My informant here was Ndate Muyunda Wamunungo of Silele Village in Senanga District. He was a personal attendant to both Lewanika and later to Yeta III, Lewanika's eldest son and successor. He left his office when Yeta III was forced to abdicate in 1945.

[2] Today individuals refer to those people who are not related to them in any way as 'Baluilui' or 'Baluyiluyi'. Hence the saying 'Muluyi ma nalikole'.

'Aluyi' were Manyengo and Muenyi. The Nkoya lived in the eastern forest, and farther south were the Mbukushu and Subiya.

I found some interesting variations to this version. The first one was that the Lozi or Aluyi did not enter the country from the south but rather from the north.[1] They came in contact with the Lunda *before* entering Ngulu or Bulozi. The Lunda proved too strong for the Lozi and to establish friendly relationship Mwambwa gave her daughter to Mwata Yamvo; then she began wandering south seeking for a new kingdom. It was pointed out to me that the fact that there were more royal graves and mounds (Liuba) in the north of the country shows that the Lozi have lived there longer than in the south. Apart from this, whenever there was trouble in the country the Lozi fled north and never south. This, my informant went on, shows that the Lozi were more acquainted with the northern countries than with the south.

The other interesting variation was in connection with Mbuyu, Mwambwa's daughter, who was given to Mwata Yamvo as hostage and wife. Some sources[2] have it that Mbuyu did live long and had a child whom she named Lusinde. The Lunda failed to pronounce this name and it was corrupted to Shinde. The Shinde who came to ask Lewanika for protection against the Luvale slave traders was a direct descendant of Lusinde. This it is held is the origin of the saying 'Kalui Mwambwa, Kalunda Mwambwa u soko wetu u mweya'.[3]

As these variations themselves suggest and as I have already said, the Lunda origin is on the whole much more strongly supported than the Rozwi origin by Lozi oral tradition. Variations to the Lunda story are very numerous, but I think one can easily pick out the significant common factors in them all.

The basic story is that Mwambwa was a Lunda princess or

[1] Information given by Mulena Mukwae Makwibi, the Queen Sister, at Nalolo in the presence of the Ishee Kwandu (the consort); the Sambi Ndopu, her Prime Minister, and Induna Saywa Mainga Wamundila. Date of interview, 26 November 1962.

[2] Information given by Lubinda Imataa Kabuku. Born 1905. Village—Nalunembwe, in Wanyau sub-district. Occupation—1933 to 1949 dug canals at Lealui; 1949 to 1953 salesman in a store; 1954 in charge of the building of the Senanga-Sitoti road; 1962 in charge of the pontoon at Lukando.

[3] Translation: 'Kalui is a child of Mwambwa, Kalunda also is a child of Mwambwa, our ancestor is the same.'

chieftainess, who with a small party broke away from the Lunda and came wandering till they reached the present Bulozi. Although the invaders were very few in numbers they successfully imposed their rule upon the original inhabitants of Ngulu or Bulozi.

The first encounter was with a people known as Manatwa who lived in Bulozi proper. These people must have been nearly exterminated or were completely fused with the invaders for apart from a mound called after them no other trace of them survives in the plain. However, someone did say that there is still a small group of Manatwa near Libonda.[1]

Once the Lozi were settled in the country, the immediate task facing them was the consolidation of their power. Mboo, the first male ruler after Mwambwa, conquered and brought under the Lozi rule, the ma-Kwamakoma, Manyengo, ba Imilangu and Mambumi or ba Mishulundu. Ngombala, the fifth ruler after Mboo, extended the Lozi kingdom further. He conquered the Mashanjo, ma-Subiya and Matotela. The Mashi people after hearing of Ngombala's prowess began paying tribute to him of their own accord.

The Lozi group flourished and multiplied and soon it was impossible for the whole group to stay in one place in the central plain. Besides the desire for empire, it was mainly this expansion process which led to the conquest of the surrounding tribes. In most cases factions went off as a result of misunderstandings within the group. The parent group of the Lozi that remained in the central plain came to be known as Mbowe or Mambowe. One group followed the young brother of Mboo called Mwanambinyi, after misunderstandings had arisen between him and his elder brother. This group came south into the Subiya and Mbukushu country in the present Senanga district. Since these people were great fishermen and had fish as their main diet, they came to be known as 'Akwandi' or 'Makwandi' (fish-eaters). Another group under another brother of Mboo, called Mange, left the main

---

[1] Mr N. S. Zaza—see note 3 on page. 241 The Mulena Mukwae of Nalolo did not put it in the same way, but did say people living near Libonda in the north talked more freely on the origin of the Lozi than any other group of people in the plain. See note 1, page 243.

group and drove away the Nkoya from the eastern forest. It is held that Mange left the main group because he was displeased when his elder brother Mboo was chosen king. Later relationships with the parent group became so bad that they began fighting. Mange's people were defeated and in the course of the war they deserted their leader. This act of desertion earned them a nickname of 'Kwangwa' or 'Akangwa Mange', which means 'they who failed Mange'. The last group to break away went west and lived by Simaa River which is a tributary of the Zambesi. These came to be known as Makwa Simaa. Hence the Mbowe, Kwangwa, Kwandi and Simaa people are all branches of the Aluyana group.

The reasons given for the breakaway of Mwambwa's group from the Lunda of Mwata Yamuo varied a lot with different groups of informants. Some traditions have it that Mwambwa was fleeing from the wrath of Mwata Yamvo after committing a breach of tradition. Women chiefs were not allowed to have children once they ascended the throne. However, Mwambwa bore two children and rather than face the punishment she fled the country. Others hold that it was not so much because queens were not allowed to have children, but because these children were born of an incestuous union. Mbuyu, Mwambwa's daughter, is said to have contracted a similar incestuous union and that is why the identity of the father of her children has never been disclosed by the Lozi.[1]

The most striking thing here is the similarity between the particular tradition and that of the Lovedu, another divine kingship society which broke away from the Karanga-Rozwi group in the early 17th century. Here a daughter of one of the Mambos—Dzugudini—has an infant son although she is not married. The girl and her mother conceal the name of the seducer from both the Mambo and the public, saying 'the father of the child of a king's daughter is not to be known'. As the Mambo becomes very suspicious, the princess and her infant son flee to the south carrying with her rain charms and the sacred beads. Tradition has it that the seducer of the princess was her uterine brother.[2] In both

[1] Information given on condition that informant's name should not be disclosed.
[2] Krige, *The Realm of the Rain Queen*, p. 5.

Lovedu and Lozi stories, then, the creation of a new people is justified by virtue of incest. It is understood that most of the mystery surrounding contemporary Lozi rituals is based on the original act of incest committed by the early ancestors—Mwambwa and Mbuyu.[1]

Details given in oral tradition concerning Mwambwa's wanderings are rather unsatisfactory, but one particular version has it that immediately after breaking away from the main Lunda group, the Lozi dwelt at Ikuyu near the confluence of the Kabompo and Lyambai. Mwambwa Njemakati was the leader and ruler of the group. When the population increased they moved on looking for a new kingdom. To begin with they moved east till they reached Ngalanganja near Ba Congo. They did not stay long here before they began moving westward. Next they came to settle in the Kaombwe swamps near the source of the Zambesi. From Kaombwe the Lozi moved south till they came to Ikuyu again. Then they came to Nayaka which was later called Sesheke. It was here that the transfer from female to male rulers took place. Mwambwa's *indunas* plotted to rebel against her in favour of a male ruler.[2] Mwambwa learned of the plot before it materialized, so she wisely abdicated in favour of her eldest son Muyunda who was later called Mboo.[3]

It is clear from the many variants already discussed that when one has penetrated behind the official story to be found in Jalla, one does not discover a single common version of Lozi origins. That would, in any case, be too much to expect. But at least these new traditions point to a reasonable answer—that the origin of Lozi political institutions has to be sought primarily in the Luba-Lunda centre, and that they reached Barotseland at some time during the Lunda diaspora described by C. N. White. The stories also point to the fact that in origin the Lozi state was a conquest state whose institutions were imposed on the pre-existing population. But the fact of the Rozwi origin occurring in a sort of minority version of Lozi tradition should perhaps warn us from an

[1] Information given on condition that informant's name should not be disclosed.

[2] By Lubinda Imataa Kabuku. See note 2, page 243.

[3] See note 1, page 242.

exclusive concentration on the Lunda origin. Barotseland, after all, lies between the Luba-Lunda and Karanga-Rozwi centres and may well owe influences to both.

One main criticism that can be made of the abundant material still waiting to be collected in the field is that the distinctions of place and time are ignored. This leads to strange distortions. Man and events are pictured not in the shape of their setting in the past but in the colours of the values of the present. A lot more work and patience are necessary before we can find a final answer to the problem before us. One other problem, one feels, is to overcome the suspicion that exists in the mind of the people and our informants. In the course of my research, it became quite plain that it was suspicion more than anything else which had led to the concealment of a number of 'true' oral traditions in favour of the façade found in Jalla. This emerged quite clearly in the questions asked by informants—'Why are you asking about where we came from? Do you want to make out that the Lunda are senior to us?' or 'Why are you asking who was here when we arrived? Do you want to give the land back to the people?'

However, historians have a rich field in Barotseland which up to now has been left almost untouched. A close examination and study of the royal graves alone, for example, would yield rich historical data.

11

THE COLONIZATION OF BAROTSELAND IN THE 17TH CENTURY

by

L. S. MUUKA

'THE origin of the Lozi' is a very contentious subject upon which political, social and cultural forces have exerted great influence. Linked with the history of the Barotse Litungas and their present claims to land and political power, it has evoked many varied interpretations. It is in the interests of the ruling class to claim that the original home of the Barotse was Barotseland itself. The Lunda–Lozi connection is dismissed as an insignificant relationship in the course of history of two tribes or nations which have been co-existent and whose territories were contiguous. If the Barotse came at one stage from the Congo it was to return to their motherland where they were neither immigrants nor invaders.

There are those who do not accept this view, however. These have been told by their fathers that the Lozi came from the Congo, that they were part of the great Lunda–Luba empire, but that somewhere in the 17th century they, under the leadership of a female leader, Mwambónjema Kati or Mwambwa, trekked down the Kabompo and the Zambesi to set up a separate autonomous kingdom on the Upper Zambesi.[1]* It is known that at this time the Lunda–Luba diaspora was taking place. The reasons for this diaspora are not so clear-cut. It is possible that there was a population explosion in this powerful and relatively more civilized state. Again it may be that many a discontented sub-leader wanted to find gratification in military campaigns which carried him far afield and, more often than not, kept him there permanently. The quest for better lands, for political power over the weak

* Superior numerals in this chapter refer to the list of sources shown in the notes on pp. 259–60.

248

tribes, and, as someone has suggested in connection with the Lozi, socio-political differences in the Lunda–Luba empire arising out of breaches of the tradition[2] on the part of Mwambwa; all these may have combined to lead to the great population movement which affected places as far afield as Barotseland to the west, Bembaland to the north and the adjoining territory of the Kazembes on the Luapula.

Nor are these the only theories on this subject. Some people have sought the ancestral home of the Barotse in the country of the Mambos[3] (the rulers of the Rozwi) in present-day Southern Rhodesia. Briefly, the story is that the head of one of the junior houses of the royal house differed with the Great Mambo and set out to the north with stolen symbols of authority. He may have gone up the Luangwa, after crossing the Zambesi, pushed over-land to the country of the Kazembes into the Congo, and finally come down to the Upper Zambesi after clashes with the Lunda of Mwata Yamvo. Alternatively, he may have led his band of warriors along the course of the Zambesi to the upper reaches, where he set up the nucleus of the present Luyana kingdom.

But on examining all these theories it would seem that the 'Lunda–Luba diaspora theory' is more defensible than any other. The interesting thing about these theories, but one which also complicates the matter, is that they are not generally held by this or that social, political or tribal group. Opinions are as divergent among the ruling aristocracy as they are among the subject tribes. Even the royal family has got no uniform 'royal interpretation of history' as such.[4] But a few surviving sociological similarities between the Lozi and the Lunda make themselves manifest. Both societies have a distinct royal family in whom all authority, earthly and spiritual, finds a common apex. Both changed from female rulers to male rulers.[5] Place names such as Imuba and Namayula are found in both territories.[6] There are a number of similarities in the instruments of authority and the regalia of king-ship. And if we believe that the splinter group, namely the Lozi, strove to maintain their independence from the mother country, then there is little difficulty in accounting for the dissimilarities which may tend to obscure the link. Splinter groups are known to be somewhat revolutionary in the realms of sociology and politics if only to establish their own identity. Above all the study of lines of communications would seem to indicate a stronger Lozi-Lunda link than the remote Mambo pseudo-link.

This numerous group of Aluyi, as they called themselves to signify their liking for and economic dependence on the Zambesi River, believed in the existence of one Great God, Nyambe.[7] He was conceived of as the creator, the merciful, the almighty and giver of all things. He was, by nature, without flesh or bones—

Kasamusimwa Kaloyangundu, Minyamisimwáenyi. Uyu natunmuka bakanwa natumuka ba kaluyango bali mwala. Tanyamaminyi unamanongwawina. Uiluteela bakimwa belukulimbulula. Kawa maci, bo kawa nungu, to li ba munu.

(True, there was none so powerful as to withstand his command when the hour came. Nor was it possible to foretell when his messenger, death, would visit, so that escape was vain.)

To him prayers were said in the morning and evening; and everyone felt it their duty to offer to Nyambe a part of all they achieved. Seeds, hoes, spears, and cattle were all dedicated to him. His abode was somewhere in the firmament, his city was called Litooma.

Once the Aluyi were in Barotseland their history becomes less obscure and tangled. There is a lot of 'spread-eagleism' of course, which particularly tries to tie up the creation of the universe with the establishment of Barotse royal kingship. Thus, we are told, the royal family dates from the time when Nyambe was on earth, and divine paternity is claimed for this family.[8] But again if we recollect what we have said before about the behaviour of a splinter group bent on asserting its own autonomy and separate identity we can easily appreciate this functional link.

On the Upper Zambesi, Mwambwa and her Aluyi built a settlement at Sifuti.[9] They later moved down to Imuba—the Great Mound—which they built with their own labour to combat the flood. It was from Imuba that Luyana power radiated to distant parts of the country. Members of the royal family, spoken of as Mwambwa's grandchildren, were sent out to rule parts of this expanding kingdom. It should be noted here that Mwambwa remained at Sifuti and her daughter Mbuyu, or Mbuywamwa-

mbwa, succeeded her as leader of the Aluyi. It was Mbuywamwambwa's children who were to play a decisive part in the expansion
of this kingdom.

Most ambitious among them was Mwanambinyi.[10] He established himself at Nayaka, close to Libonda, his brother Mboo's
village. A struggle for power had raged between these two, a
struggle which was exacerbated at a later date by Mboo's accession to power. There are a number of interesting episodes during
the course of this struggle. There was, for instance, a bull contest
and, finally, Mbuywamwambwa's dramatic intervention on Lake
Kayoyo which ended with Lubindatanga's exile to Matondo-wa-
Ngwinyi, taking with him the name of Nangula. Mwanambinyi,
together with his cattle and *indunas*, was advised to go south to
save the young state from internal strife. In so doing he helped
expand Luyana authority to the southern reaches of the Barotse
Plain. There he subjugated the Mbukushu of Katima-Mulilo and
captured the drums of their chief Lukonga. The other chiefs,
Liswani and Cute, fled away. The Subiya were also brought under
his power and he moved them from Sesheke and settled them in
present-day Senanga District. He set up his capital at Imatongo
and from here Mulia, his son, led his armies either to conquer
some weak tribe or to defend the southern kingdom from the
armies of the northern kingdom. Mwanambinyi ruled for a long
time in the south. His sister, Imafuwa, was an influential political
figure and when the northern armies threatened defeat during the
reign of Ngalama she performed the final rites to her brother who
died like a Roman in the face of superior forces. Mulia led the
remaining southern loyalists to the east along the Luyi River. He
stayed for a while in Kawingu's country, then moved on to
Bayeke country which his son conquered. In the end Mulia went
to Kalunda in the country of the Lunda by way of the Kabompo.

Important among Mwanambinyi's *indunas* was Subulwa-
Mbuyu, who later became chief *induna* at Imafuwa's court. His
original home was Simonyi near Libonda. From the same village
also was Inumekule, Mwanambinyi's chief steward who, like
Subulwa, went with Mwanambinyi to Imatongo. Yusikwa-Nam-
waka-o-Liyungu and Akende-Namwaka were his sons. His
official title was Yambwanda.

Muyunda,[11] popularly known as Mboo-Mwanasilandu, was
also Mbuywamwambwa's son. His first village was Libonda, close
to Mwanambinyi's Nayaka. The village was first called Nanguya.
When Mboo was made ruler of the Aluyi he moved south to
Ikatulama—now called Ikatulamwa. His first Ngambela was Nawa,
also from Simonyi, who was known by the official name of
Ing'uwa-Mwambwa. He was of the family of Namwaka-mbuyu.
During his term of office he was given official villages, viz.
Ngombwe and Nalimbundu. After his death one of Ikumeses'
relations was brought from Kalala, near Sifuti, to become
Ngambela. His name was Imbala-Mwambwa.

During his reign Mboo fought and repulsed the Andonyi
people—a Luvale–Lunda people who were called Ailuvale—

Ailubale ailitopolile, aimayulu mambotomana, imatako malambalala.

'To the Luyana they looked funny, the lazy Luvale, a people with
prominent noses and flat buttocks!' Nambula, a heroine in this
struggle and a daughter of Lutangu Akashambatwa (Mboo's
steward), was given a high place at court. From her came the
office of Mbimbi, during wars. Next, he fought and defeated the
Mwenyi and Mishulundu, peoples of the west. He sent Lunda-
buyu, his daughter, to rule the Mwenyi, while another daughter, Mwanamuke, took authority over the defeated Mishulundu
people, residing at Kayoka's. Ufuyoyo (now Sinde) was Lundambuyu's chief councillor and Mundandwe was Mwanamuke's.
The other councillors for Lundambuyu included Nawa, Mubita-
Namaulwa and Kongwa-Namaulwa. Her valley-village was
Sikenge. Imwandi, Mboo's son, was also given a village, Ngoyi.
The other son, Ndikusita (the home of the fish is the deepest part
of the river), was given a village of his own also (it is the village
given to Prince Yeta of Mbololwa), and yet another son of
Mboo's, Sikena, was given Mulundwe. All these villages were
centres of small dukedoms and he or she was a potentate who
controlled them.

Mboo tried many sites before he eventually settled in Ikatulama.
First, as we have seen before, he set up Libonda as a prince. Then
when he came to power he built Nakatendeokoke, another man-
made mound, and tried to settle there. Next he went near

Simonyi and settled in Kambai. A sporting ruler, he later moved to Nangelelo (sometimes called Ubeana or, as the Kololo called it later, Mutopoloeo) which had a good view of wild game coming to drink in the lakes of Sata, Nambwewewe and Satomishino. But this was some distance from the Zambesi, so he went back to Nakatende.

Yeta,[12] also a son of Mbuywamwambwa, settled at Twamona but he later moved to Nawinda to guard against the Ailubale menace. He later became ruler of the Aluyi people. He was remarkable for his kindness and, indeed, he died from remorse after condemning his Ngambela, Angulu, to death. Yeta had another village, Mwandi-u-Likuli.

Another son of Mbuywamwambwa's was given Sakalumbwa near Mukola. His name was Ing'alamwa.[13] Very little is known about him except that some people believe he was not Mbuywamwambwa's son but her brother.[14] Whatever the relationship it seems that those who hold to this rather 'dangerous' theory have reason to believe that he was the eldest of the family. Another of Mbuywamwambwa's relatives, Isimwaa, settled in Mutungi and his 'communist' approach to life is usually quoted as the origin of Aluyi kingship.[15] But this, though popularly held, does not seem to be true. Ngalama, his son, later became a ruler and brought back the Kwangwa under his power.

Inyambo,[16] another son of Mbuywamwambwa's, was left in Imuba with his mother. But when she went back to Sifuti after Mboo had become ruler, he moved to Makululalo. He succeeded to the throne after Mboo's death and made Sikuli his capital. His Ngambela was Iwake. He, too, had his fights with the western menace, the Andonyi people, now known as the Itulabo as they had by this time begun to use canoes in their night attacks on the Luyana.

Mwanawina[17] completes this list of Mbuywamwambwa's sons. Very little is known about him, but he also was given a small area to administer. His village was Nyuwe—the place of elephants. The name was changed during the Makololo period to Liaci or Nanyaci, which still meant the same thing as the original 'Nyuwe'. Hence the name Ilicima-wa-Nyuwe; hence also the term 'bo Ilicima' which is a respectful way of addressing Mboanjikana of

Libonda just as 'bo Ingangwana' is applied to the Litunga under similar circumstances. It would seem that Mwanawina's area was called Sikongo.

This brings us to yet another impressive list of Mbuywam-wambwa's children, that of the girls.[18] Senior among them was Mboanjikana who settled in Lunde. When Mboo became ruler of the Aluyana, Mboanjikana went to Libonda to take his place. She died there and was buried there. Lunde was renamed Namakundi. It is here that Akatoka lies, but this is a later occurrence. Next to Mboanjikana was Namakau of Mulundu. Her little province was called Sikata (Sikata sa moti ilufunga ngombe—a tether for cattle is very strong, impossible to uproot if one end is tied to a bundle of grass buried in the ground). The name 'Mulundu' has also changed to 'Kwandu'. Next comes Nolea, who settled at Mabumbu or Pata near Mongu. She was the mother of Manga-Minyo-Upa, the leader of the Kwangwa and the man who extended Aluyana power in the forest region of the east. It would appear that this Aluyana junior branch tried to assert its own independence and they were only re-incorporated by the sword of Ngalama. The prince, Mange, drowned himself in Makapaela after the battle of Nangula in which the Kwangwa were subdued. His mother, Nolea, was buried in Mabumbu. Another daughter, Ing'utu of Namwanga, is not often mentioned and very little is known about her. Then comes Nakatindi, who lived at Sesheke-wa-Bulozi. Kaliubu,[19] sometimes called Kayiya,[20] followed Nakatindi, but again nothing is known about her. Still among Mbuywamwambwa's daughters were two Mbuyus, dis-tinguishable as Mbuywana[21] and Nabyana.[22] Mbuywana ruled the country near Silolo. She was the mother of Namwaka-Mbuyu of Simonyi. Mbuywana's cousin, Kangundamwambwa, settled at Imaboma. The other Mbuyu, sometimes known as Nabyana, was married to Lunde or Kalunda of Kaumbu in Lundaland. Those who claim that the Aluyana have no other original home apart from Barotseland insist that this was the only link with the Lunda. They concede, however, that this marriage took place at a time when Mbuywamwambwa and her people had gone to Lundaland for a temporary period. Nabyana bore children with chief Lunda and these also became rulers of the Lunda later. Here again some

people claim that Nabyana was Mwambwa's daughter and therefore Mbuywamwambwa's sister.

It would appear that practically the whole of the northern half
of the Barotse Valley was divided up into prince- and princess-
doms. The south was ruled by Mwamambinyi from Imatongo
and his sister Imafuwa from the village called after her. The forest
region in the east was under Nolea and her son Mange. But above
all there was Mbuywamwambwa and Mboo who wielded central
authority. Both at the central court and in the districts the royalty
ruled with the help and advice of the *indunas*. Through marriages,
gifts of land and cattle and through minor political offices which
were given to subjugated peoples the process of assimilation, so
vital to centralized states, began to mould a truly Aluyana society.
The Aluyana institutions of divine kingship, royal sisters and
Queen Mothers began to be repeated even by the conquered.
Aluyana power was truly in ascendancy. Its instruments, the ruling aristocracy, are still remembered, perhaps not as much as the
royalty, but their role is clear. They are epitomized in the praise-
names and their names are still living at the Kuta and in the district
kutas.[23]

Among them were men like Kandamwambwa, who was one of
Mbuywamwambwa's chief councillors. There was Wamuyoo,
whose name was later changed to Noyoo during the era of the
Makololo. He, like Imutoko-wa-Ng'undwe, was Mboo's councillor. Imutoko's praise-name ran as follows:

Imutoko-wa-Ng'undwe uli ndume bo uli-mai, no ku utukela lubeta
kwa fwikisandambwa ndae . . .

(You are brave, Imutuko of Ng'undwe, but at the same time you are
unfortunate, for in your moment of bravery you may rush to danger . . .)

There were some unfaithful councillors too, men like Silumenonge . . .

Silumenonge namunguya, a bona katunda mutulo wa Nonge be ni
mukena mukalala ni mu Sambwa-ta Nangulwe, Amasiku a kena ni
mutalaet ul mongo wa Kambia wa twai.

(Silumenonge you are a complete fool. How could you imagine that
you should exploit your position by desiring your king's wife? Surely
you deserved it, for the following morning you were a dead man.)

Among the able councillors was Imbwae-ng'ono, sometimes confused as Imbwae-o-maeo. The list is a long one: there was Nganga-Nambwae, an ancestor of Kalonga's; there was Inyanga, there was Yakumatwi, Akapelwa-wa-Nganga and Imalumba-Mbuyu, an ancestor of Ndambo Simalumba. Those who gave advice to Mwambonjema at Sifuti included Ikumese Akalilwa, Imikendu and Kangundamwambwa as well as Ingombe. Kangundamwambwa proved an inefficient councillor and so he lost his position at Sifuti. He retired to Imaboma with his sister, Moola.

In the outlying districts there were men like Nawasilundu who was advisor to Namakau. Malikana Siminuka was at Yeta's court where Angulu was the Ngambela.

It would appear that once established the Alyuana lived a settled life. The popular theory of constant population migrations does not seem to apply here. It is true that as more territory was acquired *indunas* and princes were sent out to administer the new areas. They settled there permanently and their children acquired land there and became the future ruling aristocracy, loyal to the authority and institutions of the Litunga and the central Kuta. But by and large the earlier *indunas'* descendants still occupy the same lands and villages occupied by their ancestors. Thus villages like Nayaka, Libonda, Ikatulama, Sesheke and Imatongo are still where they were at the time of Mbuywamwambwa. Some, like Simonyi,[24] have been moved either because of floods or because of increase in population which led the villagers to look for a larger mound to contain them. But such movements have revolved around relatively short radii. The question of permanency is especially important when we realize that some of these villages, like Makono, Mbuywamwambwa's burial place, are national shrines which cannot be abandoned.

It would appear that apart from the main Aluyana incursion into the settlement of Barotseland there was an earlier wave which came before.[25] It was led by Masinda and Kaputungu, both children of Mwambwa who were the first 'bone of contention' in the 'breach of custom' theory involving regal childbirth. It seems they were sent by their mother as scouts. They came to Barotseland and drove the Kwengo—a short and stocky people with very light complexion, whose language was full of click-sounds—to the fringes of the Kalahari. Masinda and Kaputungu went farther south and settled in the Mashi region. The Kwengo, having been driven out of the way, the main Aluyana wave found it easy to establish itself in the plain. The only menace to them came from the tribes inhabiting the forest region of the west. But it was not long before they became dominant. After Mwanambinyi's era, Barotseland was, on the whole, free from internecine wars.[26] Political struggles revolved around personalities within the ruling aristocracy and never assumed a national magnitude at any time until on the eve of the Makololo invasion.

The Aluyana proper lived, by and large, in the Barotse Plain[27] —Ului-ngulu, ya ka linga na mei, na mulilo. They believed this Ului-ngulu, the Plain, could not be completely flooded over or completely wiped out by a wild fire. Just as parts of it will remain untouched by the highest of floods so also parts of it would remain untouched by a blaze even during the dry season. The Aluyana were keepers of large herds of cattle. Indeed land and cattle were the hallmark of social and political status. Thus *indunas* were rewarded for their service by gifts of lands and cattle. There were villages and herds attached to political offices which the holders of office received and retained during the term of their office. With land went weirs, fish ponds and streams in the area. Large estates meant many villages which owed local allegiance to the local landlord or chief. Such landlords were expected to raise men and provide tribute for the Litunga. On the other hand, the Litunga would treat them with respect and as a result it was not conceivable for a Litunga to wield dictatorial powers. The grandees of the court, the local chiefs and landlords, were a powerful force he could not brush off easily without serious repercussions on his position.

The political institutions began with the village headman at the base and rose in power and authority, in triangular fashion, until they found their apex in the Litunga. Thus even the conquered tribes had room in this structure although their voice was not heard at the higher court with the same volume as at the village level. The Litunga ruled with a *kuta* of *indunas* and *likombwa*, the leaders of national and royal interests respectively. His powers were very wide, but it is inconceivable to talk of the Litunga in matters of importance without associating the decisions with the Kuta. He was royal, a divine king and sometimes referred to as the earthly God. He had the powers of life and death in the entire kingdom. But the grandees were responsible for his installation and in a state where succession is a fluid matter, although it revolved within the royal family, he would not antagonize the Kuta if he hoped to rule long. Besides he needed the *indunas'* co-operation in the raising of armies, the collection of tribute and the administration of justice as well as the maintenance of law and order. Like the Queen Mother, the royal sisters and the Nata-moyo, a member of royalty who sat in the Kuta as a minister of justice and mercy, the Litunga was a sanctuary for offenders. A departed Litunga was considered to wield more power than the living one. He was the national mediator between the living and Nyambe. In the event of a famine, a drought or an invasion, the living Litunga would lead his people to ask the departed king to forward their request to Nyambe. At accession the Litunga-to-be would spend a night with a few of the grandees at Makono, the burial place of Mbuywamwambwa. Thereafter he is given the royal drums and the war drums. Then he would make a new fire for the whole nation. His name means 'The Land or Earth'. In land matters he was a trustee for the whole nation.

It has already been stated that the Aluyana were keepers of cattle. They loved milk, especially sour milk. Their country abounded with game for meat, with fowl and fish. Kaffir corn was the staple cereal until Namushi of Akenda introduced maize later. A variety of lilies, sibuyuyu, a kind of grass whose seeds re-sembled those of rice—and many different products of the valley and the forest supplemented their diet. Intoxicating drink was unknown to the Aluyana—the nearest to it was their drink made out of honey and sour milk, Ilya. The nature of the territory allowed for a great degree of specialization based on regions and this was a stimulus to trade—barter being the mode of exchange. The valley Aluyana caught fish, kept cattle and exchanged their products with canoe makers, blacksmiths and honey-collectors of the forest regions. Pottery, basketry, mat-making and wood-carving became regionally specialized occupations. Trade fairs were held during the winter months—a practice which laid the pattern for the trade fairs of the last century, during which the Mambari, agents of Portuguese ivory hunters, exchanged supplies of cheap calico, guns and gun-powder, for ivory.

The Aluyana society was free from disease. The only disease which was common was leprosy or the 'fire of God', as they referred to it. A leper was always confined and isolated in a hut on the leeward side of the village. His eating vessels were not used by anyone else. But as the kingdom expanded new diseases were introduced—especially the 'possession' type of diseases. The Kaonde brought 'Macoba', the Lima introduced 'Liyala' and 'Maimbwe'. Aluyana dances included 'Ngomalume', a war dance, 'Liimba' and 'Liwale', which dances were all performed at the Kuta.

This chapter has been based on material collected in a space of two months—a pilot survey in oral tradition among the Lozi. No attempt has been made, therefore, to supplement the information with what little has been written on the early history of the Lozi. The result is necessarily tentative and incomplete.

NOTES

INFORMANTS

Evangelist Luke M. Akayombokwa, Village Simonyi, Libonda. Over 60 years old. I stayed at his home for 2 days, 7–9 January, 1963. (Refs. 1, 6, 7, 9–13, 16–18, 20–21, 23, 24, 27.)

Gordon Muyunda from Senaga (in the south). Clerical Officer, Northern Rhodesia Government. About 40 years old. Interviewed at Mongu, 7 December 1962. (Refs. 2, 5, 14, 25.)

Mrs Mubita—claims to have been told the story by some 'progressive' family near Sefula. Interviewed on 7 December 1962 at the Barotse National School, Mongu. Not true Lozi. (Ref. 3.)

The Litunga agrees basically with A. Jalla; not so his daughter, the Princess Chief (Mulena Mukwae). (Ref. 4.)

Official informants at Lealui. (Ref. 7.)

Official informants—assigned to me by the Litunga-in-Council, theoretically available all the time. (Refs. 8, 19, 22.)

Induna Amba. (Refs. 9. 13, 16–18, 23.)

Official informants. (Refs. 9, 10–13, 15, 16–18, 23, 27.)

Induna Muleta (premier) at Libonda. (Ref. 23.)

Silenga, Village Iliuka. Former *sikombwa* (steward) to Lewanika, Yeta and Inwiko. About 60 years old. (Ref. 26.)

On life of the Aluyana: Mwene Matako, a Mbunda, who claims to have come to Barotseland some 130 years ago as a baby. Lives in Village Kabulwandila, Mabumbu. Has fought in 1884–5 rebellion, in both Shukulumbwe wars. Interviewed on 7 and 20 December 1962. The Litunga. *Induna* Luyanga.

12

BAROTSELAND:
THE SURVIVAL OF AN AFRICAN STATE

by

ERIC STOKES

'Truly the pen is mightier than the sword, and in the hands of experts . . . achieved more in Barotseland than the most potent lethal weapon in many of our less fortunate dependencies.'
—COLIN HARDING, *Far Bugles.*

AT a cursory glance Central African political systems would appear to have been too insecurely based to survive the onset of European rule. Although the region contained a relatively high proportion of centralized state systems they all collapsed or were swept aside, the governing powers of the 'paramounts' being taken over by the European district officers and the chiefs in their political capacities surviving merely as local headmen and constabulary officers of the white government. This chapter seeks to study how one kingdom, that of the Lozi, escaped the general fate, and in severely truncated and attenuated form passed into the era of modern politics.[1]

It is obvious that Barotseland's survival could have been brought about only by a particularly favourable constellation of circumstances. Of prime importance was the independent initiative taken by this fairly powerful, isolated, inacessible kingdom, to open a window on to the modern world. That initiative came at a point in time when the British South Africa Company as the main agency of northward expansion was engaged in feverishly pegging out claims for the future but was in no position to administer or settle the region north of the Zambesi. The price of the mineral rights over North-Western Rhodesia coveted by the

[1] I would like to acknowledge the assistance of a grant from the Rockefeller Foundation in the preparatory work for this chapter.

Company was protectorate status guaranteed by the British Government; and the missionary go-between, Coillard, through
whom the negotiations were conducted, provided Lewanika
with a ready-made diplomatic channel capable of ensuring that
the terms of the bargain were not lightly overridden. The protracted failure, or rather inability, of the Company to carry out
the terms of the Lochner Concession of 1890 further promoted the
survival of the Lozi policy. By the time the Company was ready
at the end of the 1890's to take up its rights its escutcheon was so
blotted by the Matabele war and rebellion and the Jameson Raid
that the British Government was forced to interpose a strict
supervision to ensure the peaceable extension of European
control.

On the strength of the Lochner Concession the British Government formally announced the recognition of a protectorate to be
exercised through the agency of the Company; but the terms of
the concession itself were never ratified and so have relevance only
so far as they were incorporated in subsequent agreements. The
negotiation of the concession is, however, worth looking at more
closely for the light it throws on the interplay of African and
European motives.

The train of events on the European side began in May 1889
when, as a result of discussions with Harry Johnston in London,
Rhodes agreed to send 'agents to the Barotse country which
would secure British supremacy in that part', while he made
£2,000 over to Johnston to be used 'in securing other claims to
the British South Africa Company between Lake Nyasa and the
Barotse country'.[1] The immediate intention was to lay claim to
as broad a swathe of territory as could be secured north of the
Zambesi between the Portuguese settlements on the east and west
coasts. Almost at the same time (June 1889), under circumstances
which have not been properly elucidated, the Barotse chiefs
granted a mineral concession to Henry Ware over the Batoka
country (the region north of the Falls between the Machili and
Kafue rivers). As early as October 1888, according to Coillard's

---

[1] Johnston to Rhodes, 8 October 1893, encl. in Johnston to Rosebery;
FO 2/55. Cited Roland Oliver, *Sir Harry Johnston and the Scramble for Africa*,
1957, p. 154.

account, Lewanika had sought to stabilize his own internal political position by asking for British protection, but had been opposed by the chiefs.[1] Following the Ware Concession Coillard was at last authorized to send a formal request for protection to the British authorities at the Cape.

Profiting from this initiative and having succeeded in buying out Ware's concession, Rhodes sent up F. E. Lochner in September 1889 to wring further concessions from Lewanika and Msidi (Msiri) in the Katanga. Rutherfoord Harris, the Company's secretary at its Kimberley office, wrote with his customary pert loquacity, that 'these missions cost practically nothing and will in future give us the whole position if necessary . . . Our great object should be, where possible with little expense, to place our finger waiting for the practical development which is sure to come.'[2] Lochner was supplied with a detailed draft treaty and instructions to secure the cancellation of the 4 per cent royalty to be paid Lewanika under the Ware Concession. By the time Lochner had reached the Barotse Valley in April 1890, the Scramble was in full career. It was now a question of producing sufficient treaty claims for the partition agreements under negotiation in Europe.[3] In May the London directors were cabling: 'It is most important secure all you can treaties with Zambesi otherwise Government do not announce British influence. Thomson must act in combination with Lochner it is most most important anticipate advance Portuguese from Zumbo.'[4] Anxiety in the Company was renewed in July 1890 when the terms of the Anglo-German agreement

---

[1] F. Coillard, On the Threshold of Central Africa, 2nd ed., 1902, pp. 329, 356. Before his death in 1888 George Westbeech had been the 'licensed' supplier of trade goods. Arrangements with Ware were partially aimed at finding a replacement for Westbeech. Cf. E. C. Tabler, ed., Trade and Travel in Early Barotseland; The Diaries of George Westbeech 1885-8, 1963, referred to hereafter as Westbeech Diaries.

[2] F. Rutherfoord Harris to Weatherley, Secy. B.S.A. Co., 16 September 1889; National Archives, Salisbury, CT 2/11/1.

[3] Loch to C.O. (telegram), 7 April 1890; F.O. Pr. 6968, encl. 2 in No. 17. Secy. B.S.A. Co., London, to Harris, 11 April 1890; Salisbury Archives CT 1/11/1/1.

[4] Secy. B.S.A. Co., London, to Harris, 2 May 1890, confirming text of telegram. CT 1/11/1/1. When it became clear Lochner would not be able to continue to Msidi's, Joseph Thomson was dispatched to Katanga via Lake Nyasa.

became known providing for German access to the Zambesi above the Falls,[1] while alarmist reports from Thomson of German and Portuguese agents making for the country west of Lake Nyasa sharpened impatience for a formal declaration of a British sphere of influence. The Barotse country was believed rich in minerals, but the immediate concern was to fix a boundary to the British northern Zambesian sphere as far to the west as possible, partly with the idea 'at some future opportunity to exchange the country to the west of Barotse for the Portuguese possessions of the east coast'.[2]

Lochner's negotiations, protracted over three months, were far from plain sailing. Lewanika excused the initial delays on the absence of many of his principal *indunas* on a war expedition. But it is clear that his own position was difficult and equivocal. Lochner appears to have been a man of the ordinary colonial stamp, 'better adapted for camp life than diplomacy', and blinkered by the obtuse race prejudice of his kind. The Barotse he thought 'very much worse than the Matabele . . . [they were] born thieves and beggars, practise the worst form of witchcraft and altogether are a most awful lot of savages'.[3] His reports lack all sensitive percipience and for the most part echo Coillard's generalities. Popular derision was aroused by his attempts to buy off opposition,[4] an opposition which had been fanned by certain white traders, Weyers (Wehas) and Sell, and by earlier rumours put about by Ware, who warned against the dangers of 'selling' the country to a monopolist group. On the Lozi side the key to the opposition seems to have been what Coillard described as 'the old heathen, conservative party', which he feared would expel the mission if it gained the upper hand. Both Coillard and Lochner

[1] Telegram to Rhodes, per Wernher, Beit & Co., recd. 7 July 1890: 'Flaw agreement—Give German access Zambesi—Colonial office fear German extend northwards—Must be checkmated. Shall we send another expedition or can you arrange secure upper and west Zambesi?' Harris to B.S.A. Co., London, 7 July 1890; Salisbury Archives, LO 5/2/2.

[2] Copy of cablegram, Kimberley Office to Home Board, 2 July 1890; LO 5/2/2.

[3] Lochner to Harris, 10 June 1890; LO 5/2/3. For Coillard's poor view of Lochner, cf. *On the Threshold of Central Africa*, p. 385.

[4] Coillard, p. 385. Coillard to Smith, 20 June 1890; Salisbury Archives, CO 5/1/1/1.

refer to the Sesheke chiefs as the central element.[1] These dozen or
so *indunas* under the Mulasiane (Morantsiane) governed the country around the Chobe-Zambesi confluence and guarded the passage across the river from the south. They had frequently been
reconstituted as a result of the internal revolutions of the Lozi;
and the most recent change which occurred after Lewanika had
recovered power in 1886, was the appointment as Mulasiane of
Kabuku, the young son of Lewanika's elder sister, the Mulena
Mukwae, Matauke. This close link with the Mulena Mukwae's
kuta at Nalolo appears to have involved the Sesheke chiefs in the
internal rivalry between Nalolo and the Lealui *kuta* under Lewanika. Although the Mukwae was regarded by Coillard as a covert
enemy of the Paris missionaries, there would not appear, from the
scanty evidence available, any formal opposition to European
influence founded on clear principle.[2] Rather was it a question of
jealousy lest Lewanika's relations with the missionaries and the
Chartered Company should give him undue advantages and so
disturb the internal balance of power.

Lewanika's apparent procrastination and his inability to adhere
to a clear line of action led Coillard to believe the king to be hope-
lessly weak; but in fact he may have been playing a clever waiting
game. Lochner had learned his political arithmetic from Coillard:

> The king is wretchedly weak, in fact the country is a republic and if
> one wants to be successful in a mission like mine the chiefs are the
> people to gain over, they don't care twopence for the king and the
> king is in mortal dread of going against them . . .[3]

The Sesheke chiefs, according to Lochner, were 'the most powerful factor in the country, and are supposed to be in opposition to
the king in his desire for protection and the advent of the white
people'. Handsome presents had got them on the best of terms.
In the event of his failure to obtain a concession over the whole
country from Lewanika and the Lealui chiefs, Lochner said he

[1] Coillard, *Central Africa*, p. 385.
[2] Coillard, *Central Africa*, p. 350. On the Sesheke *indunas* and Kabuku, cf.
Westbeech, *Diaries*, pp. 33–4, 56, 73. Some of the Sesheke chiefs appear to have
gone over to Sikabenga, the Mulasiane deposed in December 1885, when he
led a revolt against Lewanika in March 1888; Westbeech, *Diaries*, pp. 96 ff.
[3] Lochner to Harris, 10 June 1890; LO 5/2/3.

planned to bypass the latter and work the Ware Concession over the Batoka country in alliance with the Sesheke chiefs. If this, indeed, accurately represents the attitude of the Sesheke chiefs it would indicate that they were playing for their own hand in the internal struggle for power and wealth rather than fighting for the exclusion of the white man as such.

Coillard had forced Lochner to raise the terms of the concession to the comparatively large sum of £2,000 a year as an annuity, and to forgo cancellation of the Ware royalty. The £2,000, like all tribute, he had argued, would come to the *kuta* at Lealui and be apportioned among the chiefs at large, thus firmly anchoring them in loyalty to the Company.[1] Coillard, of course, had his own reasons for wanting to see British protection, even though exercised at the hands of a commercial company. Quite apart from the greater measure of security for the Mission it would afford, foreign protection was bound to strengthen Lewanika's own internal political position upon which the Mission's influence vitally depended. In addition he was quick to appreciate that immediate agreement with the Company would preserve a much ampler measure of self-government for the Lozi, a consideration important to a society whose whole experience in Basutoland had attuned it to success through a dominant grip on the chiefly structure rather than working under the less favourable and congenial conditions of direct white settler rule:

For my part I have no doubt that for the nation this will prove the one plank of safety. It was not in the power of these tribes, only bound together by the chains of an abject and disgraceful servitude, to oppose a permanent barrier to the invading floods of emigrants and gold-seekers. Today they knock at the door and ask for a treaty; tomorrow, they would have broken it down and invaded the country as masters. The Barotse are incapable of governing, and left to themselves, they would before long have annihilated each other.[2]

Despite his precautions to appear neutral in the negotiations Coillard was the moving influence, as Lochner was the first to acknowledge. The concession was given formal assent at a public *pitso* on 27 June 1890, at which Khama's authority, through his

---

[1] Lochner to Secy. B.S.A. Co., Kimberley, 2 July 1890; LO 5/2/3.
[2] Coillard, p. 388.

representative, was thrown into the scale to silence the waverers. For all his wariness Coillard was caught in the wave of reaction following Lochner's departure. Middleton, the 'renegade' Paris Missionary Society's missionary, gained the ear of the Litunga and persuaded him that he had been cheated out of the queen's protection and had bartered away his country to a group of monopolist gold concessionaires. By October 1890 Coillard was writing to Rhodes:

The King himself is in the greatest state of agitation. He pretends not to have fully understood the bearings of the question & to have been taken advantage of. Indeed he even avers that he has been wilfully deceived. He says that what he wanted & still wants is to be under the Protectorate of the Queen, & not to be at the mercy of a Gold Mining Company. It is contended by him & his advisers that the annuity of £2,000 without any royalty is a cheat and a mockery & that the concession must be broken at any risk.[1]

In June 1891 Coillard felt the situation to be so critical that he bowed to the Litunga's insistence and wrote to Harris returning the £200 which had been paid on account by Lochner as a first instalment of the Ware Concession subsidy. Coillard himself had become incensed at the Chartered Company's failure to send a resident or to take any steps to observe the terms of the Lochner Concession. That concession had only been agreed, he wrote pointedly, because of the clause implying the queen's protection, in which it had been stated 'that any agreement with the Company was to be considered in the light of a treaty or alliance made between the nation (the Barotse) and *the Government of Her Britannic Majesty Queen Victoria*'.[2]

Once more the centre of opposition in the country appears to have been Sesheke, where in May 1891 the Primitive Methodist missionary, Baldwin, and Goy of the Paris Missionary Society, were maltreated ostensibly for some breach of etiquette at the Mukwae's residence, Lewanika professed himself helpless:

The king certainly shared my feelings. He was very much displeased at the affair, and he cast all the odium of it upon the Sesheke chiefs.

[1] Coillard to Rhodes, 27 October 1890; Salisbury Archives CT 1/4/3. Also G. W. Middleton to B.S.A. Co., 27 October 1890; LO 5/2/12.
[2] Coillard to Harris, 5 June 1891; LO 5/2/12.

Mukwae, according to him, was nothing but a tool in their hands. He wanted to send them a severe reprimand, but was grieved that he had nobody courageous enough to convey his message to them. It was in vain that together we went over the principal personages of the [Barotse] Valley. The Seshekians are formidable and everybody fears them.[1]

In his journal Coillard wrote in more agitated language than that intended for publication in the *Journal des Missions Evangeliques*; he made it clear that internal politics once again lay at the root of the trouble:

'It is my impression that they wish to kill (harm?) me, & to sacrifice me to the animosity of this nation. The King is doing it to save himself. The king is accusing everybody of having made a plot against him & wishing to kill him to put Sepopa in his place.'[2]

The news of a Ndebele crossing of the Zambesi came opportunely on 15 June 1891 to end the immediate crisis. Towards the end of October official despatches from Loch at Cape Town announced the British Government's formal recognition of a protectorate and the storm clouds dispersed.[3] Yet after his experience Coillard was determined to act no more as Lewanika's intermediary.

The shaping of the colonial relationship depended partially on formal legal instruments but increasingly on political usage. The actual form of that control was worked out haltingly and piecemeal. Initially it was expected that Johnston, the Commissioner appointed to start up the administration in Nyasaland and the Nyasa-Tanganyika Plateau, would establish relations with Lewanika; but straitness of funds and difficulties of communication put this out of the question, Johnston himself expressing the view that geography placed Barotseland in the South African political orbit. In 1895 the Foreign Office agreed to hand over administrative responsibility for the sphere north of the Zambesi to the Company.

As a consequence of this decision it seems to have been assumed that the Company would establish a direct form of overrule in

[1] Coillard, 16 June 1891, *Central Africa*, p. 423.
[2] CO 5/1/1/1 f. 1060.
[3] Coillard, p. 437. Loch to Lewanika, 19 September 1891, LO 5/2/12

North-West Rhodesia, for it was arranged that Hubert Hervey (later killed in the rebellion) should proceed to Barotseland 'to obtain administrative powers from the Chief'.[1] Moreover, the British Government appeared perfectly prepared to allow the Company to exercise as full a control of affairs as it did in Southern Rhodesia, and a draft Northern Zambesia Order in Council was actually prepared to extend the 1894 Matabeleland Order in Council north of the river. In that event the Company would have been armed with sovereign powers of jurisdiction and Lewanika's position would have been sensibly weaker. But the Jameson Raid and the rebellions threw the whole scheme into the air. It was no longer possible to extend the Company's administrative powers north of the Zambesi; and though the Company continued to pay and provide officers they were subject to the authority of the High Commissioner.

Lewanika's persistent representations, and the need to ascertain Lozi claims to territory west of the Zambesi (disputed by Portugal) could not be ignored indefinitely; and led to the dispatch of an Imperial Officer, Major Goold-Adams, to visit Lewanika in late 1896. For all his discontent with the Company Lewanika agreed to confirm the Lochner Concession so long as the area reserved for him and his people were greatly extended.[2] After Coillard had again been in London, the Colonial Office confirmed that the concession did not entitle the Company to make land grants to white settlers; and when at length in September 1897 the first Resident, R. T. Coryndon, took up his post he hastened to assure Lewanika in writing: 'You are definitely under British protection. You gave a concession to the British South Africa Company. Afterwards you were afraid you had sold your country. Do not believe this: you have not sold your country.'[3]

Another factor in the altered situation was the attitude of the new High Commissioner, Milner, who while prepared to see the Company employed as the agency of administration believed in

[1] Johnston to Salisbury, 11 March 1890; F.O. Pr. 6851, No. 123. F.O. Confidential Pr. 6784, Nos. 139 and 150.

[2] Goold-Adams to H.C., 13 April 1897; C.O. Conf. Pr. African (South) 686, encl. in No. 85.

[3] R. T. Coryndon to Sec. of State, Foreign Affairs, 25 November 1897; African (South) 686, Encl. in No. 101.

the permanent maintenance of the imperial factor. Starting from the conviction that the Zambesi was 'the natural northern boundary of what will some day be self-governing British South Africa' he concluded that the ultimate goal for the north could not be white-settler rule but a Crown dependency, following 'the line of development of Uganda and the Niger Protectorate rather than of Zululand and the Transkei'.[1] The problem had presented itself to his immediate attention because of a projected trek into the Batoka country in 1899 and consequently the urgent need to establish an effective means of legal control over white men west of the Kafue-Zambesi confluence. Milner successfully urged that the source of legislative authority should be the High Commissioner and not the Southern Rhodesia Legislative Council. Hence the Barotseland–North-Western Rhodesia Order in Council of 1899 formally vested the administration in the Crown, while allowing the Company the right to nominate the officials in return for meeting the administrative expenses.[2]

Milner had assumed that the officials would exercise only those powers of government that had been expressly granted by Lewanika. And the Company on the same assumption had re-negotiated the Lochner Concession at a conference with Lewanika and some of his councillors at the Victoria Falls in June 1898. Although the Lawley Concession which resulted repeated the earlier clause that nothing in the agreement would otherwise affect the Litunga's constitutional power or authority, the Company was now given the right to make land grants to white farmers 'in any portion of the Batoka or Mashukulumbwe country to white men approved by the King' together with administrative rights to deal with 'all cases between white men and between white men and natives, it being clearly understood that all cases between natives shall be left to the King to deal with and dispose of'.[3] But Lawley's concession was at once superseded by

[1] Milner to Chamberlain, 5 April 1899; African (South) 574, No. 114.
[2] Milner to Chamberlain, 5 April 1899; African (South) 636, No. 120. Chamberlain's despatch stated that since the Portuguese boundary remained unsettled it was not considered desirable for the B.S.A. Co. to be entrusted with the administration of Barotseland; Chamberlain to Milner, 1 July 1899; African (South) 574, No. 203.
[3] African (South) 686, encl. in No. 116.

the 1899 Order in Council so far as powers of government were concerned. 'In fact for many of the purposes of the Concession', the Colonial Office told the Company, 'the Queen's authority has already taken the place of that of Lewanika, and the grants to be made by him will only be operative so far as they are ratified by Her Majesty or are not inconsistent with the Order in Council'.[1] The Order marked the loss of sovereignty. Henceforth Lewanika's authority rested, formally speaking, on sufferance and not autochthonous right.

Niceties as to the legal status of African rulers may appear as airy cobwebs that were rudely brushed aside by the harsh facts of power; and it would be unrealistic to suppose that expediency did not play the major role in fashioning the relationship between the colonial and indigenous political systems. Yet it could happen that the colonial power fettered its discretionary authority by its own legal instruments and constitutional usage. In the Foreign Office protectorates like British Central Africa formal rights of jurisdiction were limited under the Africa Order in Council of 1889 to the regulation of the external relations of protected chiefs who theoretically preserved their internal sovereignty intact. At first Johnston by virtue of the Order had jurisdiction only over British subjects and foreigners, viz. such classes as Europeans, Arabs and 'coastmen'. Even when full sovereign rights had been purportedly transferred by treaty agreements, it was held that European officials exercised jurisdiction over Africans in their capacity as agents of the chiefs and as such administered native law.[2] Fiction had no doubt later to be adjusted to fact; but in any event the formal legal status of chiefs in Nyasaland presented no barrier to the encroachment of colonial authority at its own convenience, since the chiefs either conceded jurisdiction pliantly or were so implacably hostile that the required rights were obtained by conquest. But in the case of a state like Buganda which was both powerful and friendly the juridical conception of the Foreign Office protectorate permitted the conclusion of a treaty—the

---

[1] C.O. to B.S.A. Co., 8 May 1900, para. 4; African (South) 656, No. 65.
[2] Cf. A. J. Hanna, *Beginnings of Rhodesia and Nyasaland*, p. 202. H. H. Johnston, *British Central Africa*, p. 114. Johnston to F.O., 31 December 1895, F.O. Confidential Pr. 6851, No. 54.

Uganda Agreement of 1900—which had the practical effect of
limiting the sovereignty of the Crown and took precedence over
subsequent Orders in Council.[1] Juridical status, it must be acknowledged, was never more than one element in political relations, but
insofar as it constituted a defence against the erosion of indigenous
authority it is evident that had Johnston chosen to establish relations with Barotseland by treaty before 1895 he might easily have
allowed the authority of the Crown to be permanently limited in
the same way. It is true that the Lawley Concession of 1898 (and
likewise its confirmation by the Lewanika Concession of 1900)
repeated the clause of the Lochner Concession of 1890 that 'this
Agreement shall be considered in the light of a treaty or alliance
made between my said Barotse Nation and the Government of
Her Britannic Majesty . . .'; but, as it has been seen, and was
made clear in the terms of Chamberlain's ratification, the Order
in Council of 1899 took precedence over the concession.[2]

That Order in Council sprang from the Colonial Office tradition of protectorates in Africa under which, unlike Foreign
Office protectorates, sovereign rights of jurisdiction over *all*
inhabitants of a protected territory were asserted from the outset.
The tradition was made explicit by the Bechuanaland Order in
Council of 1891 on which the 1899 Order for Barotseland was
framed.[3] Chamberlain's despatch specifically stated that it was not
necessary nor was it intended that the powers and authority of
Lewanika should be infringed any further than those of Khama
and other Bechuana chiefs.[4] But there was no question, as in
Buganda, of the Litunga asserting a residual sovereignty. Although the Colonial Office considered it both politic and just to
secure Lewanika's consent before permitting the Company's

[1] Cf. D. A. Low and R. C. Pratt, *Buganda and British Overrule*, O.U.P., 1960,
pp. 21, 186 ff.
[2] Printed in Gann, *Birth of a Plural Society*, Manchester, 1958, pp. 215–20.
[3] On the wider significance of the 1891 Bechuanaland Order in Council,
Hailey, *Native Administration in the British African Territories, Part V*, London,
1953, pp. 202–4, 217–18. For statement of differences between Foreign Office
and Colonial Office protectorates see C.O. to F.O. 13 August 1894; F.O.
Conf. Pr. 6613, No. 71. Also Farnall's Memo., 8 October 1898; F.O. Conf. Pr.
7143, No. 70.
[4] Chamberlain to Milner, 1 July 1899; African (South) 574, No. 203.

officials to exercise further administrative powers, he was left in a relatively weak bargaining position.[1]

The great object of Lewanika and his *indunas* in the Lawley Agreement of 1898 and its subsequent incorporation in the 'Lewanika Concession' of 1900 appears to have been to secure the recognition of an extensive area to be reserved from prospecting. For this, it would seem, they were prepared to reduce the (unpaid) subsidy of £2,000 a year to £850, as well as forgo the royalty on the Ware Concessiom.[2] It was a shrewd instinct and laid the basis of territorial differentiation. The missionaries would have no part in the agreement. Coillard kept his counsel, but in private permitted himself a brief, bitter comment:

Major Coryndon had come all the way from England to have the Victoria Falls agreement signed by Lewanika and his councillors. At the King's request Major C. begged me to be present at the proceedings. I went to one of the meetings but declined to put my name to such a document. Poor Natives! always eaten up by the elder stronger brother. It is mysteriously sad.[3]

The political form North-West Rhodesia should take had still to be decided. The extent of its monopoly of mineral rights was bound up with the extent of Lewanika's dominions so that the Company was obliged to acknowledge his formal sway over the whole of North-West Rhodesia and to press his claims in the disputed territory west of the Zambesi. The Portuguese considered his position had been inflated artificially for the purposes of the boundary arbitration proceedings and spoke contemptuously of 'ce grand chef qui ne le sera plus sitôt que la question des limites sera vidée'.[4] For administrative purposes, however, there was little in the South African tradition that made for a system of dual

[1] Cf. C.O. to B.S.A. Co., 21 July 1903; African (South) 717, No. 250: '. . . as a matter of policy and justice it appears to be desirable to obtain the assent of Lewanika to whatever is done in the way of conferring jurisdiction over natives upon the officers of the administration.'

[2] Lewanika to Lawley, 25 June 1898 (copy), and Lawley to B.S.A. Co., London, 1 September 1898; Salisbury Archives LO 1/1/3.

[3] Coillard to Miss C. Mackintosh, 20 October 1900; Salisbury Archives CO 5/1/1/1.

[4] G. V. Fiddes (Colonial Office) to Coryndon, 12 July 1904; African (South) 746, No. 215.

or indirect rule; so that it was perhaps inevitable that the solution to the problem of a double source of authority was sought for in administrative partition.

Here again the Bechuanaland model would appear to have been decisive. In telling Goold-Adams in 1897 that his confirmation of the Lochner Concession was conditional on a substantial increase in the area reserved for the exclusive use of himself and his people, Lewanika was possibly influenced by the much publicized interview of the Bechuana chiefs with Chamberlain in November 1895, when the tribal reserves were decided on, and a rough boundary between them and the proposed Company-administered area laid down. The views of the Colonial Office on the exercise of powers of jurisdiction by Lewanika and the Administration would seem to have run in a similar direction.[1] The 1891 and 1896 Bechuanaland Proclamations gave the white officials comprehensive judicial powers but reserved to the tribal tribunals all cases between Africans, except cases of murder or those in which an administrative officer might decide to intervene in the interests of order. This overlapping territorial and functional division of authority was no doubt envisaged as appropriate for conditions north of the Zambesi where Lewanika had conceded to the Company the right to settle white farmers in the 'Batoka' and 'Mashukulumbwe' country.

From the outset the Company regarded Barotseland proper as possessing little economic value; and for this reason Coryndon recommended compliance with Lewanika's request for a further enlargement of the reserved area.[2] He had accepted the fact that the western and north-western regions were unlikely to have much importance; on the other hand what he called the Batoka and Mashukulumbwe plateaux were high and healthy and lay athwart the proposed railway to Tanganyika. The administrative headquarters of the Company would therefore be in this region or north-east across the Kafue.[3] This initial geographical separation of Lewanika's capital from the headquarters of the Administration

[1] Cf. H.C. to Chamberlain, 24 August 1903; African (South) 717, No. 332.

[2] R. T. Coryndon to Secy. B.S.A. Co., 24 January 1901; African (South) 659, encl. 3 in No. 33. This refers to extension west of the Zambesi.

[3] R. T. Coryndon to Capt. Lawley, 23 December 1898. National Archives, Lusaka, 6/1/1. N.W.R. Sundry Papers.

was bound to shape relations and to hasten political separation. Coryndon set up the headquarters of the Administration in Kalomo in 1900, Colin Harding remaining at Lealui as Resident. Coryndon, on his return from leave at the end of 1901, could report favourably on Harding's work, while commenting that 'Lewanika and the Barotse valley are fortunately far to the West of the country we occupy'.[1] The situation contained the seeds of future dispute. Harding, like Goold-Adams earlier, travelled widely in the Zambesi headwaters for evidence in support of Lewanika's territorial claims preparatory to the arbitration proceedings on the western boundary. His visit with Lewanika to London in 1902 for the Coronation celebrations strengthened his attachment to the Lozi cause, and perhaps fostered the notion of developing North-West Rhodesia as a single protected Barotse state.[2]

Until 1906 circumstances did not make this idea seem impossible. Although the Order in Council gave the Company power to raise a hut tax, Chamberlain insisted that Lewanika's consent had first to be obtained as well as a report on the probable attitude of the people towards such a tax. He was writing at the beginning of 1902 when the South African War, as he said, made it of the utmost importance to avoid any risk of serious disturbances.[3] Coryndon was anxious to commence levying hut tax at the earliest moment since even the skeleton establishment of three District Commissioners and a small headquarters staff was estimated by him as likely to cost £21,000-odd in 1902–3, with only trivial revenue coming in from stamps and licences. The Ila-Tonga peoples had shown signs of recalcitrance and Coryndon recognized he could not begin the task until he had doubled the police force to 500.[4] Lewanika's co-operation in the circumstances was a valuable asset if hut tax collection were to go off smoothly.

[1] Coryndon to Rhodes, 27 November 1901; African (South) 702, encl. in No. 117.
[2] C. Harding, *In Remotest Barotseland*. Also, *Far Bugles* (2nd ed., 1933). In 1900 Harding patrolled eastwards as far as the Kafue-Zambesi junction taking with him four of Lewanika's *indunas*. Harding to Dep. Administrator, Bulawayo, 3 August 1900; Lusaka Archives NWR 6/1/1.
[3] Chamberlain to Milner, 31 January 1902. African (South) 702, No. 24.
[4] Coryndon to Rhodes, 27 November 1901; *op. cit.*

Lewanika accepted the idea of hut tax with alacrity; it promised him a substantial increase in his own revenue, and he wished to extend the area under tax more rapidly than even the Administration thought prudent. But the matter was to become one of bitter dispute.

The price of hut tax, as Lewanika recognized, was not merely the loss of his tribute rights over the portion of the country outside the Barotse Valley. The work of census taking and collection needed European officials; so that the whole question of his recognition as ruler over the outlying peoples was involved. Lewanika therefore took advantage of his presence in London in 1902 to approach the London board of the British South Africa Company direct. Although he asked for a percentage on collections, he appeared more anxious at this stage to be allowed, like the Bechuana chiefs, to attempt the work of collection through his own administrative system than to control the disposal of the tax. As he rather ingenuously wrote:

... I wish it to be clearly understood that what I wish is simply to have the power to collect 'hut tax' from my people, not only in the Barotse Valley, but the whole of my country, which I will hand over to the Government of Barotseland. If I find that I am not able to do this in any district I will then leave it in the hands of the Government; at present there is no reason why I should not try, as I used to get tribute from them ...[1]

The London board agreed that the hut tax should at the outset be collected by Lewanika on behalf of the Administration to whom he was to hand it over, but it was to be clearly understood that in this respect Lewanika was acting under the authority and supervision of the Administrator and that tax was to be collected by Lewanika only in those districts in which his authority was sufficient to ensure peaceable payment.[2]

Coryndon resented the concession, even though couched in such restrictive and almost humiliating terms. Lewanika had been

[1] Lewanika to B.S.A. Co., 10 July 1902; African (South) 702, encl. 1 in No. 337.
[2] B.S.A. Co. to Col. Harding, 8 August 1902; African (South) 802, encl. 9 in No. 285.

prepared to agree to a £1 tax which the Colonial Office thought unduly high. But Coryndon was rigidly opposed to honouring the London agreement. In his previous conversation with the king there had never been, he said, any question of Lewanika being allowed to collect outside the Barotse Valley. Lewanika's original proposals had envisaged placing his son, Letia, in charge of the collection in the Falls district and the Ngambela in the Batoka district. They were to have *indunas* and smaller chiefs under them who would carry out the detailed work, but Lewanika recognized that they would need white officials to assist them. The tax monies would then be brought before Lewanika and the *kgotla* at Lealui but would then be transmitted to the Administrator at Kalomo. Coryndon thought the scheme wholly inadmissible. While Lewanika might collect a fluctuating tribute—and from the outlying Batoka, Kasempa and Kafue districts he had collected almost nothing in the past five years—he was unlikely to exercise sufficient authority to collect a money tax, which was traditionally regarded in Southern Africa as the prerogative of a white government. The Administration would become involved in a host of petty fights to uphold Barotse authority or perhaps worse:

Though the Barotse authority over these distant districts is undoubted, it is vague in actual reality, and Barotse *indunas* carrying and enforcing Lewanika's direct authority have seldom penetrated of late as far east even as Kalomo, and a sudden invasion of native chiefs demanding a cash payment for huts—which is an idea quite foreign to these tribes—will result most probably in a wholesale resistance which may develop into an armed neutrality or even a war.[1]

Lewanika said his arrangement 'would show the people that he is still their king', and Coryndon acknowledged this to be his principal motive. As an alternative Coryndon proposed that a Barotse *induna* should go round with the collector of each sub-district to instruct the people on Lewanika's behalf to pay the tax but to have nothing to do with the actual receipt. The money would be sent to Kalomo and from there it would go under escort of a Barotse

[1] Coryndon to Secy. B.S.A. Co., 9 January 1903; African (South) 717, encl. in No. 76.

induna and contingent of Barotse Native Police to Lealui and then returned. This latter seemingly purposeless arrangement was proposed to meet Lewanika's special wishes. So far from apparently reducing his authority as Lewanika feared, Coryndon argued that it would greatly increase it in districts distant from Lealui. At the same time Coryndon was candid enough to admit that his proposed arrangement for Lozi co-operation in tax collection was meant to be no more than a transitional one. Later on, as in Southern Rhodesia, the people would come themselves to the collectors' camps and 'so the necessity for the Barotse *induna* who had accompanied the collector on tour would gradually cease'.

In an anonymous and undated paper of *c.* 1904 an official recognized that what he called the Lozi feudal system had suffered much derangement since the advent of Company officials in 1897.[1] That system had been based on continuous raids by the Lozi on weaker neighbours in search of slaves; the representations of the Company and missionaries had caused the raids to cease, with the consequent breakdown of Lozi authority in the outlying regions. Worthington, the Secretary for Native Affairs in 1908, gave a more settled picture of the Batoka district before European control.[2] Not only Lewanika but the Mukwae, Letia, and Akanangisna (the Mukwae's daughter) had resident *indunas* whose duties were to collect tribute and exercise a certain influence:

These *indunas* took a very active part in the internal affairs of the communities over which they presided; they exacted tribute, settled all disputes of importance, appointed the successor to a vacant indunaship, and acted as the channel through which the Paramount Chief's wishes were transmitted to the subject tribes. They performed yet another function, namely, that of teaching the Sekololo languages in pursuance of Lewanika's desire to absorb all subject peoples and create one large and powerful Barotse tribe.

This system was to be profoundly altered by the extension of European administration.

On his own responsibility Coryndon rejected the agreement

[1] Paper headed 'Census' (typed copy), from position in file probably 1904; Lusaka Archives NWR 3/14 Hut Tax 1902 April–December 1907.

[2] Memo. on Barotse Representative Indunas by F. V. Worthington, 5 June 1908; African (South) 899, encl. 2 in No. 100.

Lewanika had made in London and secured the Litunga's un-willing assent to his own tax-collection proposals. The Company, the Colonial Office, and Milner, the High Commissioner, accepted the position, although the whole of 1903 was taken up with the correspondence.[1] In the meantime Lewanika was experi-encing the descent into harsh realities from the euphoria generated by the flattering treatment he had received in England. Marshall Hole, as Acting Administrator, began tightening the hold of the Administration, seeking first to gain control over the movements of chiefs like Kasempa in their visits to Lewanika and likewise over Lewanika's *indunas* sent out into the districts.[2] He then took a sharply unsympathetic attitude over Lewanika's claims to suzer-ainty over two chiefs, Sitanda and Siankomala, quoting Val Gielgud's report that Barotse influence was practically dead throughout the entire extent of the Hook of Kafue and that no signs of effective occupation existed except at one place (Siakum-bila's). Lewanika had never before made pretensions to authority in the district concerned and expressly repudiated such authority in 1897. Now he had 'suddenly conceived the idea that he has been unjustly deprived of territory which has always belonged to him'; and Hole clearly implied that Harding, the Commandant of the Barotse Native Police, was in some way responsible.[3]

Marshall Hole visited Lewanika at this time and found him querulous and contentious. There was evidently a trial of wills over some small matters and Lewanika was refusing co-operation. He had failed to send an *induna* to reside at Kalomo as Coryndon had requested; and the main reason seems to have been his objec-tion to the proposed hut tax collection in the Batoka and Falls districts in 1904. Lewanika burst out: 'I have never been told that hut tax was to be collected in the Batoka at once. Things are done

[1] B.S.A. Co. to C.O., 8 May 1903; African (South) 717, No. 144. Lyttelton to Milner, 19 December 1903; *ibid.*, No. 452.

[2] H. Marshall Hole to Lewanika, 5 August 1903; Lusaka Archives NWR 3/19/4 Native Affairs Lewanika and Family May 1904–October 1910.

[3] H. Marshall Hole to Secy. B.S.A. Co., 14 November 1903; African (South) 717, encl. in No. 466. When the boundary between North-Western and North-Eastern Rhodesia was settled in 1905, Coryndon wrote to Lewanika that 'now Sitanda and Siankomola come within your country as you wished'. Coryndon to Lewanika, 29 May 1905, Lusaka Archives KDE 2/34/1.

in my country and I am never told of them. Coryndon and Worthington [who were present] are trying to drive me out of my country.' Later he tried to pass the remark off as a joke. Colonial Office insistence on Lewanika's consent to the collection of tax and the unsettled question of the Litunga's percentage continued to delay matters. Coryndon visited Lealui in August 1904, bringing with him several hundred Ila and Tonga chiefs so that Lewanika could give them his personal assurance that he and his council had agreed to the levying of hut tax which was to be paid to the administration. It was arranged that a principal *induna*, Iluyea, was to live at Kalomo as Lewanika's representative, and that cases between Africans in the Batoka district were to be settled jointly by Iluyea and the Secretary for Native Affairs. Lewanika was told in a letter by Coryndon confirming the arrangements that the residence of Iluyea with the Administration at Kalomo and the maintenance of five gardens at different places in Batoka had the purpose of showing the people 'that you are their king always'.[1]

The bone of contention was now Lewanika's percentage of the tax. Lewanika held out for fifty, then thirty and lastly twenty per cent, but Coryndon would not budge beyond five. Lewanika fought to save his position, breaking the rules in Coryndon's eyes by writing directly to the High Commissioner and to the London board of the Company. Even the letter sent through Coryndon to the Duke of Abercorn, barely legible and scarcely comprehensible in its broken English, is eloquent evidence of Lewanika's distress.

I am very very sorry for I can't agree with him [Coryndon] every matter is too hard to agree with me, he can't agree with me even am crying to him and my Council, he can't listen us what we talk to him; things in this country now [—] finished when the hut tax takes place. And then if we can't [—] the twenty per; the Government is going to put us down a[s?] the dust.[2]

[1] Administrator (Coryndon) to Lewanika, Lealui, 17 August 1904: Lusaka Archives NWR 3/14. Printed African (South) 746, encl. in No. 323. Also cf. F. V. Worthington to his father, Lealui, 21 August 1904; Worthington Papers, Rhodes-Livingstone Museum, Livingstone.

[2] Lewanika to President, Duke of Abercorn, 24 August 1904; NWR 3/14. Also Lewanika to Milner, 31 August 1904; African (South) 746, encl. 1 in No. 287.

Considering Coryndon's attitude as too severe Milner recommended that Lewanika should receive at least ten per cent, which was the proportion recognized in Basutoland and Bechuanaland. Lyttelton, the Secretary of State, concurred.[1] The Company, however, backed its administrator and repeated his argument that five per cent was the utmost that could be safely entrusted to Lewanika; and that, indeed, his total income from the Company should be limited to £2,000 a year, the remainder being paid into an administrative fund and not Lewanika's private purse.[2] Lyttelton compromised by adhering to the formal proportion of ten per cent of the gross receipts, but stipulated that all beyond a certain figure be paid into a fund for works of public utility for the African population, Lewanika and Council deciding on the nature of such works subject to the administrator's veto. After further months of correspondence the figure was finally fixed at £1,200, but the decision was bitterly resented.[3] As Lewanika told Selborne by letter in 1907, it 'was imposed upon us against our will and we vainly protested against it'.[4]

Lewanika was now entering the time of the troubles. Hut tax collection proceeded in late 1904 in the Batoka and Falls districts, Letia and the Ngambela, with other Barotse *indunas* taking part with the European collectors.[5] But there was mounting dissatisfaction over the matter, Lewanika's share of the receipts having to sustain not only the royal family but also his *indunas*. Early in March 1905 there were rumours of unrest and of a party hostile to Lewanika being formed under the *indunas* Kalonga and Imoana. As a precaution a patrol of forty police and a Maxim were sent up to Lealui to reinforce the Litunga's authority. His immediate reaction was to throw himself into unreserved dependence on the Administration, agreeing to the extension of hut tax 'in all that part of my country situated north and east of the Kafue River, in the Kasempa

---

[1] Milner to Lyttelton, 7 November 1904 (telegram); *ibid.*, No. 289. C.O. to B.S.A. Co., 11 November 1904; *ibid.*, No. 292.

[2] B.S.A. Co. to C.O., 5 December 1904; *ibid.*, No. 313.

[3] Selborne to Lyttelton, 3 July 1905; African (South) 763, No. 199.

[4] Lewanika to High Commissioner, 1 October 1907; African (South) 872, encl. 8 in No. 186.

[5] F. V. Worthington (S.N.A.) to Secy. Kalomo, 17 November 1904; African (South) 763, encl. 1 in No. 13.

District, the Mankoya District, and in the Sesheke District'.[1] He
likewise agreed to the collection of tax in the Barotse Valley
beginning in 1906 under European direction.

The unfavourable boundary award at the end of 1905 delivered
a severe blow to his already shaken prestige. Coryndon, who
visited him at the time, reported that the Lozi were sore at the
loss of so much tribute-paying country and so many cattle posts.
There were signs of a falling off in Lewanika's popularity. In the
Khotla (Kuta) there was an atmosphere of constraint; few of the
important *indunas* now came regularly and freely into the public
room in Lewanika's house. The Litunga went about very little
and his reception by the people was not so spontaneous or loud as
a few years ago. Coryndon thought that perhaps Lewanika's visit
to England, his European clothes and manner of life, and his
friendliness to white men had alienated him to some extent from
the people. And perhaps he was largely blamed for the numerous
irritating restrictions, such as the suppression of domestic slavery,
the hut tax, the prevention of promiscuous raiding and plundering
by which the Barotse obtained and held their supremacy. No
doubt seeing the days of tyranny coming to an end he and one or
two of his chief *indunas* had pressed on with various works using
forced labour. Lewanika was not a strong chief in the sense of
Shaka, Mzilikazi or Sebituane, and Coryndon said he did not
think 'he would be a Paramount Chief today had it not been for
the establishment of a white government which has consistently
supported his authority'.[2] Selborne, the High Commissioner who
succeeded Milner, was more seriously perturbed. Pointing out the
obvious fact that 'as a factor in the administration of the country
his loyalty to us will cease to be of any value if it is only maintained at the cost of his influence over his people', he endeavoured

---

[1] Lewanika to Coryndon, 14 March 1905; *ibid.*, encls. in Nos. 130, 131.
Cf. F. V. Worthington, *Rough Journal*, 21 March 1905; Worthington Papers,
Rhodes-Livingstone Museum, Livingstone: 'I have been very much more
successful than I had right or reason to expect. I have obtained all I was instructed to obtain and a little more into the bargain. . . .' This appears to refer
to the land concession of 8 March 1905, cited Gann, *Birth of a Plural Society*,
p. 222.

[2] Administrator (Coryndon) to High Commissioner, 19 December 1905,
African (South) 802, encl. in No. 21.

vainly to secure a modification of the unfavourable boundary award.[1]

Lewanika was about to make his greatest surrender. It will be recalled that in the Lewanika Concession of 19 October 1900 (which confirmed the Lawley Concession of 25 June 1898, and incorporated the desired extension of the reserved area) Lewanika had given the Company the right to grant land in the Batoka or Mashukulumbwe country only. On 24 August 1904 Coryndon had obtained from him a letter written by his amanuensis and without witnesses which vaguely stated that outside the reserved area he and his people 'agreed that you shall give some farms to the farmers as you asked', in response to Coryndon's request for authority 'to issue land over all your territory'.[2] The Secretary of State was not satisfied, and on 23 January 1906 Lewanika was persuaded to set his hand to a formal deed of cession witnessed by the Ngambela and Imasiku on the Lozi side, which (excluding of course the Barotse Valley and round Sesheke) 'gave the right to dispose of land to settlers, as it should from time to time be required, on whatever terms the Company consider just, the Company retaining any money received from such disposition of land'. The Colonial Office was hesitant about ratification, recognizing that the concession amounted to 'a land grant of the whole of North-Western Rhodesia, except Lewanika's own reserve'.[3] How far Lewanika understood what he was doing has remained a matter of dispute. In November 1910 he repudiated any intention of giving the Company the right to sell the land;[4] and the petition of Yeta III to the High Commissioner in 1921 strenuously repeated the claim. Some years, however, were to pass before the implications of the concession of January 1906 were made apparent.

In the meantime, a further concession was wrung from the Litunga in July 1906: the abolition of serfdom in Barotseland proper. Although a limited right to unpaid labour for the Litunga and *indunas* was retained, the concession was obtained with much difficulty, Worthington at one stage of the negotiations tearing up

[1] Selborne to Elgin, 22 January 1906; *ibid.*, No. 21.
[2] Printed Gann, *The Birth of a Plural Society*, p. 221.
[3] African (South) 802, No. 54 and encls., No. 124. Concession is also printed, Gann, *op. cit.*, p. 222.
[4] African (South) 948, encl. 2 in No. 143.

the draft proclamation and stalking out of the council chamber. In Worthington's opinion the act of emancipation 'saved a revolt' since the pressure from the slaves after the introduction of hut tax had become too powerful to contain.[1] Lewanika had had to content himself with the system of representative *indunas* as the only means of retaining an influence over the outlying districts, and had been assured by Coryndon that—so far as the 'Batoka' country at least was concerned—this would show the people that 'you are their King always'. In one sense, indeed, the system was intended as a compensation for the refusal to allow Lewanika to collect the hut tax by his own agency. But it was also employed to bridle and diminish Lozi authority in the districts which European district commissioners were seeking to bring under their own control. In January 1904, F. C. Macaulay, the D.C. Kasempa, was asking that Luyea Indambu (Ndambo) should reside permanently near the *boma* instead of paying occasional visits from Lealui. As it was, Macaulay contended, the local chiefs were taking their complaints to Lealui, a practice encouraged by Lewanika to preserve his influence. If, however, Luyea were made to reside at Kasempa, the chiefs would have to bring their complaints to him, to be forwarded to the D.C.; they would not be able to say that they were afraid to report to the D.C. since they would only have to come to Luyea. Macaulay believed there was a tussle for influence with Lewanika over chief Kasempa, who had expressed a wish to move south of the Dongwe, thus bringing him into Lewanika's reserved area.

Lewanika's *indunas* aim at poisoning the people's minds with hatred for the Government, telling them that if they stay here North of the Dongwe they will have to pay hut tax and be the whiteman's servants, and if they cross the Dongwe they cease to be under white Government, and can do as they like, paying tribute to Lewanika.

If Barotse *indunas* were stationed at Kasempa the chief could be induced to remain.[2]

[1] F. V. Worthington to Secy., Kalamo, 13 July, 1906. African (South) 802, encl. 4 in No. 177. Also Memo. by F. V. Worthington on the abolition of slavery, n.d., forwarded by Acting Administrator to High Commissioner, 22 November 1906; *ibid.*, encl. in No. 243.

[2] D.C. Kasempa (F. C. Macaulay) to S.N.A., 18 January 1904, Lusaka Archives NWR IN/1/5/5. The Administrator learned that 'twice towards the

Although Marshall Hole had indignantly repudiated Lewan-ika's pretensions to authority in the Hook of the Kafue only a few months previously, in August 1904 the D.C. Kafue District, A. C. Anderson, whose headquarters were at Mumbwa, was asking for a Lozi *induna* to be sent to assist in the settlement of judicial disputes among the people, since despite all Anderson's efforts to back them the local chiefs were powerless to settle even the pettiest matter. The immediate reply was that it was not advisable to establish Barotse representatives in other parts of North-Western Rhodesia, and that Anderson should continue to settle disputes through the local chiefs.[1] But by 1905 the Admini-stration had changed its tune. Lewanika's consent to the levy of hut tax and the need for the collection to go smoothly brought about instructions for the Hook chiefs to be sent to visit Lewanika for his orders and corresponding arrangements for three Lozi *indunas* to take up residence near the D.C. Kafue and his collec-tors.[2] Anderson was told that the system of having a representative *induna* at Kalomo had answered so well during the past year and tended so much to heighten the confidence of the Barotse in the Administration that arrangements had been made to extend the system to other districts. The good will of the Barotse, it was said, was worth much to the Administration; but there was a more cogent reason.

In November 1904 Lewanika had formally agreed to surrender powers of civil and criminal jurisdiction over Africans except in the reserved area bounded by the line of the Kabompo-Dongwe Rivers in the north, and the Machili River in the east. Within the reserved area Lewanika would retain his jurisdiction but cases of murder and any offences directly against the laws of England, such as witchcraft, would be tried by the Administrator. It was a serious loss of authority but for the moment its extent was dis-guised by Coryndon's assurance that it was not intended that 'the

---

end of last year plans were made by the *indunas* to do away with Lewanika'; Worthington to Codrington, 23 July 1907; Lusaka Archives B/1/2/286.

[1] D.C. Kafue (A. C. Anderson) to S.N.A., 16 August 1904; S.N.A. to D.C. Kafue, 19 September 1904; Lusaka Archives NWR IN 1/5/4.

[2] S.N.A. to D.C. Lealui, 8 April 1905. S.N.A. to D.C. Hook, 8 April 1905; Lusaka Archives NWR IN/1/5/4.

white Government shall interfere in small matters which concern only native custom and tradition', and by the adoption of the system of representative *indunas*. The extent of the reserved area caused concern both to Milner and the Secretary of State, since the proclamation made no provision at all for the administration of justice within it.[1] Embryo district administration had already been established within the reserved area, the whole of the new Mankoya district and part of the Kasempa district falling within it. In order to bring these districts within the scope of the Courts of Justice Proclamation (No. 6 of 1905) Lewanika had been persuaded to accept an arrangement by which the proclamation should come into force even in the reserved area on condition that a representative *induna* were attached to the European district official.[2] Iluyea's work as an *induna* at Kalomo had so pleased Coryndon and Worthington that they fell in with Lewanika's proposal to extend the system to every other district.[3]

Yet the attitude of the Administration towards it was ambivalent from the outset and that of the district officials distinctly hostile. Even while stating that a principal object was Lozi goodwill, the Secretary for Native Affairs frankly acknowledged that another was 'to place the entire Administration of natives in the hands of Officials of this Department'.[4]

Worthington later acknowledged that representative *indunas* were appointed in 1905 'with the object of delegating to one individual the duties performed in the past by many Barotse scattered throughout the country'. Thus in the Batoka district previous to their appointment, not only Lewanika but the Mukwae of Nalolo, Letia and Akanangisna (the Mukwae's daughter) had resident *indunas* who collected tribute, settled disputes, and 'who took a very active part in the internal affairs of the com-

[1] Coryndon to Lewanika, 10 October 1904; Lewanika to Administrator, 8 November 1904. Milner to Lyttelton, 6 March 1905; H.C. to Administrator, 18 February 1905; African (South) 763, No. 77A and encls. 5, 6. Lyttelton to Milner 5 May 1905; *ibid.*, No. 115.

[2] S.N.A. to D.C. Kasempa, 17 April 1905; Lusaka Archives NWR IN/1/5/5.

[3] Coryndon to H.C., 8 April 1905; African (South) 763, encl. in No. 154. Report of F. V. Worthington, Secy. for Native Affairs, 7 April 1905; *idem.*, Worthington to Lewanika (copy), 2 February 1905; Lusaka Archives KDE/2/34/1.

[4] S.N.A. to D.C. Hook, 8 April 1905; Lusaka Archives NWR IN/1/5/4.

munities over which they presided'. For 'the purpose of better administration' these petty *indunas* ceased to function with the appointment of a representative to reside with the principal officer of each district.[1] In the Mashukulumbwe there were previously, according to Lewanika, nine Lealui *indunas*, three from Nalolo, and one from Letia.[2] In June 1905 it was arranged by Lewanika to send as representative *induna* the ex-sergeant of Barotse Police, Mulonda, together with two others. Dale, the D.C., was clearly hostile to the whole arrangement, and soon complained about its working. As a result he was told in January 1906 not to 'make too much of these men' and not to 'use them overmuch in native matters'. Dale could find no outward fault in Mulonda, who was 'studiously correct' in his attitude towards him; all he could complain of him was that he 'constantly inspires a feeling of uneasiness and prompts the conviction that some adverse influence is working as an undercurrent against me'. Inevitably he made play with the foreign character of the Lozi, of their unpopularity with the Ila, and the people's resentment at Mulonda's attempt to introduce Barotse law and customs.[3]

In the Kasempa district, E. A. Copeman who had taken over from Macaulay as D.C., made no attempt to conceal his disagreement with the whole conception of the representative *induna* system; and in his memoirs he speaks of the levying of tribute going on just the same despite the introduction of hut tax until he had 'succeeded in driving Lewanika's *indunas* back into the Barotse country'.[4]

By 1907 the unequal contest had been decided. Outside the reserved area Lewanika had given up his rights of tribute and jurisdiction, and his substantial rights over the land. All that he retained was his percentage on the hut tax receipts and the shadowy influence possessed by the representative *indunas* sitting as assessors in 'native cases'. It was clear that, having served their

[1] Memo. on Barotse representative *indunas* by F. V. Worthington, 5 June 1908; African (South) 899, encl. 2 in No. 100.
[2] D.C., Lealui (F. C. Aitkens) to D.C. Siabola (Mashukulumbwe), 12 June 1905; Lusaka Archives NWR IN/1/5/7.
[3] Andrew Dale to S.N.A., 4 July 1905; S.N.A. to D.C. Mashukulumbwe, 12 January 1906. Dale to S.N.A., Report on Barotse Settlement and Representative Mulonda, 9 May 1906; Lusaka Archives NWR IN/1/5/7.
[4] E. A. Copeman to S.N.A., 2 May 1905; Lusaka Archives NWR A/3/19/11. Draft Memoirs of E. A. Copeman; Salisbury Archives CO 3/4/2.

turn, the administration was looking for a favourable opportunity to send these packing. It came in the latter part of 1907.

Some difficulties over the collection of hut tax had been encountered in 1905, when Harding's protests over hut burning as a punishment for defaulters occasioned the termination of his appointment the following year.[1] In July 1907 the collector at Mumbwa reported unrest in the Kafue district in alarmist terms, attributing it as 'entirely due to the pernicious influence of the Marotse'. The *induna* Muntumoaswani had, he said, 'been preaching a crusade against the white population, telling the people that they are fools to pay the tax, that the white men have nothing to do with the Government, which is Lewanika's alone'. Certain 'trustworthy natives' had informed him that a message had been sent all over the country from Barotseland telling the people to resist the payment of tax.[2] Worthington paid a visit at once to Lewanika telling him of the charge; and it was agreed to send three of Lewanika's most senior officers of state to make a full inquiry and deliver a stern warning against disaffection.[3] Apart from Muntumoaswani nothing incriminating was discovered, as the European officials acknowledged. For the most part the unrest sprang from unfounded rumour. In the Mashukulumbwe district the D.C., Knowles Jordan, reported that Mulonda was acquitted of inciting the people to resist tax payment. His attitude had been 'studiously correct' throughout the collection, although Jordan had 'the uneasy feeling that he is, behind one's back, doing all he can to push his own influence to the detriment of the white Administration'. In the Kafue district, Anderson, the D.C., reported that the leader of the mission of inquiry, Mukuwakashiko, was of the decided opinion that Muntumoaswani was accessory to the unsatisfactory attitude of the people in the district, but it was impossible to prove anything against him.[4]

[1] Colin Harding, *Far Bugles*, 2nd ed., 1933, pp. 140–1. Coryndon to Milner, 9 March 1905; African (South) 763, encl. 1 in No. 102. Also *idem*, 30 May 1905; *ibid.*, encl. 1 in No. 178.

[2] Collector (G. H. Nicholls) Mumbwa, to S.N.A., 3 July 1907; African (South) 872, encl. 1 in No. 151.

[3] Worthington to Coryndon, 7 August 1907; Lusaka Archives NWR 3/19/6.

[4] Report of E. Knowles Jordan, 4 October 1907. Report of A. C. Anderson, 17 October 1907; Lusaka Archives NWR IN/1/5/2.

According to the account Lewanika received, Anderson told the mission that 'all the King's representatives among the Mashukulumbwe and the Matoka' had to return to Barotse; and apparently because of this the other Lozi who had been resident in these areas 'long before' wished to return with them 'less they should be accused of any trouble'. Lewanika saw that this meant the final destruction of his influence outside the Barotse Valley and made a last despairing protest to the High Commissioner:

Now I also ask Your Excellency what is the meaning of the expulsion of all my representatives from the Mashukulumbwe and Matoka districts? Does the Company intend to take those districts quite out of my power? I understand the expulsion of Motumosoana but why the others? You can see that I have been accused without any reason at all. I have always done all in my power to keep the peace in all my country and to have all my people submissive to the Company. I am sorry to see they have so little confidence in me. And why allow such false reports to spread . . . I feel it very keenly. Oh! that we were granted to pass directly under the Government of King Edward![1]

Selborne refused to intervene for he knew the game was lost. Already in June 1907 he had proposed complete partition as the only means of saving the remnants of Lewanika's power. Recognizing that Lewanika's authority outside the reserved area had 'ceased to be more than nominal', he proposed the renunciation of all Lewanika's claims in return for direct imperial protection of the reserved area on the lines of Basutoland and the other High Commission protectorates. Such an arrangement offered the prospect of a 'well-governed native State', that would be more than self-supporting financially.[2]

---

[1] Lewanika to High Commissioner, 11 December 1907; African (South) 899, encl. 1 in No. 45. Although there was no abrupt dismissal the system of representative *indunas* was allowed to lapse. Mulonda was recalled by Lewanika and left in March 1908; Muntumoaswani left Mumbwa in October 1907. Dale to S.N.A., 3 March 1908; IN/1/5/7. Anderson to S.N.A., 5 September 1907; IN/1/5/4. Iluyea was left to his own devices when the Administration moved from Kalomo to Livingstone, being told there was nothing for him to do. S.N.A. to Administrator, 10 October 1907. Admr. to S.N.A., 10 October 1907. Res. Mag. Barotse Dist. to S.N.A., 9 October 1908; Lusaka Archives NWR IN/1/5/3. Iluyea remained, however, at Kalomo until 1921. Note of interview with Yeta III, 9 April 1921, NR B/1/2/292.

[2] Selborne to Secy. of State, 17 June 1907; African (South) 872, No. 118.

Elgin, the Liberal Secretary of State, was not to be drawn. While admitting that he had 'no doubt that an Imperial Protectorate would provide an administration less likely to clash with native interests, and more satisfactory from the standpoint of relation to Lewanika' he turned down the proposal on practical grounds, doubting the prospect of the Company's agreement or the financial self-sufficiency of such a protectorate. Beyond this was the larger principle:

The Company has been placed in possession of the assets of a wide area in consideration of the administration of that area without expense to the British taxpayer, and successive Secretaries of State have steadily refused to permit any infringement of this arrangement in spite of the good reasons which have from time to time been urged for placing this or that part of the interior under direct Imperial control.[1]

Lewanika vainly petitioned for a direct Imperial Protectorate and poured out his grievances:

Now we have been deprived of the yearly tributes that were brought into our capitals from all the tribes that are under our power; our former slaves feel no more obliged to help their headmen; we have to pay for the least service they render us; how are we to live? £1,200 would be hardly sufficient for the King's large family: are all the headmen to give up their duties as rulers and judges of the nations in order to dig their gardens and build their houses with their own hands?

We are sometimes caused to feel as if we were a conquered nation, while we have made an agreement which was said to be just like an alliance between our nation and the Imperial Government. When we say so, those of the British South Africa Company ask 'Do you want to be conquered?'[2]

The Company's response to this outburst of discontent, fomented, the Administrator professed to believe, by Jalla and the French missionaries, was to tighten its grip still further over the administration of Barotseland proper.[3] Mackinnon was appointed as

[1] Elgin to Selborne, 10 August 1907; African (South) 872, No. 144.
[2] Lewanika (with Letia, Ngambela, Nyekwa) to High Commissioner, 1 October 1907; African (South) 872, encl. 8 in No. 186. Also A. Jalla (countersigned by Lewanika, Letia, Ngambela, Nyekwa) to High Commissioner, 30 September 1907; ibid., encl. 5 in No. 186.
[3] Memo of Administrator (R. E. Codrington), 1 January 1908, para. 8; African (South) 899, encl. in No. 15.

Resident Magistrate at Lealui and in his report of September 1908 made clear that the Native Commissioners, hitherto confined to the role of tax-collectors, must henceforth travel more to extend their authority.[1]

In such a constantly weakening position Lewanika was induced in August 1909 to make his last important concession. This was an unrestricted grant of all land outside the reserved area in return for an extension of that area to the recently defined Anglo-Portuguese boundary west of the Zambesi.[2] The Colonial Office had shown some hesitancy in accepting the sweeping concession of 23 January 1906 and had pressed half-heartedly and fruitlessly for a guarantee that the profits of land sales would be applied to administrative purposes and a small percentage (5 per cent) devoted to 'the welfare of the native inhabitants'. Ratification did not occur until June 1909 when the Company, having succeeded in expunging the other restrictions, agreed to the High Commissioner having power to set aside sufficient land for the African population and to ultimate control over the removal of Africans from villages and occupied lands.[3]

The concession of August 1909 was something of a sleight of hand. The grant of 1906 had given the Company the right to dispose of the land outside the reserve to settlers only. It now wished to have unfettered disposal and as inducement offered the extension of the reserved area west of the Zambesi. Lewanika and his *kuta* were brought to rapid agreement. They must have been entirely unaware of the formal undertaking given to the Colonial Office in 1901 that, in return for ratification of the 1900 Lewanika Concession the Company would 'reserve the area referred to [west of the Zambesi] for the sole and exclusive use of King Lewanika and his people'. This condition had been expressly included in the terms under which the concession was confirmed

[1] Report by C. McKinnon, September 1908; African (South) 932, encl. in No. 16.

[2] Wallace to Selborne, 12 November 1909; African (South) 932, encl. in No. 242. The 1909 concession is printed in Gann, *Birth of a Plural Society*, pp. 223-5.

[3] C.O. to B.S.A. Co., 25 June 1909; African (South) 932, No. 142. Also *ibid.*, Nos. 71 83, and African (South) 899, No. 77.

by Chamberlain as Colonial Secretary in November 1901.[1] The
Company had brought off a double bargain and the Colonial
Office, which must have been fully aware of the position, con-
doned the transaction in silence.

Having yielded so much, the 1909 Concession, like its predecessors, was quickly challenged. From this time a fresh political
element seems to have made itself felt—the new educated élite
of the Lozi aristocracy with Letia at its head. Possessing a novel
awareness of legal right and convinced that trickery had been
practised on the illiterate Lewanika in the past, the younger generation of the royal house seems to have fanned the discontent over
the latest concession. This burst out when the 1911 Order in
Council came to be negotiated.

Selborne had acted on the assumption that the 1909 Concession marked the full acceptance of the logic of partition.
Lewanika, he said, henceforward abandoned all his claims and
interests outside Barotseland proper while maintaining Barotseland proper in the most absolute manner for the exclusive possession and enjoyment of the Barotse.[2]

The legal position could thus be simplified and the way cleared
for the unification of North-Western and North-Eastern Rhodesia, an object the Company was anxious to secure for reasons
of economy now that the railway had overcome much of the
problem of communications between the two regions. Selborne
saw no reason why the administration of the whole territory
could not be brought under a single Order in Council which
could also be made applicable to Barotseland proper without

[1] Asst. Secy. B.S.A. Co., to Under-Secy. C.O., 29 June 1901 (cyclostyled
copy), para. 7; Lusaka Archives NR B 1/2/277:' As regards the reserve area
asked for by Lewanika which is west of the "Modus Vivendi" provisional
Boundary line . . . the Company formally agree that, in the event of this area
being ultimately decided to be within the British sphere, they will, unless gold
in payable quantities is not discovered in the remainder of the King's territory
covered by this Concession [of 1900], reserve the area referred to for the sole
and exclusive use of King Lewanika and his people, will prevent prospecting
for gold within the area, and exclude gold prospectors from entering upon it.'
See also Condition 5 of the Secretary of State's confirmation of the 1900 Concession, 23 November 1901, Gann, *Birth of a Plural Society*, p. 220.

[2] Selborne to S. of S., 6 December 1909, para. 8, African (South) 932,
No. 244.

Lewanika raising any objection. The Colonial Office agreed that there could be 'no question for the present of establishing for the reserve any other system of government than that provided for the rest of Northern Rhodesia by the Order in Council'.[1] The special position of Barotseland in the new unified scheme was safeguarded merely by two clauses in the 1911 order, one providing for the non-alienation of the land in the Barotse reserve, and confirming the rights and obligations of the Litunga and people under the concessions of 1900 and 1909, and the other stating that the provisions dealing with the removal of natives should not be deemed 'to limit or affect the exercise by the Chief of the Barotse of his authority in tribal matters'.

This final incapsulation of Barotseland within a larger colonial unit raised no immediate objection, except that Lewanika never relented in his demand to come under the direct authority of the Crown. When in November 1910 Colonel Fair came to Livingstone to secure the agreement of Lewanika and his *indunas* to the draft Order in Council it was over clause 42, making explicit the alienation of all land outside the reserve, that he was assailed.[2]

It was significant that Wallace, the Administrator, felt obliged to go behind the August 1909 Concession to the letter of 23 January 1906, whose status and, at first, whose existence, the Lozi disputed. Despite the protest of the Ngambela Sope and the *induna* Mwanza that no more than the grant of 'ploughing rights' was intended—that the land was merely to be 'borrowed' not 'sold'—they were now made to face the harsh fact that the white men were forcing the wording to its limit. The 1906 letter granting to the Company 'the right to dispose of land to settlers, as it should from time to time be required, on whatever terms the Company consider just, the Company retaining any money received from such disposition of land', was held by Colonel Fair, as the agent of the High Commissioner, to cede full rights of ownership.

When the issue was pressed Wallace produced the argument

[1] Crewe to H.C., 26 March 1910, para. 12, African (South) 948, No. 41.
[2] For the record of meeting, see typescript notes [misfiled after p. 1. of record of meeting of 29 September 1911] NR B 1/2/292. Also African (South) 948, encl. 2 in No. 143.

that if the land had not been granted to the Company, then neither had the reserve to the Lozi. 'Can anybody give away that which is already given to a person?' inquired Mwanza. 'Did the land west of the Zambesi belong to the Barotse?' rejoined Wallace. 'Yes', interjected the Ngambela, 'many years before the English came.' Wallace turned upon him with a stroke which gave him the game. 'After the 1900 Concession whose was it?' 'It was the Company's,' came the reply, leaving Wallace to conclude: 'I then gave you back that land for the right we have been discussing.' The admission was long remembered.

The officials right up to Selborne and Gladstone (his successor as High Commissioner) were convinced that Lewanika had understood perfectly well what he had been about when he set his hand to the various documents, but felt that the 'less enlightened' of his followers had not previously realized the effect of the concessions. To avoid unpopularity Lewanika was seeking to create the impression that the Company claimed the land outside the reserve not by virtue of concessions which he had granted, but by virtue of an Order in Council for which he was not responsible.[1] In December 1910 Gladstone had to admit that the practical abandonment by Lewanika of all land outside the reserve was a possible cause of the prevailing discontent and of the weakening of Lewanika's authority noticeable at the time.

The outbreak when it came was promptly nipped in the bud. In March 1911 Lewanika, fearing a plot to depose him, called on the white officials to uphold his authority.[2] The alleged ringleaders were promptly arrested and arraigned before a court of inquiry under Worthington. Suspicion fell mainly on Mboo (or Fwabi) and Ikasaia.

Worthington believed that Mboo was a figurehead—an impoverished son of Sepopa (a former Litunga) and so a ready tool for malcontents. The unrest in the Barotse Valley went much deeper, he believed, and stemmed from the discontent of the people at the burdens pressing on them. Officially all tribute

[1] H.C. (Gladstone) to S. of S., 14 December 1910, African (South) 948 No. 143.
[2] H.C. to S. of S., 24 March 1911, African (South) 969, No. 39. Also B 1/1/2/286.

rights had been abolished on the institution of hut tax, and all unfree labour (apart from the annual twelve days tribute labour) had been made unlawful with the ending of slavery. In reality the people were oppressed by the double burden of the legal tax and the illegal exaction of tribute in kind and forced labour. The *indunas* felt equally aggrieved at the loss of rights and privileges consequent on the new order. 'Some regret lost freedom, others that a larger measure of it has not come to them. Both parties blame Lewanika, both imagine that a new chief would introduce a new order of things more to their liking.' Lewanika had not pressed the inquiry into the plot for fear, Worthington thought, of disclosing the underlying discontent and its cause. Rumour had it that a large number of *indunas* were connected with the plot, but 'all had retired to the background with conspicuous success'.[1]

Outwardly the Administration took steps to support Lewanika's authority. Although no proof of conspiracy could be found, Mboo and Ikasaia were sent to live outside the Barotse Valley, and Letia was formally proclaimed heir. But Worthington's reading of the situation and the inherited cast of the official mind made it one more occasion for attempting to whittle down Lewanika's power. The only way to prevent abuses, urged Wallace, was to allow a right of appeal from Lewanika's court to that of the Resident Magistrate, though admittedly this would mean 'a great diminution in the Chief's authority'. Gladstone had quickly forgotten the partition principle by which Selborne had been guided in his attempt to solve the political problem in Southern Africa; the remedy for the considerable discontent, Gladstone agreed with Wallace, was 'the gradual transfer of authority from the Chief and his headmen to the Administration'.[2]

Yet the era of formal concessions was over. The Administration had possessed itself of the main instruments of control; and for the rest had to be content with the gradual erosion of the Litunga's effective authority. In practical terms Lewanika had been reduced from the formal status of sovereign over the whole of North-

---

[1] F. V. Worthington, Report on Mboo and the Unrest in the Barotse Valley, 20 April 1911, Lusaka Archives B 1/2/286.
[2] Wallace to H.C., 21 April 1911, Lusaka Archives NR B 1/2/286. Gladstone to Wallace, 8 May 1911, NR B 1/2/301.

Western Rhodesia (as it existed in 1899) to a chief with no more than 'tribal authority' in a reserve. He had lost whatever governing powers he had possessed or could have asserted outside Barotseland proper, and even within his reserved territory he had no more than a limited subordinate jurisdiction. In this, of course, his position differed little from that of Khama and the major Bechuana chiefs. His 'authority in tribal matters' remained undefined until 1936, and his surviving judicial powers—exercised through the *kuta* at Lealui and other subordinate tribunals—similarly remained unregulated.

There were two factors which prevented the Company from closing its grip completely: an uneasy sense that any further curtailment of the Litunga's formal powers would throw into doubt the monopoly mineral rights the Company had obtained from him as the original grantee; and secondly, the counter-offensive of the educated Lozi aristocracy under Letia. The latter element appears to have asserted itself as early as 1910 when it may well have persuaded Lewanika and the Ngambela Sope that they had given away the land rights without proper monetary compensation, and so induced Lewanika to challenge the validity of the land concessions at the meeting with Colonel Fair.[1]

In 1914 there was an imbroglio over the surviving powers of jurisdiction, Lewanika supporting Letia's defiance of the Sesheke Resident Magistrate in hearing cases of cattle theft (which the Administration claimed constituted offences against English law and so fell under the jurisdiction of the magistrates' courts). Lewanika's letter was bluntly worded:

. . . as it was not in our concession with the Chartered Company in 1898 . . . we were objecting to this matter, and as it is seeming that the Chartered Company is trying as much as it can to take all matters in its hands than our agreement was made. I will be objectioned to these matters always, and I can say it is better to me and my *indunas* to know now what have left to us or to the Chartered Company. My son Litia what he did at Sesheke it is alright . . .[2]

[1] This was the interpretation of Richard Goode who was present at the meeting. Note by R. Goode, 15 April 1921, NR B 1/2/294.

[2] Lewanika to Ag. Magistrate, Lealui, 19 March 1914, African (South) 1015, encl. 1 in No. 166. Also *idem*, No. 175 and encls., No. 229, African (South) 1034, No. 9, encl., No. 19 and encls., No. 27 and encls.

Lewanika was not allowed to escape without reprimand but he had tied the Administration up in legal technicalities, and the matter dragged on until just before his death in 1916 when it was accepted that without a fresh concession from Lewanika the problem of concurrent jurisdiction could only be settled by an understanding as to the disposal of cases.

Letia's accession as Yeta III brought the educated Lozi royals to power. The inflation of the war period and the cessation of the cattle trade through the protracted pleuro-pneumonia epidemic had seriously depleted their finances. At the same time it was apparent that the days of the Chartered Company's administration were numbered. In 1918 Yeta launched an attack by petition and deputation that ceased only with the change to Colonial Office rule after 1923. He pressed his claims on every side, convinced apparently that his illiterate father had been cajoled into signing away his rights by documents whose full purport he did not grasp. In 1918 he indicted an omnibus petition in which he rehearsed Lozi grievances. Prominent was the demand for the full enjoyment of the 10 per cent share of the hut tax, for the use of the old title of king instead of paramount chief, and for the recognition of his political authority outside the reserved area. The officials thought Yeta 'very greedy for money' but Wallace, the Administrator, recognized the problem to be more deep-seated.[1] The financial difficulties of the Lozi aristocracy mirrored the general weakening of its traditional authority, as the people growing accustomed to working for wages outside Barotseland refused to render the traditional unpaid customary services. Yeta himself was finding it increasingly difficult to secure the twelve days annual free labour stipulated in the proclamation of 1906 when slavery was abolished, the *kuta* having no means of enforcing its demands. Hence his renewed insistence on being granted the whole of the 10 per cent share of the hut tax proceeds. The officials were fearful that the Lozi aristocracy, feeling 'a waning influence over the people and . . . unwilling to lose their power or diminish the state in which they live' would conduct a general feudal reaction; they were demanding greater control over

[1] Administrator (Wallace) to H.C., 29 October 1918, encl. Address and Petitions dtd. 9 August 1918, NR B 1/2/292.

movement in order to tie their former serfs to the soil and striving to wring the last advantage from their rights. They came therefore into direct collision with the efforts of the officials to stamp out the final vestiges of 'slavery' and to bring an end to all forced labour.[1] Opportunities for the exaction of tribute were also incidentally responsible for the attempts of Lewanika's 'English-speaking sons' to revive Lozi political pretensions outside the reserve. But the attempts also marked a newly educated Lozi patriotism determined to assert itself. In 1918 jealous European district officers reported Lozi attempts to 'boss up' Ila and Sala chiefs in the Kafue district and to interfere in the succession to the Mumbwa chieftaincy. Wallace had to warn his officials that Barotse political authority in these regions had never been legally abrogated, but he cautioned Yeta by word and letter against interfering with Africans outside the reserve.[2] Wallace inherited the direct-rule traditions of Company administration and saw no permanent asset in chiefly authority:

The whole of his [Yeta's] claims would die if the outside Natives refused to recognize them and we did not support them. This should come with the general breaking down of all Chiefs' powers—even in the Barotse this has begun. . . . That [Barotse] influence has been waning ever since the beginning when they had Native assessors in every Native court, and it is better to encourage this natural diminution of influence than by any drastic action to bring on a serious dispute as to our rights and theirs.[3]

It was easier thus to defeat Lozi pretensions in practical detail and not raise the question of abstract right. Formal renunciation of all authority outside the reserve might throw the Company's mineral rights into question. As late as 1905 the Company had considered the Lewanika Concession gave them a title 'more susceptible of strict proof' than that on which their claims rested in North-Eastern Rhodesia; and mainly for this reason extended the area of North-Western Rhodesia well across the Kafue in 1905.[4]

[1] See correspondence of G. Lyons, NR B 1/2/297.
[2] Wallace to Resident Magistrate, Mongu, 21 November 1918, NR B 1/2/281. Also Administrator, Reply to Petition, 10 August 1918, NR B 1/2/292.
[3] Wallace to E. S. B. Tagart, 21 November 1918, NR B 1/2/281.
[4] R. Goode to Administrator, Salisbury, 26 October 1921, B 1/2/281.

Yeta petitioned for direct Crown protection, for the cancellation of the Company's concessions, for the retrocession of the Caprivi Strip, for the extension of the reserve north of the Kabompo to the Anglo-Portuguese frontier, as well as for the whole of the 10 per cent share of the hut tax to be paid to him as paramount chief. Gone were the picturesque language and handwritten missives of Ishe Kambai, Lewanika's amanuensis. Yeta's correspondence was conducted by typewriter in concise, businesslike English. It was considered necessary to refuse him permission to bring a European lawyer to his audience with the High Commissioner in March 1921 or subsequently to conduct his affairs direct with the High Commissioner through a firm of Cape Town solicitors instead of through the Administrator in Livingstone. 'Without doubt' Yeta had 'been coached by European advisers in Cape Town', and the exposition of his case against the genuineness of the land concessions was for the first time marshalled in an orderly and convincing manner. In particular the sleight of hand of the 1909 Concession was exposed, the petition demonstrating that the extension of the reserve west of the Zambesi to the Anglo-Portuguese boundary had been explicitly made a condition by the Secretary of State of the confirmation of the 1900 Concession, and so could not validly be used as a consideration for obtaining fresh rights in 1909. The Administration could only counter feebly with the argument that the Ngambela in November 1910 had acknowledged the area west of the Zambesi to belong to the Company after the conclusion of the 1900 Concession.

For all his importunity, his stiff interviews with the Administrator, his petitions to the King of England, his audience with the Duke of Connaught as High Commissioner in Cape Town, Yeta obtained no satisfaction. The Colonial Office in July 1921 were quite firm in refusing to reopen the issues that had rankled so long. But Yeta's stand had not been altogether in vain. His aggressive counter-attack had warded off further invasion of Barotse authority; while considerations of prudence stayed the dying hand of the Company's Administration against the rough handling the Resident Commissioner in Salisbury wished to see meted out.

In 1924 the Lozi had the satisfaction of seeing Northern

Rhodesia as a whole coming under the direct rule of the Crown.
On the arrival of the first Governor, Herbert Stanley, they went
through the motions of petitioning afresh, pointing out 'with
great pride . . . that it is not many native states which came under
British protection which were neither conquered, subdued nor
annexed as this our territory was brought under the protection
of the British Crown by the free will and request of the Barotse
Council'. Stanley dealt gently with their demands, which even
now included the recognition of the Litunga's authority throughout North-Western Rhodesia. He sensed that Yeta was in serious
financial plight and that an open-handed policy would solve most
of the outstanding difficulties. Yeta surrendered the last effective
shreds of his rights outside the reserve by giving up his ivory
rights and his half share of game licence revenue throughout
North-Western Rhodesia for £850 a year, and within the reserve
gave up the right to exact unpaid labour for a grant of £2,500
(£500 of which was to go to his private purse).

The political wind was veering in favour of the preservation of
Barotseland's separate identity. Fears of a common African
nationalism springing from the disintegration of traditional
societies were now abroad. In 1927 the Reserves Commission
wrote privately to the Government:

As long as Natives are governed through Chiefs and Councils, each
Native will feel himself the member of a tribe and not of a coloured
race irrespective of tribe; his loyalty will be to the Chief of his tribe
and he will be suspicious of other tribes, and the moment when he feels
himself the member of the Bantu race pitted against the European race,
may be indefinitely postponed.[1]

The writings of experts like Loram in South Africa, officials like
Bruce-Miller, and old missionary hands like Edwin Smith who
had worked among the Ila and Tonga, gave the prevailing indirect rule philosophy a local habitation and a name.[2]

[1] P. J. McDonald, H. B. Hart, J. Moffat Thompson to Acting Gov., 13
February 1927, Lusaka Archives ZA 1/9/79.
[2] Cf. article by C. T. Loram, the South African 'separate development'
educationist, in the Christmas Number of the *Livingstone Mail*, December 1922.
Cf. Bruce-Miller, Papers in Salisbury Archives. Cf. Edwin Smith, the authority
on the Ila-Tonga peoples, *The Golden Stool*, 1926.

In the later 1920's and early 1930's there was even talk of developing Barotseland as a 'native state'. Maxwell, the 'West Coast' governor, who introduced the indirect rule measures of 1929, spoke up in this sense before the Hilton Young Commission. Worthington in retirement enthusiastically supported the idea. Throwing a liberal gloss over the founding years he conveniently forgot his own early attempts to kill the representative *induna* system, and put down the lost opportunity of working through the indigenous form of government to the lesser men who had followed Coryndon after 1907.[1] By 1932 there were discussions with the Governor at the Colonial Office on 'making Barotseland into a separate Native State'.

But the notion was at best fanciful. It was enmeshed in the complexities of white politics and the demand for settler rule; and in any event it was bound to break on the fact that modern administration had been developed in Barotseland in separation from the traditional government, which it had increasingly circumscribed. Only in the sense of removing the external threat of subjection to a settler-controlled legislature did the discussion have purposeful meaning. Self-government by Africans had to begin after 1936 on the lowly rungs of the native authority system and remained confined to cautious steps to improve and modernize the traditional government.[2] The Pim Commission in 1938 found the country stagnant and far more backward than other parts of Northern Rhodesia. It was this constant discrepancy between fact and fiction, between the reality of a poor and remote labour reserve and the pretensions and parchment bonds of a state in alliance with the British Crown, that lent the element of ambiguity to Barotseland's position and so allowed it to play a role in modern politics.

[1] Memorandum by F. V. Worthington, dated 1930, Worthington Papers, Rhodes-Livingstone Museum. Cf. Worthington to his father, 22 October 1904, *ibid.*
[2] Cf. L. H. Gann, *A History of Northern Rhodesia*, 1964, pp. 294–5.

13

THE NGONI STATES AND EUROPEAN INTRUSION

by

J. K. RENNIE

WHAT was the nature of the Ngoni states on the arrival of the Europeans? Were the varied paths by which they came under European rule determined purely by the differences between the groups of Europeans with whom the Ngoni came into contact? These are the main problems which this chapter attempts to deal with.

I

The Ngoni migrations were only part of the widespread population movements caused by the rise of the Zulu Empire. When the power of Zwide, the great Ngoni chief of the Ndandwe clan north of Zululand, was broken by Shaka, Zwangendaba preferred to migrate rather than be incorporated into the Zulu Empire. The northward migrations were not a march, but rather a gradual progression from one convenient stopping place to the next. Zwangendaba left Swaziland about 1821–2; he settled temporarily amongst the Tonga near the mouth of the Limpopo, and then moved on: finding his existence cramped by the Gaza on one side and the Ndebele on the other, he moved north-west and then north. The main body of the Ngoni crossed the Zambesi near Zumbo in 1835, this auspicious occasion being suitably accompanied by natural phenomena—the memorable beer- drink before the crossing, an eclipse of the sun which occasioned the premature birth of Mbelwa, and the parting of the waters of the Zambesi when Zwangendaba struck them with a stick. A second group of Ngoni, having crossed the Zambesi farther down, moved beyond the Shire and occupied the eastern shore of Lake

Nyasa. These Maseko Ngoni, as they were called, seem to have been an offshoot of the Ndebele rather than of Zwangendaba's Ngoni.[1]

After moving eastward and along the Luangwa plateau, the group moved north to the area between Lakes Nyasa and Tanganyika, raiding and taking captives where they could.

During the period of migration, [wrote Barnes] the Ngoni flourished. They were successful brigands on the march. Yet they were brigands in a poor land, and despite their military successes their economy remained one of subsistence cultivation, even though others did some of their cultivation for them. They were well organized for war and their enemies were not, but both they and their enemies were poor people relying on shifting cultivation with a poor technology and with access to only moderately valuable natural resources. The hinterland of Africa provided the Ngoni with an area within which they could operate successfully. . . .[2]

Up to this point the Ngoni state had remained largely intact, but in this area Zwangendaba died in 1845. A series of succession disputes followed. Again the evidence of oral tradition is conflicting, each group being anxious to demonstrate the legitimacy of their own claimant. Ntabeni went up the east of Lake Tanganyika, where we find terrible reports of the doings of the MaViti (Ngoni) in Livingstone's diaries. Zulu Gama led the Gwangwara Ngoni round the north end of Lake Nyasa and they raided the Rovuma Valley area and eventually drove the Maseko Ngoni back across the Shire. Ciwere Ndhlovu, a headman, led a group of followers to the Dowa district, where they terrorized the Cewa and Cipeta tribes.

Meanwhile in the main group the succession dispute went on; Mpezeni, Mtwaro and Mbelwa claimed right of succession on grounds of primogeniture, Zwangendaba's choice and popular opinion. Mtwaro stood down in favour of Mbelwa, and contented himself with being a chief under him; Mbelwa moved

[1] J. A. Barnes, *Politics in a Changing Society*, O.U.P., 1954, p. 17 ff. Accounts of the northward migration of the Ngoni vary considerably, and it is not possible to be absolutely sure about their movements. I have here followed the account of Barnes basically.
[2] Barnes, *op. cit.*, p. 63.

south into Tumbukaland, where he finally settled. The discontented Mpezeni moved off to the Fort Jameson district, and
Mperembe went off to raid the Bemba about 1856; he did not
have much success, and returned to be a sub-chief under Mbelwa.[1]

These disputes have been described by Bryant in typically ex-
travagant terms.[2] 'As happened in almost every case with the
great Bantu nation builders, the strong controlling hand having
let fall the reins, the unruly steeds kicked over the traces and
bolted, leaving the glorious chariot of state in shatters behind.
One after another faction fell away from Zwangendaba's tribe,
led by ambitious young headmen yearning to emulate the ex-
ploits of the master that was gone.'

This pessimistic view seems unjustified. Segmentation was a
common phenomenon in Ngoni society, and division of the tribe
seems to have helped to solve succession and any other disputes
which could not be resolved by free discussion, or killing off rival
claimants. Those who wished to secede were generally free to
leave and settle where they wished unmolested, unless they came
uncomfortably close to any other group. Any political system
intended to curb the unruly and coerce malcontents, while at the
same time preserving the 'democratic' institutions necessary for
the welfare and stability of Ngoni society, would have been both
unnecessary and too cumbersome for a migrant warrior tribe. It
may have been this view that the splitting up of a tribe necessarily meant decay and disaster which helped to foster the view
that by the time of the arrival of the Europeans, the Ngoni were
an effete military aristocracy, their pure strain weakened by
intermixture with other tribes, and that their states were hollow
shells which a mere touch would destroy. The segmentation
system, functioning normally, was like the swarming of bees,
keeping the tribe functioning harmoniously and retaining it
within manageable limits.

By about 1860, then, the Ngoni had completed their forty
years' wandering in the wilderness and their Moses had died with-

[1] Cf. E. H. L. Poole, *Native Tribes of the Eastern Province of Northern Rhodesia*,
Lusaka Govt. Printer, 1949, p. 7 ff., followed by Mary Tew, *Peoples of the Lake
Nyasa Region*, O.U.P., 1950. The above account is very oversimplified, the full
details of this dispute being very complicated and outside the scope of this paper.

[2] Bryant, *Olden Times in Zululand and Natal*, London, 1929, p. 466.

out setting foot in the promised land. The disposition of the Ngoni west of Nyasa was therefore something like this: in the north, the main group under Mbelwa, with Mperembe and Mtwaro as the main sub-chiefs; in the west, the Fort Jameson Ngoni under Mpezeni; between them, under Cabisa and Mwase Kasungu, whom Mbelwa had subdued, some Ngoni very inter-mingled with the Cewa; near the south end of the lake, Ciwere; and in the Kirk Range stretching to the southern end of the lake, the Maseko Ngoni under Cikusi and Cifisi. How were these groups organized? There are several good studies of Ngoni society.[1] There are enough similarities between the various groups to warrant treating them together for the moment, although there were important differences.

Though they were a wandering tribe, [wrote Y. M. Chibambo] yet there was one Paramount from whom proceeded the laws for the good government of the people. All the lesser chiefs and headmen received from him the leadership of the people . . . they kept their unity by messengers passing between them. The Paramount had power to call gatherings from time to time. . . . In these gatherings the old men and the men of repute who had a point to make were heard in criticism and made suggestions for the building-up of the realm. By this means the Paramount and his counsellors heard of and understood the thoughts of their people. It was in such large gatherings that the laws of the country were delivered to the people, so that they might hold fast to them and not be punished unreasonably for breaking them in ignorance. After they came back from these gatherings, the headmen and men of standing gathered together their villages . . . and told them carefully about the laws . . .[2]

There was a hierarchy of courts, the most simple being decided at village level, ranging upwards to the trial of serious cases like murder and witchcraft at the Paramount's court. Some measure of good and fair rule was ensured by the position of the village head-man, who had to maintain his popularity by giving fair judg-ments, and at the same time prove his fitness to rule to the Para-mount, on whose goodwill his position depended. Cases were

[1] Barnes, op. cit.; M. Read, The Ngoni of Nyasaland, O.U.P., 1956; M. Tew, op. cit., pp. 107-17.
[2] Quoted in Read, op. cit., p. 88.

generally decided by free discussion until full agreement was reached, time being no obstacle. If any party was dissatisfied with the result, the decision was referred to a higher court.

The Ngoni political system was not the arbitrary autocratic system which European administrators later represented it as being; it had a built-in system of checks and balances. There was a definite conception of law, and of authority as emanating from a person; there was a system of communications throughout the state which functioned in between the great *indabas* held once or twice a year.

Central to Ngoni culture were war and cattle. From herd-boy days the young warriors were trained in the art of weapons, encouraged in mock battles and disgraced if they were cowardly. They were drilled and armed in typical Ngoni fashion, and were organized into regiments on an age-set basis. Young men were not allowed to take part in the great annual games and dances until they had 'washed their spears' and at the great after-war dances a man's prowess and therefore prestige was reckoned by the number he had killed. It was on their military feats that the Ngoni based their sense of superiority over other tribes, and the functions of men in the society were included almost wholly in fighting, managing political affairs and supervising the welfare of the herds. In the Northern Ngoni there seems to have been a distinction between civil and military functions, Ngonomo being Mbelwa's 'war-minister'.[1] Mpezeni apparently made no such distinction.

Cattle were equally essential to the cohesion of the tribe; they were held in common, and their possession meant everything— wealth and status (because the ability to give generous gifts and hold feasts was reckoned important); they were necessary for lobola and for sacrificing to the ancestors of the tribe.[2]

The relation of these Ngoni groups to one another was usually one of peaceful coexistence although apparently not of active cooperation. Each recognized the sovereignty of the others in their own sphere and were kept well informed about other Ngoni events. As late as 1897 we find a summons from Mpezeni's Ngoni

[1] D. Fraser, *Winning a Primitive People*, 1914, p. 32.
[2] For this account of Ngoni culture cf. Read, *op. cit.*, Part II, Ch. IV.

to Mbelwa's Ngoni to combine in revolt to drive out the Europeans. Although this was not answered it can be noted that it was thought worthwhile to make the invitation. Sometimes, as with Cikusi and Cifisi, lack of room for expansion compelled them to live in hostile proximity, but this was exceptional.

However, the conciousness of a common ancestry does not seem to have been sufficient to foster co-operation in the face of a common enemy. Mpezeni did not help Cikusi, Cifisi or Ciwere against the Europeans; the Northern Ngoni did not combine with Mpezeni, Cabisa or Mwase although the opportunities presented themselves.

From the organization of politics and the relations of the Ngoni states to one another, we must now turn to the more problematical subject of their relations with the tribes whose lands they invaded. Accounts differ greatly depending on whether the sources are Ngoni or not. The Ngoni on the march raided the surrounding tribes for food and assimilated large numbers of captives into their society—first the Limpopo Tonga, then the Karanga, then the Senga, Cewa and Tumbuka peoples. These became thoroughly assimilated although still conscious of their position as 'Ngoni from the south of the Zambesi', 'Ngoni from the march', etc. Each of the Ngoni groups began to extend its influence over the tribes in the neighbourhood of the area in which it settled—Mpezeni over the Cewa, Undi, Bisa and Senga; Mbelwa over the Tumbuka (who, says Fraser,[1] had once been a strong centralized people but had by this time become decentralized and scattered), Kamanga, Henga, Senga, Cewa, Cipoka, Nkonde and Tonga: and the southern groups over the Nyanja, Yao, Cewa and Cipeta tribes. The nature of their rule is represented by themselves as being enlightened and beneficial, and by their subjects as brutal and almost wholly destructive. Ishmael Mwale said of the Central Ngoni states:[2]

Before the Ngoni came to this country the villages were small and isolated from one another. There was constant pouncing on people to catch them as slaves, and there was no redress. . . . Most people never went beyond the boundaries of their own village. . . . So no one had

---

[1] Fraser, *op. cit.*, p. 117.   [2] Cited in Read, *op. cit.*, pp. 88–9.

any wisdom beyond that of his own village and family. When the Ngoni came they had one law for all people and they had courts to hear cases where this law was enforced. There was freedom to travel in the land . . . because they had peace within their boundaries.

On the other hand, the 'wise rule' which Y. M. Chibambo spoke of [1] seems to have consisted, in part at least, of driving the unhappy Tonga and Cipoka tribesmen to the cliffs and escarpments bordering the lake, where they eked out a precarious existence on almost inaccessible crags or behind waterfalls, thoroughly cowed and terrified until they were found and given back a measure of their self-respect by the European missionaries; the Southern Ngoni terrorized the weaker of the Yao and Nyanja chiefs of the Kirk Range foothills and the Shire highlands: Mpezeni drove away the Cewa so that a population vacuum denoted his sphere of influence—his constant raids for captives made cultivation in the vicinity a decidedly risky proposition. The missionaries' reports, and those of people like Glave, show clearly the havoc and terror which even the suggestion of a Ngoni raid could cause. The picture of Ngoni cruelty may be overdrawn, however; the reports are by people who were either anxious to justify a speedy pacification of the country, or anxious to demonstrate to a doubtless responsive audience the need of a ferocious and pagan tribe for the civilizing effects of Christianity; and they in their turn as often as not got their information second-hand from people anxious to elicit sympathy, guns, or protection. Reading between the lines of a book such as Elmslie's,[2] one can see that the Ngoni did not completely wipe out whole villages so much as conduct small-scale raids involving perhaps a few hundred warriors and twenty or thirty deaths, and their purpose was to capture food and captives rather than establish political supremacy for its own sake. Besides, when Laws visited Cikusi's Ngoni in 1876 he was told that the worst raids were not by the Ngoni themselves, but by the 'scum' of the subject tribes who had become detribalized and uncontrolled though skilled in warfare.[3]

[1] Y. M. Chibambo, *My Ngoni of Nyasaland*, London, 1942.
[2] W. A. Elmslie, *Among the Wild Ngoni*, Edinburgh, 1899.
[3] Cf. Elmslie, *op. cit.*, p. 98. It has been suggested that the raids could not

Sometimes the Ngoni became involved in the local politics of other tribes, and not always to their own advantage. Kacinda-moto gained Mponda's help against Gomani in return for his lending warriors against the Makandanji clan and Cindamba's Yao in particular.[1] But one feels that Mponda had the better of the bargain, gaining both protection from Cindamba and profit from slaves captured in the raids on the Kirk Range foothills.

Did the Ngoni themselves engage in the slave trade? Johnston and Sharpe were both quite certain that they did. Not very much credence can attach to these reports alone: in the first place, there was a dearth of reliable information, and no distinction was ever made between raids for captives to be incorporated into the tribe, and raids for captives to sell; and secondly, allegations of slave trading were very useful to Johnston as a justification for his 'energetic' policies and coming quite clearly within Johnston's terms of reference. Neither had the means or the inclination to inquire closely into what was happening. A report of Glave's[2] was admittedly written by a man with more detailed knowledge, but he did not make the distinction between captives and slaves either, nor did he give any figures or detailed information, although he painted a grim picture of Ngoni devastation. So perhaps some credence can be given to the views of Wiese and the Ngoni tradition that the main object of the raids was not to get slaves to sell again but for captives to be assimilated.[3] A point in favour of this argument is the scarcity of guns and cloth amongst the Ngoni, noted both by the missionaries to the North-ern Ngoni and by Hawes on his visit to Cikusi;[4] since the Ngoni

have been for food because the Tonga staple diet is cassava, which is not reaped and stored like maize, but ripens underground and is not easy to raid. But since the raids were most frequent at harvest-time, it is reasonable to suppose that the Tonga, who were originally maize-growers, may have begun culti-vating more cassava at this time to discourage the raids, which nevertheless continued for captives and because of Tonga 'insubordination'.

[1] Johnston to Salisbury, 24 November 1891; F.O. Pr. 6337, encl. 1 in No. 74.
[2] Glave to Edwards, 14 June 1894, in F.O. 2/108, p. 27 ff., and F.O. Pr. 6968, No. 50.
[3] Cf. Barnes, op. cit., p. 79.
[4] Hawes' report May–June 1886, F.O. 84/1751. The scarcity of guns is also evident from the military reports of the campaigns against Cikusi and Mpezeni, where the few obsolete guns they did have were hardly used.

engaged in small ivory trade with the Arabs some of their cloth and guns would have come from this.

The treatment of the captives captured in these raids seems to have varied from group to group. Mpezeni assimilated his captives individually, whereas Mbelwa incorporated captured youths into regiments depending on the tribe of their origin, and appears to have allowed some measure of indirect rule.[1] Amongst Mpezeni's Ngoni, the captives belonged to the Paramount who then allocated them to their particular segments: the captors in the northern group were allowed to keep some of their captives.[2] Mbelwa was subsequently troubled by insubordination amongst his subject tribes, whereas Mpezeni was not. The question of the assimilation of large numbers of captives raises the question of the strength of the Ngoni states on the arrival of the Europeans; for it was well known that the Ngoni were intermixed with many other tribes, and it seems to have been a widely held view that the pure Ngoni blood was being defiled by interbreeding, that the tribe was becoming weakened and effeminate.[3] This argument does not bear examination, for the Ngoni had assimilated large numbers of other tribes on their northward migration: these had all become wholly members of the Ngoni tribe, and there is no evidence of any possible decline in power until after 1875.[4]

Evidence on the subject here is very slender, and the whole question is largely one of conjecture; but it can be held that until European intrusion, Ngoni power was being consolidated; that this intrusion took place at a critical juncture, providing a rallying point for enemies, or disaffected and unsubdued elements, or weakening the hold of the chief over his people; and that European presence prevented Ngoni reprisals and reassertion of control.

Mpezeni had been defeated by the Bemba (who were formidable opponents because of their Arab alliance), and Cikusi had suffered occasional reverses at the hands of the Yao, but both had settled in areas where they would be unmolested. In 1875 there

[1] Chibambo, *op. cit.*, Ch. 6.
[2] Fraser, *op. cit.*, p. 37, cited in Barnes, p. 30.
[3] This is the view held by Bryant, *op. cit.*, and followed by Lane Poole, *op. cit.*, and implicit in the term 'Bastard Zulus' used elsewhere.
[4] Cf. Read, *op. cit.*, p. 10.

had been a successful revolt of the Lakeside Tonga under Man-kambira against Mbelwa. His contention that the missionaries had given him medicine to make the revolt successful[1] was effective in frightening the Ngoni, and it did not make the task of the missionaries any easier, but it gives force to the argument that European presence encouraged the Tonga. Chibambo considered the decline equally due to the loss of ethnic purity and to the work of semi-assimilated 'agitators'. This second element is borne out by the studies of van Velsen,[2] who has shown that certain groups of Tonga were profoundly influenced by the proximity of the Ngoni, especially in matters of war, and returned to encourage and lead their suppressed brethren. However, even the presence of the missionaries was not enough to remove the threat from Bandawe; there is no reason to suppose that, failing the arrival of the Europeans, these minor revolts would have been anything but temporary, or have resulted in more than producing a few more scattered pockets of independent but terrified people.[3]

Other rebellions against Mbelwa were mostly suppressed. Be-tween 1876–9 the Kamanga and Henga rebelled, and in 1880 the Tumbuka revolted. However the years 1880–1 saw a revival of Ngoni power: the Tumbuka, Kamanga and some of the Henga were defeated, and when the missionaries arrived at Mbelwa's in 1881 they found the ground littered with the whitening skeletons of the Tumbuka rebels.[4]

There were two other possible sources of weakness. The fact that the Ngoni began to settle in a particular area does not seem to have affected the stability of the tribe, and Mbelwa's Ngoni were a strong enough society to be able to survive the transition from a military way of life. Mbelwa successfully prevented any attempt at secession or revolution caused by his cessation of raid-ing: and after his death the tribe, instead of splitting up, held together for six years without a paramount chief. Despite the increasing divergence of interest between him and his people, Cikusi kept his country under control for ten years after trans-

---

[1] W. P. Livingstone, *Laws of Livingstonia*, London, 1921, p. 153.
[2] In *Rhodes-Livingstone Institute Journal*, No. 26, 1960.
[3] This is the view held by W. P. Livingstone, *op. cit.*, pp. 185–6.
[4] Cf. Chibambo, *op. cit.*, Ch. 8.

Shire raiding was stopped; and Mpezeni's Ngoni preserved their tribal structure for more than thirty years after the Europeans thought they had smashed the system completely. As far as the structure of society goes, there are indications of a cohesiveness far removed from the rotten fabric which European conquerors imagined it to be.

The other possibility is that the Ngoni would have been prevented from building up strong states by more powerful neighbours. This is admittedly more of a possibility. The Bemba were a match for the Ngoni but relations were peaceful as long as there was enough distance between them to allow for this. Mbelwa's relations with Mlozi and the other Arabs at the north end of the Lake were not particularly good but were certainly not hostile. Too ambitious raids over the Shire might have brought Cikusi into conflict with Kawinga, Zarafi, Makanjira, or other powerful Arabized Yao chiefs with guns, but neither was in a position to destroy the other; and if the Ngoni had needed guns, they were in a very strategic position to engage in the slave trade. The speculation is interesting: if European intrusion had been delayed by ten years, they might well have encountered much stronger and better-organized resistance. A tradition of Ngoni superiority might have lessened the likelihood of revolt, and in turn made their rule less violent and more acceptable. As it was, however, the Europeans arrived to find the means of weakening the Ngoni states at their disposal, whether accidentally, or for conscious use as policy.

II

The theme of Ngoni history from the arrival of the Europeans to the turn of the century is the story of their gradual absorption into a larger social and political unit; of the effects this had on Ngoni society; of how contact with different groups of Europeans with differing aims and interests affected the path which this absorption took. At this point it becomes convenient to separate the histories of the Central African groups of Ngoni. The European contacts of the Northern Ngoni were almost exclusively missionary; from the beginning they realized the trickiness of their position with regard to local politics, and the attempt that was being made to include them in it.

In all the other districts the missionaries were hailed as the friends and protectors of the people, [wrote Elmslie, one of the first Livingstonia missionaries] . . . they gladly welcomed the missionary, hoping that his presence would prove their safety from their enemies. In no single case did they welcome him on account of his message, and the trouble in those early days was that he was pestered for medicine, guns and powder to kill their enemies.[1]

The Free Church established a mission at Cape Maclear and later at Bandawe in 1879 among the Tonga, who looked to the missionaries to take arms and lead them against their oppressors. Alone, they could do little. 'The Ngoni are like a snake, we are like a frog,' they said.[2] Laws had learned from earlier mission mistakes, however, and did not take sides. He said he was prepared to visit Cikusi and ask him to stop raiding; they were incredulous: 'You cannot hold a discussion with a wild beast,' they said.[3] Laws visited him in 1878, but was not very successful in establishing contact. The presence of the missionaries undoubtedly strengthened the Tonga, however, as it was obvious that Cikusi was extremely afraid of the Europeans; and Cipatula and Mtwaro had been impressed by Stewart's display of shooting. Laws, however, drew the line at leading a Tonga army against the Ngoni.

Then in 1879 James Stewart wrote that Mbelwa wanted the mission to come—he wanted an exclusive alliance. 'They have lost both power and prestige within the last two years, and may be resolving to gain both,' he informed Laws. '. . . Mombera and Cipatula and their headmen are desirious of peace and invite us still to come among them, while Mtwaro and Mperembe wish to recover their power by force of arms.'[4] Mbelwa was visited in 1881, and again in 1882, and a mission was established at Ekwendeni, the missionaries finding the ground littered with the whitening skeletons of the slaughtered Tumbuka rebels. For the

---

[1] Elmslie, *op. cit.*, p. 135.
[2] *Bandawe Mission Journal*, 17 November 1881; Elmslie, *op. cit.*, p. 99.
[3] Livingstone, *op. cit.*, p. 191.
[4] Quoted in Elmslie, *op. cit.*, p. 123.

Ngoni no less, this was an attempt to draw the missionaries into local politics; they saw their advantage, and Elmslie was asked for medicine to make slaves more obedient, headmen longer-lived and raids more successful. And when those were not forthcoming—'their pride would not allow them to think that in any way a white man or two could be of any profit to them.' The disillusionment which followed their arrival can be seen in the treatment they received. They likened Laws to an unfaithful wife who had two husbands and ran from one to the other, because he attempted to keep on good terms with the Tonga and the Ngoni. Perhaps the simile is significant, indicating the light in which they viewed him. The early missionaries claimed that the Ngoni treated them like slaves. When Dr Elmslie tried to induce them to give up raiding, they called him a child, and said he could not speak the language properly.

Nevertheless, Mbelwa agreed to leave the Bandawe Tonga alone. This decision, because it did not coincide with a decision to stop raiding westwards, cannot really be viewed as a decision of principle, but only as a concession of deference or fear—or both—to the missionaries. Until 1887 there was a sort of uneasy truce. Following the tradition of most missions in strong centralized societies, they made no converts for a long time—their first two baptisms were in 1890. On one occasion the mission at Bandawe was burned, and although the missionaries lived under a hardly intermittent threat of war, they were in fact largely unmolested.

Why was this the case? Ngoni society from the early 1880's until after 1887 was apparently undergoing tension and strain, because the missionaries had upset the balance of local politics. We have reports of surprising number of disputes over wives, perhaps because it was in the missionaries' interest to demonstrate the unworkability of polygamy, but also perhaps because of the decline in raiding and the subsequent strain on military organization. The medical work of the missionaries may have undermined the work of the native doctors. In 1886 a large body of armed youths staged a minor riot, barring Mbelwa from entry to the kraal until he gave them permission to go on a raid; but permission was successfully withheld. Mtwaro, one of the more important chiefs, fearing that if he remained under Mbelwa's jurisdiction his power would be reduced, tried to regain his power by attempting a revolt in 1886, but the kingdom was maintained intact. A crisis in 1887 seemed to set the work of the mission back several years. The Tonga wives seceded, taking with them their children; the future of the tribe was threatened; they could not be recovered except by a raid. For ten days war-dances were danced each day; it looked as if the moratorium on Tonga raids would be broken and the missionaries expelled from Ngoniland. Elmslie made dramatic nocturnal preparations to evacuate the mission, burying his medical stores and hiding the freshly-dug earth. Eventually Mbelwa agreed to punish severely any future attempts to raid the Bandawe Tonga, and the Lakeshore missions were safe, although raiding continued westwards for some time.[1]

Under these circumstances, one must ask why Mbelwa chose to stick to his original decision, and how he was able to do so in the face of opposition, both within his own group and from others such as Mtwaro's. It was not easy. W. P. Livingstone[2] says that he was compelled to be friendly to Laws in private and hostile in public. In the first place, he must have realized that any attack on the Tonga would bring him into conflict with forces stronger than he could cope with—a fact which his subjects probably did not appreciate. Secondly, between him and Laws had grown up a friendship of mutual esteem rather like that between Robert Moffat and Mzilikazi. Thirdly, he must have found in his tribe a sufficient element to support his decision, bearing in mind the structure of politics in Ngoni society. This pacific element must have been partly due to the influence of the missions, whose work expanded slowly until 1886; and this influence in turn due to their increased fluency in the language, and partly to the Xhosa evangelist William Koyi. The missionaries were quick to perceive that evangelization would most easily and effectively be carried out by Africans themselves, and William Koyi, by living amongst the Ngoni and yet constantly indentifying himself with the white missionaries, saying that if they were to be killed, he must be killed too, exercised a tremendous influence in the missionaries' favour. In addition, apart from the Tonga revolt of 1887, there

[1] Cf. Elmslie, *op. cit.*, Ch. XI.   [2] Livingstone, *op. cit.*, p. 230.

were no other attempted insurrections after 1881; and there was an exceptionally good harvest in 1889, following a rainy season which apparently a prayer meeting produced when the tribal rain-makers failed.[1] The missionaries claimed that the assimilation of less warlike local tribes was weakening the Zulu strain and lowering the moral tone of the tribe by introducing 'dances, beer, indiscriminate mixing of the sexes, looser family ties, rebelliousness to authority'.[2] As we have seen, the assimilation of great numbers of less warlike tribes during their migrations did nothing to make the Ngoni effeminate; but what may have happened is that by the introduction of people from other cultures where war was not a necessary part of life nor bravery the supreme status symbol, the tribe was laid open to the acceptance of the missionaries' insistence that raiding was senseless destruction. Besides, the missionaries attempted, even if only on a very small scale, to provide industrial training and education, and there was always a labour market in the south.

The last reason for Mbelwa's being able to keep to his decision for so long must surely be that the society was not on the verge of collapse: that despite the tension and unrest his position was secure enough to enable him to enforce his decision where it was unpopular. The 1887 crises marked the end of instability; Mbelwa, who had suddenly become unwilling to give up raiding the Tonga, was overruled in council.[3] Mtwaro agreed provided he could have a mission, which further paved the way for missionary influence. In 1891 Mbelwa died, but instead of a general disruption of the tribe when no successor was chosen, the tribe held together for five years under a regency. Ngonomo, the unruly *induna*, tried to gain the chieftainship for himself; his section of the Ngoni had not given up raiding, nor had Mperembe's. They knew of the declaration of a Protectorate, of the Administration's activities in the south. They had been left alone—perhaps Johnston was afraid of them? Yet their chance came, and was rejected. First Cabisa and then, when he failed to get their support and took refuge at Mpezeni's, Mpezeni himself, tried to gain their support in rebellion. A collision with Johnston seemed imminent.[4]

[1] Livingstone, *op. cit.*, p. 229.   [2] Fraser, *op. cit.*, p. 33.
[3] Elmslie, *op. cit.*, pp. 245-6.   [4] Elmslie, *op. cit.*, p. 289.

Ngonomo was the only *induna* to favour support, and he was finally dissuaded from actually joining in, although he drew the line at handing Cabisa over to the Protectorate government. At a great *indaba*, Cabisa, Ngonomo and many of the old men tried to get the others to agree to go to war, but the young men refused —a curious inversion of what might have been expected! 'It was then demonstrated to the old men that their voice was no longer a power in the tribe. . . . All the young men . . . rose up and left in a body to attend the (church) service,' wrote Elmslie with justifiable pride.[1]

Was the cessation of raiding then due to a decline in Ngoni power? Sections of the Ngoni continued to raid westwards into Bemba country until 1894, (and even into the Administration's province to the south[2]). Glave wrote:[3]

The Angoni attack in overwhelming numbers, and constitute a power with which the Wanyika, Wasenga, Watshewa cannot cope . . . [The Angoni] are masters of this country, from some villages they collect tribute in slaves, cloth, and ivory, and when so inclined, murder, pillage, and enslave. On the map this whole country is embraced by distinctive limits and marked '*British Protectorate*'. The whole thing is a farce. Where is the protection? . . . if the B.C.A.A. does not come to the relief of the Wasenga, Watchewa, and Wabisa in the near future all will have passed into the hands of the Angoni. Already a host of villages . . . have . . . given themselves up to live as slaves of the Angoni. The Angoni have no stockaded villages, such protection they deem unnecessary as no enemy can be strong enough to attack them. If they get the 7 and 9 pounders playing on them some day they will get the kinks taken out of their ideas I am thinking.

He was writing of the area raided by Mpezeni's and Mbelwa's Ngoni, so this is hardly consistent with a view of the decline of Ngoni power. All that happened was that the missionaries, by their presence, had altered the balance of power between the Tonga and the Ngoni.

With these facts in view there is no more reason to seem surprised at the peaceful incorporation of Northern Ngoniland into the Protectorate than at the violent subjugation of the other groups.

[1] Elmslie, *op. cit.*, pp. 294–5.   [2] Swann in *B.C.A.G.*, 1 April 1895.
[3] Glave, *loc. cit.*

Here again, the influence of the missionaries played a large part, only this time it was a more conscious effort. They introduced the Government agent Crawshay to Mtwaro and ensured his friendly reception.[1] Until 1896 they caused the Administration no trouble, but on the defeat of Mlozi, Johnston wanted to bring the whole of Northern Nyasaland under direct administration.[2] Laws, one of the few Scottish missionaries whom Johnston could stomach, wrote quickly to Johnston explaining that the time was not yet ripe and that the Ngoni were managing their affairs quite well. He felt any attempt at exercising jurisdiction would mean a military expedition, and this would ruin the mission's credit with the Ngoni.[3] 'We may not get the credit for it,' he wrote to Swann, 'but there is a preparation for British rule going on in Ngoniland which may yet make it the easiest transfer of power in British Central Africa.'[4]

So Johnston waited, and Elmslie and the other missionaries worked assiduously to spread the idea that it would be a good thing to have Victoria as Chief. Perhaps because of disorder in the tribe,[5] or because of the threat of a take-over by the Administration, Mbalekelwa was chosen Paramount Chief *de jure* and ruled from 1897-1915, when he was deposed for his part in Chilembwe's rising. The disorder cannot have been very great because although his legitimacy was very doubtful his succession was never seriously challenged. It is also significant that the ceremony on his accession was specifically Christian.[6]

On the defeat of Mpezeni it was felt in Government circles that the Northern Ngoni would now see resistance to European occupation was useless.[7] There were, however, other reasons than the fear of physical force. Between 1897 and 1904 Ngoni society

---

[1] Crawshay to Johnston, 8 August 1893, F.O. Pr. 6482, encl. in 261.
[2] Johnston, *Report on B.C.A. Protectorate 1895-6; Parliamentary Papers*, 1896, 1 August, p. 437, Johnston to Salisbury, 24 April 1896; 'our action in regard to these people [a section of the Northern Ngoni] is much embarrassed by the fact that the Livingstonia Free Church Mission has many stations in their territory. Was it not for this, I should have been disposed after the conclusion of the Arab War, to have dealt decisively with one of the Northern Angoni chiefs . . .' Cf. Livingstone, *op. cit.*, p. 283.
[3] Cf. Livingstone, *op. cit.*, p. 283.   [4] Quoted in Livingstone, *op. cit.*, p. 284.
[5] Fraser, *op. cit.*, p. 49.   [6] Elmslie, *op. cit.*, p. 296.
[7] *B.C.A.G.*, 26 February 1898.

gradually and peacefully altered. As usual, one of the first toe-
holds the Government got was with discontented litigants apply-
ing to the Boma for redress. Gradually, as the older chiefs died
off (Mtwaro, for example, in 1897) the tribal restraints began to
break down and the new generation seemed more willing to
accept British jurisdiction. The advantages of this were brought
home to them when a filibuster fled from the country after in-
sulting and shooting some of the Africans. A raiding party to
fetch him and punish him would have been out of the question—
it would have brought them into conflict with Sharpe. Laws used
the occasion to point out the advantages of British administration.[1] Sharpe wrote to him, 'Write and tell me when you are
satisfied, and I will act at once,'[2] and in 1904 Laws suggested the
time was ripe. Sharpe travelled north unescorted except for his
wife, and this prudent act of faith stood him well. It must have
been one of the most unusual assumptions of political control.
Thousands came to the great *indaba*, and Sharpe carefully explained that British control would mean no interference with the
running of tribal affairs. The chiefs seemed glad to accept this; and
a Resident was sent and Native law applied where possible. So it
was that, thirteen years after the declaration of a Protectorate
over the country, Northern Ngoniland passed finally under
British jurisdiction.[3]

Not as a result of this change, but because of much earlier-
based forces, the culture gradually changed. In the first place,
Christianity began to have a very great influence on culture,
helped by the growth of an indigenous church. The influence of
the tribal doctors was undermined.[4] Ngoni was gradually replaced by Tumbuka as a language. The Ngoni were drawn into
the Shire Highlands labour and trading complex, and also were
recruited for mine labour in the south, with the result that a
further cultural interfusion and weakening of tribal ties took place.
The recruitment of labour was not easy at first. Some sections of
the tribe claimed they had not agreed to come under British
jurisdiction; some people fled, believing that the Administration had come to take away their cattle (doubtless the legacy of

[1] Fraser, *op. cit.*, Part I, Ch. 9.   [2] Quoted in Livingstone, *op. cit.*, p. 314.
[3] Cf. Livingstone, *op. cit.*, IV, Ch. 9.   [4] Elmslie, *op. cit.*, p. 153.

the Mpezeni campaign). Cash became increasingly part of the economy, as was shown by the increasing amount of hut-tax paid in cash.[1]

III

The case of the Southern Ngoni further bears out the theory that it was not until the arrival of the Europeans that a decline in power set in; and that this decline is directly attributable to the growing conflict of interests between the chief, his people, and the administrators. The Maseko Ngoni, as they were called, had been driven back across the Shire by the Gwangwara Ngoni, and now ruled over a considerable stretch of forest and plain bordering the lake, the Kirk Range, and the plateau to the west. The soil was fertile and well-cultivated. Separated from them by a 'no-man's-land' was Mponda, who paid them tribute and bought protection from Makanjira's onslaughts. Between Mponda's and Cikusi's was a two-way traffic of Ngoni labourers selling their services in return for salt, which was very highly prized, and meal. Liwonde was another tributary; and they afforded 'protection' to the Maravi on the west. The tributaries of the Ngoni were (naturally) amicably disposed towards the British, and in this position the Ngoni were not free to raid without coming into conflict with stronger peoples—the British, the Portuguese or the other (stronger) Ngoni groups.

From about 1875 we have reports of the Cikusi's trans-Shire raids, with the disorganized and divided Yao an easy prey. The Ngoni were armed as usual with spears, clubs, bows and arrows, and a few old muzzle-loaders presumably obtained from the Arabs, which seem never to have been used. After the 1880 raids the Makololo chief Kasisi built a chain of fortified villages along the left bank of the Shire as a protection, but Nyanuka, one of Cikusi's headmen, bribed a Nyanja headman to let the Ngoni through in 1884, and they ravaged the Zomba area, coming very close to Blantyre. Then, on representations from the Blantyre missionaries, they withdrew to the west of the Shire. The following year Hawes visited Cikusi to try and persuade him to trade instead

[1] *British Central Africa Protectorate Report*, 1905-6.

of raid. Hawes' impressions confirm the theory that at this time the Ngoni state was strong. 'The whole country is under perfect control,' he reported, 'and the greatest respect is shown to the King. . . . He has absolute power, and is reported to be most cruel. . . . Disobedience is punished by death.'[1] Throughout his stay the Consul was shown the utmost courtesy, which he contrasted with the 'unbearably rude' Tonga of Livingstonia. Cikusi swore in the presence of his headmen to discontinue raiding, and promised to send an agent to Blantyre to discuss trading with the African Lakes Company. Nothing seems to have come from the latter venture. Cikusi's decision seems to have been based partly on deference to the Europeans (he was on good relations with Clement Scott of the Blantyre Mission) and partly on a healthy respect for their power. (Hawes made a point of saluting him with an impressive three-gun volley.) Four years later he was visited by Sharpe, who with Johnston was attempting to bring the whole of British Central Africa under British control, in a rather frenetic attempt to keep out the Portuguese. Johnston accordingly attached great importance to the treaty. 'He is altogether the most powerful chief between the Zambesi and Lake Nyasa,' he wrote enthusiastically to Lord Salisbury, 'and his adhesion to our protectorate is of very great local importance.'[2] It is doubtful if this optimism was justified. Cikusi's state was not the highly organized machine that Mpezeni's or Mbelwa's was. Cewa influence was predominant and Ngoni as a language dying out.[3] In any case, it is unlikely that Cikusi himself considered he had given away much, and we find Johnston saying the following year that he hoped to get Cikusi to cede his sovereign rights now that he was impressed by the defeat of Kawinga.[4] Maguire and Buchanan were dispatched, but apparently nothing came of it; the British Central Africa Administration had no control over southern Ngoniland until they conquered it by force; this was made possible by a decline in Cikusi's power caused by a succession dispute and a weakening of his authority. On Cikusi's

[1] Hawes' report, May–June, 1886,! oc. cit.

[2] Johnston to Salisbury, 10 June 1890, F.O. 84/2052, fo. 48 ff. Sharpe's treaty with Cikusi forwarded with this letter is not reproduced.

[3] Laws, op. cit., p. 122.

[4] Johnston to Salisbury, 10 December 1891, F.O. Pr. 6337, No. 43.

death (1891), Kacindamoto refused to recognize Gomani Kwendi as Paramount and moved towards Mponda's. The rival groups were too close for comfort, however: fighting ensued, Mponda making full use of the division. Then Gomani gained Mponda's help, and Kacindamoto appealed in desperation to the Administration. Major Edwards, who felt that the only people really benefiting were the Arabs and Yao, and that the Ngoni were in danger of being submerged by the Yao,[1] managed to restore harmony at Dedza without loss of life;[2] but there can be no doubt that the split weakened the Ngoni in general and the prestige of the chiefs in particular.

A far more important reason for the decline of Gomani's power was the increasing divergence of interest between him and his people. Both Gomani and Kacindamoto wished to be on good terms with the Administration, but neither wanted his authority over his subjects diminished, or wanted European settlement.[3] It is therefore understandable that they objected to the migration of their subjects across to the Shire Highlands to find work; for they would be beyond their jurisdiction there, and would have vastly increased status by virtue of their few shillings earnings when they returned. Besides, each wished to keep his fighting strength up; and each attempted to draft all the able-bodied men into fighting units.[4] The policy of the Administration, which was to protect settler interests, was directly opposed to this. Porters were in universal demand, for without them commerce was hamstrung; labour was needed for the coffee plantations; and the settlers had discovered that labourers removed from their environment worked harder and were more reliable. Migrant Ngoni labourers were therefore very much sought after, the more so since there had only been a trickle across the Shire—about 3,000 in 1893; and Sharpe's attempts to regulate the flow of labour by a pass system had made their passage more difficult. It was obvious to the settlers that local tribal politics were responsible for the scarcity of labour, and that many of the tribesmen themselves

[1] B.C.A.G., 14 December 1894.
[2] In true British fashion, he solemnly made the chiefs shake hands and promise to be friends.
[3] Nicoll in B.C.A.G., 28 June 1894.   [4] B.C.A.G., 15 July 1895.

were anxious to come and find work. Edwards' 1894 peace-making was followed by an immediate increase in the labour supply; and it was hoped that negotiations would be enough. They were not.

Further parties of labourers were forwarded by Codrington when he visited Ciwere; Ciwere, obviously terrified, gave in to an influential section of his tribe which had been pressing for some time for increased contact with European Administration, and agreed to pay taxes and let Europeans build on his land.[1] There was still a shortage of labour in 1898 when Ciwere admitted to Devoy, the collector, that he was having trouble with his sub-chiefs because of his close contact with the Administration,[2] of whom they were afraid (two years previously more than half his tribe had construed as military a peaceful expedition and fled).[3]

The next to give in to the Administration were the people of Cabisa and Mwase Kasungu. Cabisa closed the Luapula route and refused Swann's demand to reopen it. In January 1896 he was defeated and fled, and the 'industrious inhabitants of the country' were free to work in the Shire Highlands coffee plantations,[4] although Cabisa still caused the Administration, who knew of his activities at Mbelwa's and Mpezeni's, some little concern.[5]

Gomani must have been worried by these developments. In 1896 parties of Ngoni warriors began to threaten the villages in the foothills of the Kirk Range who had previously owned allegiance to them and were now paying taxes. The raid on the Kirk Range foothills and Zambesi Industrial Mission at Ntonda was an expression of hostility at growing European influence, and an attempt to reassert Ngoni power. Sharpe said that missions, and villages known to pay tax, were especially attacked and persons holding tax receipts were speared.[6] There was anxiety in Government circles; a few months before they had been saying that Gomani had always been amicably disposed; now they

[1] Codrington in *B.C.A.G.*, 15 September 1896.
[2] *B.C.A.G.*, 21 May 1898.   [3] *B.C.A.G.*, 15 June 1896.
[4] Report by A. J. Swann, undated, in Johnston to Salisbury, 24 January 1896; F.O. Pr. 6851, encl. in No. 84.
[5] Swann in *B.C.A.G.*, 15 April 1897.
[6] Sharpe to Salisbury, 15 October 1896; F.O. Pr. 6911, No. 117; also *B.C.A.G.*, 15 October 1896.

announced that he had always been hostile to British rule, and
that he would be dealt with. A force left Zomba and broke the
Ngoni power with ease, meeting with very little resistance.
Gomani, refusing to submit, and saying that the Shire Highlands
people were his and that he would not have them under British
law, was captured, shot for murder, and his villages were burned;
a new Ngoni chief was selected.

Hopes expressed that this would bring peace were ill-founded.
Raiding continued into Maravi country,[1] and there was a further
rising at Domwe in April 1898, described in the *Gazette* of that
month as 'serious'; but after Mandala, Msekandiwana, Jovalema
and Kwaila were picked off, it was obvious the Ngoni were no
longer a military power and that the people were defecting from
the chiefs for the attractions of the European economy.[2]

IV

The position of Mpezeni was somewhat different. Whereas the
Southern Ngoni territory was invaded and conquered by a European armed force, because a Ngoni state was an incompatible
neighbour for the Shire Highlands, the pattern of events as far as
Mpezeni is concerned follows the framework of events of, say,
the Shona rebellion. His country was surrounded, and infiltrated
without his permission; the suppression of the rebellion which
followed gave the Europeans control of the country.

Mpezeni encountered Europeans, not in the shape of religion
or administration, but as capitalism; for his territory was rumoured
to have gold in it, was healthy, and good for cattle; but his first
contacts were with the Portuguese. There had been occasional
Portuguese explorers, ivory hunters, and mineral prospectors
traversing the region before he settled there, and there was a
Portuguese military post to the north of his territory, abandoned
before the Ngoni crossed the Zambesi. Apart from a few missionaries and freebooters, few were interested in his country until
about 1887. An exception to this was Carl Wiese, a German con-

[1] *B.C.A.G.*, 15 August 1897.
[2] *B.C.A.G.*, 21 May 1898. Cf. Manning to Salisbury, 22 April 1898, F.O.
Pr. 7074, No. 77.

cession-hunter. Evidence about him is very conflicting, due to the
fact that he was in a very strategic position and different parties
tried to use him for different ends at various times. He seems to
have arrived at Mpezeni's about 1885, and to have befriended him
and received by verbal treaty a grant of about 10,000 square miles of
land in which to conduct his operations. He established a number
of trading posts, and lived with a black Portuguese woman, Doña
Romana. Mpezeni gave him a number of captives whom he employed in his plantations and ivory hunting. He went round
making treaties with other chiefs, extending his claims over an
area of something like 25,000 square miles. He obtained a position
of great influence as one of Mpezeni's most trusted advisers. Because of this both Portuguese and British tried to buy his services.
He helped lead de Solla's expedition in 1888 and distributed flags,
and thereafter Mpezeni looked on the Portuguese with favour,
because apart from this formality they left him very much alone.[1]
The following year Sharpe visited Mpezeni, and was unsuccessful
in trying to conclude a treaty. Mpezeni obviously felt he did not
need the support of the British. 'He is under the impression that
he is the most powerful monarch in the world, except possibly
Mombera,' wrote the aggrieved representative of Her Majesty,
'and the suggestion that it would be a good thing for him to have
(in case of a future war) so powerful a friend as the Queen,
created great amusement.'[2] The next on the scene was Thomson,
employee of the British South Africa Company, who was received with such hostility by the Ngoni that he had to shelter at
Wiese's house and flee under cover of darkness. How was Johnston to surmount this difficulty? Sharpe's attempts to buy Wiese's
services had failed; an embassy of Mpezeni's to him at Kota Kota
in January 1890 had been inconclusive; they had merely said that
Mpezeni had not made and would not make a treaty with the
Portuguese. At first Johnston pointed out[3] that existing treaties
with Undi and Cikusi cut him off from the Zambesi; but the map
accompanying this showed his country as a large unclaimed gap
in an optimistically large pink British area. He said Mpezeni was

---

[1] Cf. Barnes, *op. cit.*, p. 73 ff. [2] F.O. 84/2052, pp. 274–315.
[3] In an undated memorandum of 1890 in F.O. 84/2052, pp. 143–8 (? 9
August).

not hostile to the British; that 'being a good-tempered sort of chief' he had not refused Sharpe an interview; Sharpe had used up his stock of presents and had been unable to see him. 'In any case,' he concluded, 'the Portuguese *must not be allowed* to establish them-selves at Mpezeni's, if we are to hold any dominions north of the Zambesi.'

This position gradually changed. In a memorandum to the Foreign Office in 1897 he explained his early policy; finding Mpezeni obdurate, treaties had been made with surrounding chiefs, and his authority was not recognized. A few years previous he wrote,[1] 'Perhaps if in 1889, 1890, or 1891 Mpezeni had chosen to enter into friendly Treaty with Her Majesty the Queen, I might have been inclined to recognize his authority. But . . . [he] always declined . . . I therefore refuse now to recognize Mpezeni as ruling chief.' Mpezeni did not seem unduly worried about Her Majesty's Consul's non-recognition of his authority, which was tangible enough without it at that stage. It is worth pointing out, however, that he was neither informed that his country had been placed in the British sphere of influence, nor that Rhodes and Johnston had in a house in London early in 1891 arbitrarily drawn a line which put part of his people in the Protectorate. At that stage it did not matter; he was not hemmed in and Glave's report of 1894 showed him still raiding within the Protectorate.

In April 1891 Mpezeni formalized his lease of 10,000 square miles of land to Wiese, for a consideration of £200 per year; it provided 'mineral, wood and water rights, agriculture, grazing and navigation rights'. Being superstitious, he refused to put his mark on paper; so de Solla, the Portuguese who happened to be at Mpezeni's at the time, signed it for him. It seems quite probable that Mpezeni knew what he was doing and was quite prepared to give his friend the privileges claimed; so the treaty was morally, if not legally valid. At any rate, it was more valid than any other claim.

For about five years nothing happened. Mpezeni was perfectly aware of what was going on in other territories under British control. Ndebele refugees started to reach the Fort Jameson area

[1] Johnston to Lt.-Col. Warton, 3 March 1894; F.O. Pr. 6537, encl. 2 in No. 146.

after 1893—in fact he heard of the news of Lobengula's defeat before many of the Europeans in Nyasaland. Wiese was off in Europe somewhere, and when he next came back it was with an expedition from Tete, the leader of which, Colonel Warton, had been introduced as a brother of Wiese's. On these grounds Mpezeni accepted them. When they asked if they could dig for gold, he replied that he had already given all the gold in his country to Wiese—on the strength of his recommendation they could enter his country. After all, they would help to keep the British out. He had been rather alarmed at the recent sudden extension and exhibition of British power. They had separated him from Mbelwa by their campaign against Cabisa and Mwase Kasungu in 1896. He had heard of the vigorous campaigns against the Yao chiefs. This Portuguese expedition would help him to keep his independence. It was not until a year later that he discovered the deception that had been practised on him, and by then it was too late to do anything about it. Wiese, one of his most trusted advisers, had betrayed him into admitting the British South Africa Company, the very people he had attempted to exclude from his territories!

The story behind the North Charterland Exploration Company's 1896 expedition is a long and sordid one, and too tortuous to examine in detail here. Briefly, Wiese had been unable to get his concessions ratified because of Johnston's obstructionist tactics. Johnston supported the rival claims of the British South Africa Company to the region; but he could not get the Foreign Office to accept that Wiese's claims were invalid. The deadlock was broken by Wiese selling out his option, and his concessionaires forming a new company, the North Charterland Exploration Company, which was controlled by the British South Africa Company and was to exploit the region formerly claimed by the British South African Company under Sharpe's treaties.[1] The North Charterland Exploration Company's expedition left Tete even before agreement had been reached. Loud disclaimers were later made by the Company and by Warton that an attempt had been made to disguise the British nature of the expedition. The Union Jack had been flown, they declared, and Warton had

[1] Cf. *North Charterland Concession Inquiry—(Maugham Report)*, Col. 73, July 1932.

been merely represented as a friend of Wiese's and not as his brother; but the evidence to the contrary is strong. In the first place, the choice of Tete for departure instead of the much more natural way *via* Blantyre; secondly, a report by Hugo Genthe, in a semi-official publication:[1] 'Since travelling in British territory, though "made in Germany", I have always taken with me the Union Jack. I was requested by the N. Charterland Coy. not to take this with me now . . . they were afraid it would cause a row. There is no flag at the N. Ch. Coy's. station.' Thirdly, there is a private letter from Warton which says, 'Mr Wiese is regarded by the Angoni as almost one of themselves. . . . Personally I am known as Wiese's elder brother.'[2]

From the realization that this was British South Africa Company rule, and from Warton's illegal attempts to administer the country, and from the growing threat caused by the loss of independence of Cikusi, Cifisi, Ciwere and Cabisa, of whom the latter took refuge at Fort Jameson and tried to foment rebellion, dates the loss of Mpezeni's prestige, and the progress towards the rebellion of a discontented section of the tribe. Mpezeni chose to accept a *fait accompli*; the Matabele and Mashona rebellions had failed; the Northern Ngoni would not co-operate; he was bribed by an offer of a percentage of the hut tax; he was getting old (probably over sixty) and disinclined to violence. In 1896 the British South Africa Company requested him to punish a party of warriors which had raided a caravan of porters on the way from Kota Kota to Fort Jameson (at that time Fort Partridge). This was done. In the same year he sent to Zomba for a British flag, but the request was ignored. In his place, his son, Nsingu, who was much more inclined to revolution, gained support, particularly as news began to filter up about the Matabele rebellion, and when Mpezeni did nothing to support Cabisa's rebellion. The unrest was growing, as we can see by the appeals of the prospectors to Kota Kota for help. Johnston, however, felt that the time was not yet ripe. Any attack on the Ngoni must be provoked by the Ngoni themselves. Meanwhile, perhaps to encourage the prospectors to remain there

[1] Genthe in *B.C.A.G.*, 1 August 1897.
[2] Quoted in Lane Poole, *op. cit.*, p. 13. I have not found this letter referred to anywhere else.

as much as for any other reason, the British South Africa Company offered a reward of £10,000 to the first person to find workable gold. Forbes wanted to bolster up Mpezeni's power and saw Wiese as the key to the situation. He wrote to the London board, pointing out that it would be a good idea to employ Wiese with a force of Tonga police 'with which he can, by supporting Mpezeni, not only keep the North Charterland Company's territory quiet, but can extend the authority of the British South Africa Company for a considerable distance to the west.'[1] But before the telegram of the London board sanctioning his appointment arrived, Wiese had tactfully disappeared for a time into the west; he must have realized that any credit he had with the Ngoni had gone; henceforth his only friend was to be Mpezeni. The situation was further complicated by the importation of arms (legally and otherwise) by the North Charterland Exploration Company which made armed conflict more probable.

From here events moved swiftly. In May 1897, Mpezeni's people started moving over the border into the Protectorate, hoeing gardens and building temporary villages there. It was obvious that they realized the difference between Protectorate and Company rule. The Foreign Office and the Colonial Office both recognized any attempt at administration as illegal, and had ruled that if Mpezeni did not let the Charterland Company administer his territory they should withdraw. But Mpezeni obviously did not know of this support from higher circles, and wrote a pathetic letter to Sharpe asking to settle to the west of the Kota Kota district. 'I wish no war. All Chipeta was mine, and now you say it is not. Mwasi was my slave and you killed him in war . . .'[2] He would agree to pay taxes and obey the laws. Sharpe was amenable, as Mpezeni would now be more 'get-at-able' as he termed it.[3]

The actual rebellion need concern us little here. It is discussed quite fully from the Government angle in the military reports, the only moot point being whether or not Nsingu's 'rebellion' was caused partly by the presence of government troops before any hostilities had actually taken place. Manning in particular seems

---

[1] Lane Poole, *op. cit.*, p. 14.
[2] Reproduced in F.O. Pr. 7010, No. 11, enclosure.
[3] Sharpe to Salisbury, 13 June 1897, in F.O. Pr. 7010, No. 13.

to have been inclined to precipitate action. The poorly armed Ngoni were no match for the Maxim gun and the troops, who understandably perhaps were prepared for a second Matabele war, had a surprisingly easy victory, due no doubt to the disunity they themselves noticed amongst the *indunas*.

The results of the defeat have been described by Barnes, and one can only summarize his fairly detailed conclusions here. There was not the same incentive for the peaceful alteration of society as there had been in the case of the Northern Ngoni. Once raiding was abolished and the rebellion quelled, the same absorption into a larger social and economic unit began to take place. The Ngoni were recruited for the British South Africa Company, and were used to suppress the Shona rebellion. They went south, to work on the mines and farms. Tax had brought in the need for a money economy, and a new value-pattern, based on material possessions, clothes, and so on, grew up, incurring, naturally, the resentment of the chiefs, who still held positions of authority, but now as government servants. Little attempt was made to develop the region, which was regarded as a labour and cattle reserve. The further breakdown of tribal institutions was encouraged by the ban on carrying weapons of war; and the regiment-system which had been one of the mainstays of social organization, disappeared. Perhaps a more serious blow was caused by the seizure of cattle. Learning nothing from the lessons of the Matabele Rebellion, Manning wrote to Salisbury[1] that nearly 12,000 cattle had been captured. 'I do not imagine the total cost to the British South Africa Company will be more than £2,000. This will be covered ten times over by the value of the cattle captured by the expedition, so that the ... Company will reap a handsome profit.' Eventually the wishes of the Colonial Office prevailed and many of the cattle were handed back, but the damage was done. By 31 March 1900 only 1,200 remained;[2] the rest had been sold, looted or slaughtered, and another tie making for the cohesiveness of the state was gone. Large villages disappeared, many of them were burnt by the Company's troops and never rebuilt.

There was more resilience in Ngoni society than its conquerors

[1] Manning to Salisbury, 17 February 1898, F.O. Pr. 7074, No. 48.
[2] Barnes, *op. cit.*, pp. 93–6.

supposed, however. They considered that in one fell swoop they had completely smashed the whole tribal organization but more than thirty years later an Order in Council provided for a more 'indirect rule' type of judicial administration, the establishment of native courts something along the lines described in an earlier part of the paper, where original Ngoni society was discussed, except, of course, that now all the officials were paid government employees.

V

What conclusions must we come to, then? In the first place, we have found no evidence to support the theory that Ngoni society was on the decline before the arrival of the Europeans, and that until that time the position of the chiefs was fairly secure. On the Europeans' arrival, however, the balance of power in politics began to change. The Northern Ngoni were forced to give up raiding their Tonga neighbours, and partly from the inherent strength of their society, and partly from the nature of the contact with the Europeans, they survived the change without revolution. The influence of the Southern Ngoni chief was undermined by the presence of a Shire Highlands European community, and their need for labour; so that his attempts to retain his people caused disaffection, and made the task of European conquest an easy one, for resistance was only partial. In the case of the Western Ngoni, Mpezeni was tricked into admitting the Europeans, his acquiescence causing loss of authority and tribal division; hence although there was finally resistance to the Europeans it was again no more than partial.

14

THE AFRICAN—A CHILD OR A MAN

*The quarrel between the Blantyre Mission of the Church of
Scotland and the British Central Africa Administration
1890–1905*

by

REV. ANDREW C. ROSS

Mr Commissioner Johnston in his despatches advised that
there would be no permanent and satisfactory state of things
with regard to this mission until two missionaries, the Rev.
D. C. Scott and the Rev. Alexander Hetherwick were removed
from the country. . . . I am sorry to say that this mission has
entirely returned to its old practices . . . the missionaries are
taking a course that makes them appear in the eyes of the
natives of this Protectorate as an Opposition Party to H.M.
Administration.' (Acting Commissioner Sharpe to Lord
Kimberley, 31 October 1894; F.O. 2/67.)

THIS judgement by Alfred Sharpe, Johnston's locum while he
was on leave, is, I think, an accurate judgement. The role he
assigns to the Blantyre Mission is one which they did in fact enact
from the setting up of the Administration until the First World
War, but here I intend to confine my study to the last decade of
the 19th century. This role of opposition to the Administration
was one which was forced on the Blantyre Mission by its close
association with the African people of what is now the southern
region of Malawi. This association led to their being in a real
sense a mouth-piece for the people: it was forced on them by their
understanding of the value and potential of African society, and
of the individual African.

The Shire Highlands had been the scene of increasing European
penetration and influence from the time of David Livingstone's

first visit in 1859. That same year had seen the arrival of the Ngoni people to settle in the hill country to the west of Lake Nyasa, and increased penetration of the Shire Highlands by the Yao.

The Universities Mission to Central Africa was the first body to attempt settlement—under Bishop McKenzie at Magomero near Zomba. But the very high death rate and acute problems of communication led McKenzie's successor, Bishop Tozer, to withdraw the mission in 1863. In 1875 a mission of the Free Church of Scotland settled at Cape Maclear at the south end of the Lake, on land given by the Yao chief Mponda. The very next year, on land given by another Yao chief, Kapeni, a Church of Scotland mission, the Blantyre Mission, settled on a ridge near Ndirande Mountain. There followed these groups various Europeans, hunters and prospectors; but also some planters and one considerable trading company, the African Lakes Company. This body was founded by evangelical Glasgow businessmen sympathetic to the Scottish missions and was aimed at answering Livingstone's call to combat the slave-trade by Christianity and commerce.

The British Protectorate had its tentative beginnings in 1889 when John Buchanan, the British Acting Vice-Consul for the Shire Highlands, declared the Shire Valley to be under British protection. Buchanan took this step in order to forestall its occupation by Portugal through the agency of Major Serpa Pinto's 'scientific expedition' of seven hundred Zulu riflemen. During the months following Buchanan's declaration, Johnston, the British Consul at Mozambique, aided by Buchanan and Alfred Sharpe, signed treaties with many chiefs, bringing most of what is now Malawi and Zambia under British protection. Months elapsed before the final boundaries with Portuguese territory were confirmed and an Administration was set up. During this period there was a greatly increased influx of Europeans, many of whom made speculative land purchases.[1]

The dual threat of Mlozi and the other Arabs at Karonga and of the Portuguese had united British interests in the late 1880's in a campaign to gain some kind of British protection. This campaign in Britain had been led by the anti-slavery organizations

---

[1] *Life and Work in British Central Africa.* Issues for 1890 and 1891 *passim*, Edinburgh University Library.

and the Scottish Churches. The missionaries campaigned by letter
if they were in Nyasaland, and in person if they were in Britain on
furlough. Alexander Hetherwick worked especially hard at this
task.[1] The missionaries of both Churches were full of joy when a
Protectorate was secured. It seems surprising, therefore, that we
should find the ensuing decade one of great tension between the
Administration and the Scottish missions, especially the Blantyre
Mission.

Professor A. J. Hanna refers to this tension, but only during the
very hysterical period of 1892–3. His book, *The Beginnings of
Nyasaland and North-Eastern Rhodesia 1895-95*, is based primarily
on official sources for the study of this quarrel, and so he finds
references mainly to this period of 1892-3 when undoubtedly
feelings were so bitterly aroused that unfair accusations were made
by the missionaries. However, had he been able to consult the
complete edition of the monthly mission magazine *Life and Work
in British Central Africa*, now in the Edinburgh University Library,
or the Letter-books of Dr McMurtrie, Convener of the Church
of Scotland Committee for the African Mission, now in the
National Library of Scotland, he would have seen another side to
the tension, as well as how much longer and more deep-rooted it
was. Dr Hanna makes a good deal of the personality of Alexander
Hetherwick, who was certainly a difficult person. But the man
who in white tie and tails was the star of a Blantyre concert,
singing 'The Man who broke the Bank at Monte Carlo', was not
simply a narrow fanatic.[2]

D. C. Scott, Hetherwick and their leading associates saw
Africans as people. They saw African society as something valid;
something to be built on and not something to be destroyed. They
believed individual Africans to be capable of absorbing western
culture, which was not something to be left for their far-distant
descendants. They did not just speak and write these things, but
acted on them. When Hetherwick went on his first furlough in
1888 he left John Bismark in sole charge of the school and of the

[1] McMurtrie to D. C. Scott, 18 February 1891, Church of Scotland Foreign
Mission Committee Convener's Letter-books, M 1, National Library, Edinburgh.
[2] Emily Booth Langworthy, *This Africa was Mine*, p. 47.

church services at Domasi. For years on end in the 1890's Ce Rondau was in charge of the station at Chiradzulu. When work was begun among the Ngoni of Cikusi in Ncheu, it was begun and developed by Ce Harry Kwambili Matecheta with only occasional help from European members of staff. For a while in the mid-1890's he had two female missionaries working with him. They were in his sole care in an area not yet policed; this to the dismay of both local European opinion in Nyasaland and of the Church authorities in Edinburgh. The very mission magazine, *Life and Work*, which was to be the bane of the Administration and of many Europeans, was produced in a printing house staffed solely by Africans under Mungo Chisuse. Ce Chisuse and John Kunje spent 1896-7 in Edinburgh, Chisuse finishing his hitherto very informal printing apprenticeship in the famous House of Nelson's. Of this time in Edinburgh, D. C. Scott wrote:

The Messrs. Nelson received Chisuse into their well-known printing establishment, and treated him with kindness for which we cannot be grateful enough. He was introduced not only to the beautiful touch of the great firm's workmanship but to the stalwart band of Scottish workers who took to Chisuse as he took to them. This fine manly intercourse is especially good for our mission material. It brings about an inter-racial communion without in any way destroying dispensational difference and respect. Mutual respect is the lesson we so much need at this time—and we say nothing in the inter-relation of races as to which side holds most of the dispensation power.[1]

It must be noted that Matecheta, Chisuse, Kunje and many of the others of the African Christians given such responsibility were Yao, the tribe which Johnston saw as the main enemy of the peaceful development of the Protectorate.

On the basis of the actual abilities and good character of people like Mungo Chisuse, the mission constantly appealed through the columns of its magazine to the European population to act and live in a spirit of brotherhood and mutual respect with the African people. Their appeals, their Cinyanja classes, seem to have had little effect on the Europeans, many of whom saw Africans as 'niggers' and 'kaffirs'. There were reasonable Europeans, however, the most outstanding being Commissioner Johnston. Their

[1] *Life and Work*, December 1897.

attitude was also far from that of the mission. Johnston believed that in three generations it might be possible for the African to assimilate modern culture. He admitted that the 'clothed negro' was, from the Adminstration's point of view, an improvement on the untutored tribesman, but was otherwise scathing about the products of the missions. He could accept that people like Chisuse could become printers, but could not accept the reality of his Christianity or of his moral integrity.[1] Johnston was undoubtedly far more sympathetic than most of his contemporaries, and yet so far from D. C. Scott. This difference between them extended to African society as well as to the individual African. By 1891 the Scots missions had lived with the chiefs and people without the benefit of a European administration for fifteen years, Scott personally for ten years. The missionaries had found this possible, had seen the African people as 'constitutional' people working through the *mlandu* according to traditions and laws. They saw the Arab and Swahili visitors as the disturbers of a society that could develop peacefully. To Johnston, however, the Yao chiefs especially were 'robber' chiefs and 'inveterate slavers', to be dealt with before the Protectorate could be made real.

These are the root differences between mission and Administration which led to the mission's opposition role, and which it is the purpose of this chapter to explore.

A secondary source of real difference was the mission's deep hostility to rule by a Chartered Company. Scott and Hetherwick were alarmed by the possibility of such rule even while they campaigned for British protection from the Portuguese. This fear was well founded since the British Government was at this time expanding Britain's empire by the expedient of chartered companies, Treasury stringency preventing more direct forms of control. The African Lakes Company had begun to prepare itself for such a contingency by making treaties with chiefs throughout Nyasaland in 1885. At Glasgow in 1886 the Scottish Churches conferred with the Company, which was asking for a charter, and persuaded them to desist, counting the treaties as void. The attitude of the Churches in Scotland was the result of reports

---

[1] H. H. Johnston, *British Central Africa*, chapters entitled 'Missionaries' and 'Natives of British Central Africa', *passim*.

received from the missionaries in Nyasaland. Now, in 1890, the danger of Company rule was much greater. Salisbury was determined to resist Portuguese advances, but how could he finance a British Protectorate except from Rhodes's Company so long as the Treasury remained unyielding? Throughout 1890 every edition of *Life and Work* contains some reference to this danger. Scott had hoped that no European political authority would be necessary for the Shire Highlands and the Lake area, but the threats from Arab and Portuguese had made him call on Britain. However, if that call was to be answered with a Chartered Company, it would appear tantamount to a betrayal; in the missionaries' eyes a Chartered Company was simply an additional threat to African development, alongside that posed by the Arabs and Portuguese. This was especially so since Rhodes's Company was, as they put it, a 'Cape' company.

... a Chartered Company is not a government and never can be. To be ruled by such is to be ruled for commercial ends by absentee directors and shareholders whose real interests are only served by tangible dividends.[1]

Very little ground in Cape Colony belongs to the natives and no advance has been made without some Kaffir war. We have here very different antecedents and very different relations, and we look forward to the settlement of questions in this land without wars and without bloodshed.[2]

This last statement is of the greatest significance when we look at the mission's attitude to the Administration's wars with the Yao, for opposition by the missionaries and the Churches to the Chartered Company was an important factor in the decision to divide the area north of the Zambesi into a British Protectorate, directly under the Foreign Office, and a sphere under the Chartered Company. The solution did not clear up the fears, however. H. H. Johnston was to be not only Commissioner of the British Central Africa Protectorate, but also the Administrator of the Chartered Company's sphere. Furthermore, the only money available to the new Administration was a subsidy from Rhodes. The result was a constant fear of Company rule, and a constant

[1] *Life and Work*, October 1890.   [2] *Ibid.*, August 1891.

suspicion of Johnston as an agent of Rhodes. Today, reading Dr Hanna's book and Professor Oliver's biography of Johnston, we can see what was going on, but confusion and suspicion in the minds of Nyasalanders of the time is understandable.

When Johnston instituted taxation in certain areas we find Hetherwick writing to the Church authorities at home asking them to enquire of the Foreign Office whether the new taxation was for the benefit of the Company or the Administration.[1] This suspicion can also be seen in a letter sent by Dr W. A. Scott to Dr McMurtrie, the Convener of the Church of Scotland Committee for Africa, in which he says of Johnston:

If he can lift ivory and taxes when and where he pleases in the interest of the B.S.A. Co., we demand on behalf of the natives some independent power to watch their interests.[2]

Suspicion and fear continued in the minds of the missionaries until the two administrations were clearly separated in 1894, Rhodes's speeches doing nothing to allay them. In April 1893 *Life and Work* reported him as saying in England that he had an understanding with the British Government that the Company would gradually relieve the Government of their responsibilities in Nyasaland. Scott ends the article thus:

The Makololo, the Yao, the Machinga, the Angoni chiefs have signed treaties to the Queen of England. Every treaty, purchase, transfer has been made out under her name alone. The Protectorate was declared in her name and the signatures received the joyful assurance that the name covered the chiefs, the people and the people's friends.

And yet in face of all this Mr Rhodes claims the reversion of the lands.

His boast that he has met no one that he cannot deal with or fight reminds one of some Goliath prizefighter with 'ideas and money' for shield and spear; we shall prevail against him we are persuaded with this sling and with this stone, in the name of Africa's God.

Apart from this suspicion of Johnston as a possible agent of Company rule, the missionaries had other reasons for being wary

[1] Hetherwick to McMurtrie, 13 June 1892, C. of S. F.M.C. Convener's Letter-books, M. 1.
[2] W. A. Scott to McMurtrie, 7 June 1892, C. of S. F.M.C. Convener's Letter-books, M. 1.

of him. Among these was not his often-boasted agnosticism. Indeed, nowhere in the Convener's Letter-books nor in *Life and Work* have I been able to find any reference to Johnston's belief or lack of belief, or any criticism of his character. On the contrary there is a letter from Dr McMurtrie to Johnston assuring him that despite the quarrels over taxation, punitive raids and so on, his name was not impugned.[1] The first of these other reasons was that Johnston, before coming to his post as Consul at Mozambique, had been the British representative at negotiations at Lisbon which gave the Shire Highlands to Portugal. The fact that, under pressure from Scotland, the British Government had not accepted this agreement did not alter the fact that Johnston had been enthusiastically for it. Again, in 1890, Johnston had written an article in the November issue of *The Fortnightly* in which he showed great enthusiasm for the use of Arabs in the governing of British Central Africa. This was to be done by the subsidizing of Arab 'sultans' like Jumbe of Kotakota, and the possible use of Arab police. Since the missionaries insisted that it was these Arabs and Zanzibaris who were the source of the slave-raiding and not the Yao who, without their presence, would desist, the Scottish Churches were rightly upset. On this article Dr McMurtrie wrote to D. C. Scott saying:

We here are opposed to this policy, and are determined to resist it by united action, even if we should have to go to Lord Salisbury and rouse the public.[2]

But let us return to the root difference between the Blantyre Mission and the Administration, that is, the difference in attitude towards the African and his society. Because they believed in the validity of African society, and the potential of individual Africans, the mission saw the paramountcy of African interests as being the key to any future development. They had hoped that this would happen without the intervention of European political authority, as we have seen already. But before Serpa Pinto had disabused his mind of that possibility, D. C. Scott had written in the August and November issues of *Life and Work* for 1888 of the future as lying

[1] *Ibid.*, McMurtrie to H. H. Johnston, December 1892.
[2] McMurtrie to D. C. Scott, 5 March 1891, C. of S. F.M.C. Convener's Letter-books, M. 1.

with the development of 'native power' towards a civilized Christian society, and emphasized that this growth was to be 'a growth of the community upon its traditional basis'. They saw the role of the white man to be that of a helper to aid the African people to move forward in that direction. This view of the European role received its clearest statement when Johnston talked of introducing Indian settlers to fulfil a role he believed the Africans incapable of fulfilling. Of this idea D. C. Scott wrote:

We believe it to be fatal to the true interests of the country and of the people who live in it both black and white. Africa for the Africans has been our policy from the first, and we believe that God has given this country into our hands that we may train its peoples how to develop its marvellous resources for themselves.[1]

The first direct quarrel with the Administration as such was over taxation. We have seen that the suspicion of the proceeds being sent to the British South Africa Company was a factor in this difficulty. However, just as important was the mission's contention that it was too great in amount and imposed too precipitately. The way of imposing the new tax was wrong, they believed, and would have been wrong even if the amount had been reasonable. They felt that the only valid basis for taxation or any new thing imposed by the new Administration could be the agreement of the chiefs and the people affected. Already, before Johnston had arrived, Scott wrote in the May 1891 issue of *Life and Work*:

We are in doubt as to the new régime. Strange rumours reach us of taxation . . . and the strong hand of power. Power there is here, neither lately formed nor of small amount, a power which lies in the constituency of approving minds.

In the November issue of the magazine Hetherwick analysed the economic enormity of the new taxes. Johnston recognized this and reduced the amounts by half the next year, 1892. But again Hetherwick comes to the point that the amount of the tax is not really the main issue but that it was imposed with no consultation of the African people. He wrote:

[1] *Life and Work*, January 1895.

We ask too for a constitutional mode of dealing with the native life around us. We ask that the authority and influence of the native chiefs in the country be recognized and their counsel sought in dealing with the people. The African, if he is anything, is constitutional—no change or step of importance is taken without first open 'mlandu' in which the opinion of all is fully sought and expressed. We hope to see the same constitutional methods continued in all future changes. The native recognizes and obeys them, and when similar modes are followed he will obey the new power as readily as the old. *The nature of native life must be developed and not crushed.*[1]

These opinions, which could be read by Nyasaland Africans and were also expressed to those friendly chiefs who consulted the missionaries about these problems, were obviously an embarrassment to Johnston. The fundamental difference of principle between the Mission and the Administration can be seen again in their difference over Johnston's first campaign. This was against Chikhumbu, a Yao chief who ruled the western slopes of Mlanje Mountain. The Blantyre Mission had had trouble with him in the past, but the influence of Robert Cleland and W. A. Scott had brought a measure of peace not only with the Mission, but also with the Nyanja of Chipoka, Chikhumbu's neighbour. Johnston saw him as a 'robber chief' whom he would have to deal with, and indeed had made up his mind to do so when he was on his first visit to Nyasaland while still Consul at Mozambique, before he became Commissioner.[2] Chikhumbu was one of a list of chiefs whom he saw as needing to be 'induced or compelled to give up the slave-trade before our Protectorate could become a reality'.[3] These chiefs were all Yao and to the mission were men who could be dealt with 'constitutionally' except for the bad influence of the Arab or Swahili, the same people who stood so high in the opinion of Johnston at this time. The consequence of this attitude of Johnston's was, as Hanna puts it, 'one little war after another'.[4] In almost every case except for the large campaign against the Arab Mlozi at Karonga, the Blantyre Mission was to some degree critical. This vocal opposition was so galling to Johnston, that we

---

[1] *Life and Work*, November 1891 (my italics).
[2] Johnston to F.O., 29 December 1891, F.O. 84/2114.
[3] *Ibid.*   [4] A. J. Hanna, p. 288.

find the Foreign Office complaining to the Foreign Mission Committee of the Church of Scotland in Edinburgh. As a result McMurtrie wrote to D. C. Scott in August 1893, saying:

Sir J. V. Lister is entirely on Mr Johnston's side. I defend you against Mr Johnston's charge that our mission is disloyal to the Administration, but I cannot defend page 4 of your May number, in which currency is given to at least two uninvestigated rumours of the mis-doings of the Administration.[1]

However, to return to the first campaign, that against Chikhumbu. It was not a war to check slave-raiding, but Johnston sought to 'bring Chikhumbu to reason'[2] because of the complaints of European planters. They complained that in addition to the initial payment for the land, the chief was asking for repeated payments of increasing amounts. This gave Johnston the opportunity to crush a chief already on his list of those to be disciplined. Of this campaign D. C. Scott wrote:

Chikhumbu has got into difficulties with some of the planters . . . the mission sent a responsible capitao and their best English-speaking teacher to offer to act as a go-between in the settlement of the difficulties; but the planters had already put the matter into Mr Johnston's hands and refused to accept the proffered help. Our motive in the offer of mediation was two-fold—Firstly knowing the difficulties of the case we felt it a necessary thing, that some one with a knowledge of the language greater than newcomers could be supposed to possess, should be there to help to avoid difficulties. . . . Secondly although Chikhumbu is excitable and imperious, some of his men are the finest specimens of Yao we know. We thought it would be an immense pity if anything that could be avoided with a little timely patience and aid, should occur to destroy hopeful and helpful relations with them. . . . Mr Cleland spent a long time in Chikhumbu's and won the respect of all and of Chikhumbu himself. He succeeded without power or force of any kind whatsoever except that of a firm kind will and a brave character. . . . It is our opinion that from our experience of native custom and from our relations with Chikhumbu, that what seemed to call for the initial use of force could without much difficulty *have been settled by Mlandu*.[3]

[1] McMurtrie to D. C. Scott, August 1893, C. of S. F.M.C. Convener's Letter-books, M 1.
[2] H. H. Johnston, *British Central Africa*, p. 99.
[3] *Life and Work*, August 1891 (my italics).

Johnston's next campaigns against Mponda, Makadanji and Makanjira were commented on more favourably by the mission magazine. These chiefs had been raiding because of the presence of Arabs from Kilwa. But it is to be noted that Mponda, with whom Johnston did have a real discussion, a *mlandu*, did remain loyal for some considerable time afterwards. Indeed during the crisis late in 1891 and 1892, after the defeat and death of Captain Maguire, Mponda even helped to defend Fort Johnston, the administrative post in his area. 1892 was a difficult year for the Administration for some Yao chiefs undoubtedly became very aggressive, notably Makinjira, whose prestige was high because of his defeat of Maguire. The presence of Arabs and also, as the missionaries believed, the news of the defeat of the Germans by the Hehe, lay behind this. Johnston complained that it was just at this time that the Mission especially troubled him, and troubled him in a way which seemed to him to be utterly unfair. Certainly it was during 1892 and 1893 that the complaints, many of which were only based on rumour, did occur, about which Hanna comments so severely. The reason for the almost hysterical note at this time was that the Mission saw a fairly happy relationship between European and Yao falling to bits because of Johnston ignoring all that they believed to be good in African society, and ignoring the channels of *mlandu* and discussion that had been open when he arrived. It is also to be remembered that at this time Johnston's relationship with Rhodes was still suspect, and the fear of the Company taking over was great. On this problem we find McMurtrie writing to Hetherwick saying:

He [Lord Rosebery] also sent a copy of a letter from the F.O. to the A.L.C. defining Mr Johnston's position towards the South African Company [sic]. Lord Rosebery suggested that a copy be sent to the missionaries. The definition is not to my mind clear but you will judge for yourselves.[1]

The occasion of the letter was to report to the missionaries that their complaints of 'indiscriminate punishment' had been listened to by the Foreign Secretary, Lord Rosebery, who had asked

[1] McMurtrie to Hetherwick, 3 October 1892, C. of S. F.M.C. Convener's Letter-books, M 1.

Johnston to desist from using this technique in dealing with the people. The incident which triggered off the missionaries' complaints was one referred to by Johnston in his *British Central Africa* in treating of the 'high-way robbers' of Mount Chiradzulu. That there was highway robbing going on everyone had to admit, but the punishment of this by the destruction of Chief Mitoche's village caused a great deal of anger. Hetherwick wrote:

I saw the ruins and the half-burned maize lying scattered over the ground—and a sore sight it was, when one thought of the famine of last season—and yet the administration boast they administer English Law.[1]

The missionaries believed that this raid was to do with taxation and could have been dealt with differently. Letters from Dr W. A. Scott at Blantyre, H. E. Scott at Zomba, and Adam Currie at Mlanje all talk of chiefs coming to consult them about the meaning of this raid, which was without any preliminary *mlandu* or European trial. The Reverend H. E. Scott, who was usually more favourable to the Administration than the others, writes how appalling was the destruction of grain-stores because there was no way of replacing their contents that year. Malemia and Kumtumanje, the main Yao chiefs of the area, had come to see him and pointed out the unfairness of the Administration's actions, making H. E. Scott feel ashamed of his race.[2] Adam Currie wrote that Ce Namonde and other Mlanje Yao chiefs had had an all-night consultation with him about this action of the Administration.[3] In all of these letters there are also references to planters including Buchanan, who was also an Administration official, using this same technique of grain-store burning to compel villagers living on land bought by the planters to work in their coffee fields. It is to Johnston's credit that as soon as he was free from campaigning he turned to the land problem and tried to ensure that this could not happen again. With regard to his own administration, after the reproof from Rosebery he seems to have seen to it that the

[1] Hetherwick to McMurtrie, 13 June 1893, C. of S. F.M.C. Convener's Letter-books, M 1.
[2] *Ibid.*, H. E. Scott to McMurtrie, 14 June 1892.
[3] *Ibid.*, Currie to McMurtrie, 12 June 1892.

indiscriminate technique of punishment was not used in 'police' affairs. This period of 1892–3 was the period, as we have seen, when an unfair and unsubstantiated element entered into the criticisms made by the mission; Johnston, however, matched them in his despatches. In these he accused the Blantyre missionaries of being useless as missionaries, of mis-using mission funds, and of intolerable arrogance.[1] His attacks of this period are in contrast with his basically favourable reports before and after the period, as well as in his book, *British Central Africa.*

Like on occasion their descendants, the African nationalists of the mid-20th century, the missionaries were at this time spoiling a valid case by exaggeration, allowing Johnston to dismiss their whole case on the basis of rebutting certain inaccuracies. However it must be noted that even on the clear issue of indiscriminate punishment he is unable to appreciate their point. He said:

In almost every issue of the monthly paper of the Blantyre Mission there appears . . . a perversion of some trifling incident of Police routine into 'a great crime', 'a serious disaster'.[2]

The missionaries were being consistent with their principles. Mitoche was a chief, not just a 'robber leader'; he and his people did deserve some sort of *mlandu* before being punished. Some attempt ought to have been made to discriminate between guilty and innocent, otherwise they were being reduced to the level of being not people, but some kind of nuisance. The conferences between Yao chiefs and missionaries show how seriously the African people viewed these 'trifling incidents of Police routine'. Such conferences were initiated by the chiefs, who naturally turned to men they had known for a good many years, who spoke their language, and had sat with them in *mlandu* in the past. So often this natural coming together of the African people and the Blantyre Mission was completely misunderstood by the Administration. To Johnston it was the arrogance of Hetherwick and D. C. Scott still trying to cling to a civil authority they had tacitly held before the coming of the Administration; it was their

[1] Private letter of Johnston to Lister, 4 June 1893, F.O. 2/54.
[2] Johnston to Rosebery, 19 September 1892, F.O. 84/2197.

'meddling in politics'; it was 'intrigue with the natives'. Johnston even goes so far as to say:

The plain fact is, that all this trouble arises from the presence in this country of two men—the Reverend D. C. Scott and the Reverend Alexander Hetherwick.[1]

By early 1894 Johnston's despatches talk of better relations between mission and Administration until, during Johnston's absence on leave, another incident of 'indiscriminate punishment' took place. A trial did take place but the whole village was punished 'Mitoche' style for the action of a few men. The mission criticism of this action led to the despatch from Sharpe, the Acting Commissioner, with which this chapter opened. The village was Malunga's, a Yao village on the slopes of Ndirande. Highway robbery had been rife on the Matope road which skirted Ndirande, and Malunga's people were tried, convicted, and their village destroyed. The missionaries insisted that there was no reliable proof that men from Malunga's were responsible, W. Scott showing fairly convincingly that the police witnesses were not reliable, and that the wildness of Malunga's people in the old days was the real basis of the Administration's case. Even if some of his men were guilty, was it right for a whole village to be punished? The missionaries were especially angry because at Malunga's was the first real village school, and the first baptized Christians who were involved in normal village life and were not in a community dominated by a mission institution or missionary-minded Europeans like the African Lakes Company managers.

At this time the Matabele war, conducted by the South Africa Company, was arousing feeling among the missionaries, and when Nkhanda, a Yao chief of Mlanje, was crushed by the Administration, an article in *Life and Work* expressed a very critical attitude to British rule north of the Limpopo:

We do not find in history a people who loved their conquerors, it would be unnatural, and we do not look for it to be reversed in Africa. Can we thrash a man and expect him to thank us for it, and have we not practically thrashed the native out of power and possession, and for no tangible reason; our war-cry is the slave-trader, but the slave-

[1] Johnston to Lister, 4 June 1893, F.O. 2/54.

trade has little to do with it; the real motive power is gold thirst and land grabbing.

That unjust scene of blood in Matabeleland was to protect the Mashona slaves. Our late attack on Mkhanda was reported at home as an attack on the slave-trade. Where then are our merits for gratitude which we grumble at not getting?[1]

Because the exaggerated tone of criticism in *Life and Work* ceased after 1894, mention of this criticism in official despatches also ceases to be frequent, and so there is no more reference to opposition in Professor Hanna's book. But the role of opposition played by the Blantyre Mission did not cease; it went on. The opposition was not simply confined to the unbalanced period of 1892–3 but was a much deeper matter, beginning, as we have seen, in 1890, before the Administration actually commenced. If we review this opposition's effectiveness up until the end of 1894 we find that it had some success. Firstly, indiscriminate punishment ceased to be a technique of the Government; secondly, the whole taxation structure was made more reasonable. The third was probably the key victory in the eyes of the missionaries—this was conceded by Johnston in a letter to Sir Percy Anderson at the Foreign Office:

As to the revival of the 1885 treaties [those of the A.L.C. already referred to in this chapter] the thing is an absolute impossibility, it cannot even be argued about. Practically therefore, the situation is this: that the bringing of the Protectorate under the British South Africa Company is almost impossible. These detestable Blantyre Missionaries and almost all the now numerous band of planters out here are dead against it.[2]

But, on their most basic point of the acceptance by the Administration of African society as a valid structure on which to build a new state, the mission had failed.

This basic belief of the mission was also contradicted by the land situation in what is now the southern region of Nyasaland. From the time in 1889 when it became clear that Britain would extend some kind of authority over Nyasaland, there had been a considerable influx of land speculators and planters. After the

[1] *Life and Work*, September 1894.
[2] Johnston to Sir H. P. Anderson, 23 March 1893, F.O. 2/54.

setting up of his administration Johnston stopped any more direct buying from the chiefs. However he further complicated the issue by declaring to be Crown land, that is land at the disposal of the Crown, all the land of chiefs who had signed treaties with the Queen, although the chiefs had only intended the ceding of sovereignty. Also, he adopted the attitude that the land of those Yao chiefs with whom the Administration considered it necessary to fight, was at the disposal of the Administration. Some of this land was not occupied, but much of it was. When sold, what **was** to be the relationship between the new owner and the dwellers on the land who had participated in the old communal ownership? Although Johnston, after the end of the initial campaigns, did turn to this problem and did try to ensure their protection, the status of the villagers was, as Hanna says:

merely that of legally protected squatters on private estates, and time was to show that the protection of the law was far less valuable and permanent than he had intended.[1]

From almost the beginning there was not much protection for people who had had what was really their land sold over their heads. In 1892 D. C. Scott chided his old friend John Buchanan for using force to get villagers on his land to work in his coffee fields. To David Clement Scott, this problem was another facet of the problem of the recognition of the validity of African traditional law and of the paramountcy of African interests. In the December 1894 issue of *Life and Work*, he wrote:

Our contention is that if the Europeans take the land they practically enslave the native population. There is no law to help the native in his distress; but there is power to put into the European's hands to force the native to work. We have heard it said, 'a good thing too,' followed by invective against the native character but we beg to say the native does work and work hard, and that the invectives are cowardly and untrue: and we uphold that no civilized power can come into a country, more especially under Christian promises, and turn the natives into slaves on their own holdings . . . we cannot treat the land as conquered country, and we must in every case of confiscation or annexation have the very best proof to show that no other way than fighting the natives was possible. We have all along believed and believe still that the

[1] Hanna, *The Beginnings of Nyasaland and North-Eastern Rhodesia*, p. 233.

British Government could rule and develop this whole African Empire, in all questions really native, without striking a blow.

We grant that it needs endless tact and patience and a real grip of native language, life, customs and history, but this is obtainable; Africa won't be ruled without trouble and much 'palaver', but what country is?

These and many other protests on the land issue bore little fruit. What was done was done, and the problem of land and the villager on the estate went on to be a factor in the Chilembwe rebellion, and to be still a problem today. Again one must notice how Scott brings the discussion back to the issue of the chance of development based on the fundamental reasonableness of African society, contrasted with the conception of its essential 'savagery' as manifested in the actions of the Administration.

This issue led to another open rupture in 1898 between Mission and Administration over the crushing of Mpezeni's Ngoni. Once the bad feelings between the Chartered company administrator and the Ngoni had reached the pitch it had, the Mission admitted that war was inevitable; but need that situation have been reached? Neil MacVicar, W. A. Scott's successor as mission doctor and the first man to train Africans to run rural dispensaries, wrote in *Life and Work* in January 1898:

For the information of home readers we should explain that the whole of Mpeseni's country and much more is marked red on the maps, and is being administered by the South Africa Co., and the Charterland Company. It is quite outside our tight little Protectorate. But the Rhodesian Companies are not yet able to 'administer' very much. A white man in a fort with a few armed natives cannot effect much, living beside chiefs like Mpeseni, who are quite able to 'administer' their own countries, and who do so according to their own ideas and generally according to native laws and traditions. What a representative of a Chartered company can do depends on what sort of a man he is.... If he is foolish he will find endless ways of getting into trouble.... The true history of Central Africa may one day be written, perhaps by a native and the beginnings of these wars, by which 'the slave-raiding chiefs' who 'required smashing' were 'dealt with' will be made known.

By the late 1890's that 'Cape' influence, which the missionaries had so feared might come in by Company rule, was coming in anyway through the European community which was now considerable in the Southern Province. They were not dominant and did not control the Administration, but they were there and the mission resisted them. A fear of the results of African education and a desire to keep the native in his place were the dominant ideas.

Race feeling of this sort—little as our up to date colonies think it—is an antiquated idea. Colonials are today expressing, in a rather intenser form, the sentiments of our great-grandfathers, who in their hearts thought the 'blacks' were not really human. . . . When the true colonial arrives in B.C.A. and finds natives in places of responsibility, who can write and yet do not forge cheques, he can only explain the mystery by saying 'Ah, you seem to have a different kind of native.' Are our natives then so much the creme de la creme of savagery that they can bear to be treated as no other savages can? Are the Maori or the Zulu not as fine races? No! It is not a difference of raw native but a difference of treatment. The people here have not yet to any extent been repressed. Their native pride remains in them . . . yet we are not free from danger, for the colonial sentiment is among us. 'Some day', it says, 'we will have to repress too'.[1]

It was just at this time that colonial influence came into Nyasaland with a vengeance with the agreement made to allow labour recruiters for the mines of Southern Rhodesia and the Rand to recruit in the territory. From March 1899 until 1905, when the issue seems to have been given up as hopeless, the mission, through its magazine and its influence in Scotland, tried to have this permission withdrawn. The first article on the subject struck the notes that were reiterated for years. Firstly, labour for plantations and industry in Nyasaland was often short; secondly, Nyasas were often employed at cut rates to undercut the local people; thirdly, as being more important, the article went on:

Native races attain their true development in their native country. The country—its resources and the development of its productions—and the people to whom we look for this development, must grow together. Transportation of labour acts deleteriously both on the labour itself and on the soil and country which is thus deprived of it. Every pair of hands drafted south means a pair of hands less in the develop-

[1] *Life and Work*, January 1899.

ment of their native soil and its products, and the effects on the labour is demoralizing. . . . South Africa has notoriously failed with its own native question that we are fully justified in protesting against its interference.[1]

Aurora, the magazine of the Livingstonia Mission added articles giving a careful description of the bad effects on villages created by the taking of their men in this way. However, on this issue, the combined campaigning of the Blantyre and Livingstonia missionaries and the church leaders in Scotland failed to achieve any significant result.

Turning again to the words of Alfred Sharpe quoted at the beginning of this study, that the Blantyre Mission was 'in the eyes of the natives of this Protectorate . . . an Opposition Party to H.M. Administration', we can see that the Africans of Nyasaland had made a substantially correct estimate of the mission's role during the period of our study. This was always a 'loyal' opposition, and was not simply made up from bad personal relationships between missionaries and administrators. Such bad relations did exist for a time in the period 1892–3, but this must not obscure the fact that the mantle of opposition, or at least of critic, was assumed as early as 1890 and continued into the 20th century. Neither should these temporarily bad human relations obscure the fact that the critical position of the mission with regard to the Administration was based on fundamental differences over principle. The issue of principle was twofold: first, was the African of the day capable of becoming a responsible and 'civilized' individual, and secondly, was African culture capable of being the foundation for modern development?

[1] *Life and Work*, June 1899.

15

MALAWI POLITICAL SYSTEMS AND THE INTRODUCTION OF COLONIAL RULE
1891–1896

by

ERIC STOKES

WHEN in 1903 Hector Duff reflected on the manner in which colonial rule had become established in Nyasaland after 1891 he was struck by two aspects[1]: firstly, 'that, with the exception of Jumbe of Kota Kota, no chief of any power or standing in the whole country from the Songwe to the Ruo was induced to submit to the authority of the new Government without a recourse to arms'; and secondly, that with the partial exception of the Northern Ngoni, 'not even a vestige of political unity remains among the so-called tribes, or any sort of real authority with their so-called chiefs'.[2] Official reports then and since have laid emphasis on the disintegration of the traditional political institutions and have usually attributed it to the necessity of using military coercion to suppress the slave trade.[3] Within a few months of the formal establishment of the infant protectorate in 1891 the Blantyre missionaries accused Johnston, the first Commissioner, of needless violence and a wanton destruction of African authority. Johnston's defence—that his course of action was dictated by local conditions—has generally been accepted by later writers. For them it appears axiomatic that Nyasaland's high

[1] I would like to acknowledge the assistance of a grant from the Rockefeller Foundation in the preparatory work for this chapter.

[2] H. L. Duff, *Nyasaland under the Foreign Office*, 1903, pp. 18, 97. Duff's statements have rightly been criticized as inaccurate and exaggerated. Griff Jones, *Britain and Nyasaland*, 1964, p. 277, n. 43.

[3] Annual Report 1903–4, cited Hailey, *African Survey*, 1938, p. 62. Report on Closer Union in Eastern and Central Africa, 1929, Cmd. 3234, pp. 77, 287.

degree of ethnic and political fragmentation, itself both the cause and consequence of endemic slave raiding and warfare, produced a situation in which the introduction of colonial authority was bound to be met with violent resistance, and yet one in which the indigenous polities were too small and unstable to emerge as viable units within a system of British overrule. Johnston's biographer, Professor Roland Oliver, has drawn the picture of a man unusually sensitive to African life and anxious to preserve its institutions, yet compelled by the logic of circumstance to shatter the power of the larger chiefdoms and to rely on force as his constant instrument.[1]

The trend of the contemporary Afrocentric approach is to see the historical initiative in African and not European hands. Its focus is the interplay of African politics in which the colonial factor comes into view as a subsidiary element caught up and exploited by the local situation. The old notion of imperialism has been stood on its head. It is no longer possible to look on European intrusion as a compulsive movement issuing from within Europe and blindly imposing its will on Africa as though it were but 'clay in the potter's hands'. The forcible subjugation of African peoples is now portrayed as rather in the nature of a reluctant reaction to the unexpectedly violent resistance many of them offered. For, so the argument runs, the European powers sought initially no more than a light, inexpensive consular control to keep out rivals; only the necessity of putting down internal resistance led them on to become the conquerors of Africa in their own despite. The initial adjustment of political relationships between African and European is therefore considered as a pragmatic process in which the 'local crisis' was the key determinant, and in which the type of historical interaction can be broadly predicated from the local type of African society.[2]

In placing the *primum mobile* so firmly in African hands the danger to be averted is an over-correction of the older distorted view. If the aim is—in Nadine Gordimer's pointed phrase—to

---

[1] Roland Oliver, *Sir Harry Johnston & the Scramble for Africa*, 1957.
[2] The view has been stated in its most extreme and generalized form by Ronald Robinson and John Gallagher in 'The Partition of Africa', *New Cambridge Modern History*, vol. XI, chap. xxii, p. 617 ff.

'present Africans as people invaded by the white West, rather than as another kind of fauna dealt with by the white man in his exploration of the world', then European activity has to continue to be treated as an independent variable. This may seem a truism, but its consequence is that European activity cannot be seen purely in terms of a reflex to an African stimulus. Due allowance has to be given to an important element of European purposiveness and premeditated design, not to perpetuate old-style colonial history but to construct a new-style African history. For without it imperialism as part of the African's deepest experience is stripped of its essentially aggressive meaning, and one historiographical distortion is replaced by another.

Indeed in many ways the old Europocentric view, in its desire to exculpate imperialism from the charge of a deliberate destruction of African institutions, leant towards the same error as the Afrocentric. While, of course, seeing the colonial period exclusively through the eyes of the white man, it too suggested that he was a prisoner of local circumstance. The constraint lay elsewhere: not in the character of African societies but in the paucity of means at the disposal of colonial rulers. So that, as in the case of Lugard's decision to preserve the Northern Nigerian emirates after conquest, 'indirect rule originated . . . not from any considerations of deliberate policy but out of sheer local necessities'.[1] Now in fact Lugard was more abundantly supplied with troops and money than any previous West African administration and so was able to carry through a radical change of policy. In contrast the Niger Coast Protectorate or Lagos Colony were given no significant imperial subventions and were forced to finance their expansion out of their own slowly expanding customs revenue. The extension of their authority in area and scope was consequently a more gradual process, and in the end one more destructive of indigenous political forms. Lugard proceeded from strength, equipped with a standing army unparalleled in other regions. By means of it he was able to knock out the military resistance of the emirates with a few swift blows, oust the old rulers and instal pliant successors, all in so short a space of time that indigenous

[1] Lord Harlech, *British Native Policy in Tropical Africa*, 1941, Witwatersrand Branch of the South African Institute of International Affairs, p. 5.

political systems retained much of their old cohesion. Elsewhere the military power of white administrations was a more exiguous affair. Since the relatively powerful African polities could not be quickly overwhelmed, it was enough to meet the day-to-day needs of security by reducing their potential threat through the detachment of dependent peoples or groups. Such methods not merely weakened the more powerful structures but bred in them an irreconcilable hostility. The ultimate reckoning had usually to come by force against states too weakened or too dangerous to be permitted to survive. It is true, of course, that the powerful state organization of the Nigerian emirates had few analogues else-where, yet it is remarkable that even where larger political sys-tems were to be found—with the Ashanti in the Gold Coast, or Jaja, Nana, and Benin in the Niger Delta, or the Arabs, Ngoni, Bemba, and even Yao—they were almost invariably smashed up or swept aside.

It has therefore to be recognized that the prospect of survival for such systems in Nyasaland was doubly reduced, firstly by poli-tical fragmentation, and secondly, by the paucity of means with which Johnston commenced his administration. Yet this is not a sufficient explanation of the speed with which the systems broke down or of the manner in which colonial authority was asserted. However much the product of expediency and day-to-day deci-sion policy was also fashioned by certain implicit assumptions which acted as an independent causal factor.

From the mid-1880's when the extension of British influence over the African interior became a matter for practical decision a debate opened on the principles that ought to govern the adjust-ment of relationships between the colonial and African political systems. The innate tendency of the west coast administrations was to work, however slowly, towards the extension of the Crown colony system and the consequent obliteration of autochthonous jurisdictions. The most effective and obvious method of accelerat-ing the process was to clear the ground by force. It was not until after 1895 when Chamberlain took charge of the Colonial Office that the 'military school' was finally given its head and Cardew in Sierra Leone, Maxwell and Hodgson in the Gold Coast, and Moor in the Niger Coast were allowed to initiate aggressive forward policies. Only then did an opposition view make itself fully articulate. Although far from constituting a consistent viewpoint, the voices of protest that came from people like Holt, Chalmers, Mary Kingsley and E. D. Morel were unanimous in denouncing the Crown colony system and arguing instead for a light, colonial overrule which could be established for the most part with African consent and which would leave the indigenous systems intact.

The debate had, however, begun much earlier, and Johnston, with his experience of carrying things with a high hand in the Oil Rivers in 1887 and 1888, was an important participant. In January 1889, before taking up his Central African appointment, he addressed the Royal Colonial Institute. European control he regarded as the essential agent of African modernization, though he fancied there were still 'a few ignorant, narrow-skulled fanatics existing in England ... who still cherish the notion that it is kindest and best to leave the uncivilized and the savage to wallow in their half-animal existence'.[1] In terms of natural evolution the African was at least two thousand years behind the European. But scientific control of natural forces now made it possible to 'deliberately raise races of our backward fellow-men out of the Stone Age into the age of Steel'. Often the process could not be accomplished by peaceful persuasion: 'we must—if I may thus put it—educate the negro by force if necessary, leaving him to thank us and understand us afterwards, when by our teaching we have raised him to a condition to do so'. The West African had to be taught to develop the material resources of his country, and the principle of the process was to be avowedly that of assimilation, 'to educate him gradually and thoroughly in the principles of civilized society by which we ourselves are governed, and so assimilate his views and sympathies with ours that we may be indissolubly bound together with ties of commerce and empire'.

Professor Oliver rightly points out that Johnston's views on African capacities were in constant development, and he himself has preferred to give emphasis to the later, more liberal Johnston.

---

[1] 'British West Africa and the Trade of the Interior', by H. H. Johnston. Paper read before the Royal Colonial Institute, 15 January 1889, Royal Commonwealth Society Library—West African Pamphlets, 43/3.

But it would be wrong to suppose that in his early career the man was merely echoing the loose-tongued prejudices of the day. His was a deliberate view, so sharply put that in the discussion which followed his address to the Royal Colonial Institute, C. S. Salmon, an old Gold Coast official, rose to protest against Johnston's strictures on the African character and on the methods of strong-armed coercion he proposed.

Why don't we make allies of the people? The great English nation can surely make better use of the instruments given her. Instead of knocking them down, we ought to make use of these native powers . . .

Johnston saw himself as a radical negrophile but he thought misplaced sentimentalism about African society the great hindrance to progress. In place of bolstering effete indigenous systems he wanted the most rapid introduction of modern administration, leaving Africans to participate in government by way of progressive advancement in the civil service.[1]

So far, therefore, from coming to his task in Nyasaland in 1891 with a mind disposed towards some form of indirect rule, Johnston was quite clear that his aim was to introduce a Crown colony system at the earliest opportunity.[2] That is not to say that he did not recognize the immediate necessity of gradualism and consequently of a temporary *modus vivendi* with some of the more friendly local powers. His attitude was put most clearly in a memorandum he submitted on the future administration of the Oil Rivers protectorate which he was to cite a few months later as a rough model for Nyasaland:

This, of course, must be a gradual policy, this sapping of the power and influence of the native Chiefs; indeed the whole policy of the Oil Rivers Administration must be cautious, conciliatory and 'opportunist', but the end steadily held in view and patiently striven for must be the substitution of European government for negro rule. As I have repeatedly stated on other occasions I do not think the negro race will be competent to rule itself or others for at least another century . . .[3]

[1] Cf. Johnston, *British Central Africa*, 1897, p. 183.

[2] Within less than two years from the founding of the Protectorate Johnston could speak of the territory as 'what no doubt will become before long a Crown Colony'; Johnston to Rosebery, 31 January 1893; F.O. Pr. 6482, No. 80.

[3] Johnston's Memo. on the Administration of the Oil Rivers, 11 August

The clarity of Johnston's purpose in Nyasaland has been clouded, partly by the verbal smokescreen he put out to disguise the deliberate nature of his moves towards Crown colony government, and partly by the weight of the factors making for the breakdown of indigenous rule. These latter factors need to be looked at more closely. Quite apart from the *kleinestaaterei* that characterized the country, Johnston's actions were bound to be circumscribed by the historical growth of relationships between African societies and missionary agencies since 1875. The missions and African Lakes Company had become deeply involved in local politics; their stations had been set up among the weaker, more receptive peoples along the overstretched line of communication that ran from the Shire to Lake Tanganyika, and in their efforts to defend their charges against the threat of the slave trade they had found themselves increasingly at odds with the more powerful polities, like that of the 'north end' Arabs under Mlozi, or of the Yao ruler Makanjira, at the south-east end of the Lake. The prior establishment of European coffee estates in the Shire highlands meant that the country was already launched on an export economy whose foundation was European enterprise rather than peasant production. Gathering demand for plantation labour was to act as a spur for the extension of the directly administered region and at the same time to bring the Administration into conflict with slaving interests of the Yao chiefs and the manpower needs of the Ngoni military system.

Of perhaps more immediate moment was Johnston's weakness in men and money in the founding years of the Protectorate. If there were validity in the argument which states that paucity of means conduced towards a light colonial overrule and the preservation of indigenous systems, then Johnston's administration should have provided the example *par excellence*. No other administration in what became British tropical Africa started out with such slender financial and military backing. The subsidy of £10,000 a year from Rhodes, free transport by the Lakes Company steamers, and consular salaries met by the British Treasury,

1890, F.O. Pr. 6004. Cf. Memo. on Administration of Nyasaland, 7 October 1890, F.O. 84/2052. Dr Low notes Johnston's 'direct rule' tendencies, D. A. Low and R. C. Pratt, *Buganda and British Overrule*, 1960, pp. 45 ff., 57 ff.

provided no more than shoe-string government. Moreover, though it would be wrong to set too much store on constitutional forms, the legal framework of the Foreign Office protectorate would appear to have been the most favourable framework for the growth of an indirect rule system. In complete contrast with the sovereign powers the Colonial Office gave to Lugard ten years later, the Africa Order in Council of 1889 granted Johnston little more than an extended consular authority over British subjects and foreigners, the theory being that the protecting power regulated no more than the foreign relations of protected states and left their internal sovereignty intact. Even when Johnston had purported to secure powers of government from local chiefs by treaty agreements ceding sovereign rights, the Foreign Office insisted that such powers could be exercised only under the fiction of a delegated agency to British officers and could not be enforced under British law or through the consular courts.[1]

Johnston's instructions followed the spirit of limited liability infusing the Africa Order in Council. He was told 'to consolidate the protectorate of Her Majesty over the native Chiefs; to advise these Chiefs on their external relations with each other and with foreigners, not unduly interfering with their internal administration; to secure peace and order, and by every legitimate means in your power, to check the Slave Trade'.[2] Sir Percy Anderson cautioned him not to attempt too much at first and consider himself rather as the pioneer of administration. If he could manage to raise a certain income by local duties, he might provide 'subsidies to native Chiefs which, judiciously employed, might be our most effective method of keeping the peace'.[3]

Despite these instructions Johnston launched out immediately on his arrival as Commissioner with a whirlwind campaign of punitive expeditions. Although the Blantyre missionaries rightly sensed that 'the policy of the Administration is to crush and

---

[1] Johnston to Salisbury, 10 December 1891, F.O. Pr. 6337, No. 43. Cf. A. J. Hanna, *Beginnings of Nyasaland and North-Eastern Rhodesia*, 1956, p. 202. Also Johnston, *British Central Africa*, p. 114. Johnston to Salisbury, 31 December 1895, F.O. Pr. 6851, No. 54. Minute of Gray, 11 May 1894, F.O. Pr. 6537, No. 158.

[2] F.O. to Johnston, 24 March 1891, F.O. Pr. 6178, No. 9.

[3] Sir H. P. Anderson to Johnston, 20 December 1890, F.O. 84/2050.

destroy all native authority and independence',[1] it has to be recognized that Johnston was not a completely free agent. If he had possessed a field force of battalion strength in 1891 or even the force he disposed of in 1895, he could have afforded to ignore the strictly military problem. As it was his policy could not fail to be narrowly influenced by considerations of immediate security. When he later came to defend himself against the charge of needless warmongering he pointed to his responsibility for repressing the slave trade. At the same time he denied that he had embarked on a permanent crusade but had restricted himself to safeguarding the security of the settled districts and the lines of communication northwards.[2] So that he was first led to think in terms of establishing a small directly administered enclave in the Shire Highlands which could be progressively extended, a nuclear Crown colony settlement spreading itself like an oil stain over the hinterland.[3] Equally his military weakness was in part responsible for the spoiling policy of weakening, dividing and wearing down every indigenous political system that possessed any capacity to menace or resist. Although he recognized the need to find temporary allies—he was attracted at the beginning to the Arabs[4]—it was essentially a policy springing from weakness and its informing principle was *divide et impera*:

Dissociate the personal interests of the various native chiefs and Arab Sultans as far as possible; discreetly encourage their mutual rivalries (though stopping short, of course, of inciting them to civil war); bind over the more influential men to your interests by small money subsidies, and you will easily become the unquestioned Rulers of Nyasaland.[5]

Johnston's immediate strategy was to isolate the two leading slaving powers on the Lake, the north-end Arabs and Makanjira.

[1] McMurtrie to Salisbury, 24 March 1892, F.O. Pr. 6337, No. 64.
[2] Report on First Three Years' Administration . . . of . . . British Central Africa, 1894, C. 7504, p. 30. Cf. Oliver, *Johnston*, p. 253.
[3] Cf. Johnston, Memo. on the Administration of British Central Africa by a Chartered Company, 17 July 1890, F.O. 84/2052, f. 380. Also Memo., 7 October 1890, *ibid.*
[4] Johnston, Report on Nyasa–Tanganyika Expedition, 17 March 1890, FO 84/2051, f. 199. Cf. Hanna, *Beginnings of Nyasaland*, p. 154.
[5] Johnston's Memo. on the Administration of British Central Africa by a Chartered Company, 17 July 1890, F.O. 84/2052.

By treaty engagements he aimed to detach the west coast chiefs whose harbours were also important as refuelling stations on the line of steamer communications. The greatest reliance was placed on Jumbe of Kota Kota, who was subsidized by the Lakes Company at the substantial rate of Rs. 3,000 (c. £200) a year; and during the same period in 1889 Johnston concluded a treaty with the Yao chief Kazembe, a relative of Makanjira's, who held the terminal of the southern ferry as Jumbe held that of the central ferry. This was already to support the weak against the strong and presupposed that Johnston was capable of warding off the external and internal threats which had doubtless induced both Jumbe and Kazembe to place themselves under European protection in the first instance.

From the accounts we possess it is clear that the Marimba sultanate over which Jumbe III (Mwene Kusutu) ruled from about 1875 was far from possessing the characteristics of a centralized state. Jumbe's predecessors had established themselves by force over the Cewa population organized under some eight chiefs and a paramount, Malenga, and they had also allowed the settlement of Arab and Yao elements with whom power and revenue had to be shared. The reports speak particularly of one principal supporter, a Yao chief, Baruku, whose nephew succeeding under the same name greatly increased his power until half the population of Kota Kota acknowledged his sway. A more formidable figure was another Yao, Ciwaura (Tshiwaura), who in his rise to influence had leagued himself with Makanjira, and who was the only one of Jumbe's sub-chiefs who refused to sign the 1889 treaty.[1] According to local tradition 'Jumbe (I)'s system was to give his *indunas* and the old local chiefs full power as long as they brought him sufficient tribute in the form of slaves and ivory. . . . Jumbe was regarded as the head of the Arabs and Zanzibarees . . . in all judicial matters, whereas the Achewa resorted to their Native Ndunas.'[2] To the south, Kazembe, the so-called sultan of

---

[1] *British Central Africa Gazette*, referred to hereafter as *B.C.A.G.*, 20 August 1894. Johnston's Report on the Second Makanjira Campaign, 9 December 1893, F.O. Pr. 6537, encl. 1 in No. 31. Both of these make use of Major Edwards to Johnston, 17 July 1894, F.O. Pr. 6613, No. 137.

[2] Kota Kota (Marimba) District Note Book, [1907], f. 37: National Archives, Zomba. Entry appears to be in the hand of A. J. Swann.

Rifu, enjoyed a much narrower measure of autonomy and power. His dominion had originated out of the colonizing activities of Makanjira II and III and the severing of this allegiance through his treaty with Johnston in 1889 made him more immediately dependent on European protection.

Makanjira had turned hostile to the Europeans at the time of the Arab War at Karonga in 1888, and his hostility was fanned by the subsidizing of the west coast chiefs. By October 1890 his activities were proving so detrimental to the mission work of the U.M.C.A. that Buchanan thought that the question of a subsidy ought to be considered unless there were prospects of stationing a gunboat on the Lake to curb him. Johnston disliked 'placing a premium on disorder'; at the same time, as an index of his comparative impotence, he was averse to strengthening his rival, Jumbe, since if the latter became too powerful it would be necessary 'to set about controlling him'. 'Our policy in Nyasaland in our present state of weakness must be "Divide and Rule".'[1]

In the event Johnston's policy fell between two stools and his touch proved fatal to friend and foe alike. He commenced his administration in the latter part of 1891 with the object of obtaining firm control over the Upper Shire region between Zomba and the Lake. But the deceptively easy successes that were won by his tiny force in a brisk series of petty actions led on to disaster when operations were extended to the Lake itself in a campaign against Makanjira. The repulse that led to Maguire's death in December 1891 left Johnston without any sure hold on the southerly portion of the west coast for a full two years, and gave a lingering death blow to his system of subsidiary alliances. The immediate result of Makanjira's resurgence was his despatch of an expedition across the Lake. Kazembe who had defected to Makanjira earlier in the year and then reverted to his British alliance when Johnston visited him in force on 31 October, was now driven out and a woman ruler, Kuluunda, installed in his place. From this base Makanjira supplied his ally Ciwaura in Jumbe's country, until open revolt broke out in August 1893 which found support among an Arab element in Kota Kota itself.[2]

[1] Johnston's Memo. on Makanjira, 29 December 1890, F.O. 84/2052.
[2] As early as 20 February 1892, Johnston had confessed that 'even here there

Jumbe then fled, a king across the water, to seek succour from his British allies at Fort Johnston. The second Makanjira Campaign of November 1893 restored the exiled rulers to power, but by now they were men of straw. Johnston's comment on Kazembe was that: 'Although rather a weak man, he has a good disposition, and, if properly supported, will probably prove a fair specimen of a native Ruler.' On Jumbe his remarks made clear that the beginning of the end was in sight:

Until such time as we have the funds to administer Jumbe's country directly, I cannot think of any better arrangement that it should continue under the mild rule of Jumbe, who is, for an Arab, an excellent man, and thoroughly attached to the English. . . . His Nyasa subjects are thoroughly attached to him, and I believe he is sincere in his determination to put down the Slave Trade.[1]

At the same time Johnston had to acknowledge that since 1891 Jumbe had twice asked to abdicate and spend his declining days at Zanzibar. The difficulties of both rulers in securing internal support may perhaps be gauged by the fact that within a few months both were found to be slaving. Jumbe was dealt a warning; but because of his co-operation with the outlawed Makanjira's supporters on the other side of the Lake, Kazembe was summarily deposed.[2] By July 1894 the aged Jumbe was dead, and his headmen asked for a government agent to administer affairs. This in itself, from subsequent events, was probably a measure of the internal strains within the disintegrating political structure. On his return Jumbe would appear to have made his chief support the Cewa headmen. The new Jumbe, Mwene Khere, was according to Johnston, not an Arab in any sense, being the son of a slave wife of Jumbe I, and threw in his lot with the Yao element. On Jumbe's death Sharpe had agreed to the appointment of Nicoll as Government Agent to control the ferry traffic and collect dues;

---

are some disintegrating forces at work. Jumbe himself is becoming weary of controlling the turbulent Arabs and Mahomedan Yaos, whom he calls his Captains ("Akida"), and sent a letter to this effect.' Johnston to Salisbury, 20 February 1892, F.O. Pr. 6337, No. 90. On Kazembe, cf. Hanna, p. 186.

[1] Johnston's Memo. on the Second Makanjira Campaign, *op. cit.*

[2] Sharpe to Rosebery, 20 April 1894, F.O. 2/66. *Idem*, 9 May 1894, F.O. Pr. 6613, No. 3.

but it was not intended to interfere with the internal affairs of the district, these being left to the new chief and his headmen. By December 1894 Mwene Khere's doings were regarded as insupportable and he was removed from office. Nicoll claimed to have discovered a plot by him and 'the more youthful element of Kota Kota, almost entirely composed of young Yaos . . . to kill all the recent Jumbe's Headmen, and to oust the Administration from the place'.[1] Sharpe advised that the best course now was to appoint no Jumbe at all but for Nicoll 'to directly take charge of the whole of that country, and govern it through the Council of Headmen', since Nicoll had found no difficulty in administering affairs through the headmen but had found the presence of a sultan a great drawback.[2] Johnston endorsed the advice. The Arabs had nearly all gone, the Yaos had been expelled and direct administration through the headmen therefore meant that 'the land reverts to its original A-Nyanja inhabitants'.[3]

Such was the effect of Johnston's attempt to make use of overtly friendly local rulers as allies. With the less amenable Yao chiefs his policy tended to operate with the same disintegrating effect. Admittedly the Yao political organization was a highly fragmented one and would not have sustained more than a local government system. The real question was the position of the Yao chief, whose prestige, as Mitchell has suggested, depended largely on his economic and military functions in connection with the coast caravan traffic.[4] In 1891 Johnston was powerful only to hurt but not to overawe or subdue. His protracted failure to retrieve the repulse suffered in December at the hands of Makanjira, combined with a less important reverse dealt by Jalasi (Zarafi) shortly afterwards, must have encouraged an unrealistic attitude of defiance which, set firm and reciprocated, was later almost impossible to alter. The most powerful of the Yao chiefs, Makanjira and Jalasi, never submitted and continued to operate with their

[1] Sharpe to Kimberley, 15 January 1895, F.O. Pr. 6688, No. 113.
[2] *Idem*, 5 December 1894, F.O. 2/68. The chief headmen appear to have been Malenga, Mausa as well as Baruku and Mwene Waziri (Jumbe I's brother). Cf. *Life and Letters of A. F. Sim*, 1897, pp. 139, 148, 155, 159, 169–71.
[3] Johnston to Kimberley, 19 May 1895, F.O. Pr. 6784, No. 15.
[4] J. C. Mitchell, 'The Political Organization of the Yao of Southern Nyasaand'. *African Studies*, viii, No. 3, September 1949, p. 142.

confrères from beyond the Portuguese border until after 1900. On the British side, there was the same tendency for early postures to harden rapidly into fixed attitudes. It became axiomatic with the Administration that its authority was to be extended by defeating each resistant polity in detail and expanding the directly-ruled area proportionately to the means made available by the annual growth in revenue. In this there is a parallel with the tradition which set in with Moor in the Niger Coast Protectorate once expansion into the interior began after 1896.[1]

If Johnston lacked the power to subdue he was also lacking in the means to persuade. Jumbe's handsome subsidy of £200 a year (partly in compensation for the surrender of customs dues) was not matched elsewhere. All Johnston felt able to offer was a small royalty on mythical mineral deposits and an allowance of up to 10 per cent on hut tax collections. The total estimated revenue from hut tax as late as 1896–7 was still only £2,300, not all oι which, of course, was subject to the deduction for chiefs; while the nominal entry for subsidies was £250.[2] These figures make abundantly plain how little Johnston had to play with, and what negligible means he possessed to induce the Yao chiefs to give up the slave and gunpowder traffic and settle down as dependent rulers.[3]

He was therefore reduced to the tactics of striving to drive a wedge between a chief and his people by detaching the sub-chiefs and headmen. One of the best examples of this was Mponda. After Mponda's first brush with the Administration he appeared to be not dissatisfied with his submission:

[1] J. C. O. Anene, 'The Establishment and Consolidation of Imperial Government in Southern Nigeria 1881–1904', London, M.A. thesis, 1952, pp. 199 ff.

[2] Revised Estimates 1895-6, F.O. Pr. 6784, No. 11.

[3] Mponda was given a subsidy of £100 a year and a 5 per cent mineral royalty. Jalasi and Makandanji were each given £50 a year. A. J. Hanna, *Beginnings of Nyasaland and North-Eastern Rhodesia*, 1956, p. 191. Also Johnston to Salisbury, 10 December 1891, F.O. Pr. 6337, No. 43 and encls. In the Report by Commissioner Johnston on the First Three Years Administration of the Eastern Portion of British Central Africa dated 31 March 1894, c. 7504, p. 29, Johnston states: 'With the exception of the percentage on the taxes which is paid to most of the Chiefs, there are no direct payments of subsidies made to them by the Administration.' The only exceptions were Jumbe £200, Mponda £100, and Kanga £40.

The fact was that before our coming Mponda's position was rather uncertain. He had but little control over his people and his own tenure of power was menaced by rival and more legitimate claimants to the throne, besides the threatened attacks of the Angoni and the Makandanji clan. Our fort [Fort Johnston] therefore and our alliance gave him a more secure position in the country. He has certainly ever since been remarkably friendly and helpful.[1]

In the early part of 1892 he withstood the attack of the Yao confederacy of Jalasi, Likoro, Mkata, Makandanji and Msamara, who were all prompted by Makanjira.[2] But despite a subsidy of £100 a year to keep him faithful, Mponda eventually returned to his slaving activities, though this meant withdrawing westwards to the hills from his town opposite Fort Johnston. The Administration then put his son in charge of the town to help rally the headmen.[3] By October 1895 Johnston could report that 'the Mponda difficulty is rapidly melting away as Mponda is deserted by nearly all his people who have settled down near Fort Johnston'.[4] The coup de grâce came in November when Mponda took advantage of the Jalasi campaign to attack the Monkey Bay settlement, provoked a punitive expedition, surrendered and was deposed. It is indicative of Johnston's state of mind by this time that he felt it necessary to justify his decision not to abolish the chieftainship:

... it may be thought that perhaps I might have done more wisely to have caused the native Chieftainship to cease with the deposition of Mponda, but I felt that, in view of the persistent support that we had received during four years from a large section of Mponda's Headmen and people, and especially from the mother of the young Chief, who is the rightful heir, it would be decidedly unfair to deprive them of a privilege they much value—being governed in their own internal affairs by themselves. As all the people referred to have for several years past paid the hut tax and comported themselves in a thoroughly friendly manner, it is evident that they should not be treated as a conquered people, but as allies, and be treated quite differently to the

[1] Johnston's Report on Measures to Suppress the Slave Trade in British Central Africa, July to December 1891, F.O. 84/2114.
[2] Johnston to Salisbury, 16 February 1892, F.O. 84/2197.
[3] Sharpe to Rosebery, 9 May 1894, F.O. Pr. 6613, No. 3.
[4] Johnston to Hill, 5 October 1895, F.O. 2/89.

recalcitrant Yaos who hung about Mponda and gradually weaned him from his friendship with the British.[1]

This pattern was to be repeated in many other instances. Johnston played on the conflict of interests between the settled agricultural population and the military trading elements, especially among the Yao groups, where the conflict often corresponded to a large extent with the ethnic difference between the immigrant Yao and the indigenous Nyanja. In his contest with Makanjira he encouraged the claims of Kumbasani, a woman rival, and on Makanjira's expulsion from his town in November 1893 installed her instead, contending that though she had 'never succeeded in getting her claims to power accepted by the Yaos ... she seems to have conciliated the sympathies of the much larger Nyasa population which ... numbers about 16,000 people, as against 4,000 or 5,000 Yaos and Swahilis.'[2] 'By rooting out the Yao chiefs on our eastern frontier,' he argued, 'we restore the country to the peaceful Mananja, who are a most industrious people and well worthy of our protection.'[3] On Kumbasani being killed in January 1894 in a raid by Makanjira, aided by Jalasi and Makandanji, the British then made use of a Yao chief Ciwaura who supplied them with 400 fighting men.[4] In November 1895 Makanjira still had some 25,000 people settled under him, although this appears to have consisted in part of 'a large Arab and coast population'.[5] The effect of the long spoiling warfare with the more powerful Yao chiefs like Makanjira and Jalasi was to unseat them from the territories where they were slowly building up settled dominions and to transform them back into their old role of migrant warlords. Jalasi, who had withdrawn to his fastness on Mangoche Mountain, still had some 25,000 people about him when he was attacked

[1] Johnston to Salisbury, 13 November 1895, F.O. Pr. 6851, No. 25.

[2] Johnston's Report on the Second Makanjira Campaign, 9 December 1893, F.O. Pr. 6537, encl. 1 in No. 31. The old Makanjira (IV) had died and had been succeeded by the young Makanjira V.

[3] Johnston to Rosebery, 4 February 1894, *ibid.*, No. 105.

[4] *B.C.A.G.*, 7 April 1894. This Ciwaura is to be distinguished from the Marimba Ciwaura killed in the expedition to Kota Kota in November 1893, Johnston, *Briish Central Africa*, p. 124.

[5] Major Edwards' Report of Military Operations ... against ... Matapwiri, Zarafi, Mponda, and Makanjiri ... during September, October, and November 1895, F.O. Pr. 6851, encl. 2 in No. 58.

and driven across the border in November 1895. Johnston commented:

The bulk of Zarafi's [Jalasi's] people belong to the Anyanja stock and with all these we have now made peace, and they have come to settle down in their old homes. The dominant race, however, was Yao, and most of them have fled with Zarafi, and may not care to return under the very stringent conditions of disarmament which I shall feel compelled to impose.[1]

Johnston reported that after Jalasi's flight all his minor chiefs except one had come forward to make peace and the chieftainship was made over to Mkata.[2] A year later Sharpe described an attack against Katuri north of Fort Mangoche, when after the chief's capture large numbers of his people requested to build near the Fort under British protection. 'It is the Yao Chiefs who give so much trouble,' Sharpe remarked. 'The people themselves, when once they have made up their minds to accept our rule, become good subjects.'[3]

The treatment of the Yao chiefs varied according to their disposition and relative strength. Mponda, Liwonde and Matapwiri were deposed: Kawinga was allowed to return from across the border after peace had been made with his sub-chiefs and he himself had aided the attack on Jalasi by the provision of guides. One cannot doubt that in any event the old political units had been completely disrupted and that the surviving chiefs were 'not really chiefs any longer, but only headmen under British control, with an authority more or less nominal over inferior headmen in their vicinity'.[4]

The same clash of interest between a chief and a large section of his people reappeared in the case of the Southern Ngoni under Gomani Kwendi (Cikusi). At the commencement of Johnston's administration in 1891 Gomani, who had just succeeded to the chieftaincy, proved friendly, partly because of internal strife with Kacindamoto (Cifisi) who had allied with Mponda to raid Gomani's country in the foothills of the Kirk Range for slaves. He

---

[1] Johnston to Salisbury, 13 November 1895, F.O. Pr. 6851, No. 25.
[2] Johnston to Salisbury, 13 November 1895, ibid., No. 26.
[3] Sharpe to Salisbury, 29 September 1896, F.O. Pr. 6911, No. 99.
[4] H. L. Duff, *Nyasaland under the Foreign Office* (2nd ed. 1906), pp. 194-5.

allowed missions and later coffee-planters to establish themselves in this area. The Southern Ngoni soon became the chief source of labour supply for the Shire Highlands; so that when the supply appeared to be threatened by continuing internal war at the end of 1894, Sharpe sent Edwards to negotiate a reconciliation. Gomani late in 1893 had induced Mponda to change sides, and together with other Yao chiefs in Central Angoniland like Tambala and Mpemba, had succeeded in driving Kacindamoto to the south-east arm of the Lake. The corollary of the new alliance for Gomani was fresh participation in slaving.[1] But more important, the increasing seasonal flood of Ngoni labour across the Shire was evidently clashing with Gomani's need for warriors.[2] By November 1895 there were reports of trouble in Gomani's country, part of which lay over the Portuguese border. People were being forbidden to pay taxes and their tax papers destroyed.[3] A series of attacks on mission property and villages paying taxes coincided with the Matabele rebellion and was sufficient inducement for Sharpe in October 1896 to instruct his forces to lose no time in breaking up Gomani's power.[4] In keeping with the new rigour that had made its appearance with Mlozi's execution, Gomani after his defeat was tried and shot. The immediate result was that 'the headmen of 210 villages representing some 30,000 people' asked to come down and settle in the low country under the immediate rule of the Administration. According to Sharpe they had for long wanted to do this, 'but they have always feared the chief himself who has been opposed to British interests'.[5] There followed the settlement of large numbers in the Upper Shire District together with an increased flow to the plantations in the Shire Highlands, some 5,000 being employed by March 1897.[6] As Johnston no doubt correctly pointed out the bulk of these

[1] *B.C.A.G.*, 28 June 1894, 28 July 1894, 26 October 1894, 21 November 1894, 14 December 1894, 15 July 1895. Also Edwards to Sharpe, 31 October 1894 and 20 November 1894, F.O. Pr. 6688, encls. 1 and 2, in No. 30.
[2] *B.C.A.G.*, 15 July 1895.
[3] *B.C.A.G.*, 15 November 1895.
[4] Sharpe to Salisbury, 15 October 1896, F.O. 2/108.
[5] Sharpe to Salisbury, 10 November 1896, F.O. 2/108.
[6] Sharpe to Hill, 1 December 1896, F.O. 2/108. Report on . . . B.C.A. Protectorate, 1896–7, F.O. 2/127.

so-called Ngoni were in fact Cewa agriculturalists; and it may be guessed that as with the Yao principalities the smaller Ngoni states were coming apart at the ethnic or rather occupational seams on account of indirect European influences long before the Administration stretched out its arm.

The absorption of Southern Ngoniland came, however, late in the day, when the determination of the Administration to knock out the surviving rulers possessing any real power had become open and determined. In the earlier period Johnston was at pains to deny the missionary charge that 'the policy of the Administration is to crush and destroy all native authority and independence'.[1] In his defence he employed not only the familiar argument that his military campaigning was directed solely against intrusive foreign oppressors, but contended that taxation was never imposed without carefully explained treaty agreements. In ordinary cases, he said, he offered a choice to the chiefs; where they were unable to keep order or where they specifically requested him to do so, then they had to surrender their sovereign rights and pay hut tax: 'If, on the other hand, you do not wish to cede your sovereign rights nor to pay taxes to the Administration: very well then, you need not; but you must, in that case, rule your own country wisely and well, must keep the peace with your neighbours, and protect yourself if attacked; and you must lend no countenance to the Slave Trade.'[2] As late as March 1894 he could publicly promise that: 'No native taxes are at present levied in any other portion of British Central Africa nor will they be so levied until the Chiefs and people have been approached on the subject and have voluntarily signed Treaties agreeing to pay.'[3]

These professions were doubtless necessary to assuage the fears of the Foreign Office and rebut the charges of the missionaries. But they were the product of opportunism, not principle. Until 1895 he was in no financial position to extend the administered area outside the Shire Valley, and he reinstated Jumbe in late 1893

[1] McMurtrie to Salisbury, 24 March 1892, F.O. Pr. 6337, No. 64.
[2] Johnston to Salisbury, 10 December 1891, F.O. Pr. 6337, No. 43. Cited Hanna, p. 242.
[3] Report . . . of the First Three Years' Administration . . . 31 March 1894, C. 7504.

MALAWI POLITICAL SYSTEMS, 1891–1896   371

avowedly as a *pis aller* 'until we have funds to administer Jumbe's country directly'.[1]

In August 1895 he was planning to establish administration and taxation in Central Angoniland. Though his professions were by this time sounding distinctly hollow, he still chose to enunciate his earlier principle;

> On this point I have not changed the policy I pursued from the commencement of my administration, which is, that where a district . . . does not continually seek our help in the management of its affairs, or does not assume an aggressive attitude towards the British administration in the Protectorate, I prefer to leave it untaxed and ungoverned; but where from one cause or another I am obliged to place officials and erect stations, I think it only right that the natives, in return for the protection and assistance they thus acquire, should contribute their reasonable share towards the expenses of Administration.[2]

This, of course, is Johnstonian cant. Johnston entered upon the administration of Central Angoniland and left Northern Angoniland alone purely because it was expedient to do so; because in the one instance 'the progress of the Protectorate and the continued immigration of Europeans bent on mining enterprise render it necessary', and in the other, because it was politic to leave the Livingstonia missionaries' empire untouched.[3]

Although Professor Oliver rejects the charge as 'an odious insinuation' Sir Clement Hill was not so wide of the mark when he minuted: 'Sir H. Johnston's method is simple: treaty or compulsion, your money or your life. It answered well in Central Africa where all recalcitrant chiefs were improved away and where the area was comparatively small; but it was preceded by many small wars.'[4]

Following the crushing of Mlozi in the north the confused

---

[1] Report on Second Makanjira Campaign, 9 December 1893, F.O. Pr. 6537, encl. 1 in No. 31.

[2] Johnston to Salisbury, 5 August 1895, F.O. Pr. 6784, No. 118.

[3] Johnston to Salisbury, 27 August 1895, F.O. Pr. 6724, No. 145. Johnston had recognized the African Lakes Company's treaties in C. Angoniland conferring mineral rights in order to transfer them to the B.S.A. Co. The B.S.A. Co.'s title was confirmed by F.O. to B.S.A. Co., 27 November 1894, F.O. Pr. 6613, No. 228.

[4] Oliver, *Johnston*, p. 299.

jumble of Yao, Cewa and semi-Ngoni states in the Central Angoniland and Marimba districts was brusquely 'pacified' during 1896,
Cabisa, Mwase Kasungu, Tambala, Odete and Ciwere being
brought to heel on the grounds that they were disturbers of the
peace with their continued slaving and their blocking of the
labour supply to the Shire highlands.[1] Johnston saw his work as
done. 'The native labour question,' he wrote in his final report, 'is
almost the most important question which can now claim the
attention of those administering the Protectorate ... All that
needs now be done is for the Administration to act as friends of
both sides, and introduce the native labourer to the European
capitalist.'[2] Sharpe who succeeded him in May 1896 watched
without regret the crumbling of the vestiges of authority possessed
by the more powerful chiefs. Observing how the hut tax receipt
was freeing the people from 'the oppression of their Chiefs' he
welcomed the signs that during his first year of office there had
been 'a marked diminution of the autocratic power formerly held
by native Chiefs throughout the Protectorate'.[3]

A policy that rested so squarely on European enterprise rather
than peasant production was bound to have as its corollary a
system of 'direct rule' but later observers noted how intensive this
rapidly became.[4] But a description in terms of 'direct' or 'indirect'
rule is too crude for the subtler realities of political relationships.
It is not to be supposed that indigenous political systems were
struck out of existence, but rather that they were overlaid and
submerged by colonial authority while their social and political
functions were fundamentally altered. European administration
remained, however, too limited in aim and personnel to be capable
of reconstructing society anew. Where it did make radical changes
was in the effective dismantling of the larger-scale systems and the
displacement of the political and coercive authority of centralized
institutions and paramounts. At the level of the local headman
and local 'chief' little direct change might occur. In all this the
difference between the northern region (beyond Kasungu) and

[1] Cf. Swann's Report, January 1896, F.O. Pr. 6851, encl. in No. 84.
[2] Johnston's Report on the B.C.A. Protectorate 1895-6, 29 April 1896,
F.O. Pr. 6851, No. 142.
[3] Cited Hanna, p. 244.
[4] Sir Philip Mitchell, *Journal of African Administration*, viii, No. 2, p. 5.

the conquered, more developed, more ethnically confused south has also to be borne in mind.[1]

It seems indeed to have been the aim of the Administration to preserve the indigenous system at the purely local level for its own purposes. In the early years Johnston claimed that he did 'not seek to interfere more than necessary with the rule of the native Chiefs over the people', and he appears to have given instructions 'to uphold as much as possible the power of the Chiefs'.[2] Oliver also says he was 'anxious to preserve the Yao chieftaincies throughout the northern half of the Shire Province . . . because they provided him with a ready-made chain of command, a manageable number of local government units in place of the plethora of village heads with whom the administration would have to deal if the Yao were driven out or demoted'.[3] In fact, however it seems that Johnston wanted to retain the indigenous organization only in its intermediate ranges and not at the more recalcitrant level of the larger chieftaincy. Oliver himself quotes Johnston on the malleability of the smaller chiefs and the refractoriness of the big, and Hector Duff saw with philosophic eye that the attempt to stabilize indigenous authority at an intermediate level in the interests of security and administrative convenience had resulted in a more general disintegration than was desired:

The tribal body was intolerable to us, for a directly opposite reason. It was too large, too powerful, too aggressive to exist side by side with a European administration, and accordingly it was dissolved. But in the Shire Highlands the process of dissolution had gone a little too far—far enough at any rate, to make it difficult and nearly impossible to carry out effectively the true theory of a Protectorate—viz. government through native chiefs. It is an ideal theory, this, and yet I doubt whether it can be put into complete practice among people like the Central Africans. I do not think that anything can permanently arrest the tide of political decentralization among them at least at the exact point which such a system requires.[4]

---

[1] Cf. Griff Jones, *Britain and Nyasaland*, pp. 70- 1.
[2] Report of the First Three Years Administration, 31 March 1894, C. 7504, p. 29. J. O. Bowhill, 'A Statistical Account of the West Shire District', 1 October 1893; *British Central Africa Gazette*, 1 January 1894.
[3] Oliver, *Johnston*, p. 206.
 H. L. Duff, *Nyasaland under the Foreign Office*, op. cit., p. 288.

Whatever the tenour of his early instructions Johnston viewed the passage of authority from African to European hands with equanimity. By 1897 he was writing to the Foreign Office:

For some time we endeavoured to support the power of such native chiefs as were willing to exercise it under our protection but with very few exceptions their ideas of law-giving and law-enforcing were found to be so incompatible with justice and humanity that our officials were obliged to take their places as magistrates. Now we administer justice to the natives throughout the whole Protectorate with the exception of a small portion of the West Nyasa district and we do this in the name of the native chief and either as the result of treaties concluded with that chief or because we have conquered the country from its alien invaders and have no native chief to deal with.[1]

Johnston was of course guilty of typical exaggeration in stating that European officials had taken over the entire work of the administration of justice; for this was true only in a formal sense. Lugard in Northern Nigeria had seen before his arrival that the preservation of indigenous authority required its formal definition and support by colonial authority; and indeed the real difference between 'indirect' and 'direct rule' systems of administration in the former British areas of Africa lay precisely in this feature. Indirect rule regulated 'native authorities' while direct rule merely permitted them to function *sub silentio* at the whim of the local European official. In March 1897 the Foreign Office recognized that it had to be prepared 'for the gradual extinction in practice of native rule' and wanted to devise a properly regulated system of native authority courts. On Sharpe's advice, however, the provisions for 'Courts of Local Native Chiefs' were dropped and indigenous jurisdiction left to function as best it could.[2]

Things had fallen out as they were bound to fall. Johnston had brought the whole territory under administration with a speed exceptional for the period and for many years later; and this result must be attributed to that convergence of circumstance and 'ideology' which we have outlined. A recent writer has it that

---

[1] Johnston, Report on a suggested transference of the African Protectorates to the Colonial Office, 31 May 1897, F.O. 2/128.
[2] Minute note by F. B[ertie ?] on Sharpe to Salisbury, 17 March 1897, F.O. 2/127. Cf. Sharpe, Memo., 29 August 1898, F.O. Pr. 7143, No. 47.

'administration made a virtue of the necessity to reduce the powers of chiefs'.[1] That is a way of putting the matter which at least recognizes such a convergence. The attitudes of colonialism have their place in the historical reckoning. At the outset of colonial rule Johnston's 'aggressive imperialism' helped reduce the power of the traditional élite and dominant warrior peoples in decisive fashion.

[1] Griff Jones, *Britain and Nyasaland*, p. 75.

16

SOME EARLY PRESSURE GROUPS IN MALAWI

by

J. VAN VELSEN

I

IT is surely a testimony to the pioneering quality and the excellence of Sundkler's work *Bantu Prophets in South Africa* that it should have inspired so many historians, sociologists and others to examine religious movements for aspects of social and political protest. The impact of this work has been such that there seems to be a tendency to expect the beginnings of social and political protest movements to appear only in a sectarian guise. In this chapter[1] I will discuss some early, secular associations in Nyasaland whose express aim was to bring to the notice of the Government, in the days before any form of popular, political representation existed, the desires and complaints of the ruled.

It should be noted that in their earlier stages such associations were only concerned to bring pressure to bear upon the Government to alleviate current problems within the prevailing political and administrative system. There was then little thought of tackling these problems at their source by demanding greater influence in, or control over the country's Government. It is not until after the Second World War that we see a shift in emphasis from gradual social and economic reform towards a demand for a political 'take-over' in accordance with Dr Kwame Nkrumah's well-known injunction to seek first the political kingdom. However, here I am concerned with the *roots* of political nationalism in

[1] This paper is the result of research in the National Archives in Zomba, Malawi (formerly Nyasaland). Financial assistance from the University College of Rhodesia and Nyasaland has greatly facilitated this research.

the erstwhile Protectorate of Nyasaland, of which the present sovereign state of Malawi is the off-spring.

Shepperson and Price in *Independent African* and Gray in *The Two Nations* have already indicated the politically catalytic role which various Malawians have played over several decades in South and Central Africa. It is hoped that this chapter will contribute further data which may lead to a greater understanding of why this relatively small and essentially agrarian country should have taken such a prominent political lead.

Most of the pressure groups took the form of Native Associations.[1] From the available records it would appear that the North Nyasa Native Association[2] (N.N.N.A.) and the West Nyasa Native Association[3] (W.N.N.A.) were formed respectively in 1912 at Karonga (by A. Simon Muhango) and in 1914 at Bandawe —barely twenty years after the establishment of the Nyasaland Protectorate in 1891. Other Native Associations of note[4] were the Mombera Native Association (M.N.A., founded in 1920);[5] the Chiradzulu District (later 'Native' was added) Association (C.D.N.A.) which was founded in 1929 by Dr Daniel Malekebu[6] and the Nyasaland (Southern Province) Native Association, which was founded in 1923.[7] This last one apparently later split into the Mlanje Native Association (Ml.N.A.) and the Blantyre Native Association (B.N.A.). There was also a Zomba Native

[1] See also Gray, pp. 171–6.

[2] Statement encl. in Abraham to H.C.S., 24/3/21, on S1/1481/19. All file numbers in this paper are those of the National Archives, Zomba. Apart from the initials for the various Native Associations I have also used the following: H.C.S. (the Honourable the Chief Secretary); A.C.S. (Acting Chief Secretary); P.C. (Provincial Commissioner); S.P.C. (Senior Provincial Commissioner); D.C. (District Commissioner—D.C.'s were earlier known as Residents).

[3] Yesaya B. Bhango to H.C.S., 4/10/35, on S1/2065/19. Levi Z. Mumba and Yesaya Murray Jere to H.C.S., 26/11/33, on NAT 12/3, also mentions: 'From the time of their institution [i.e. of the Native Associations] 20 years ago . . .'.

[4] Or rather those on which I have found substantial information in the Zomba Archives. Foulger to H.C.S., 25/7/35, on NAT 12/3, encloses a list of all Associations (including Producers' Associations) known at the time in the Northern Province. For some of them (e.g. the Central Province Native Association with George S. Mwase as President) I have not found any records.

[5] Encl. in Moggridge to A.C.S., 19/2/20, on S1/210/20.

[6] Minutes of C.D.N.A., 12/11/29, on S1/1598/29.

[7] Minutes of N.S.P.N.A., 23/12/23, on S1/3263/23.

Association, but I have found only a few documents relating to it.

It is interesting to note that the Native Associations of the north preceded those of the south. Although the north had its own problems (particularly the large number of its men absent in the Rhodesias and South Africa[1]), one would have expected that formal pressure groups would have originated in the south where there were even greater and more immediately pressing problems of land shortage and the insecurity of the so-called 'squatters' on the European estates.[2] I cannot offer an explanation for this apparent paradox.

The year 1929 also saw the formation, in Zomba, of the Representative Committee of Northern Province Native Associations (R.C.N.P.N.A.), which consisted of members of the N.N.N.A., W.N.N.A. and the M.N.A., most of whom were working in Zomba.[3] Although most of these men were civil servants (who had their own Association) they still felt the need to retain a collective interest in Northern Province affairs. Moreover, even as civil servants they had their own particular problems due to the long distance to their homes and their relatively short periods of leave.

The moving spirit behind the formation of the R.C.N.P.N.A. was Levi Z. Mumba who had been secretary of the North Nyasa Native Association since its inception in 1912. He had a part in the formation of the Native Civil Servants' Association. We meet him as Corresponding Secretary of the Lilongwe African Welfare Society,[4] and later he became the first president of the Nyasaland African Congress. It was not only in the sphere of voluntary associations that he established a reputation. He also made his mark in Government circles. When the chairman, Haythorne Reed, of the North Nyasa Native Reserves Commission wanted 'a really competent Native clerk, typist and interpreter', he requested the services of Mumba.[5] And later he was appointed on to the Advisory Committee on Education.

[1] Cf. *Emigrant Labour Report.*   [2] Cf. *Land Report, 1921* and *Land Report, 1946.*
[3] Jere to S.P.C., 7/1/30, on NAT 12/3.
[4] Memorandum of 26/5/38, on S1/262B/37.
[5] Reed to H.C.S., 22/3/29, on S1/1519/28. I have come across a reference to an article by and a biography of Mumba in the *International Review of Missions* (p. 362), but have not yet been able to trace it.

It is important to note that these Native Associations were not tribal either in purpose or in outlook. They were not interested in maintaining tribal identity *per se*. Indeed, the northern Associations initially tried to keep chiefs and headmen out because it was felt that they represented a conservative, tribal way of thought. Native Associations were regional rather than tribal. This is also clear from their names which refer to Districts rather than tribal units. That Native Associations could operate successfully across Districts and on a supra-tribal level is shown by the existence of the Representative Committee of Northern Province Native Associations which functioned in the south and had its effective headquarters in Zomba, the seat of government. This was very active and vocal not so much in matters of particular concern to the Northern Province but rather in administrative, social and economic issues which were the concern of the majority of the Protectorate's citizens. In other words, the R.C.N.P.N.A. was geared to the emergence of Nyasaland as a new nation. Indeed, in spite of its regional name the R.C.N.P.N.A. functioned more like a national pressure group, the first of its kind. It could thus be considered as the forerunner of the nationalist movement of the Nyasaland African Congress which was formed in 1944.

It is clear that the outward looking, supra-tribal attitude of the Native Associations was not fortuitous; it was very much part of their *raison d'être*. For instance, the rules of the Nyasaland (Southern Province) Native Association, adopted at its inaugural meeting in 1923, state that one of the objects is 'to keep in touch with other similar Native Associations'.[1] And a minute of a meeting in 1930 of the N.N.N.A. mentions a 'Union of Associations'; it had been agreed in 1923 that the Northern Provincial Associations needed a 'united power'.[2] This question was also raised at a meeting of the Mombera Native Association in 1924.[3] Although such a union was never formed in the north, the objective was at least partly realized in the south through the formation of the R.C.N.P.N.A.

Whilst the R.C.N.P.N.A. was an example of the formal

[1] Meeting of 23/12/23, on S1/3263/23.
[2] Meeting of 14/8/30, on S1/1481/19.
[3] Meeting of 12/6/24, on S1/1365/24.

co-ordination of the Associations' activities, there were also instances of informal co-operation. For example, members of one Association were frequently present at meetings of another. But an even more telling example is the similarity between, or, indeed, the identity of the rules of the various Associations. Both the Chiradzulu and the Nyasaland (Southern Province) Associations had as their object 'to keep in close touch with other similar Native Associations'. They also shared the following objects (the wording, too, was identical):

(1) to assist the Government in every way, especially by keeping it informed of Native public opinion.
(2) to assist the Native by representing him in all political matters, by keeping him informed of and explaining the object of legislations both new and already in force.
(3) to organize public meetings for the discussion of subjects of general and special interest.[1]

Likewise the rules of the Associations in the north show clear signs of close contact. The stated aims, in identical wording, of the Mombera and the West Nyasa Native Associations were also, as in the south, to 'adequately express their [i.e. "of our people"] desires and needs to the Government; and being educated it [the Association] could fully explain the mind of the Government to the people.' But they went further:

It aims at making the people understand the necessity and value of order, and the importance of becoming law-abiding citizens and also of the value and importance of industrious labour—and in short the value of civilization as against ignorance, laziness, disloyalty and anarchy.

In order to follow intelligently and loyally the doings of the Government, the Association would esteem it a favour to be supplied monthly with the Government *Gazette*, for which it shall duly pay the sum of 7/6d. annually.'

As to membership, both Associations' rules stated that it was open to 'persons of good knowledge and character. It is also an open question for educated Chiefs and Europeans either to attend or

---

[1] S1/3263/23, *loc. cit.* and meeting of 12/11/29, on S1/1598/29.

join it as full members thereof [the last four words are not in the Mombera rules], if they choose to do so.'[1]

The insistence on education and the half-hearted acceptance of chiefs should be noted. The membership qualifications of the southern Associations, however, were less selective: there is no educational requirement and the only condition is permanent or temporary residence in the Associations' respective areas.

We are dealing, then, with communities which had only comparatively recently entered the era of colonial control and unification and which had responded in remarkably similar ways to the new challenges. The values of the Associations[2] and their founders did not echo the glories of the past nor did they appeal to tribal loyalties. Instead, they were a response to the social and political consequences of a newly introduced money economy and industrial employment. And the loyalties they appealed to were those of common membership of an embryonic national entity.

The 'new men' who ran these Associations were thoroughly involved in the new ways of life: they were educated men and most of them were teachers, ministers of religion or civil servants. They were suspicious of the conservatism of the chiefs. The Associations clearly bore the stamp of the 'new men' who founded and ran them. Meetings generally opened and closed with Christian prayer; office bearers were selected by vote; minutes were kept, often typed on paper with the Association's own printed letter-head, and so forth. Each person contributed his own experience. Consequently one finds in the records a mixture of biblical and civil service phraseology.

II

I will now make a selection—necessarily limited—from the many issues which were raised by the Native Associations and others. I will try to recreate the impression made by the records

---

[1] Encl. in Resident Chintechi to H.C.S., 6/11/19, on S1/2065/19 and meeting of 7/1/20 on S1/210/20. I have described the relations between the W.N.N.A. and the Tonga chiefs in van Velsen, 1962.

[2] I am here mainly concerned with the regional Native Associations. There was, however, also a Native Civil Servants' Association. I intend to discuss this Association on another occasion.

of their meetings, their memoranda and correspondence with Government officials.[1] The variety and wide range of issues which attracted the members' attention and provoked their serious discussion is striking; so is the keen realization of the implications of apparently insignificant events, or decisions of Government. This in turn illustrates the lively interest which these new, leading men took in their own and the country's problems. Their achievement is the greater when one realizes that the average standard of formal education was so much lower than it is now.

Education was, indeed, among the most frequently discussed issues at meetings and the subject of numerous complaints, memoranda, etc. addressed to Government. The Associations were continuously pressing for more educational facilities, i.e. more of what they had already, namely primary education, but also secondary education.[2] At its meeting of 27 July 1920, the North Nyasa Native Association passed the following resolution:

The Associations and all other natives feel very grateful for the help which the Government has been giving [i.e. to the missions which were then, and for some time to come, still the only educational institutions] for a good many years past for the education of the natives, and since the hut tax has been raised, they will be doubly grateful if the Government would see its way to increase this grant.[3]

This resolution is typical of the many other requests from this and other Associations for increased education. It was widely realized that the 'new life' required a new system of education. This point comes out very clearly in the record of a meeting of the Mombera Native Association, held in September 1920. Mr Yesaya Chibambo pointed out that the old Ngoni system of education had been suitable for the conditions under which they were living at the time. It succeeded in moulding the children of the conquered tribes into proper Ngoni. But, he adds:

[1] It is possible that the picture is not complete. The only records in the Zomba Archives relating to the Native Associations which I have been able to find so far, are those documents which entered Government offices in the course of their administrative dealings with these Associations. There may also have been correspondence within Associations or between them.
[2] The first secondary school in Nyasaland was not opened until 1940 (in Blantyre). It was independent with its own board of governors.
[3] S1/1481/19.

The country is now in a new era with a new life, new knowledge, new resolutions, new laws and new customs which can be learnt through education; it would be foolish and ridiculous, if people of this country dislike the civilization. The old life differs greatly from the present life and it would be wise for the people of this country to aspire to have education, which alone leads them to civilization.[1]

The demand for Government to spend more money on education in view of the Africans' contribution to the country's revenue had been persistent for many years. At a conference on education in Blantyre on 16 August 1920, attended by representatives of Government and missions,[2] the Governor, Sir George Smith, observed that:

... the Native already ... contributed the larger part of the public revenue and was entitled to ask for more to be spent on his advancement ...

However, there was a growing awareness among the African leaders that the more satisfactory educational system they wanted was more than merely a question of larger Government grants. Whilst they were careful to express their appreciation for the missions' past efforts in getting the educational ball rolling, they were nevertheless of the opinion that the time had come for Government to take over this responsibility from the missions. The demand for state education was influenced by several factors. Firstly, there was the knowledge that the missions' financial means were limited. Secondly, there was the fact that the educational aims of the missions were also limited with regard to secular and/or the religious aspects of education.

At the Blantyre conference on education the representative of the Universities Mission to Central Africa, the Rev. Hand, stated that for the U.M.C.A. secular teaching had always been subordinated to the teaching of the Christian faith and practice; they were a religious and not an educational body and if they allowed Mohammedans to enter their schools without attending the religious courses, they would be abandoning their principles. As for the secular aspects of their education, the Rev. Hand remarked that the U.M.C.A. 'did not want to advance education beyond

[1] S1/210/20.   [2] S1/1494/19.

a certain point generally. Boys were apt to get swollen heads through over-education and were consequently spoilt.' These views found general support from the representatives of the Roman Catholic and the Seventh Day Adventists missions. Against this, the Governor and to a lesser extent the Scottish missionaries, Laws and Hetherwick, favoured a greater degree of Government control over education to balance the increased Government grants.

The Native Associations had a fairly clear idea of the issues involved. In their resolutions and memoranda they did not limit themselves to negative opinions about the existing conditions. On the contrary, they attempted to get to the root of the trouble and come up with suggestions for improvement.

An interesting example of this is the 'Memorandum on Native Education' submitted in January 1932, by the Representative Committee of Northern Province Native Associations to the Director of Education.[1] The memorandum, which also quoted from the minutes of meetings of the Mombera and West Nyasa Native Associations, raised the question of the inadequacy of mission education from both the educational and the religious angle. The main complaint was that the mission schools did not take education far enough and the memorandum wanted the Government to start a high school.

The Director of Education in his reply expressed his sympathy with the Committee's desire for more school places but complained that even the existing schools did not get adequate support from parents and children 'who will not in many cases attend school if he or she has to walk far'. He mentioned that, 'The majority of the children leave [school] before they complete class 8.' And he added that the Committee 'will be interested to learn that the Government school at Liwonde will have to be closed shortly unless it is more adequately supported by the Headmen and the parents.' (Liwonde lies to the north of Zomba in an area with a large Muslim population.)

The Committee replied reiterating their request that 'the Government beside grants to Missions should directly take its share in education' so as to provide education for 'those who are not

[1] NAT 12/3.

adherents of any *Church*'. On the point of pupils failing to finish their courses, the Committee suggested that this is 'not always due to apathy for education' but possibly the result of the incompetence—and often the youth—of the teachers.

Regarding the poor attendance in Government schools the Committee suggested that these schools were mostly in Mohammedan areas where 'the teaching of English characters and books to the exclusion of Arabic is considered as a sop to make them forget by relegating to the rear the reading and recital of their Islamic religious books'.

The Associations wanted Government also to take over from the missions the responsibility for medical services. Their objections were not to mission hospitals as such but rather to the fact that the missions charged for their services whereas Government hospitals gave free treatment. However, Government medical services did not escape criticism; complaints about their poor standards or the total lack of such services in certain areas were frequent.

Other subjects discussed by the Native Associations were of a less general nature and reflected their regional character. For instance, one finds in the records the Associations' concern about the alleged laxity with which tribal law is applied in the local courts. This applies particularly to laws regarding marriage. However, in 1926 the Mombera Native Association came out strongly against the custom of 'forced weeping' at funerals. It wanted 'to stamp out this old custom and have a new one instead'. The same Association also spoke out strongly against 'witch finders' who went around deceiving people by professing his or her 'bad smelling', and they advocated that the Resident should be asked to impose heavy punishments on such people when found guilty. Careless herdsmen, who allowed cattle to destroy people's gardens, were also condemned.

On the lakeshore where the Tonga were more concerned with fish than with cattle, the West Nyasa Native Association often discussed the question of Government royalties on trees. The Tonga needed large trees for their canoes and they objected to the payment of a fee for the permission to cut down a tree which they considered was after all a gift of nature.

The people of the North Nyasa District were exercised by a very different problem in the years following the First World War. It would appear that in this area in particular the recruitment for the army and carrier corps had been heavy. As a result the records of the North Nyasa Native Association of the early post-war years show all the signs of the existence of the usual post-war problems of returning soldiers and carriers, of war widows and of the proper recognition of war services in the form of medals. At a meeting of the North Nyasa Native Association in June 1919, a plea was made that war widows should be treated with leniency by Boma messengers on their tax-collecting rounds. (This was a reference to the practice of arresting women as hostages if they or their husbands failed to pay hut tax.) The minutes of this meeting would appear to contain polite hints of the disappointment experienced by returning African soldiers after the 1914–18 war (and, indeed, again after the 1939–45 war). They expected that their services as the country's *soldiers* fighting for 'King and country', would have been rewarded with greater recognition as the country's *citizens*.

III

Economic issues, together with education, worried the Associations more than most other subjects. We are after all dealing with a country with a minimum of development where the opportunities for earning cash in the locality of a person's residence either through wage employment or through the sale of produce were very severely limited. On the face of it, it would seem paradoxical that under those circumstances there should be a shortage instead of a surplus of labour available for hire. Part of the answer is of course that those looking for wage employment were not restricted to the Protectorate. And, indeed, it is well known that for several decades now many thousands of Nyasaland's men have gone abroad in search of employment.

The fact then is, that so long as there have been employers, whether Government or private, of wage labour in the Protectorate, so long have there been complaints about shortages of labour. And just as the problem of finding sufficient labour made its persistent appearance in the Government's files as far as they go back, so the discussion of poor conditions of employment, including low wages, found its way into practically every Native Association meeting.

The Africans accused Government of making up its labour deficiencies by forcing Africans into its employment very often by bringing pressure to bear on chiefs and headmen to supply Government's local agents, either the Resident (later called District Commissioner) or the officer in charge of a local section of the Public Works Department. The matter was raised in a meeting of the Mombera Native Association, held on 25 May 1927.[1] The M.N.A.'s secretary, the Rev. Charles Chinula, forwarded the minutes containing the complaint about forced labour (locally referred to as *chibaro*) to the Resident; from there they went to the Provincial Commissioner and ended up at the Secretariat, Zomba. Usually such minutes were forwarded to the P.C. for information, but it would be the Resident who would reply directly to the Native Association. Alternatively, the P.C. might communicate his reactions to the minutes to the Resident who would then reply accordingly to the Native Association. This happened when the minutes contained an important point of principle or policy.

Apparently, the complaint about *chibaro* raised in the meeting of 25 May was considered particularly important, and it was the P.C. himself who replied in a letter of 14 July 1927, to the secretary of the M.N.A.

Public Works Recruits. I think that your Association, which is composed of the educated Natives of the district, should encourage the uneducated Natives to accept work offered by the Government and not sympathize with their efforts to evade. I am sure the Principal Headmen and Councillors are not dealing harshly with the Natives, but they are only bringing pressure to bear to induce lazy men to accept work down country [i.e. in the Southern Province where the shortage of labour was always greater] on terms that are good. You interpret this pressure as harsh and unjust. Even if Chiefs have, as you say, 'forced' men to go to the Boma, there is no reason why they should have signed on for work when they get there if they did not want to work, because the Government does not force them to sign on.

[1] S1/1365/24.

On the same day the P.C. wrote to the Chief Secretary acquainting him with his views regarding *chibaro*. He repeated the argument that chiefs' pressure to get men to the Boma did not constitute *chibaro* because they were under no obligation to sign on.

The Rev. Chinula in his reply wondered how the reluctance to work for the P.W.D. could possibly be ascribed to laziness when in fact 'People throng to South Africa and elsewhere in skins and barkcloth, not afraid of being laughed at by prosperous people'. As for the P.C.'s denial that people were forced to enter employment, Chinula countered: '. . . do you yourself know how Principal Headmen and councellors get recruits. . . . I met many in gangs, tied around their necks. . . . You do not arrest, but Chiefs, afraid of losing their good name [i.e. with Government and thus lose Government support], do compel people. . . . This trouble will not cease . . . unless wages and treatment and P.W.D. can really satisfy . . .'

The P.C. in his letter commented: '. . . Chas. Chinula greatly exaggerates. It is extremely difficult for the Chiefs and Headmen to respond to a call for labour [i.e. from the Resident] unless they bring some sort of pressure to bear, and if Residents try to prevent it, the Headmen would in future make no attempt to get labour.' He made the same observation in his reply to the letter from the Resident, Mzimba, quoted above.

The M.N.A. and the Rev. Chinula had touched on a very sore spot—and they were probably well aware of it. For this question of forced 'voluntary' labour in order to satisfy P.W.D. demands had been the subject for many years of much correspondence within the Government, and between it and the Colonial Office. For example, the P.C. of the Northern Province in a letter of 4 February 1925,[1] to the Chief Secretary reported on a meeting of Residents at which the labour problem was discussed. The Residents agreed that voluntary labour for the P.W.D. could not be obtained and 'that if they had to continue to send down compulsory labour it should be legalized. The natives now realize that they have the right to refuse to engage for work which they dislike, provided they have paid their taxes.' The only solution the

[1] S2/5/25.

meeting could think of was to bring into force those sections of the District Administration (Native) Ordinance which allowed the use of compulsory labour for certain purposes. As for making employment by the P.W.D. more attractive the Residents suggested 'the issue of good blankets, better and more food and better housing' but they were dubious about the effect of an increase in wages. An increase in Government wages would tend to affect the country's whole wage structure and 'the public [presumably the European public] would object to anything which would tend to raise these wages generally'. Moreover, the Residents were of the opinion that 'The native will not go to work (there is no pressure of existence on the ordinary villager), unless it suits him, even if he is offered an increase in wages'.

In a minute relating to this correspondence the Chief Secretary addressed himself to the Governor and stated that the problem of labour shortage was an old one, but that still no solution had been found. Although 'there are thousands of natives available for this work, none will work without compulsion'. However, the Secretary of State for the Colonies had disapproved of compulsory labour for ordinary maintenance work of the P.W.D. The C.S. admitted that the Residents disliked to use their Headmen as labour recruiters, 'but I think the situation should be clearly faced and the Headmen told that the provision of labour for essential State works is one of their first duties, and that the Headman who cannot produce his share of labour is worth neither his position nor his salary'. If this were made clear to the Headmen 'the supplies of labour will be forthcoming—as they have done hitherto when Residents have been firm enough'.

The Governor in a despatch of November 1925[1] to the Secretary of State took the same view. He admitted that both Residents and headmen had resorted to compulsion to recruit labour: it had been a practice without a legal basis. The Secretary of State replied on 5 February 1926 that any extension of the powers for compulsory labour recruitment would involve 'a wide departure from the policy of His Majesty's Government'. He was unable to approve of the Governor's request to be allowed his powers of labour conscription.

[1] S1/1550/25.

It may be interesting to note the comments of the Chief Judge (Haythorne Reed) on the P.W.D. wages. In a minute of 1 January 1928, addressed to the Chief Secretary, he wrote: 'If I may say so, the situation in Nyasaland seems to be that thousands and thousands of natives prefer the danger and discomfort of trekking hundreds of miles to work in the Union, Northern and Southern Rhodesia and Tanganyika, rather than here, simply because the wages here are so inadequate.'

The Judge's words were but the echo of Chinula's. Indeed, I have dealt with this issue in some detail because it provides a striking example of the fact that the Associations and their leaders knew on the whole fairly well what they were talking about and often managed to attack the Government at its weak spots. It is also clear that there was often a good deal more uncertainty about the legality or mere correctness of some Government actions than Government officers would allow to appear to the outside. In brief, the allegations and suspicions of the Mombera Native Association and its secretary, the Rev. Chas. Chinula, have been proved substantially correct with evidence based on the Secretariat's inner workings. As for the Administrative officers out in the country, they had a tendency to consider people like Chinula and the Native Associations as meddlesome trouble-makers over whom they had so much less control than over the chiefs and headmen. This was one of the reasons why they were often so reluctant to accept the Associations as at least one form of public opinion. Instead, they made every effort to channel this *new* form of a *new* public opinion through the District Councils which were dominated by the chiefs and which were, at least theoretically, the preservers of traditional values.

Finally, perhaps the most suitable comment on the kind of labour conditions exposed by the M.N.A. and the Rev. Chinula, is: 'To speak of the dignity of labour and yet not to be ready to reward adequately the good worker, it is to speak but idle words.'[1]

This was not the only kind of labour problem which worried the Associations. They were also very concerned about the exodus of able-bodied men to the Rhodesias, South Africa and elsewhere.

[1] An Address of Welcome for the Governor from the North Nyasa Native Association, Governor's Baraza of 4/3/30, on S1/629/30.

There were two aspects of labour migration which troubled them. Firstly, there was the very fact that it should be necessary at all for all those thousands of men to go so far away from their homes for long periods in order to earn cash for the necessities of the 'new life', such as clothes, blankets, school fees and tax. All of these could only be acquired with cash but local wage-earning opportunities were rather limited and at unsatisfactory rates. Hence the numerous suggestions at meetings of the Native Associations for the promotion of cash crops and other means of reducing the need for long-distance labour migration. I will return to this point below.

Secondly, accepting the need for migratory labour, there were still the many unpleasant consequences of the men's prolonged absence which might be alleviated. The Associations did make some very useful suggestions. And although they were declared at the time to be impracticable by the Government, some were in fact later adopted.

At a meeting of the Blantyre Native Association on 14 November 1936,[1] it was suggested that the Government should take steps to arrange for compensation for workers who had been disabled whilst working in the South African mines, and for deferred pay and family remittances. They were in fact instituted sometime after the war.

The payment of the hut tax by the dependants of absentees was another problem that caused a great deal of hardship. This tax was levied per hut and whoever occupied the hut was responsible for its payment. This meant that if the husband were absent or dead, it would be his wife or widow who would have to pay the tax. But since she was often left without any source of cash, she might find herself in trouble with tax collecting messengers or indeed be taken to the Boma as a 'hostage'. We saw that this point was raised in connection with the war-widows of the North Nyasa District. The Mombera Native Association also brought this matter up several times. On one occasion the Acting Chief Secretary admitted that the practice existed but added that it was 'as distasteful to the Government as to themselves [the tax payers], but sometimes necessary'.[2] On another occasion when the M.N.A.

[1] S1/3263/23.   [2] A.C.S. to P.C., Nkata, 24/10/21, on S1/210/20.

had complained that 'the wives of the *machona* [i.e. men who have been abroad for a number of years] etc. are being taken as hostages for non-payment of hut tax', the P.C. in a letter of 21 July 1924 to the Chief Secretary denied that wives of *machona* were any longer taken as hostages for their husbands' failure to pay tax.[1]

Apparently, the practice was legal but, like the P.C. quoted above, many in the Government disliked the practice, particularly that of taking women hostages. However, one suspects that the practice was more wide-spread than many Government officers realized or wanted to admit.[2] Indeed, as late as 1935 its alleged existence led to an editorial in the *Nyasaland Times* (26 February 1935) and to a question in the House of Commons (reported in the *Nyasaland Times* of 25 April 1935). Just as in the case of the recruitment of compulsory labour necessity tempered legal scruples, so here it tempered moral scruples.

Whatever the official attitude might have been, the Africans seemed to be quite certain that the practice existed. They probably realized that as long as the 'necessity' was there, there would be little hope of having the practice abolished. Instead, at a meeting of the M.N.A. in July 1925,[3] it was suggested that the Government consult the 'Rhodesian Government' (i.e. Southern Rhodesian Government?) about the possibility of getting Nyasaland workers in Rhodesia to send their tax to Zomba. The Chief Secretary's reaction to this suggestion was that 'The Government of Southern Rhodesia would not be prepared to assist in the collection of Nyasaland hut taxes'.[4] In fact, some such arrangement was agreed to many years later (I think it was in the late 1930's).

People intending to go abroad—generally to seek work—had to get a pass from the Boma. At a meeting in May 1926,[5] people complained that 'instead of getting passes free of charge, people are compelled to work for some hours, before they get the desired passes, and so the Association asks: 'Is there a law that a person before getting a pass should work for some hours or a day before he can get it? . . . The Association humbly requests the local Resident to explain whether or not there is a law, so that all those

[1] S1/1365/24.   [2] S1/377/24 deals with this practice.
[3] S1/1365/24.   [4] S1/1365/24.   [5] *loc. cit.*

who complain may be advised to be content.' The P.C., Nkata, forwarded this meeting's minutes to the Chief Secretary with a covering letter dated 29 June 1926, in which he commented: 'It has for a long time been the custom at Mzimba to make applicants for passes weed grass whilst they wait for the passes to be filled in, otherwise they sit outside chattering and become a nuisance. If there are many applicants, they may be detained in this way from 9.0 a.m. to noon.' The Acting Chief Secretary's reply of 28 July 1926 to the P.C. stated: 'His Excellency cannot approve of the custom of requiring applicants for passes to weed grass on the station while they are waiting for their business to receive attention.'

Any form of centralized government experiences the difficulty of maintaining effective control over its agents who operate away from the centre. As long as its agents efficiently fulfil their tasks (e.g. forward the required amount of labour or tax), the centre is not likely to be too strict as to whether its agents are also always acting within the bounds of legality. Central government usually rests content provided its agents remain loyal and do not provoke political disaffection among their charges through too much efficiency and too little legality. However, it is the citizens who will exploit any means available to them to force the agents to act legally. One way of doing this is to keep the lines of communication open in both directions between the centre of government and the citizens. This assumes that the citizens are confident that the central government is interested in their well-being even if its agents are not.

That to me is the significance of the three issues of compulsory labour, women as hostages for tax and 'passes for grass'. In all three instances ordinary citizens managed to alert the Secretariat that its agents were in the process of sacrificing legality for the sake of efficiency. This had been possible because the citizens had managed to reach the Secretariat whom they assumed were interested in their welfare. That the lines of communication between the citizens and the Secretariat were still open in both directions, was not a matter of chance; it was the result of a long continous battle on the part of the Native Associations. I will presently describe some aspects of this battle.

The Native Associations were not merely interested in minimizing the harmful effects of labour migration. They also wanted to minimize the incidence of labour migration itself by creating the kind of economic conditions which would enable men to earn their cash locally and live at home. To that end they rarely lost an opportunity to impress upon the Government the desirability of actively promoting cash crops, especially cotton and tobacco. The Associations clearly did not expect charity; there was no question of expecting cash crops on a silver platter. They merely wanted Government to help to create the right conditions for commercial farming: agricultural instructors, markets, roads and so forth.

The following data regarding tobacco growing give some idea of the Africans' desires and frustrations.

In 1932 African tobacco growers in the Chiradzulu District brought to the notice of Government, through a resolution of the Chiradzulu District Native Association,[1] the unsatisfactory state of affairs in the markets where they had to sell their tobacco. The Director of Agriculture drafted a reply to the C.D.N.A. in which he admitted the validity of some of the complaints and promised some improvements including the setting up of special markets. This draft was submitted to the Governor for his approval, which he gave.

The Director of Agriculture was also chairman of the Native Tobacco Board and it was in that capacity that he declared his intention of opening tobacco markets in the Southern Province. These markets would be run by the Native Tobacco Board which had been operating such markets in the Northern Province. This would have been the first time it had markets in the south. However, the scheme fell through. In a letter, dated 9 August 1932, addressed to the Acting Chief Secretary, the chairman of the Native Tobacco Board wrote:

It is admitted on all hands that the markets are desirable, particularly as a means of ensuring to the grower a cash return for his efforts to maintain or improve the quality of his leaf, but their establishment has met with opposition from the buyers [who, if I am correct, were mostly, if not all, European], who contend that under present con-

[1] Quoted in P.C., Blantyre, to H.C.S., 5/7/32, on S1/1598/29.

ditions the S[outhern] P[rovince] industry cannot carry the extra overhead expenses involved in the markets. [The passage 'who contend . . .
the markets' was marked A in the margin.] The Board has therefore
decided to postpone the question of establishing S.P. markets and to
re-open it in a year's time.

The letter suggested that the Chief Secretary in his reply to the
Chiradzulu District Native Association should inform the Association of his decision regarding the markets.

The Acting Chief Secretary's comment on this letter, in a
minute addressed to the Governor was: 'The only argument
adduced—at A . . .—does not appear very convincing, unless we
are to be told later that it applied equally to the N[orthern]
P[rovince]. I should have thought that if the remote markets in
the N.P. can stand the overhead charges, those in the S.P. also
could. The advice of the Board must, however, presumably, be
accepted.' The Governor minuted back to the A.C.S. on 12
August 1932: 'Has A . . . been established to the satisfaction of the
N.T.B. by facts and figures, as opposed to vague generalizations?'
The chairman of the Board replied in the affirmative. He explained that the establishment of the markets would involve the
buyers in too much extra expenditure. He added that the quantity
of the Northern Province tobacco was four times that of the
Southern Province and that the quality was better.

One is inclined to share the apparent suspicion of the minute
writers in the Secretariat as to the real reasons for the reluctance
of the tobacco buyers to regularize the buying of African tobacco,
particularly when one considers that neither of the two crucial
bodies controlling the production and the marketing of African
tobacco (i.e. the Native Tobacco Board and the Nyasaland
Native Tobacco Exporters' Association) had a single African
representative. This fact may add significance to the following
minute from the Acting Chief Secretary addressed to the Governor. This minute referred to the one from the Chairman of
the Native Tobacco Board, from which I have just quoted. 'I
may say that whenever this question comes up for discussion at
meetings of the Board I have always strongly advocated the establishment of markets, but have failed to convince the other members of the possibility of doing so, although they all admit the

desirability.' It should be noted that the Native Tobacco Board
consisted of white officials and non-officials. Clearly, the Government felt unable to push this matter further and the Acting
Governor in his reply of 16 August 1932 to the above minute
wrote: 'Accept the Board's advice.'

From the complaints raised by the C.D.N.A. at a meeting held
on 12 May 1934, it would appear that little progress had been
made towards the solution of the problems discussed at the meeting two years previously. Some of the following statements show
that the African tobacco growers also had their doubts whether
they got a square deal from the buyers or, for that matter, from
the Government.

The minutes of the May 1934, meeting[1] recorded:

Mr J. Chiwayula stated how hard it was this year for the people to get
good prices for their tobacco. Some years ago the buyers were saying
that tobacco was not properly cured, then we asked the Government
to give us people who could teach us how this could be done. Still the
buyers are saying, the tobacco was not good, what could be the trouble
now with the supervisors that they know their business? We ask that
the buyers inform the seller how much a man's tobacco was worth . . .
it was moved and seconded to put before the Government the following:
that markets be limited and properly restricted; that Native Authorities
have their capitaos at each market to see that justice is done to growers;
that Government should inform people of what other economic crops
to grow besides tobacco. This was unanimously carried.

The Executive of the same Native Association met on 22
December 1934. The resolutions of this meeting were communicated to the Chief Secretary in a letter from the secretary, Dr
D. S. Malekebu. Again, the Government's attention was drawn
to the difficulty 'to find money'. The District Commissioner commenting on these resolutions wrote: 'The past year was not a
difficult one [for finding money] for the Chiradzulu Natives. The
tobacco industry alone brought approximately £9,500 to the
Chiradzulu District. The best year in this respect the district has
ever had.' However, the total population of the District at that
time was estimated at 80,000[2] so that the value of the tobacco
crop represented only about 2s. per head of the total population.

[1] S1/1598/29.   [2] See Murray, p. 169.

A year later, the Blantyre Native Association at its meeting on 25 February 1936,[1] protested against the Government rules regarding the uprooting of tobacco:

When the natives were preparing their gardens the Native Tobacco Board did not attempt to give or measure areas for each native to plant his tobacco in order to control the over-production, and now after the natives have done their utmost, Government gives power to uproot native tobacco plants . . . [These are not] well-considered rules . . . [and] will also cause much dissatisfaction and people to look with mistrust to Government policy. It would also happen, however, that sometimes the persons so empowered will cause to uproot native tobacco from even personal misunderstanding with the natives, since the powers are so wide.

After pointing out that on several occasions the Governor had encouraged the people to clear larger gardens, the letter continued:

Now when the natives tried to enlarge their gardens to get enough for their needs, Government order that their crops should be uprooted if they have large areas is therefore not understood. We also ask the Government to give us native representatives on Native Tobacco Boards, as we want more protection for native growers, so that we may understand better such rules and thus make us trust the Government more.

This request was passed on to the Board for its consideration. The minutes of the Board's meeting on 20 March 1936 recorded that the Board had 'no objection to native representation on the Board if Government considered it desirable'. This decision was communicated by the Chief Secretary in a letter to the B.N.A. in which it was also stated that the tobacco uprooting rules lapsed on the 31 March and 'if other rules with a similar object are considered desirable in the future, proper consideration will be given to the views of the Blantyre Native Association'.

The Chief Secretary's letter was discussed at a meeting of the B.N.A. on 9 April 1937, and Mr J. K. Somanje was nominated as the B.N.A.'s representative on the Native Tobacco Board. However, the Acting Chief Secretary, in a letter dated 31 July 1937, informed the Secretary of the B.N.A. that

[1] S1/3263/23.

the Acting Governor has decided not to proceed with the proposal for the appointment of a native representative as a member of the Native Tobacco Board. I am to add, however, that the Chairman of the Native Tobacco Board has been advised of the desirability of inviting a suitable native representative to attend meetings of the Native Tobacco Board for the consideration of specific questions which may arise from time to time.

I have not been able to find any indication of the reasons for this sudden reversal except for a general but often veiled opposition on the part of European planters to Africans growing tobacco in the tribal areas lest increased prosperity in these areas should interfere with the African villagers' willingness to work for wages on the European estates. It would appear from the Native Associations' records which I have been able to find, that the subject of representation on the Native Tobacco Board was not pursued.

The Associations frequently voiced the people's desire for Government assistance in creating opportunities for 'finding the money', as we noticed in one of the quotations above. Government control over and assistance in the production and marketing of cash crops was one of the themes of the Associations' records. But not all demands for markets were as ambitious as those of the Southern Province tobacco growers. Particularly in the north, Africans frequently asked for simple markets where people could sell whatever surplus food crops they might have available to raise, say, money for tax.[1]

Similarly, there was a constant demand for more roads which together with markets would open the country up for greater economic activity. The Blantyre Native Association minutes of 25 September 1937[2] indicate that this Association at one stage even attempted to build a road itself. But apparently this was a fiasco and it lost money over it.

Other examples of the Associations' concern with economic problems are complaints about the inefficiency of the post office at Livingstonia and an objection to 'the new and *Heavy Duties*

[1] See, for instance, the Minutes of the Mombera Native Association of 1 and 2 September 1920, on S1/210/20.
[2] S1/3263/23.

charged on goods imported for native use and on goods exported'.[1]

IV

It is clear, then, that the Native Associations wanted a hand in the ordering of their own welfare. This meant not only that they were concerned with conditions of employment, the establishment and marketing of crops and so forth, but also that they felt free to comment on legislation directly affecting the majority of the population. This further meant that they wanted to be kept informed of any new legislation. And, finally, they were most anxious that their views, which they considered to be representative of the views of the bulk of the people, should reach the centre of Government (i.e. the Secretariat in Zomba) and should not be held back from the Secretariat by agents of the central Government interposed between the people and the Government at Zomba.

A striking example of protest at unjust laws is found in a letter, dated 29 September 1930, from the secretary, Isaac Mkondowe, of the North Nyasa Native Association, addressed to the Chief Secretary.[2] It complained that a new law concerning offences against morality (No. 22 of 1929, Section 129) was discriminatory in that it penalized illicit sexual intercourse between a white woman and black man. This measure was intended for the protection of the white women but it did not extend similar protection to black women vis-à-vis white men. A letter, dated 29 December 1930, from the secretary of the Representative Committee of Northern Province Native Associations, Zomba, and addressed to the Chief Secretary 'for the consideration of his Excellency the Governor', supported the request for an amendment of this law.

These letters caused some consternation and, indeed, indignation in the Secretariat. There followed a discussion, in the minutes, within the Secretariat on the question of how minutes

[1] Both came from the North Nyasa Association, in minutes of 9 August 1926, and 13 March 1935, respectively, on S1/1481/19.
[2] S1/1481/19.

and letters from the Native Associations should be brought to the notice of the Government. The conclusion was that such communications should use the proper administrative channels. This conclusion was embodied in a letter from the Acting Chief Secretary to the Provincial Commissioners of the Northern, Central and Southern Provinces, dated 30 January 1931. It recalled a letter of November 1926, which 'laid down the procedure to be adopted in regard to the activities of Native Associations. His Excellency is of the opinion that it is the duty of the better educated natives to place the benefit of their education at the disposal of their fellows in general and of their Chiefs in particular, and he considers that any question of policy which it is desired to bring to his notice should pass through the channels of the District Councils and not only through those of the Native Associations.' The Provincial Commissioners were therefore urged to inform the Native Associations in their areas that although they could 'continue to send copies of the minutes of their meetings to the District Commissioner, their resolutions will not receive the Governor's consideration unless they are supported by their respective District Councils'. This appears to have been the first official response to the Associations' letters about the new penal code: an attempt to restrict the Associations' direct access to central Government.

In the meantime, on 27 January 1931, the District Commissioner for North Nyasa commented on the Association's remarks in a letter to the P.C. of the Northern Province. The D.C. located the source of 'this propaganda' at Livingstonia, naming an African minister who 'possesses a copy of the Penal Code, as he subscribes to the Government *Gazette*, and has it carefully bound'. The letter continued: 'The request does not spring from any moral standpoint, but from one of equality and equal rights. . . . At the back of their minds is an intolerance of the European and their creed is "Africa for the Africans".' The writer thought that this was at least in part due to the wrong kind of education at Livingstonia in the past but also to close contact with South Africa. He considered this new law unnecessary for Nyasaland. He considered that 'the bare fact of the morals of white women being discussed by Native Associations is deplorable . . . the time for equality in matters sexual has not arrived and the Government holds itself free to enact whatever legislation it considers fit and proper for the protection and punishment of the women of its own race'. Finally, the D.C. argued that African women were adequately protected under other sections of the Code.[1]

The P.C. enclosed this letter in one of his own to the Chief Secretary. The P.C. signified his general agreement with the D.C.'s comments and suggested that 'in view of the fact that the matter has been taken up by other Native Associations, . . . a reply should be drafted by the Attorney-General'. He also informed the Chief Secretary that: 'The irregularity of his [i.e. of the secretary of the N.N.N.A.] action in transmitting the Association's Minutes to you instead of to this office through the District Commissioner has been brought to the notice of the Association's Secretary.'

These letters were forwarded to the Attorney-General who commented in a minute addressed to the Chief Secretary:

I fully appreciate the logic of the Association's Minute if they assume the absolute equality of races.

I associate myself with the arguments [of the D.C.] . . . and also with the P.C.'s reply, while doubting the policy of so baldly stating the fact that the ruling race may take any action it thinks fit to protect its women folk.

I am of opinion that the Association should be informed that the Penal Code is a model code for all the East African colonies. That experience in other colonies has convinced the Secretary of State of the necessity of such a provision, though the occasion for putting such a provision into operation may not actually have arisen in Nyasaland.

This minute reached the Governor *via* the Chief Secretary and the former ordered that: 'The P.C. should be asked to reply accordingly.' The P.C.'s reply to the N.N.N.A. incorporated almost *verbatim* the last paragraph in the Attorney-General's minute.

I have described this episode in some detail since it highlights

---

[1] The unequal treatment in law of the sexual relations between a white woman and a black man on the one hand, and between a white man and a black woman on the other hand had been a subject of protest not only in the meetings of the Associations but also in public meetings with Government officials in the Mombera, West Nyasa and many other Districts.

several points of interest in relation to the Native Associations as pressure groups.

I quoted earlier on in this paper some of the aims and rules of the Mombera and West Nyasa Native Associations and we noted that 'In order to follow intelligently and loyally the doings of the Government' they wanted to be supplied with the Government *Gazette*. Apparently, the supply of the *Gazette* was not always very regular and hence the frequent reminders from these and other Associations in their minutes and letters to Government. One cannot help feeling a certain, covert reluctance on the part of Government officials in their response to such requests. The idea that the business of administration and government should be left to the Protectorate Government and its officials without the meddlesome interference from the 'better educated natives' and their Associations, seemed to be firmly held by at least some individuals. This is clear from the D.C.'s remark quoted above in relation to the Rev. Manda's 'carefully bound' copy of the Penal Code.

Moreover, the new élite did not merely want themselves to be acquainted with the laws under which they were living; they desired that those who did not read English should also have this opportunity. Thus the Representative Committee of Northern Province Native Associations in a letter,[1] dated 18 July 1936, to the Chief Secretary referred to the recently published *Land and Agricultural Bank Report*. This report dealing with land had naturally roused a great deal of interest and suspicion in a situation where land was a very touchy problem, especially in the Southern Province. Referring to the report's recommendation that Europeans should be able to acquire Native Trust Land on leases of up to 99 years, the Representative Committee felt 'all the more the need and necessity of a vernacular publication of the Native Trust Land Order in Council, so that natives may know where they stand in the matter'. This request set off a prolonged discussion on the pros and cons of such a translation both within the Secretariat, in minutes, and outside, e.g. in correspondence with missionary language experts. Apart from the obvious problem of translating English legal phraseology into the various vernac-

[1] NAT 12/3.

ulars, another point which kept appearing in the Secretariat minutes was the question why the 'educated natives' should want translations of this or other laws.

The paternalistic attitude of many of the administrators went so deep that they completely missed the point of the originators of the idea, namely that a large a number of the ruled, who were literate in English or any other language, should be given an opportunity to familiarize themselves with the rulers' laws. However, there were others who saw some merit in the idea even if only for tactical reasons. For instance, the Acting P.C. of the Southern Province, Eric Smith, minuted on 27 July 1936: 'Still any refusal in such an important matter to Natives as the Native Trust Lands O. in C. might be viewed [by the Natives] with unfounded suspicion and I submit that the request of the Native Association for the translation . . . be approved.' This, again, shows that the Associations' views were frequently respected. The Governor, in a minute of 2 August 1936 to the Chief Secretary, took a similar line: 'The Order-in-Council is so important, that I think a vernacular translation would be a good thing . . .' Finally, after many technical difficulties of translation, the Native Trust Lands Order-in-Council was printed, in the latter half of 1937, in the Yao, Nyanja and Tumbuka languages.

The demand for greater African participation in public ceremonies was also an expression of the same desire for a greater recognition of the fact that it was after all the Africans who formed the large majority of the population. For instance, Levi Z. Mumba writing on behalf of the Representative Committee to the Chief Secretary in a letter dated 10 April 1935[1] wondered why Africans were not allowed to play a more prominent role during the celebrations on the occasion of the King's Birthday or the swearing-in of a new Governor 'who is specially appointed' to protect the interests of the Africans.

We thank the Government for the consideration given to chiefs and headmen on this day but being deficient in education we are not sure that they appreciate the importance of the event without the assistance of their educated men. . . . That such an important Government function should ignore or fail to find a place for even its few senior

[1] NAT 12/3.

African officers . . . including some well-to-do and respectable Africans, who can be of help in explaining the meaning of the occasion to others later, has created the wrong idea that they are not wanted there, and adds to their perplexities.

The Committee added that they were aware that

natives are considered as children in these matters, and so they are, but it is as children when they can better be initiated into what is demanded of them when they grow up.

We see here the Committee making a distinction between the greater sophistication of the 'educated men' on the one hand, and the simplicity of chiefs and headmen on the other hand. A similar contrast is drawn by a Government officer in the letter quoted above (p. 400) in which it was stated that the Governor held that it was 'the duty of the better educated natives to place the benefit of their education at the disposal of . . . their Chiefs in particular.' From this letter and related correspondence it was clear that the Government, or at any rate a certain number of Government officials, wished to limit the effectiveness of the Associations as spokesmen of certain sections of African public opinion, by deny-ing them direct access to the centre of Government, i.e. the Gov-ernor and the Secretariat, and forcing them to work through the Native Authorities or the District Councils which were largely the chiefs' preserves. The Native Associations had always fought very hard against any attempt to restrict their right—as citizens, if not as Associations—of direct access to the Secretariat. One might call it 'the battle of the minutes' because the battle was generally fought over the question of the proper channels for the transmission of the Associations' minutes, resolutions and letters to the Secretariat. This 'battle of the minutes' is a very frequently recurring theme in the records of all the Native Associations and its outcome was bound vitally to affect the efficacy of the Native Associations as pressure groups.

The basic issue from the Associations' point of view was that they wanted the Governor to know what was happening to 'his children' and that they were afraid that the Government's agents such as D.C.'s and P.C.'s might prevent this knowledge from reaching him. The following few quotations illustrate this point clearly.

In a letter of 26 November 1933, addressed to the Chief Secretary,[1] the Representative Committee of Northern Province Native Associations took up the point about 'the duty of the better educated natives', made in the letter mentioned earlier (p. 400). After pointing out that in the twenty years of their existence the Native Associations had always placed 'the benefit of their education at the disposal of their fellows and of the chiefs in particular' and that Native Associations, in contrast to Chiefs' Councils, were 'fully representative of all classes of natives', the Committee continued:

Chiefs' Councils will for a long time remain conservative in their aims, while Native Associations on account of their education are aspirants to a progressive policy. Our Committee therefore consider that the existence of Native Associations, apart from any Chiefs' Councils are a necessary adjunct for expression of opinion and they think their case is well supported . . . [i.e. by the minutes of meetings of the West Nyasa and the Zomba Native Associations].

With regard to the submission of questions of policy for His Excellency's consideration [see p. 400 above], as far as we know these are sent through the District Commissioners and Provincial Commissioners of the districts concerned who may make what comments they deem necessary, but Native Associations insist that their minutes should not be mutilated en route and that they should be submitted intact to His Excellency as they fear that His Excellency the Governor does not know all what he should know about his children the Africans.

A Secretariat minute addressed to the Chief Secretary suggested that the reply to this letter should simply restate the old policy, namely that the proper medium between Africans and Government in view of indirect rule was the Native Administration, i.e. the chiefs. On 21 March 1934, a letter along these lines was sent to the Representative Committee. The Chief Secretary, in his minute to the Governor, Sir Harold Kittermaster, supported this line of argument. The Governor, however, did not support it. Eventually, the following compromise was adopted: the proper channel of communication would still lie through the Native Administration but at the same time the Associations and the Representative Committee would be allowed to send their

[1] NAT 12/3.

minutes etc. directly to the Secretariat which would, however, merely formally acknowledge receipt, whilst if any action was called for, this, again, would still be taken through the Native Administration.

Because there had been so many changes in policy on this point in the course of years, it was decided to issue a circular along these lines which was sent to all Native Associations. However, about a year later (in May 1935) the Governor returned to the subject in a minute addressed to the Chief Secretary: 'I am not sure whether I agree with the circular issued last year. It is a difficult subject.' In the same minute he instructed the Chief Secretary to arrange for Levi Z. Mumba to see him. Mumba had written to the S.P.C. asking for an interview in order to have some points in the circular clarified. Mumba had his interview with the Governor on 12 May 1935. According to the Governor's notes on this interview, Mumba had two objections to conducting all business through the Native Authorities: the one was that they were more conservative and the other was 'that the Associations being in closer touch with Europeans were better able to express opinions in a comprehensible way than the N.A. [Native Authority] but that the Associations got no opportunity of speaking at N.A. meetings'. On the former point the Governor admitted that there was some truth in it, but disputed that all Native Authorities were conservative 'and I was able to quote to Mumba (in Angoni) the Zulu equivalent of *festina lente*. It should be the work of the more educated natives to induce the N.A. to move forward. In any case it is highly impolitic to act in such a way as to force these Associations into an attitude of opposition as has happened in Kenya particularly among the Kikuyu. We should try to use them by encouraging their activity if possible on useful lines.' With regard to the second point the Governor replied that he could see what Mumba meant, but he was not sure whether he was correct.

This new conciliatory approach (which would appear to have been largely the result of Kittermaster's influence) was communicated to the president of the Representative Committee in a letter dated 20 May 1935. The enthusiastic reply from the Committee, signed by their secretary, Levi Z. Mumba, shows how important this victory in the 'battle of the minutes' was to them: 'Words

would fail me to express our deep gratitude to His Excellency for
the direct and unhampered access to the Government on native
matters which he has allowed to my Committee ... a move which
is further proof of the Government's readiness to hear all sides of
native feeling and opinion.'

I have only been able to touch upon a limited selection of the
multifarious activities of the Native Associations. Sometimes their
pressures upon Government showed results and sometimes their
pressures were in vain. But if they succeeded at all as pressure
groups it was largely due to the fact that the direct line of communication between the Associations—the 'new men'—and the
Secretariat had remained open. I have suggested that this was not
a happy accident but rather the result of the Associations' 'battle
of the minutes'.

V

Before I summarize the foregoing account of early pressure
groups in Malawi I want to emphasize that it is essentially a preliminary note. Moreover my main concern has been to provide as
much detail about a secular protest movement as is possible within
the compass of a short chapter. (Shepperson and Price in *Independent African* have concentrated on protest movements of a religious
nature.) The field of African political pressure groups in the early
days of colonialism has so far hardly been explored—certainly in
East and Central Africa—by historians, whilst political scientists
do not seem to have turned their attention to it at all yet.

Before one can venture generalizations and begin to think comparatively on an Africa-wide—or even wider—scale, a body of
basic descriptive data is needed. The stimulus for the research on
which this paper is based stemmed from a feeling of the inadequacy of the generalizations and/or assumptions which I
have found in the literature. I am referring to the all too frequent
premise that African tribal societies were so baffled by and so
incapable of dealing with the political might and sophistication of
the European powers which had arrived on the African scene that
political interaction between the new European rulers and the traditional African rulers and the African masses was an asymmetric

one of, on the one hand, the Europeans creating all the pressure
for the Africans to conform with the aims and desires of the new
white rulers, and, on the other hand, the Africans *either* accepting these new forces without too much demur *or*, at the other
extreme, putting up armed revolt as the only alternative. This
approach, this basic premise is quite explicit in Hanna's writings
on Central Africa.[1] It is also present, but much more by implication in, for instance, Barnes' book on politics in changing Ngoni
society.[2]

Although this paper has been largely descriptive and confined
to Malawi, it raises several issues of more general interest. Indeed,
the starting point of the paper was to draw attention to the danger
of assuming that the political conditions in all colonial situations
were such that political protest could only be expressed in the form
of religious protest, i.e. sectarian movements. Malawi's early
colonial history shows a comparatively successful *secular* political
protest movement of a non-violent nature.

The success of this movement was the more remarkable considering the fact that it started within twenty years of the establishment (in 1891) of the Protectorate Government. In other words,
within twenty years of their first contact with a modern bureaucracy there arose voluntary associations which were organized
with the express purpose of creating a popular counter-force to
this bureaucracy. It should also be remembered that this movement, which was non-tribal and, indeed, very soon inter-tribal,
occurred in a country with a large number of small tribal units
which had hardly begun to be welded into one national unit. I
have pointed out that these associations were consciously anti-
traditional and in some respects suspicious of the conservative influence of the chiefs. The leaders of these Native Associations
were quite explicit in their desire to create a new society—they
were very much 'new men' themselves. Hence their preoccupa-
tion with increasing the amount and improving the quality of
formal education.

I raised the question why the initiative in this political protest
movement should have come from the north rather than the

[1] Hanna, 1956 and 1960.   [2] Barnes, *passim*.

south. It is and was the south more than the north which provided the classic conditions for political protest. It was in the south that there was great pressure on the land, a pressure, moreover, caused by European alienation of land and further aggravated by massive African immigration from Mozambique (this immigration was encouraged by the European farmers). At the same time there was proportionately less African emigration to the employment centres of the Rhodesias and South Africa than in the northern part of the country. In the north there was no land problem and, as a result of the scarcity of European settlement, there was less economic, political and administrative interference in the life of the African population. I have raised the problem but I have so far not been able to find a satisfactory explanation. For instance, I do not consider that the larger proportion of labour migrants from the north meant that the north was more susceptible to political influence from, say, South Africa. There were, after all, many labour migrants in South Africa from the southern parts of Malawi also.

It would appear that in Malawi organized political protest appeared earlier than in the other Central African territories. (It is possible, however, that similar political stirrings took place elsewhere at the same time but that they are still awaiting description.) If this is so, it might be argued that this early political activity was due to the country's Protectorate status. But this would leave us with the question why we do not find similar activities in the neighbouring Protectorate of Northern Rhodesia (now Zambia). Here again, I am unable to offer a satisfactory answer to this question. However, there is one factor which may explain the success of the pressure groups in Malawi and which was only *indirectly* the result of being a Protectorate: and that was the fact that there were many Africans employed in the civil service in jobs which in other countries (e.g. Southern Rhodesia and, possibly to a lesser extent, in Zambia) were filled by Europeans. Thus in Malawi, even in the early days, Africans and their leaders had access to information as to the Government's political intentions and its economic policies which is a *conditio sine qua non* for a successful anti-Government political organization.

Implicit in my description is a refutation of the very frequent assumption that African organizations (especially political organizations) which were a response to the new economic and bureaucratic conditions which followed colonial occupation, were wholly the result of a process of *borrowing* the appropriate organizational techniques from the new white rulers. I do not have the space here to discuss this problem in detail but I merely want to throw out the suggestion that many of the methods, tactics and techniques used by these early political leaders were the result of (if I may borrow a term from the argument about the origin of man) polygenesis—in other words, they arose 'spontaneously' from the very economic and political conditions in which they found themselves. An interesting example of this is a strike among the teachers at Bandawe mission which occurred in the early 1890's. I have found no evidence that this strike was the result of 'agitation' and organization by men who had learned the technique in, say, South Africa. Rather, it was a spontaneous, and indeed, obvious reaction by teachers in what one might call a 'full-employment' situation, knowing that they were irreplaceable in the short term and knowing that their services were much needed by their employers. In more humdrum situations of daily life one would say that they were merely playing 'hard to get'.

I have described in some detail the very great importance which the leaders, and their followers, of the Native Associations attached to maintaining direct lines of communication with the Central Government. This was due to their strong conviction that the Governor and the people in the Secretariat were genuinely concerned about the welfare of the masses (in this case the Africans). They considered the Governor as their real 'father' but thought that his local agents were too involved in the local situation to be fair and objective: they were at best 'stepfathers'. A similar belief is very strikingly and repeatedly expressed in the late Patrice Lumumba's book *Congo, My Country*. Here too we find that he and his political colleagues refused to believe that all the disabilities, humiliations, etc., which the Congolese Africans suffered at the hands of the local administrators were the intended policy of the Central Government or, even if it had been, that it could have been the policy of the Belgian home Government. And hence, again, their repeated attempts to get through with their complaints to either the Congo Central Government or the Belgian home Government.

Finally: I have drawn attention to the fact that in Malawi, just as in other colonial territories, the beginnings of the early nationalist movements were rebellious in character rather than revolutionary.[1] That is, they accepted the prevailing political structure but tried to obtain fairer opportunities within it. They simply wanted a fairer share of the cake but there was no question or wanting the whole cake and doing the sharing out themselves; that came later in Malawi as elsewhere.

One final point by way of postscript relating to my sources. As regards unpublished documents my account has been limited to a consideration of the records in the National Archives in Zomba. These records, generally, start in 1919 due to a fire in the Secretariat which destroyed most files. At the moment there are no other sources available to me which might explain the wider context (and especially the timing) of the rise of the Native Associations. However my search for documents and other sources of information is continuing and I hope to be able to describe and analyse Malawi's early political activities at greater length in the future.

BIBLIOGRAPHY

I

The following documents are all in the National Archives, Zomba, Malawi.

S1/1481/19 North Nyasa Native Association.
S1/2065/19 West Nyasa Native Association.
S1/210/20 Mombera Native Association.
S1/1365/24 Mombera Native Association.
S1/1598/29 Chiradzulu District Native Association.
S1/3263/23. Native Associations in the Southern Parts of Nyasaland.
NAT 12/3 Representative Committee for Northern Province Native Associations.
S1/262B/37 Royal Commission Memoranda from Associations and Public Bodies.
S1/1494/19 Education.
S1/629/30 Governor's Barazas.
S1/377/24 Tax Defaulters—Taking of Women as Hostages.

[1] For a discussion of this distinction, cf. Gluckman, pp. 109–37

S1/1550/25 *P.W.D. Labour—Inability of P.C., Central Province, to fulfil Requirements.*
S2/5/25 *Method of Recruitment of Labour for the P.W.D.*

II

J. A. Barnes, *Politics in a Changing Society*, Oxford University Press, London, 1954.

Emigrant Labour, Report of the Committee Appointed to Enquire into, Government Printer, Zomba, 1936.

M. Gluckman, *Custom and Conflict in Africa*, Basil Blackwell, Oxford, 1955.

R. Gray, *The Two Nations*, Oxford University Press, London, 1960.

A. J. Hanna, *The Beginnings of Nyasaland and North-Eastern Rhodesia, 1859–95*, Clarendon Press, Oxford, 1956.

A. J. Hanna, *The Story of the Rhodesias and Nyasaland*, Faber & Faber, London, 1960.

Land Report, 1921, Nyasaland Land Commission, Government Printer, Zomba, 1922.

Land Report, 1946, Report by Sir Sidney Abrahams, Government Printer, Zomba, 1947.

Patrice Lumumba, *Congo, My Country*, Pall Mall Press, London, 1962.

S. S. Murray, *A Handbook of Nyasaland*, Crown Agents for the Colonies, London, 1932.

George Shepperson, and Thomas Price, *Independent African*, Edinburgh University Press, 1958.

B. Sundkler, *Bantu Prophets in South Africa*, 2nd edn., Oxford University Press, 1961.

J. van Velsen, 'The Establishment of the Administration in Tongaland', *Historians in Tropical Africa*, Proceedings of the Leverhulme Inter-Collegiate History Conference, University College of Rhodesia and Nyasaland, Salisbury, 1962.

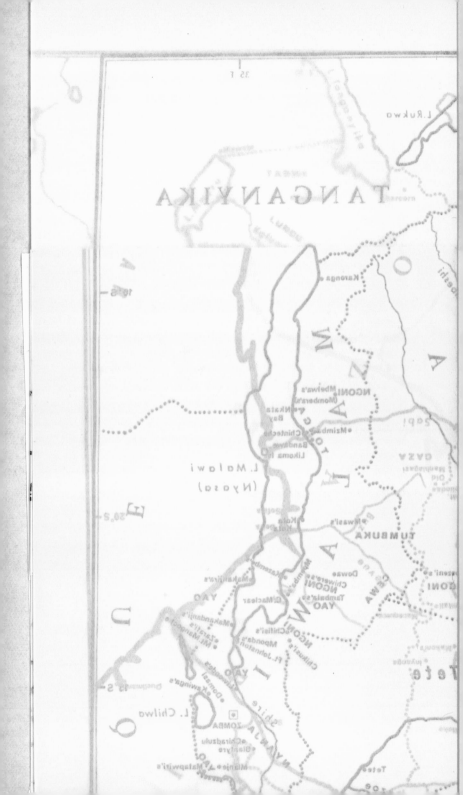

INDEX

Alternative spellings are placed in ordinary parentheses; descriptions and definitions in square brackets.

Kazembe—*contd.*
  Johnston cited on, 363
  deposed, 363
Khama (Kgama) [Bechuana ruler],
  co-operates with British, 67, 70
  boundary with Lobengula, 72
  character of Br. protectorate over,
    75, 184
  Pioneers road, 89
  Lochner Concession, 266–7
  juridical status, 272, 296
Khami [ruins site], culture, xvi, 3–4,
    10, 11, 12, 18, 21, 22, 23, 24, 26
  pottery, 4, 5, 6, 14, 16, 21
  Rozwi, 3–4, 23, 103
  Mwari cult, 103
Kololo (Makololo) [people], conquer
  Lozi, xix, xxx, 253, 257
Korekore [people], xxxiii
  oral tradition on Mutapa dynasty,
    31
  dynasty, 37
  and Rebellion, 120
  religious aspects of political succes-
    sion among, chap. 6
Koyi, William, 315
Kunzwi [Shona chief], rôle in Rebel-
  lion, 125, 131
Kuta (Khotla, Kgotla) [Lozi state
  council], 256, 257, 258, 265, 266,
  277, 282, 296, 297
Kwengo [people], pushed back by
  Lozi, 256–7

Labour Migration
  Bemba, xxix
  Lozi, 297
  Ndebele, 92–3, 172, 176, 190, 192–3
  Ngoni: Mpezeni, 330–1; Southern,
    xxv, 322–4, 369
  Nyasaland, 350–1, 358, 372, 390 ff.,
    409
Labrecque, E. D., cited, 203n, 204n,
  209, 214, 223
Lacerda, expedition to Kazembe
  (1798–9), 228, 231, 239
Lala [people], Bemba attacks on,
  xxvii
  acquire Bemba chiefs, 203, 205

Lamba [people], 203, 230
Land question, Southern Rhodesia
  Land Commission (1894), 101
  Ndebele grievances, 172, 178–9
  Privy Council petition (1914], 185
  Privy Council judgement, 187
  Carter Commission, 191
  Land Apportionment Act, 139, 163,
    191
Lawley Concession (1898), see under
  Lozi
Laws, Rev. Robert, and Ngoni, 308,
  313, 314, 315, 318, 319
  on education, 384
Leopard's Kopje, culture, xvi, 8, 9,
    11, 13, 14, 16, 20, 23, 25
Lewanika, 21, 184, 242n, 260n
  origin of name, 240
  character, 265
  attitude to European encroach-
    ment, xxx, xxxi, 70, 71, 265
  Lozi opposition to, 267–8, 281–2,
    294–5
  B.S.A. Co. and Protectorate: Loch-
    ner concession, 262, 263, 264–7,
    269, 274; Lawley concession, 270;
    Lewanika concession, 272, 273;
    land concession (1904 and
    1906), 283; land concession
    (1909), 291–2; repudiates conces-
    sions, 283, 296; judicial conces-
    sion (1904), 285–6; order in
    Council (1911), 293, 294; loss of
    sovereign rights, 271–2, 295–6;
    power of jurisdiction, 285, 295–7;
    hut tax, 275 ff.; representative
    indunas, 277–80, 284 ff., peti-
    tions for Crown prot., 289, 290;
    authority outside Reserve, 279,
    285, 287, 289
Lewanika Concession (1900), see
  under Lozi
Likoro [Yao chieftaincy], attacks
  Mponda, 366
Lippert Concession, 92
Litunga [Lozi ruler's title], see also
  under individual Litungas, e.g.
  Lewanika, 254, 256, 257–8, 281,
  282, 283

Matapwiri [Yao chieftaincy], deposed, 368
Mauch, Carl, 31, 34, 71
Maund, E. A., 83, 85
Mavudzi [Rozwi medium], 132, 133
Mawewe [Soshangane's son], 48, 49
Mbalekelwa [N. Ngoni ruler], 318
Mbelwa (Mwambera, Mombera) [N. Ngoni ruler], xxiv, 305
  accession, 303-4
  raiding, xxvi
  assimilation of captives, 310
  and Mpezeni's Ngoni, 307, 327
  revolts against, 311
  and Arabs, 312
  attitude to missionaries, xxvi, 318 ff.
  death, 316
Mbire [people], migrate S. of Zambesi, 33
  dynasty, xv, 9
  Mbire-Shoko, 10
  and Mwari cult, 34
Mboanjikana [Lozi princess], 253, 254
Mboo [Lozi ruler], 244, 245, 246, 251, 252, 253, 254, 255
Mboo (Fwabi) [Lozi induna], plot against Lewanika, 294, 295
Mbukushu [people], subjugated by Lozi, 243, 244, 251
Mbuyu (Mbuywamwambwa) [Lozi ruler], 242, 243, 245, 246, 250, 254, 255, 256, 258
Mhlope, Nganganyoni, cited on Rebellion, 105, 107, 109
Mhondoros [Shona spirit mediums], and Shona political system, xxxiii, 137 ff. chap. 6
  rôle in Rebellion, 125 ff, 143
  among Korekore, chap. 6 passim
  in Shona political history, chap. 2
Milner, Sir Alfred, apptd. high commissioner, 282
  on future of Barotseland, 269-70
  on Barotse tax, 279, 281
  on Lewanika's jurisdiction, 286
Missions, Christian, see also under individual missionaries, e.g. Laws, Coillard

influence on colonial encounter, xx, xxv
  Catholic, xix, 384
  Protestant, xix-xx
  Blantyre (Church of Scotland), xx, 69, 320-1, chap. 14, 352, 35, 370
  Livingstonia (Free Church of Scotland), xx, 69, 308, 309, 311, 312 ff., 333, 351, 371, 400
  London Missionary Society (L.M.S.), xix-xx, 66n, 68-9, 81
  Mission de la Suisse Romande, 60
  Paris Missionary Society (P.M.S.), 265, 266, 267, 290
  Primitive Methodists, 267
  Seventh Day Adventists, 384
  Southern Rhodesia Missionary Conference, 191
  Universities Mission to Central Africa (U.M.C.A.), 333, 362, 383-4
  White Fathers, xxviii, xxix, 219
  Zambesi Industrial Mission, 323
Mitoche [Yao chief], punitive action against, 344, 345
Mjaan [Ndebele induna], cited on Rebellion, 100
Mkata (Nkata) [Yao chieftaincy], attacks Mponda, 366
  turns pro-British, 368
Mkwati [Ndebele high priest], rôle in Rebellion, 105, 107, 108-17, 121, 124-5, 127, 128, 131
Mlimo, see also Mwari, 102, 105, 106, 107, 108, 109, 110, 112, 113, 114, 115, 116, 117, 121, 122, 124, 133, 134
Mlozi [Arab leader], 312, 318
  hostility to Br., 333, 358
  Br. campaign against, 341
  shot, 369, 371
Moffat, J. S., Matabele mission, 68
  negotiation of non-alienation treaty, 72-5
  negotiation of Rudd concession, 76-9
  returns to Matabeleland, 91, 92
Moffat, Rev. Robert, 315
Mombera, see Mbelwa

Ngoni—*contd.*
Ngoni; origins, 302–3, 305, 320;
political system, xxv, xxvi, 321;
and Yao and Cewa, 308; visited
by Laws, 308, 313; and Blantyre
missionaries, 320–1; split after
Cikusi's death, 322; Zambesi
Industrial Mission, 323; attack
Mponda, 366; come under Adm.,
370; see also under Cikusi
N'Gono, Rev. John, 181
Ngonomo [Ngoni *induna*], 306, 316,
317
Nguboyena [son of Lobengula], 175,
176, 177, 181
Nguni [peoples], migrations, xviii, 47
and Rozwi, 5, 32, 34
Ngwenya, Rev. P. S., 192, 193
Njube [son of Lobengula], 175, 176,
177, 181
Nkole Wa Mapembwe [Bemba
ruler], and migration from Luba,
203–7
descent from, 208, 212, 216, 220
Nkolemfumu [Bemba chieftaincy],
origins, 197, 207, 217–18
Nkonde (Ngonde) [people], and
Ngoni, 307
Nkula [Bemba chieftaincy], xxvii,
xxviii, 197, 207
Nkweto [Bemba chieftaincy], 197,
219
Nkoya [people], 243
Nombate [Ndebele *induna*], 97
North Charterland Exploration Co.,
327–9
Northern Rhodesia, Order in Council
(1911), 292, 293
Nsama [Tabwa chieftaincy], 233,
234. 235
Nsenga [people], xvi, 159, 204
Nsingu [son of Mpezeni], 328, 329
Nyamanda [son of Lobengula], seeks
recognition as king, 178–91
Nyamwezi [people], 226, 229, 233,
234
Nyanja [people], xvi, xxi
and Ngoni, 307, 308
and Yao chiefs, 367

Nyasaland, see Malawi

Oliver, Roland, cited, 338, 353, 356,
371, 373
Oral tradition
Bemba, chap. 8
Korekore, 31, 138–9
Lovedu, 245–6
Lozi, chaps. 10, 11
Ngoni, xxiv, 309
Rozwi, 32–8, 44, 240

Pacheco, A. M., cited, 30, 36n, 45
Pim Commission, and Barotseland,
301
Pinto, Major Serpa, 333, 338
Pioneers, Mashonaland, xxv, xxxi, 53,
91
Political Systems, Central African,
classification, xxi–iv
centralized, xii, 97, 255
'sudanic', 238–9
religious systems, xxxii–iii, 94
and colonial encounter, xxii ff., 261,
354–5, chap. 15
decline of chiefly authority, 372–5
Bemba, xxiii
Korekore, 139 ff.
Kotakota (Marimba), 361
Lozi, xxiii, 238–9, 246, 249, 255 ff.,
261, 278
Lunda, xxiii, 239, 249
Ndebele, xxiii, xxxi, 63, 65, 93, 97,
98
Ngoni, xxiii, 304 ff., 311, 312, 321
Rozwi, 98, 104
Shona, xxxiii, chap. 2 passim, 96,
98, 117 ff., 137 ff.
Yao, 364, 367, 370
Zulu, xxiii
Ponde [Bemba chief], xxix
Portuguese
early penetration of Zambesi valley,
xv, xix, 31
and British: rivalry, xxi; draft de-
marcation treaty (1890), 54–5;
final treaty (1891), 55–6
and Gaza, 48ff., 59–60
and Kazembe, 226, 228, 231, 232